The Great Fights

The Great Fights

A Pictorial History of Boxing's Greatest Bouts

by Bert Randolph Sugar and the Editors of RING magazine

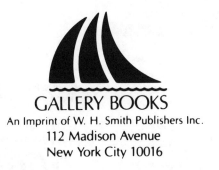

GALLERY BOOKS
An Imprint of W. H. Smith Publishers Inc.
112 Madison Avenue
New York City 10016

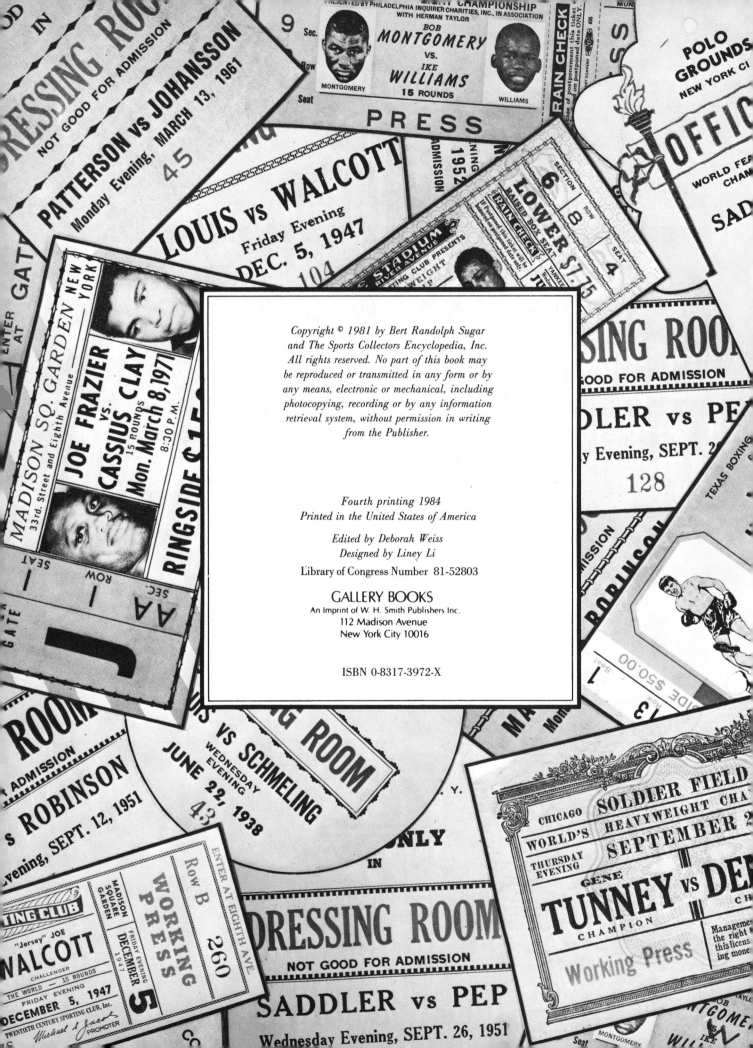

Fourth printing 1984
Printed in the United States of America

Edited by Deborah Weiss
Designed by Liney Li

Library of Congress Number 81-52803

GALLERY BOOKS
An Imprint of W. H. Smith Publishers Inc.
112 Madison Avenue
New York City 10016

ISBN 0-8317-3972-X

To the memory of Nat Fleischer,
founder of The Ring,
and to the millions of fans he nurtured
in the name of boxing.

Contents

Preface

Religious contemplatives in medieval times were wont to argue over the number of angels who danced on the head of a pin. Boxing contemplatives—called fans—go through many of the same esoteric exercises. Only their arguments have less to do with ecclesiastical issues than with the more mundane questions centering around boxing. Where the boxing fan is concerned it is usually an argument based on totally subjective standards, and beginning with the adjective "greatest," meaning singular, important, meaningful. The most common questions therefore are, "Who is the greatest fighter?" and "What was the greatest fight?"

In general, any discussion of the "greatest" starts as a discussion at the local tavern between two of the more knowledgeable savants of the sport. The subjects range anywhere from a four-rounder someone witnessed at the local emporium down to, and including, a recent to-do between two attendants at the corner parking lot. From there it is a short hop, skip, and jump to the "greatest" fights of all time.

But most participants, no matter how many fights they have personally witnessed or what they know about "the sweet science," come totally unarmed for battle, and soon begin manufacturing names and fights, unsure of their footing or their facts. Names like Robinson, Dempsey, Ali, Louis, and some others come out easily enough. But against whom? And when?

In the end most boxing fanatics have merely reinforced their own imperfect recollections, whether personal or second hand, and it will take the efforts of a friendly observer, or perhaps the bartender, to gingerly move those engaged in such a discussion back to their respective neutral corners in hopes of preventing the debate from becoming yet another of the "greatest" fights of all time.

It was to settle those time-honored contests that *The Ring* magazine went to the 50 members of its International Ratings Panel—experts from around the world who, each month, rate the fighters in the 12 weight classes—and asked them to vote on which fights they felt were the "greatest" of all time. Their answers were surprising; not in their collective outcome so much as in their individual selections, some of which were not the answers some wanted to hear.

Among the 58 bouts proposed, the panel of experts named fights that occurred in all ten decades of modern-day boxing, with the 1950s and 1970s leading the parade with 11 apiece. The 1940s were right behind with 10, and 2 were selected from the present decade. They included heavyweights and non-heavyweights alike, with all eight of the traditional divisions named. They named title fights and non-title fights, KOs and non-KOs, bouts where the title changed hands and where it was successfully defended. In fact, it was a veritable boxing smorgasbord.

However, in addition to those fights, the editor has exerted what might laughingly be called his editorial prerogative, and more properly be called his heavy-handed preference, to select a few "wild card" fights he believes are deserving of the accolade "greatest," using as his barometer their place in boxing history, their excitement, their participants, or their conclusions. There are those who might also add, not unfairly, that he also employed more than a cup of kindness to transport himself back with misty eyes to the nostalgically romantic past for a fight or two as well.

And while he was at it, the editor called upon several people to help in pulling this volume together, people like Joe Bruno, Richard Chudnoff, E. J. Gary, Jimmy Jacobs, Mike Katz, George Kimball, Steve Losch, Mike Marley, Harold Rosenthal, and Debbie Weiss, all of whom added their flair and their touch to make this book take form and flight.

All in all, *The Great Fights* is a look at the history of boxing as told through specific pugilistic encounters, from the first to the last, from the fight selected most often by the experts—the Joe Louis-Billy Conn fight—down to those selected by only a few so-called experts or by the editor. But they were all winners. There were no losers. And boxing is far richer for them all. And so will you, the reader, be as you have a chance to relive them. And use them as cannon fodder for your next "all-time greatest" discussion.

Bert Randolph Sugar

Greatest Fights of All Time

1 Joe Louis-Billy Conn (1941)

2 Jack Dempsey-Gene Tunney (1927)

3 Joe Frazier-Muhammad Ali (1971)

4 Tony Zale-Rocky Graziano (1946)

5 Rocky Marciano-Jersey Joe Walcott (1952)

6 Archie Moore-Yvon Durelle (1958)

7 Muhammad Ali-Joe Frazier (1975)

8 Rocky Graziano-Tony Zale (1947)

9 Sugar Ray Robinson-Jake LaMotta (1951)

10 Willie Pep-Sandy Saddler (1949)

11 Henry Armstrong-Barney Ross (1938)

12 Carmen Basilio-Sugar Ray Robinson (1957)

13 Roberto Duran-Sugar Ray Leonard (1980)

14 Jack Dempsey-Luis Firpo (1923)

15 Jake LaMotta-Laurent Dauthuille (1950)

16 Joe Louis-Max Schmeling (1938)

17 Sandy Saddler-Willie Pep (1948)

18 Joe Louis-Jersey Joe Walcott (1947)

19 Ike Williams-Bob Montgomery (1947)

20 Larry Holmes-Ken Norton (1978)

John L. Sullivan—Jake Kilrain

July 8, 1889

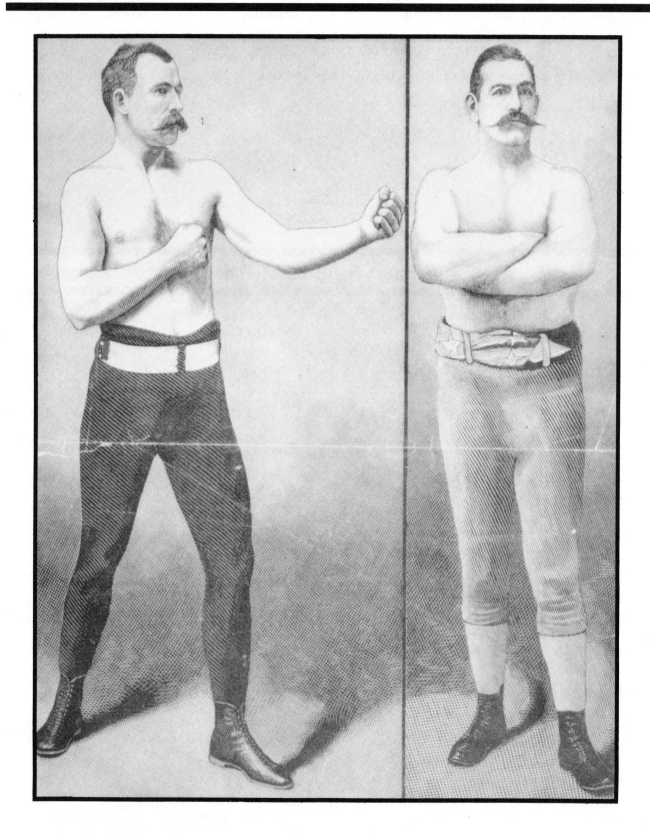

The first American worthy of the title of "boxing promoter" was neither an American nor a promoter of boxing. He was an Irishman who used the sport as a promotion to sell his publication.

Richard Kyle Fox was a penniless 29-year-old who came to the United States from Dublin in 1874 and found work with a New York newspaper. In two years he had saved a couple of hundred dollars. Adding this to a few hundred more that he borrowed, he purchased a moribund publication called the *National Police Gazette.* Once a vital weekly dedicated to scandal and sensation, the *Gazette* was now more weak than weekly. It needed more than an infusion of capital. It needed a first-class publisher with a talent for promotion.

Fox proved himself to be a promotional genius, giving away more than a quarter of a million dollars in cash prizes, medals, belts, and trophies to boost the *Gazette*'s circulation and to promote himself. He used the word "champion" to describe anything and everything that moved, as long as it moved the *Gazette*'s circulation. Fox's mustachioed face adorned various cups and medals he sponsored as he commemorated men who allowed their craniums to be sledgehammered through blocks of iron, strong men who lifted the *Police Gazette* Ferris wheel on their chest, bartenders who could make a *pousse-cafe* with the most layers, barbers who clipped hair the fastest, and champion rat-catching dogs. Under Fox's direction, his publication was less journalism than an early-day *Guinness Book of World Records.*

But even with his promotions bombarding the American public like misdirected buckshot, it was the targeting of his ten-cent weekly to the wants of the American people that was to earn him a place in history. The first thing Fox did when he took over was to add his name, "Richard K. Fox, Editor and Proprietor," to the masthead. The second was to add a sports section to the pink pages of the *Gazette,* bringing—in the absence of any such feature in the daily newspapers—accounts of races and prizefights to the thousands of Americans who were fascinated by such news.

Although in 1880 prizefighting was illegal in every one of the 38 states, Fox believed that many people were interested in it—interested enough to buy the *Gazette* to read about it.

The astonishing success of the *Police Gazette* and its sports section attracted the attention of other papers, now aware of the circulation value of sports coverage. First they merely assigned general reporters to cover sporting events. Then, as the publishers gained expertise in the field and circulation rose, they assigned reporters to sports exclusively and soon began to feature separate sports sections. Seeking readers for his penny New York *Herald,* James Gordon Ben-

nett began to publish the results of races and fights, and so did Benjamin Day in the New York *Sun.*

But it wasn't the fact that he had unwittingly spawned the sports pages that would serve as the anchor of Fox's fame. Rather it was because Fox, motivated only by his enormous ego, was to set the course for boxing in this country and serve unofficially as America's first boxing promoter, all because of a slight he suffered at the hands of John L. Sullivan.

While Paddy Ryan proudly wore both his mantle as American champion and the *Police Gazette* belt—"Presented by Richard K. Fox, Proprietor"—a new claimant was gradually making his name known, first in the Boston area and then nationally. That claimant was a 23-year-old bully, braggart, and boozer named John Lawrence Sullivan. Knowing little about the niceties of boxing, he had taken on all comers at the Dudley Street Opera House, Boston Music Hall, and the Howard Athenaeum in what were called "sparring exhibitions" in order to stay inside the law and outside the grasp of the Boston constabulary. Knocking out most of his on-stage opponents and even several offstage, John L. Sullivan gained the reputation of a knockout puncher. One opponent likened the impact of Sullivan's punch to "a telephone pole," which "had been shoved against me endwise." "It was like being kicked in the head by a runaway horse," said another.

As Sullivan's reputation grew, so did the demand to see him in action. Sullivan toured the vaudeville circuit, offering $50 to any comer who could last four rounds, building his reputation and his growing list of victims in Cincinnati, Philadelphia, Chicago, and finally New York. During his stopover in New York, late in March 1881, Sullivan dropped into a public house known as Harry Hill's Dance Hall and

Opposite: *The Great $20,000 Prize Ring Battle—vanquished Jake Kilrain (left) and victor John L. Sullivan.* Above: *Early in the fight, John L. Sullivan (right) lands a right to Jake Kilrain's chin.*

11

Boxing Emporium. Harry Hill's was a group of two-story buildings on Houston Street at the edge of New York's famed Bowery, where wrestling and boxing exhibitions were offered as a divertissement for the many stage and sports personalities who frequented the place, including its landlord P. T. Barnum, as well as Diamond Jim Brady, Lillian Russell, James Gordon Bennett, and of course, the most influential sports figure in the country, Richard K. Fox.

Sullivan had just beaten a certain Steve Taylor in two rounds on Hill's oversized stage, saving himself $50 which he was reinvesting in drinks for friends and hangers-on, when Fox, seated just two tables away, beckoned his waiter over and told him to instruct Sullivan that "Mr. Fox would like a word with him." But Sullivan was not up to being granted audiences, even by so influential a man as Fox, and bellowed back at the waiter—loud enough for Fox and everyone in the place to hear—"You tell Fox that if he's got anything to say to me he can Gahd-damn well come over to my table and say it!" No one had ever addressed him like that before. And Fox never forgot it.

This affront caused Fox to crusade against Sullivan. It was to keep John L.'s name in the limelight for the next dozen years. After Sullivan had disposed of John Flood, a New York gang leader who had never failed to "get his man," Fox started a search for a boxer who could "get" Sullivan.

There now appeared on the scene a native of Long Island christened John J. Killion, who fought under the name Jake Kilrain. During the early 1880s Kilrain fought, and beat, some of the best of the heavies, including Jack Burke, Jack Ashton, Frank Herald, and Joe Godfrey among others, and had fought a four-round draw with Charlie Mitchell. The undefeated Kilrain, with Fox and the *Gazette* noisily urging him on, repeatedly challenged Sullivan to battle. When the champion failed to respond, Fox declared Kilrain the champion and give him a belt as the American champion with the understanding that he would fight Jem Smith, then champion of England, with $5,000 a side and the belt going to the winner. Fox, of course, put up Kilrain's $5,000.

The match against Smith took place in des Souverains, France, and after 106 rounds of no-holds-barred fighting, the battle was declared a draw. Kilrain returned to the United States with a claim to the world title and the belt.

Now with a legitimate claimant on his hands, Fox's campaign against Sullivan picked up momentum and viciousness. Sullivan's fans in Boston took up a collection and presented him with a belt of his own, fancier, if possible, than Fox's. Sullivan, who had no use for either Fox or Kilrain, contemptuously sneered, "I wouldn't put Kilrain's belt

around the neck of a Gahd-damned dog," and made plans to go to England to take on the best there. When asked by a reporter why he was going abroad when the most worthy challenger for his crown was here in America, Sullivan took off the wraps and verbally took off after Fox: "I've been abused in the papers. I've been lied about and condemned by men who, for commercial reasons, wanted to see some true American, a son of the Stars and Stripes, whipped by a foreigner. So now I'm intending to get even by unfurling Uncle Sam's victorious flag in the land from which my enemies brought men they hoped would conquer me."

With few worlds left to conquer after a victorious six-month tour of England and the continent, Sullivan returned to the United States in April 1888, and immediately took refuge in the only other world he ever knew: the bottle. After several bouts with a far more formidable opponent than any he had ever met in the ring, Sullivan was finally

Artist's depiction of Sullivan's seventy-fifth-round knockout of Kilrain.

rendered senseless for the first time in his life. For four months, he was confined to bed, suffering from delirium tremens combined with physical collapse, cirrhosis of the liver, and a touch of typhoid fever thrown in for good measure.

The time seemed ripe for Fox to pluck the crown away. The weekly pink pages of the *Gazette* beat out a monotonous one-note story—that the once-proud physical specimen was now a physical wreck. There was a question whether John L. would in fact survive; if he did, would he ever fight again? Everywhere the *Gazette* went—livery stables, barber shops, saloons, fire halls, police stations—controversy was sure to follow. Was the sick Sullivan refusing to meet the "real champion?"

Within a month of leaving his sickbed, Sullivan accepted the long-standing challenge of Kilrain and Fox and posted $5,000 in New York to fight Kilrain, $10,000 a side, for the championship and possession of the belt, with "the ring to be pitched within two hundred miles of New Orleans."

Almost before the ink was dry on the contract, John L. took off on another prolonged bender. With the bout only months away, the champion was informing all present in any

bar he entered that he would win easily. But his bloated 240 pounds gave lie to his braggadocio. Sensing their hero was beyond the realm of self-discipline, Sullivan's backers hired William Muldoon, the wrestling champion and physical-fitness fanatic, to wrestle John L. back into shape. Finding Sullivan quaffing down a stein of straight bourbon in one of his normal hangouts, Muldoon physically dragged him from the premises to his health farm at Belfast, New York, for a period of rest and rehabilitation.

In a scant six months Muldoon did the impossible. It almost equaled resuscitating Lazarus. First Sullivan's eyes cleared, then he regained his wind, and finally he recaptured his style and power. Under Muldoon's watchful eyes, the flabby 240 pounds turned into a fighting 207 pounds. John L. was ready for "any son-of-a-bitch-in-the-house" again. But particularly, he was ready for Fox and his hand-picked gladiator, Kilrain.

As the date for what was to be the last bare-knuckle fight in the history of boxing drew closer, thousands of the faithful were drawn to New Orleans. A robust, rollicking town, the New Orleans of 1889 was renowned for its jetties, its Cotton Centennial Exposition, and its infamous Storyville

Crowds came from miles around to witness boxing's last bare-knuckle championship bout.

13

section. But prizefighting was as illegal in Louisiana as anywhere, so great secrecy surrounded the movements of the principals and their backers. Only the promoter of the fight, a New Orleans sportsman named Bud Reneau, and a few others, knew the exact location of the fight. So, when just after midnight on July 8, 1889, the special train pulled out of the Queen and Crescent Yards, filled to overflowing with fans from every walk of life, only a few among them knew the exact destination.

Not until daylight after a slow and tedious all-night ride did the passengers know for where they were bound. Finally, around 8 A.M., the train lumbered into Richburg, Mississippi, a lumber camp 104 miles north of New Orleans, where a ring was set up in full view on the 30,000-acre estate of pines owned by Colonel Charles W. Rich. As it came to a stop, the train disgorged its human freight, all of whom made a dash to the specially constructed wooden arena.

A few minutes before 10, Kilrain and his cornermen, Charlie Mitchell and Mike Donovan, together with their timekeeper, Bat Masterson, pushed their way down the aisle. After tossing his hat into the ring, Kilrain entered wearing green trunks anchored with an American flag that served as a belt. Then, to the roars of the crowd, Sullivan appeared and, after the ceremonial toss of his hat, entered wearing a green robe. Discarding it immediately, he stood resplendent in emerald green knee breeches, flesh-colored long stockings, and high-topped black fighting boots. His waist was also encircled with an American flag, together with his own colors, green and white.

Sullivan hardly looked the man the *Police Gazette* had been depicting for the past several months. He appeared quite fit except for a small protuberance in the lower belly. But the unanswered question was how long could he go, especially against a wrestler like Kilrain? Pulitzer's *New York World* had ventured an opinion: "According to all such drunkards as he, his legs ought to fail him after twenty minutes of fighting." Still, Sullivan was the betting favorite at ringside.

The Police Gazette *belt awarded to John L. Sullivan.*

At exactly 10 minutes after 10, referee John Fitzpatrick of New Orleans hollered "Time!" and the two adversaries advanced to the mark. They circled quickly. Kilrain threw a long left, grabbed Sullivan by the shoulders, and threw him over his heel to the ground. The first round had taken exactly five seconds. The pattern of the fight began to take shape in the second round as the enraged Sullivan chased Kilrain, who kept his distance and employed the defensive tactics of his cornerman Mitchell: jabbing, holding, and wrestling. By the fourth round, which took 15 minutes and 21 seconds, a frustrated Sullivan could only stop momentarily to snarl, "Why don't you fight, you son-of-a-bitch? You're the champion, huh? Champion of what?" But Kilrain didn't take the bait. He only laughed and went back into his shell. All the while Kilrain's corner, especially Mitchell, kept up a steady stream of abuse, trying to goad Sullivan into anger. Kilrain's strategy was obvious: wear down the bigger man and exhaust his energies, no matter how.

It seemed to be working. In the seventh, Kilrain landed a roundhouse right to Sullivan's ear and tore it open. "First blood, Kilrain," announced Fitzpatrick, and an exchange of bills accompanied the announcement of first claret. But this was to be the last time the supporters of Kilrain were to take heart, as the champion, not John L., began to wilt in the 104-degree heat. Sullivan's determination and condition were attested to by the fact that he refused to sit down between rounds: "Why should I? I only have to stand back up again." After the twelfth round, when Muldoon asked him how much longer he could "stay," Sullivan snarled, "Till tomorrow morning, if necessary."

As the fight wore on, the result became more and more apparent. The question was no longer whether John L. could survive Kilrain's attacks or even if he could win, but *when*. By the end of the seventy-fifth round, Kilrain's head was rolling loosely on his shoulders as if his neck were broken, his back was covered with beet-red blisters, and he could no longer stand up, let alone throw a punch. A physician took his second, Mike Donovan, aside and advised him, "Kilrain will die if you keep sending him in there." As Kilrain uncertainly made his way back out to the center of the ring to toe the mark for the seventy-sixth round, Donovan tossed in the sponge.

The last championship bare-knuckle fight was over. The proud line of champions that had begun fighting in 1719 on a wooden stage at James Figg's Amphitheater ended in a clearing on a lumber estate in Mississippi some 170 years later. John L. Sullivan was still the champion, and the proud possessor of the *Police Gazette* belt, "Presented by Richard K. Fox, Proprietor."

James J. Corbett—John L. Sullivan

September 7, 1892

"Shake the hand of the hand that shook the hand of John L." was one of the proudest boasts of a proud nation of boasters back in the 1890s, an era when Americans were confident and cocksure, already convinced of their place in history, and their heroes.

And there never was a bigger hero than the man called "the Great John L." To those who now know him only as a name in yellowing newspaper reports, his is a name that serves as a benchmark for the progress of boxing. But he was more, much more. His name gave color to his age. His was a name that was larger than life, spoken in reverential terms and serving as an institution in the days when "men were men" and all men wanted to be just like the man who boasted, "I can lick any son-of-a-bitch-in-the-house." Like Gladys Gooch in Auntie Mame, he lived, particularly in the minds and hearts of his followers—followers who numbered in the millions.

For the year and a half following Sullivan's victory over Jake Kilrain in the last bare-knuckle fight in history for the undisputed title and belt, he had toured the country in a play specially written for his limited talents, titled *Honest Hearts and Willing Hands*. Finally, after performing all over the world, "Sully," as he was known by his followers, ran out of villains to dispose of on-stage and now looked to dispose of those critics in the tabloids who were savaging him in print, taking out whole pieces of his hide with each passing editorial. Thoroughly piqued by the many shafts thrown at him by the literary Lilliputians, Sullivan issued one of his famous proclamations in the papers to quiet those critics:

I hereby challenge any and all bluffers to fight me for a purse of $25,000 and a bet of $10,000. The winner of the fight to take the entire purse. I am ready to put up the first $10,000 now. First come, first served. I give preference in this challenge to Frank P. Slavin of Australia, as he and his backers have done the greatest amount of blowing. My second preference is that bombastic sprinter, Charles Mitchell of England, whom I would rather whip than any man in the world. My third preference is James J. Corbett, who has uttered his share of bombast. But in this challenge I include all fighters. The Marquis of Queensberry must govern this contest, as I want fighting, not footracing, and I intend to keep the championship of the world.

Yours truly,
John L. Sullivan
Champion of the World

The first of the three to come forward was the dapper bank clerk from out of the West, "Gentleman" James J. Corbett. Corbett, first seen in the East fighting a four-rounder against Dominick McCaffrey at the Fifth Avenue Casino in Brooklyn in 1890, was to show the cynics his "stuff," as he constantly pumped his left into the face of his confused and outclassed opponent with the efficiency of a piston rod, and thoroughly puzzled the slower-moving easterner with his lateral movement—something neither McCaffrey nor the sporting gentry of New York had seen before in a man the size of Corbett. Finally, in the fourth round, McCaffrey waved Corbett off in an early-day version of "*No más, no más,*" acknowledging himself beaten.

The name Corbett was now linked to that of Sullivan. Added to his impressive record—which included wins over tough fellow-San Franciscan Joe Choynski in 27 rounds, and the same Jake Kilrain Sullivan had beaten in 75 rounds in just 10—Corbett had firmly established his credentials as a contender. Now the Corbett "hype" began with ringsiders participating in the time-honored sport of matching up the winner of a fight they had just witnessed with the champion—a practice which has continued, unabated, to the present day.

Not content to rest on his laurels, Corbett began to use the press to further his cause. He wrote a tract entitled "Boxing East and West," putting to paper his new method of what he called "scientific boxing." He then added further fuel to the fire by comparing himself favorably to Sullivan. "Confidence is half the battle, and it is that excellent characteristic which has enabled John L. to win most of his victories. I don't think I have ever lacked that quality, and, like the 'Big Fellow,' I have never met with defeat. The worst I ever did was a draw, and Sullivan had the same misfortune: He 'drew' with Charles Mitchell of England, and I with Peter Jackson of Australia. On the score of 'records,' therefore, I think we are about even."

Preceding page: *James J. Corbett ("Gentleman Jim") (left) and John L. Sullivan ("the Great John L.") face off in 1892. Right: Gentleman Jim takes advantage of his opponent.*

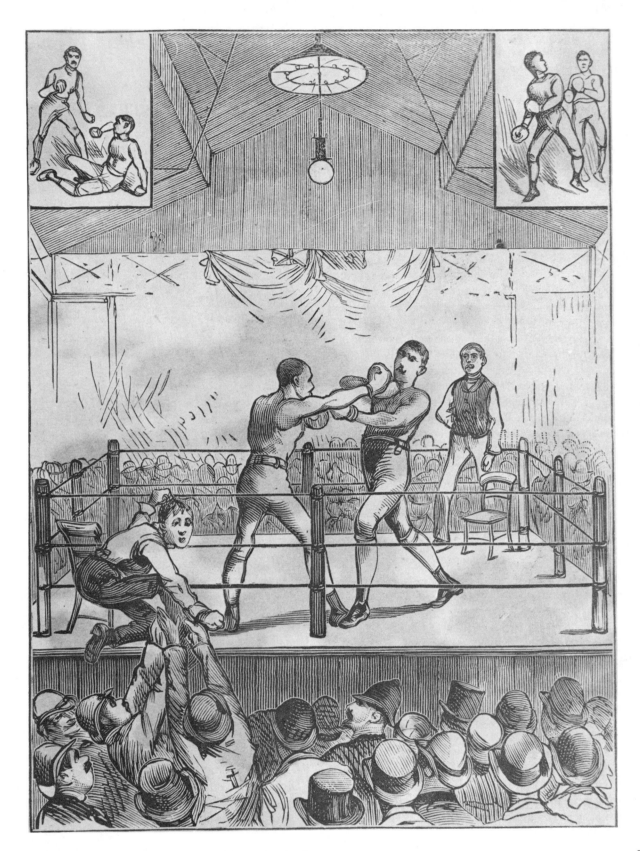

Sullivan fared well against Alf Greenfield in 1885, but the Englishman stayed four rounds.

All of this didn't set too well with John L. Nor his backers. What he called Corbett's "bombast" won for Corbett, as it was to win for a brash youngster out of Louisville named Cassius Marcellus Clay some 72 years later, a crack at the biggest prize in all of sports, the heavyweight championship.

On March 15, 1892, Corbett accepted John L.'s challenge, posting $10,000, winner take all, with the fight to be held under the Marquis of Queensberry rules at the Olympic Club in New Orleans six months later, on September 7, 1892.

Sullivan, who had gone to bloat and had not donned a pair of gloves—save for a few exhibition bouts, including a four-rounder with Corbett—since he last fought some 33 months before, now had a battle of his own before he ever got into the ring. He had to whip himself back into fighting shape, his once Adonis-like physique the casualty of carousing and many hours spent in the company of bottles and women.

Sullivan, with somewhere close to 225 pounds awkwardly and embarrassingly distributed over his 5-foot 10-inch frame, took his added avoirdupois to a place near Good Ground, Long Island, to set up training. But "training" was hardly the word for the activities performed by the 34-year-old champion, who found greater nourishment in being surrounded by sycophants and hangers-on than in getting his overaged, overweight body ready for the fight.

One of those who "worked" with him, his trainer Phil Casey, was to remember in later years, how Sullivan "trained": "I could not get the big fellow to do one-tenth enough road or any other work to prepare him thoroughly. He would not work, and the only thing left to do was to fix him up the best way we could. Many a time when he would start out of his quarters for a long road jog, he would not go more than a couple of miles. Then he would sit down, and after a rest would march back again." And when he did deign to jog, he almost always was seen trotting in the company of a fetching local beauty, a Miss Clara Tuthill, who trotted alongside him for company. Such was Sully's training. "All his fine appearance," his trainer confided years later, was "done by rubbing."

Corbett, on the other hand, had taken up training in Asbury Park, New Jersey, under the watchful eye of trainer Billy Delaney, who instituted a rigorous program. It included such activities as ball punching, pedestrianism, and bathing, or, whatever they called it 90 years ago.

Despite his training—or lack of it—it was thought that if John L. could catch lightning in a bottle and recapture just 75 percent of his youthful ability and condition, he would be no match for the Gentleman from California. And

When Jim Corbett Won Title
Sullivan Praised Conqueror
WHICH?

"I Did It Once Too Often."
—John L. Sullivan, after the fight.

the betting odds supported that contention, with Sullivan installed as the 4-1 favorite with no takers.

Dedicated in 1883 to create "a respect for manly spirits, a respect for honest unafraid muscle . . . [and] teaching the frank lesson that a fist is courage, and a pistol cowardice . . . ," the Olympic Club had quickly become one of the meccas for boxing in America, hosting the Andy Bowen-Jimmy Carroll fight in 1890, the Bob Fitzsimmons-Jack Dempsey fight in 1891, and the Bob Fitzsimmons-Peter Maher fight in early 1892. In fact, with only three states actually having legalized the sport by 1892, it was *the* mecca.

Built in a French Renaissance style, the arena amphitheater covered an area of over 163 square feet, with a seating capacity of over 9,000, where, according to an excerpt from the program book the night of the fight, "Every person who obtains admission to the arena will have a seat [without] discomfort or crowding, and every visitor will be at ease and able to enjoy the fistic exhibitors with absolute serenity."

The night of Wednesday, September 7, 1892, was to be the climax of a three-day boxing "carnival" put on by the Olympic Club; the most ambitious undertaking in boxing history and one which was to rival Madison Square Garden's "Carnival of Champions" 40 years later. Beginning on Mon-

After his loss to Corbett, Sullivan's flamboyant lifestyle was the subject of cartoons such as this appearing in the New York Morning Journal.

day night, September 5, the Olympic Club put on the light-weight-championship bout between the undefeated champion Jack McAuliffe and challenger Billy Myer, with McAuliffe winning by a knockout in the fifteenth. The next night, featherweight champion George Dixon defended his crown, knocking out challenger Jack Skelly in eight. The Sullivan fans were delirious. Not only did the 8–1 quinella on the three champions look like a good bet, but an omen could be found in the fact that all of the champions were winning. The unflappable Corbett merely said, "I guess I'll have to change that."

He started by winning the coin toss on the afternoon of the fight, a toss to select the corner. Both of the previous nights' champion-winners had won the toss and selected the southeastern corner. Now Corbett did the same thing, winning the corner where McAuliffe and Dixon before him had sat. Now it was Corbett's backers who had a good luck omen as they began hunting for Sullivan money, bringing the odds down to 3–1 in some quarters.

But while the representatives of the two combatants were meeting to toss a coin, Sullivan was paying it "no never mind," for at five o'clock—four hours before the bell—he could be found swimming in the Olympic Club's 35-foot by 75-foot swimming pool, or, as it was called, "natatorium." After swimming around for five minutes, his trainer concerned lest Sullivan expend too much of his energy, called out for him to "Come out of there, you bloomin' seapig." Sullivan, true to form, went right on swimming, staying in the pool another 15 minutes. Then it was time to go back to the hotel, take a nap, and get ready for the fight.

The big arena, which had been doing a brisk business all day, with reserved ticketholders coming in through the Royal Street entrance and general admission ticketholders filing in from the Chartes Street entrance—began to fill up by seven o'clock, still two hours before fight time. Most of those in attendance not only identified with Sullivan, they carried Sullivan's colors as well, a broad band of green silk with an American eagle in the center. At 7:35 George Dixon, the winner of the previous night's fight, came into the arena, the first black man ever to be seated in the Olympic Club, a distinction denied even the great Peter Jackson, who was turned away at the Fitzsimmons-Dempsey fight.

By 8:30 both participants had entered the building, Sullivan first, having taken a carriage and driven leisurely down the back streets of New Orleans on his way to the arena. The local constabulary cleared a path for the champion and he entered the Club at the head of a little band of followers, which included lightweight champion Jack McAuliffe and trainer Casey. Sullivan looked every inch a champion—and a fighter. He wore a dark suit and a heavy sweater with an even-heavier cowl collar peeking out from under his jacket. Corbett arrived 15 minutes later. But, instead of looking the part of a fighter, the "dudish" Corbett, attired in a straw hat and sporting a walking stick, took on the air of a man out for an evening on the town.

Sullivan came out of his dressing room first, with Corbett, playing one-upmanship, staying in his room until the last minute and then standing in the aisle to make sure Sullivan was denied his prerogative as a champ—that of entering the ring last. Only when Sullivan had entered the ring did Corbett make his way down the aisle, going immediately into his "lucky" southeastern corner, and sit on a wooden stool, while across from him the champion's ample frame was arranged regally on a high-back chair of polished wood.

Called to the middle of the ring by the referee, Professor John Duffy, for the first time the crowd could see the sizable difference in the two. While John L. stood mighty like an oak at an announced 212 (with some cynics hinting it was 2 to 10 pounds more)—his squat size set off by his green trunks and high-topped fighting shoes—his opponent, now standing next to him for the first time, looked insignificant by comparison. For Corbett's alabaster skin and statuesque features, outlined by his drab-looking trunks and a cummerbund made up of the American colors, showed off his trim 178-pound figure. If size alone could tell, Sullivan's immense weight advantage dictated that he was a winner, and the odds backing him could easily have been more than a mere 3–1 or 4–1, depending on the action, if any could be found.

Looks, also, could tell, almost kill. Sullivan was staring right at Corbett. Corbett, for most of the mid-ring instructions, did not lift up his eyes to meet those of the

James J. Corbett

19

champ. Now, as the instructions wound down, he raised his eyes and met those of Sullivan. Filled with confidence, they shone brightly. When the ritualistic instructions had come to an end, Corbett broke tradition by asking a question. "Do you mean," he asked, reaching over to Sullivan's throat and pushing his forearm into John L.'s Adam's apple, "that this is a foul?" The referee assured him it was. Corbett nodded. Sullivan glowered. And the fight was on.

Sullivan roared out of his corner, still smarting from Corbett's ploy. He threw one of his powerful lefts, but Corbett backed out of harm's way. Another bull-rushing left and then a right. But by the time they reached where Corbett had been a nanosecond before, he was gone. Corbett danced around Sullivan, in a tantalizing, taunting manner, only encouraging the champion to charge him again, this time rushing the challenger to the ropes. But again he landed no punch as Corbett ducked away. Sullivan rushed again, missing with his right. The scenario was repeated time and again, but at the bell, not one punch had been landed.

The second round was more of the same, almost as if the two warriors were negative charges in an electromagnetic field. Every time Sullivan advanced forward, Corbett danced backward. Now the crowd, strongly pro-Sullivan, began hisses, sending out the derogatory cry of "Sprinter," almost in unison. But Sullivan kept charging, angry as a lion. And Corbett, now smiling, merely danced away, content to play the waiting game, never throwing a punch. Then, just at the bell, Corbett pushed his left hand into Sullivan's open stomach, the first punch of the fight for either. The crowd loudly cheered even this scintilla of action.

By round 3 the challenger's game plan was evident to all, except Sullivan. As the hisses and catcalls continued, Corbett turned his back to Sullivan and cried out, "Give me a chance for a few rounds." Before he turned back to face his adversary, Sullivan had run in and hit him with a glancing blow off his shoulder. It was to be the only punch Sullivan would land all night. Corbett continued to turn his back and run, ducking when pinioned against the ropes.

By the sixth round Corbett was openly laughing at Sullivan's awkward thrusts, his bull-like rushes. Playing the matador, Corbett stepped in with a hard right which not only broke the champion's nose, but drew first blood, an ancient betting line which rivals today "go-no go" on Vegas' crap tables. The crowd went wild. And a second later, when Corbett backed Sullivan into his own corner, men stood on chairs, hats were thrown in the air, and pandemonium swept the Club.

Sullivan was tired. He had been fanning the air for a full six rounds, trying to find, let alone hit, the sprinting challenger. Now his condition, or the lack of it, began to tell.

After the seventh round, one of Sullivan's handlers told his friends, seated nearby, that it was "100-to-1" against his man.

But still, Corbett played a waiting game, not quite sure of what his opponent had left. For Sullivan kept coming back, determined to catch the mongoose in front of him. But all he caught was air, and a few lefts to the pit of the stomach for good measure.

In the eleventh, Sullivan threw a round-house right and missed, turning completely around. All he got for his effort was a left in the face. This pattern continued, with Sullivan missing, although less now that he was throwing fewer punches—and Corbett connecting, more now as his confidence and opportunities both increased.

Finally, in round 20, sensing that the man in front of him was a shell of what he had once been, Corbett rushed Sullivan to the ropes and landed a fusillade of punches. Rights and lefts, too quick to follow, crashed to Sullivan's mouth, leaving him groggy and his mouth a bloody mess. At the bell, a dazed and bloodied Sullivan, his eye closed and nose broken, had to be led to his corner.

The bell for the twenty-first found Sullivan slowly rising from his chair. For the twenty-first consecutive round he got off first, leading a weak left. But like all of his previous leads, this one, too, missed, as Corbett moved back. But only momentarily. Corbett leaped in and caught Sullivan with a right to the nose. He pulled back out of danger's way and then jumped back in with a right to the head that made the soon-to-be-ex-champ close his eyes. Now Corbett was atop him, raining blows to his battered features in nonstop motion. Sullivan wobbled around the ring from the effects of the punches. And Corbett threw a right to the ear and a left to the jaw as Sullivan hung in the air for a second, then pitched forward flat on his nose. He was out.

Corbett stood over his fallen foe, unsure of what had happened. As Duffy counted "10," Corbett's trainer, Billy Delaney, had to run into the center of the ring and pull him back to his corner. Jim Corbett was the new heavyweight champion at 1:30 of the twenty-first round.

No sooner had the word "10" split the air then those who had come into the arena bearing John L. Sullivan banners began raining them down into the ring, covering the fallen champion with his own colors like a funeral shroud.

Sullivan finally came to and, looking up at his second, lightweight champ Jack McAuliffe, asked, "What happened, Jack? What happened?" McAuliffe told the fallen warrior, who then staggered to his feet and went over to the ring ropes where he addressed the crowd, "The old man went up against it just once too often. He was beaten—but by an American. Yours truly, John L. Sullivan."

Robert Fitzsimmons—James J. Corbett

March 17, 1897

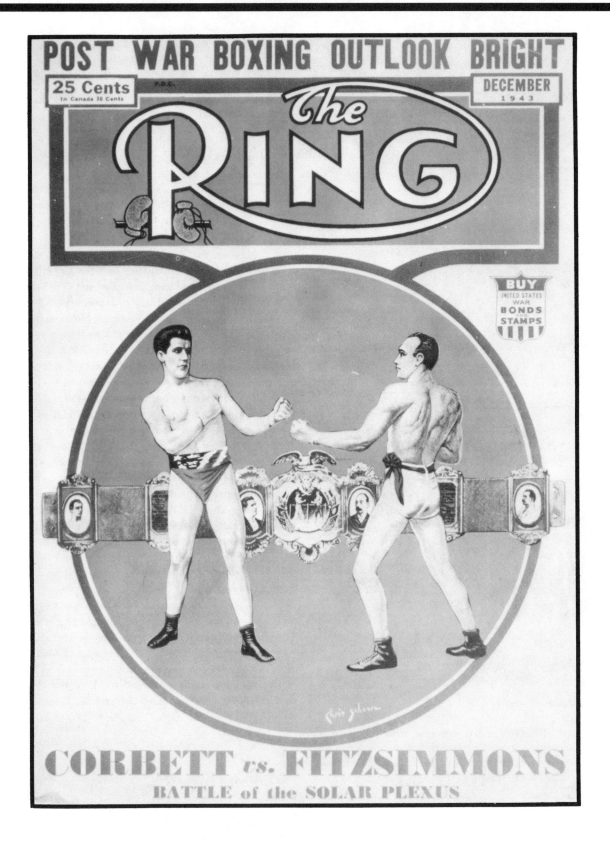

Mention the words "solar plexus" to a doctor and he'll give you a learned treatise on "the large network of sympathetic nerves and ganglia located in the peritoneal cavity behind the stomach and having branching tracts that supply nerves to the abdominal viscera." Mention those same words to the man on the street and he'll give you a more earthy answer: "the pit of the stomach." But if you should but mention those same words to a boxing fan, he'll answer, in a conditioned response, "Fitzsimmons and Corbett." And therein lies the tale of a fight, and a phrase.

Within a month after beating the idol of America, John L. Sullivan, and assuming his mantle as heavyweight champion, James J. Corbett also appropriated another of those opportunities available only to champions—he took to the stage in a vehicle written especially for him, a thinly disguised potboiler entitled *Gentleman Jack*.

The purpose of the show was less to exhibit Corbett's wares as an actor than it was to exhibit Corbett. It bothered neither Corbett nor his manager, William Brady—who sensed a "merchandizability" in Corbett, and the crown—that the reviews, at best, were lukewarm. It was an opportunity for exposure.

One night in Taunton, Massachusetts, Corbett found out just how good his acting was. The morning after opening night the heavyweight champion went down to the dining room of the hotel where he was staying and found the service bad and the food worse. Later he attempted to get one of the bellboys to do an errand for him, but the bellboy promptly forgot Corbett and the errand. In exasperation,

Preceding page: *A 1943* Ring *magazine cover illustrates the featured fight.* Top: *Souvenir magazine from the fight shows Corbett (left) and Fitzsimmons cameos.* Above: *Bob Fitzsimmons demonstrates why he was called "the Blacksmith."*

Corbett went to the desk clerk, who was calmly standing behind the desk, chewing on a toothpick. "This is the worst hotel I have ever stayed in," protested Corbett. Without removing the toothpick dangling from his slack jaw, the desk clerk slowly turned to the heavyweight champion and provided the best critical appraisal anyone ever made to the face of the champ, "Just like your show."

But regardless of Corbett's lack of ability on the stage, he kept everlastingly at it, touring the country for the better part of a year. Twice he posted monies for fights with contenders, Charley Mitchell of England and Peter Jackson of Australia. And twice the bouts fell through.

Finally, in January 1894, Corbett fought the same Charley Mitchell who had embarrassed the great John L. Sullivan in a 39-round draw six years earlier. This time it

was Mitchell who was embarrassed, being knocked out in the third round. That left only one man on the heavyweight horizon—Bob Fitzsimmons, the middleweight champion.

Bob Fitzsimmons, called "Ruby Robert" by many, a description he earned because of his light auburn hair that served as a tonsure around his balding head, was called "Freckled Bob" by others, in attestation of the freckles that covered the upper part of his torso, so much so they took on the appearance of a sheet of interconnecting spots. John L. Sullivan had still another name for him—"a fighting machine on stilts," a reference to his long angular build, which was hardly the prototype of what a heavyweight contender should look like.

In fact, Bob Fitzsimmons was almost everything a heavyweight contender should not be. He was long and sin-

Wrapped in robes of anticipation and confidence, Fitzsimmons and Corbett pose before their confrontation.

24

Above (top and bottom): Fitzsimmons' "solar plexus" punch finds its mark as Corbett sinks to his knees trying to regain his footing and his breath.

ewy, with his skinny legs forming almost two-thirds of his body and supporting the muscular shoulders of a blacksmith—which is exactly what he had been in his youth. He weighed only between 150 and 157½ pounds, some 30 to 40 pounds less than most of the heavyweights he was fighting, and beating. And he was anything but youthful. His age, depending upon whom you talked to, ranged anywhere from 28 to 34 the night he won the middleweight championship from "Nonpareil" Jack Dempsey, making him 34-going-on-40 the day he met Corbett for the championship. But, that's getting ahead of our story.

On that January 1891 night when Fitzsimmons soundly beat Dempsey, he established his bona fide credentials as a "fighting machine." But it was as a middleweight fighting machine. Nobody seriously considered the man whose frame was laughingly described as that of a "sandhill crane," and who looked to his manager like "a long pair of tongs with a little round knob at the top of the handle," as anything more than a curiosity piece. And an unusual looking one at that.

But Fitzsimmons was a curiosity piece in boxing even without considering his looks. In a day dominated by the slugger, where, in the true John L. Sullivan fashion, men would still attempt to club their opponents to the ground, swinging batlike sweeping punches with either hand, he stood alone.

Whereas Corbett had pioneered in the contribution of "science" to the manly art of self-defense, making it, in fact, self-defense rather than self-destruction, Fitz's contribution was more stylistic than substantive. For unlike Corbett, Fitzsimmons was still a member of the old "give-and-take" school. Except his giving took the form of short murderous hooks that traveled only a few inches.

Using his body—which was a broad, rippling collection of muscles that tapered to a 28-inch waist—as a catapult, Fitzsimmons could deliver either hand from scant leeway with amazing violence.

Fitz's favorite stratagem was the left shift, a move where he repositioned his feet—much like changing from the conventional right-handed stance to a left-handed stance—in a split second, and delivered his left hand, full force, to his opponent's now-exposed midrift. It was a trick in ringmanship he had learned when, according to Dan Hickey, the one-time middleweight champion of Australia, he watched "a couple of schoolboys about to settle some argument with their fists. One of them was a natural left-hander. But he boxed with his left extended in the conventional style. During the melee he swung his right, and then suddenly switched his style, banging a left to the wind." That not only settled the dispute, but it planted a seed in the mind of the auburn-haired 28-year-old watching the fight.

Declaring he would fight any man in the world, regardless of weight, Fitz took on a collection of heavier men. Always the results were the same. Hurt by their bludgeoning fists in the early going, the tall, lanky redhead would get inside their roundhouse punches and cut them down to his size with his shorter, and more deadly, punches.

A man of few words, Fitzsimmons put his fighting credo into a memorable phrase, "The bigger they are the heavier they fall," a phrase that was later changed to read, "The bigger they are the *harder* they fall." But regardless of its poetic value, its meaning was all too clear. Especially to the heavyweights Fitzsimmons met—and felled.

Almost from the moment the Cornishman, by way of Australia and New Zealand, stepped onto American soil, he had sought to make the heavyweight championship his turf. But the titleholder, James J. Corbett, evaded him, first treating his challenges with contempt, then with amusement, and finally with callous disregard. Corbett even went so far as to "retire" to "devote his full attention to the stage," designating Peter Maher, a man whom Fitzsimmons had previously knocked out, as his worthy successor.

And so, while Corbett played in the *Naval Cadet*, Fitzsimmons burned. "If he's so damn good as an actor," asked the frustrated challenger of no one in particular, "why did he ever become a fighter?"

Fitzsimmons' (right) is held off by the ref as Corbett grasps the ropes in a futile attempt to rise.

Twice, while stalking Corbett and the heavyweight crown, Fitzsimmons had cornered the champion long enough to get him to post monies for title defenses. But both proposed bouts ran afoul of the law—once in Dallas, and once in Hot Springs, where, for his troubles, Fitzsimmons had been arrested for "conspiring" to break the Arkansas law against prizefighting.

Finally, after disposing of Corbett's hand-picked successor, Peter Maher, for the second time—this time in less than one round, leaving the 230-pound Maher senseless for 18 minutes with one devastating hook to the jaw—Fitzsimmons flushed out Corbett, who "un-retired" and came back to defend "his" title against the only man left in the division he was personally decimating.

Meeting at the Bartholdi Hotel in New York, the two men signed papers for a "fight to the finish" to be held on St. Patrick's Day, 1897, at a place to be determined. The stakes were to be a $15,000 purse and a $2,500 side bet. The place became the capital of the newest state to legalize prizefighting, Carson City, Nevada. This time nothing—except Jim Corbett, himself—would stand in the way of Fitz's quest for boxing's golden fleece.

Almost from the very moment the bell rang at 12:05 P.M. on that hot St. Patrick's Day, Fitzsimmons sought to avenge all the real and imagined indignities that Corbett had subjected him to for the past six years. Refusing to shake hands, he came at Corbett, seeking to reach him on the inside, as he had so many other opponents.

Before the fight, Fitzsimmons had told reporters, "I've licked Dempsey, Jim Hall, Peter Maher, and Dan Creedon with short blows on the jaw and in the stomach, and I think I can do Corbett just as easily!" But Corbett had other plans, and the dancing master kept his distance, letting his faster feet and hands do his talking, continually outpointing and outclassing Fitz in the early going.

Still, the man the reporters called "the Speckled One" kept coming forward, attempting to pressure the champion to get him to go for one of his feints and open up his middle to one of the challenger's vaunted punches. Looking smaller than his 158 pounds and older than his announced 34 years, the challenger's face acted as a magnet for what seemed like the steel in Corbett's gloves. Corbett even resorted to hitting on the breaks and spinning his lighter opponent, all in the name of "scientific" boxing.

Corbett altered his attack, thumping Fitzsimmons in his exposed rib cage every now and then for good measure. Fitzsimmons, hindered by a pain in his right thumb—and his inability to reach the champion, switched his tactics, feinting to the head and then going to Corbett's body. But he soon found that all he got for his efforts were two or three crisp punches to the head. Forcing his way in, Fitz found that every time he got close to the champion, the champion would dance out of harm's way, leaving, as a calling card, two or three jabs to the face. On the few times the challenger did manage to inveigle his way inside, Corbett would tie him up, thumping him to the body.

By the fifth, Fitz looked tired. Corbett, scoring with a quick one-two to the head, brought first blood, ripping open Fitzsimmons' lip. Excited by the sight, Corbett picked up the action, even taking the time to laugh at Mrs. Fitzsimmons seated at ringside. Corbett caught Fitz coming in and bloodied his nose as well. The odds, 10–6 Corbett at the beginning of the fight, were now any price against Fitz.

The sixth was the turning point in the fight. Fitzsimmons now sought to stem the tide of Corbett's attack. He swung at the now-you-see-him-now-you-don't figure dancing in front of him like a mirage, and missed wildly. Corbett made him pay for his folly with a right uppercut. Fitzsimmons fell to his knees, where he stayed for six seconds, holding onto Corbett's knees. The referee, George Siler, instructed Corbett to step back from the fallen fighter. Corbett did and Fitzsimmons regained his feet almost immediately. Corbett was now atop his challenger, pummeling him with lefts and rights to the head. But Fitzsimmons, who had taken heavier punches from Maher and others, and had shown his amazing recuperative powers, now held his ground and evinced them again. The bell soon rang, ending Corbett's high-water mark. From now on, the bout belonged to Fitzsimmons.

From the seventh through the twelfth, Corbett looked the more tired of the two, the more spent. His blows seemed to have lost their force; his movements seemed less evident and fluid. He was playing for time, resting. But even though Corbett had perceptibly slowed down, letting Fitzsimmons control the fight, he still retained his cleverness, and Fitzsimmons could not penetrate his defenses on the inside.

At the end of the twelfth, with Fitzsimmons in control and looking far the fresher, Fitzsimmons' wife called out to him, "Remember, Bob, the thirteenth is your lucky round! Don't let him whip you."

Refreshed by the rest and reassured by the encouragement, Fitzsimmons took the battle to the by-now tired champion, who was no longer able to hold off the onrushing challenger, his punches beginning to fall short. But even though it was supposed to have been Fitzsimmons' "lucky round," the most damage he could effect came from a forearm to the windpipe, that is if you don't count the psychological damage done to his vanity by Fitzsimmons having knocked out two of the champion's gold teeth, a loss that Corbett noted with a look somewhere on the scale between

26

pure terror and outright embarrassment.

The fourteenth saw Fitzsimmons come running out of his corner only to be hit with two right hands that caught him flush. But Fitzsimmons kept coming back, flailing away to the body with his left when in close and going to the head from the outside. Corbett tried a right and Fitzsimmons, stepping back, cracked him with a right, then feinted him with another, bringing Corbett's hands up to his head. It was an overreaction that momentarily laid bare the champion's midsection. That moment was enough. Fitz quickly went into his patented left-handed shift and planted his left, full force, into Corbett's exposed stomach, directly under his heart. Corbett pitched forward, stricken, his wind gone. As he fell past Fitzsimmons, the soon-to-be-champion threw another left behind his ear for good measure. But it was just a postscript. The damage had been done.

Corbett fell to the floor, paralyzed. As he lay there, Fitz venomously spat out, "How do you like the view from there, you son-of-a-bitch?" But Corbett didn't respond. He couldn't. He was twisting in agony, trying to catch his breath and crawl, crablike, toward the ring ropes to right himself. As the referee reached the count of eight, Corbett blindly

groped for the rope beside him, missed it, and fell on his face. It was all over.

What wasn't over was the discussion which surrounded the bout, and its ending. Most of those at ringside had not seen the blow. Others had seen only the punch to the head, delivered while Corbett was already on his way down, even partly on the floor. And even those who had seen it hadn't understood it, or how it was delivered. Even Fitzsimmons explained it as "a left-handed shift on his wind." In reality, it was what was described in bare-knuckle days as a punch "to the mark."

It remained for Bob David, a journalist for the New York *Journal*, to put the fight—and the punch—into the history books. The day after the fight he heard two San Francisco physicians discussing the punch, describing it as one which had landed to the "solar plexus." Davis liked the sound of the phrase, and, after turning it over in his mind, not only included it in his follow-up account of the fight, but stressed it. Today, thanks to Bob Fitzsimmons, two physicians, and Bob Davis, "solar plexus" is a part of the folklore of boxing, the two-word description of one of its greatest fights.

Fitzsimmons' knockout of Corbett is depicted by noted cartoonist Bob Edgren.

27

Joe Gans—Battling Nelson

September 3, 1906

The 1904 Nevada strike was but one of a string in a state rich in precious metals. Created by the discovery of the rich Comstock Lode in 1859, a strike that produced almost $400 million in silver, the state of Nevada was admitted to the Union in 1864 because it possessed enough silver to provide much of the funding for the Civil War. Fourteen years after its first strike, the Comstock Lode produced another, the "Big Bonanza." The year 1900 saw a strike of rich silver ores in the southwestern part of the state, near Tonopah. And four years later and 40 miles farther south, the discovery of gold in the vicinity of the aptly named town of Goldfield precipitated yet another rush.

Everyone seemed drawn to Goldfield. A group of high-powered press agents pumped out story after sensational story to a nation suffering through its second major depression in 10 years. The good news—one mine produced more than $5 million of gold-bearing ore in three months—worked the same magic as a carnival barker, attracting thousands to the tent city pretentiously called "the greatest mining camp ever known." One of those who migrated there in 1904 was Tex Rickard.

With their first taste of self-promotion, the town fathers sought new and more spectacular ways to draw the world's attention to their dusty little Golconda. A meeting of the leading citizens and merchants was called. One merchant pitched unsteadily to his feet and suggested that a man-made lake be constructed on Main Street to be filled with beer every morning. A mine owner wanted the town to hire a hot-air balloon to circle the city with a basket filled with 10-dollar gold pieces which would be tossed overboard to reinforce the belief that there was gold on Goldfield's streets. Another wanted a racetrack stocked with camels imported from the Sahara. And so on. Tex Rickard suggested a prizefight.

Stimulated by Rickard's suggestion, the men formed the Goldfield Athletic Club on the spot and in less than an hour raised $50,000 to back a fight. Then they began jockeying for the most prestigious titles.

As one man after another, all bursting with pride like pouter-pigeons, jumped up and offered himself for one exalted position after another, only one man in the room didn't volunteer. That was the man who had put forward the idea, Tex Rickard. With no one desiring to have anything resembling work get in the way of his honorary title, Rickard was appointed to the positions of treasurer, "promoter," and number-one honcho. He would see to it that the fighters were found, contracts negotiated, and an arena erected. In short, Rickard was to do all the work.

Opposite: *Challenger Battling Nelson (left) and champion Joe Gans shake hands before their encounter.* Above: *Gans goes to the canvas after being fouled by Nelson.*

But he was to have the last laugh. As the promoter, his name would become known far and wide. Equally important, he was to learn how to use other people's money—O.P.M.—something any promoter worth his calling must do.

Rickard immediately turned his sights to the newest sensation, Battling Nelson, who had just beaten Jimmy Britt for "the white lightweight championship of the world," and wired him an offer of $20,000 for a "finish fight" against the recognized titleholder, the black great, Joe Gans. There was no answer.

But Rickard never took "no" for an answer. Unable to ferret out Nelson, he turned his attention to the champion, Gans. Locating him in San Francisco, where he had just knocked out "Twin" Sullivan, Rickard wired him with the offer of $20,000. Gans was destitute and immediately wired back his acceptance, agreeing to any terms Nelson demanded.

With Gans in the fold, Rickard felt reasonably assured of the fight and headed to Reno to purchase the lumber needed for the construction of an arena. There he heard that although his offer of $20,000 was the largest guarantee ever offered, an emissary from Sunny Jim Coffroth's famed San Francisco Fight Trust—the number-one fight promoter in the country, who got his nickname not for ruddy coloring but for his fabled luck with the weather for his outdoor fights—was heading east to meet Battling Nelson and offer him even more. Realizing he was fast becoming the almost-promoter of an almost fight, Rickard increased his offer to $30,000. That did it! When he returned to Goldfield a telegram awaited him. It was from Nelson's manager accepting the bid, with his man to get two-thirds of the guarantee.

Prophetically christened Oscar Battling Matthew Nelson, the man more simply known as "Bat" or "the Durable Dane" had amassed both a record and a reputation. Using the time-worn cliché, he came to fight, taking few survivors and usually three punches—preferably to the head, where it was said he was invulnerable—to every one he landed. His favorite shot was a vicious punch to the kidneys. Time and again, Nelson would take everything his opponent had to offer, then pick up the tempo, resorting to continued and often dirty in-fighting, and then knock out the thoroughly dispirited and discouraged fighter.

Joe Gans, on the other hand, was one of the classic boxers called—even today—the greatest boxer pound-for-pound and punch-for-punch of all time. In 144 fights before Goldfield, Gans had scored 49 knockouts and lost just 5 times. Three of those losses were tainted, supposedly to satisfy the betting whims of a crooked manager, since departed. But without his manager, the impoverished "master" was having trouble getting fights. For this reason, he agreed to

each new division of the guarantee Nelson's manager demanded, finally settling for $10,000 to Nelson's $23,000.

As the fight date approached—September 3, 1906—the ballyhoo increased in decibels and Rickard's plans increased in deliberateness. The streets of Goldfield began taking on the look of a midway, with every exhibitionist for hundreds of miles around descending on the town to offer his specialty, whether it was a cakewalk and watermelon dance, or bull-sticking. They were all there. And so were thousands of fans of the gentlemanly art of self-defense, spilling out of hotels, bars, and brothels, all searching vainly for a place to eat and sleep.

The day of the fight burst forth bright and it was typically dry and hot. After the prefight preliminaries that usually took place in any small fight town—including rock-drilling and races between humans and burros—almost 8,000 fans of all stripes and stations, among them 300 women, made their way into the newly constructed arena.

Gans, seriously weakened by having to make the weight just minutes before the fight at the insistence of Nelson's manager, was the first to enter the ring, just after three o'clock. He was clutching a poignant telegram he had just received from his mother in Baltimore: "Joe, the eyes of the world are upon you. Bring home the bacon!"

Then, it was Battling Nelson's turn to enter the 18-foot ring. This was yet another concession to Nelson's manager, who was positive the smaller-than-regulation ring would help his boxer.

Referee George Siler, a Chicago newspaperman, called the contestants together and the fight was on. For the first 10 rounds, his lithe black body glistening under the boiling Nevada sun, Gans struck and hit, struck and hit, pummeling Nelson in a masterful display of boxing skill. In the eleventh, Bat gained control with his stylized roughhousing, which consisted of a steady diet of butting, cuffing, and gouging. Nelson's fight plan including using every bone in his body.

By round 41, it was obvious even to Nelson that his fouling technique wasn't working. He was desperate. In round 42, while Gans smothered Nelson's infighting in a clinch, the challenger began raining blows somewhere south of Gans' beltline. As referee Siler issued a warning, Nelson drove his right hand into Gans' groin with everything he had left. Gans fell to the ground, rolling over, and shivering convulsively. Siler pushed Nelson to his corner, returned to the stricken champion, and raised his arm. Gans was the winner on a foul in the forty-second round.

Gans returned to his dressing room, still the champ, and composed a wire to his mother. It read, "Mammy, your boy bringing home the bacon with lots of gravy on it."

Jack Johnson—James J. Jeffries

July 4, 1910

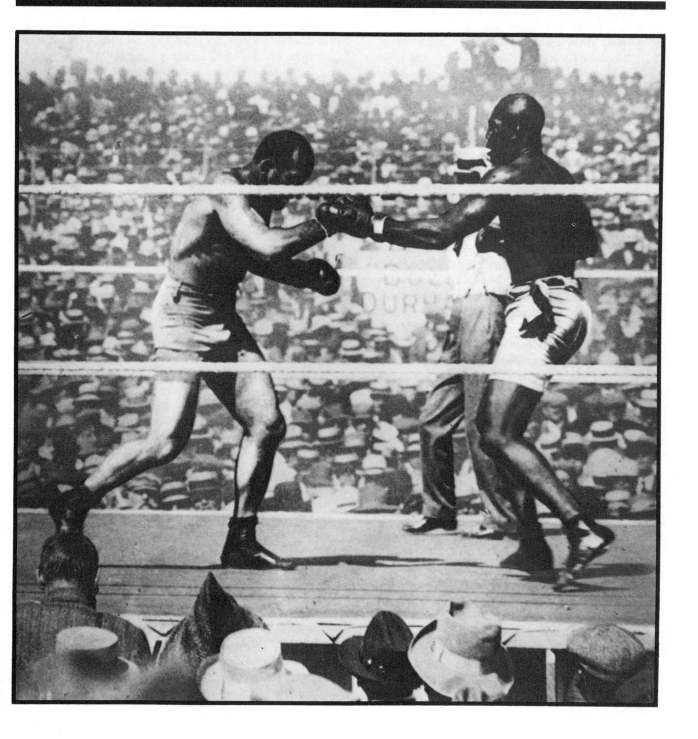

On "Boxing Day," the day after Christmas 1908, a large black cat played with a small white mouse in a boxing-match-cum-race, less for nourishment than for sadistic pleasure. The winner not only took the heavyweight championship of the world, but unleashed a dammed-up wall of hatred. For on that day in Sydney, Australia, the "Galveston Giant," Jack Johnson, outweighed, outpunched, and outgunned little Tommy Burns, and took the heavyweight championship of the world.

This wasn't merely a changing of the guard in the manner of Corbett beating Sullivan, or Fitzsimmons dethroning Corbett, or Jeffries knocking out Fitzsimmons. This was a black man beating a white man. Judgment Day had come. The "White Man's Burden" had become his master.

Johnson underlined the importance of his victory by the manner in which he achieved it. He rubbed the collective Caucasian noses in the resin. He talked to the audience and taunted his foe from the opening bell. ("Come on leddle Tahmmy!" bam—bam—bam; "Come right here where I want you," bam—bam—bam; "No good, Tahmmy! I'll teach you," bam—bam—bam.) Between rounds he expectorated with unerring accuracy over the heads of his seconds onto a vacant space at ringside the size of a handkerchief, between members of the disbelieving white press. And throughout he grinned, smiling at the 20,000 white faces in the Sydney stadium, teeth agleam. He was insufferable.

The helpless Burns was knocked down in the very first round and unable to land a blow throughout. By the fourteenth, he was hanging onto the ropes with his jaw dangling open, drooling. The local police stopped the fight. Jack Johnson had become the world's heavyweight champion. And the rallying point for a great white crusade.

Seated at ringside in Sydney, Jack London sounded the initial call to arms in the final paragraph of his story in the New York *Herald:* "One thing remains. Jeffries must emerge from his alfalfa farm and remove that smile from Johnson's face. Jeff, it's up to you!" The call went out, from public and press alike, for the unbeaten James J. Jeffries to return and avenge the defiling of the white Desdemona by putting this black Othello back in his place.

But Jeffries, who had not fought since 1904, had become bloated sitting on his farm in California. He saw no reason to leave it now. He refused to fight Johnson, invoking his right as an American citizen to "draw the color line." Hatred crescendoed as Johnson marched through the land disposing with equal ease of brave plowboys, willing white women, and tall glasses of rum. Only the invincible Jeff, the chosen representative of the white race, could answer for the real and imagined slights the Caucasian psyche was suffering at the hands of this black man who was living life to the

fullest and flaunting his color in the white man's face.

Jeffries finally succumbed. Whether it was because he heard the call for a standard-bearer, the tinkle of money, or the skin-pricking jibes of the devil-may-care Johnson, who had disposed of Jeffries' brother in five rounds in Los Angeles some eight years before, and now mocked, "I've got Jim's number," is not known. One thing is known: the first so-called "Battle of the Century" was about to take place. It was more than a morality play. It was an allegory: black versus white; invader versus avenger.

No one grasped the marketing potential of the match better than Tex Rickard. And he eagerly sought to become its architect. But he was not alone. Others saw its inherent drama and profit. Representatives of Johnson and Jeffries met and agreed to a bout to be held in July 1910. They stipulated that all bids for the bout must be submitted to them on December 1, 1909, in New York. And the "promoters" came out of the proverbial woodwork. There was Sunny Jim Coffroth and his Fight Trust from San Francisco; there was Hugh D. ("Hugh Deal") McIntosh of Sydney, who had promoted Johnson-Burns; there was Eddie Graney, premier referee with promotional aspirations; there was Uncle Tom McCarey of Los Angeles; and, of course, there was George Lewis ("Tex") Rickard.

More than 25 promoters, participants, press, and predatory hangers-on crowded in the room at Meyer's Hotel in Hoboken, New Jersey, where the auction for the rights to the fight were held, all sipping the free champagne provided them. Sealed envelopes with bids quickly made their way to the head table. Eddie Graney offered a guarantee of $70,000 plus all film rights; Fat Jack Gleason, speaking for the San Francisco Fight Trust, offered a Chinese menu of choices, either $125,000 with no film rights or $75,000 plus two-thirds of the film rights; the Australian, Hugh McIntosh, offered $55,000 for the fight if it was staged in America or $100,000 and a quarter of the film rights if held in Australia; and Uncle Tom McCarey offered "on behalf of the Pacific Club of Los Angeles," the entire gate receipts and one-half (50 percent) of the film rights.

Finally it was Rickard's turn. Like a good poker player, he had patiently waited. Now he came forward and dropped a bulky envelope on the table, cautioning the stakeholder to "Be careful with this one, it's got real money in it." When it was opened, the contents spilled out: fifteen $1,000 bills, a certified check for $5,000 more, and a piece of paper that read, "We offer the fighters the price guarantee of one hundred and one thousand dollars with sixty-six and two-thirds percent of the movie rights. The bout will be staged on July Fourth in California, Nevada, or Utah. In addition to the twenty-thousand dollars contained in the enve-

lope, twenty thousand will be deposited sixty days before the fight and an additional fifty thousand forty-eight hours before the encounter." The reading of the offer was superfluous. Jack Johnson kept staring at the bills and asked permission to touch them. "Those checks may be all right," he said, "but they don't look so good to this baby as those bills with big numbers on them." Everyone had talked big money. Only Rickard had produced it. The battle of the century was his for $101,000—plus $10,000 bonuses for each fighter under the table.

California didn't want him, but Rickard's old home state of Nevada did. He received offers from Goldfield, Reno, and Ely. Rickard now proceeded to Nevada to hear the three towns make their presentations. Each of the delegations had brass bands out to meet Rickard when he disembarked at the Reno station. Adjourning to the nearby Golden Hotel for the presentations, he emerged within the hour to announce his decision: "Boys, it's gotta be Reno because more railroads junction here."

It wasn't the train service alone that influenced his thinking. Reno had promised to build a 20,000-seat stadium to accommodate the fans who would turn out for the battle of the century.

Everyone who was anyone descended on Reno that Independence Day in 1910: writers, miners, land and cattle barons, swells and sports, pickpockets, society ladies and ladies of the street, promoters, thieves, millionaires, boxers, beggars, butchers, bakers, and Indian chiefs. It was a clan meeting of the great, the near-great, and the not-so-great. And all came bearing Jeffries' money. How could the Boilermaker, the man who had entered the ring 23 times and never lost, lose to a black man? The odds climbed to two-and-a-half to one, with no Johnson money to be found anywhere.

A hopeful crowd of 15,760 crowded into the stadium, chanting, "Jeff, it's up to you." This would be their day, the white man's day, in the Armageddon between the forces of good and evil. In those innocent days before World War I, the outcome was preordained. It was as simple as black and white.

But as a gleeful Johnson strode into the ring, a haggard and seemingly unnerved Jeffries slowly moved up the aisle. Some at ringside sensed that the hoped-for miracle

might not take place. Maybe some of the fighters who had been criticizing Jeffries' training methods had been right. Maybe their prejudice and emotionalism had blinded them to the fact that the once-great symbol of white supremacy had been robbed of his skills by the loss of 70 pounds and a six-year absence. Still, he was the invincible Jeff, or so the miracle workers hoped.

As the scheduled 45-round bout began, all of their misgivings took form. The huge black man played with the 35-year-old former champion and mouth-fought with those in his corner. For 14 rounds Johnson muffed everything Jeffries threw, playing pattycake with him. He picked off every blow and drew the frustrated white champion-turned-challenger into clinches, all the while taunting him with, "Now stop lovin' me like that, Mr. Jeff," and "How do you like this jab, Mr. Jeff?"

In the fifteenth round Johnson did the unthinkable. Springing at the shambling form in front of him, the pantherlike Johnson sent Jeffries reeling to the ropes with a quick series of blows. Then he drove the dazed hulk in front of him to the canvas with a series of short, snappy punches to the head. For the first time in his career, Jeffries was down. He staggered to his feet only to be hit by two more jolts to the jaw and knocked down again. As the obviously hurt Jeffries fell to his knees, the crowd screamed, "Stop it! Stop it! Don't let him be knocked out!" hoping to save themselves and the Caucasian race the embarrassment of having their standard-bearer so simply disposed of. But Rickard waved the two fighters together again, oblivious of the pleadings of the stricken crowd. As Johnson landed unanswered blow after unanswered blow on Jeffries' vulnerable Nordic jaw, he sank to the canvas for yet a third time, one arm wearily hanging over the middle strand of rope. One of Jeffries' cornermen started climbing into the ring. Without finishing his count, Rickard walked over to Johnson and placed his hand on the champion's shoulder. The black man had won. The crusade had failed.

Rickard, who had grossed $270,715 from the Battle of the Century—far below his original expectations of a half-million gate in the 30,000-seat bowl he had originally constructed in San Francisco—was now hailed as the "King of Sports Promoters." Tex, who never kept books and never knew until he had tabulated the gate receipts how he fared, never disclosed his profit. Johnson collected $120,000—$70,000 from Rickard; and Jeffries retired back to his alfalfa farm with $117,000—$50,000 of it Rickard's.

Finally, Rickard's promotional victory was bittersweet in the face of his idol Jeffries' downfall. He swore he would never again promote a fight between a black man and a white man.

Johnson (left) was the clear victor in this pugilistic morality play.

33

Ad Wolgast—Joe Rivers

July 4, 1912

Those were the days, my friend. Great days filled with great fights fought by great fighters. It was a colorful time and boxing was different then, not as antiseptic and regulated as it is now. Dirty tricks and scams were all a part of the game—in the ring and out. There were no ring judges and no guidelines for scoring. The referee was the supreme arbiter—the judge and jury. No boxing commissions yet existed to question his authority or overrule his decisions. Fights could be won or lost, and championships change hands on *his* word alone. Integrity and competence was of paramount importance. It was the Judge Roy Bean school of the referee's word serving as law; nothing more, but never anything less.

That's the way the fight game worked when the famous lightweight championship battle took place between Ad Wolgast and "Indian" Joe Rivers on Independence Day, 1912. To this day, it remains a source of controversy for boxing fans and historians alike. A once-in-a-lifetime ending.

Rivers was 19 and making his first appearance as a lightweight after compiling an impressive record as a featherweight. He was a quick-thinking, fast-punching boxer with a faultless, deadly left hand.

Born Joe Ybarra of Castillian and Indian ancestry, Indian Joe changed his name with the help of Charlie McHugh, the secretary of the Pacific Athletic Club. Upon hearing Ybarra's name, Charlie asked the fighter where he lived and was told, "Down by the river." "Well," said Charlie, "I want to introduce you as Joe Rivers." The name stuck.

Rivers was trying to wrestle the title from Ad Wolgast, "the Michigan Wildcat," who had won it in 1910 in a 40-round bloodletting with the aptly named Battling Nelson. Wolgast had lost only once in 86 fights, and that in his third fight. Never knocked out, he had knocked out 30 men.

Wolgast was a "stand and slam" fighter who trained for his bouts by "roughing it" in the tradition of James J. Jeffries. For weeks he would cloister himself in the mountains, and, regardless of the weather, strip down to the waist and spend hours running up and down mountainsides, throwing rocks, and chopping trees to strengthen his lungs and heart.

In agreeing to give Rivers the first shot at his title, Wolgast compelled the Mexican to accept Wolgast's choice of Jack Welch as referee. Welch, from San Francisco, had several times expressed himself in favor of Wolgast's slam-bang style as opposed to the "scientific" methods of defense. He was known as a referee who not only permitted, but indeed favored roughhouse tactics. In short, Welch believed that his job was to give the spectators what they'd paid to see—an out and out brawl.

A few months earlier, Welch had refereed a fight be-

tween Frank Klaus and Jack Dillon in which both men had refused to abide by the rules and were repeatedly admonished by Welch. Lacking the courage to disqualify either man, he left the ring, refusing to participate further in the contest. The battle continued with both fighters resorting to dirtier tactics. When it was over, although he had removed himself from the contest, Welch returned to the ring and awarded the verdict to Klaus on points. It was in Jack Welch's hands that the history of the lightweight division rested that day.

Eleven thousand fans crammed into the Vernon, California, open-air arena—suffering the glare and heat—to view the championship contest. Rivers was impatient and went right to the champion as soon as the bell rang to start the battle. As if it were a greeting, they exchanged right-hand blows to the face. Rivers stood erect in a classic boxer's pose, while Wolgast fought from a crouch. It was immediately apparent that Wolgast was not in the best of shape—slow to react and flat-footed. Perhaps he figured that his experience, together with his referee, would be enough for him to win.

Wolgast's ear was cut in the second round and blood coated the Mexican's gloves as he pounded the champ from all angles. Wolgast spent most of his time swinging wildly while the challenger continued to reach the champion with his jab, connecting to the face and the heart. Wolgast began to slow down even more. By the fourth, Ad's cut ear had company, a new wound over the left eye which swelled, becoming just a thin slit.

But now Indian Joe was beginning to slow down, too, from the number of punches he had thrown. It was Wolgast's turn. Fighting as much with his mouth as his fists, Ad taunted the Mexican, calling him every dirty name and showering him with every insult he could think of. It might have been this great spending of energy that tired Wolgast, but whatever the cause, it was apparent to both the champion and his handlers that if he were going to win, he had better do it in a hurry. For "tire" was also a four-letter word, and the most important one for Wolgast now.

Wolgast began to wrestle Rivers in order to stop the backpedaling craftsman. The tactic worked, and soon Wolgast began scoring well, turning Joe's body the color of an overripe tomato. Tremendous punishment was inflicted on both sides. Onlookers wondered how much longer the fighters could take so much abuse.

The battle seesawed, with first one man and then the other taking control. Both men were weak in the knees. The general consensus of those at ringside was that Rivers was ahead, but beginning to fade. Joe's face was puffed up like a turnip by the end of the ninth round. In the eleventh, both

Champion Ad Wolgast (left) appears to have Indian Joe Rivers heading upstream in the early going.

combatants nearly fell through the ropes during one extremely torrid exchange; and as soon as they had again found their footing, they began to go to it again. They kept everlastingly at it, slugging each other around the ring till the end of the twelfth round. The next round was when Jack Welch took control.

Wolgast, knowing that he was fast becoming a beaten man, decided not to answer the bell for the thirteenth round. His cornerman, Herman Stizel, threatened to bean him with a beer bottle if he didn't reconsider his decision. Ad must have realized that he stood a better chance against the Indian than against Herman's bottle.

Rivers rushed the hulk of the champion. But Ad held on and both men began to wrestle. Suddenly, Ad went into a crouch and sent a terrific left to the only area visible to him, directly over Rivers' groin. At that exact instant, Rivers let fly with a picture-perfect left-right combination to Wolgast's jaw. Incredibly, both boxers fell, with Rivers dropping first and Wolgast heaped on top of him.

Screams of "foul, foul" filled the arena. Welch ignored the cries. The referee looked at first one and then the other downed fighter. He counted out the numbers, lifting Wolgast from the canvas. Ad drooped as Welch dragged the champion tucked under one arm, to his corner. Through it all, the referee kept up his count. And when he had reached the fatal "10," he lifted Ad Wolgast's arm in victory.

Without waiting for the crowd's reaction, Welch bolted from the arena to a waiting car. It was weeks before he was heard from again.

At ringside all was chaos. An angry mob rushed into the ring and the police were called to quell the riot. Long after the fight had ended they were still there, shouting, threatening, and arguing among themselves. They had borne witness to what was perhaps the rarest incident in the history of boxing—a double knockout. But now, it seemed that no one could agree on exactly what they saw!

Three weeks later, Welch surfaced to tell his version of what happened.

As he saw it, Wolgast's punch was the first to land— if only by a fraction of a second. Still, it was the first blow and, there being no rule or precedent governing such an occurrence, he felt it necessary for one man to be the winner. Not only had Ad struck first, but he had gone down last. Welch saw it as his duty as the third man in the ring to help the champion up and to his corner. Since Rivers was also unable to beat the count, there was only one thing for him to do: declare Wolgast the winner and still champion.

Welch's story made sense to some people, but it didn't make sense to many more.

Al Harder, the official timekeeper, stated publicly

that it was impossible for Rivers to have been counted out because the thirteenth round ended when Welch's count reached nine. Three doctors who examined Rivers after the battle agreed that Joe had indeed been fouled by a Wolgast low blow—probably the one that had sent him to the canvas. The majority of sportswriters present also corroborated Rivers' version and supported his claim that he had been unjustly denied the title.

Earl Rogers, Rivers' attorney, released a statement which read, "It was the most gigantic swindle and the most wholesale bit of robbery that has come to my notice. As early as ten o'clock this morning I learned that a plot was afoot

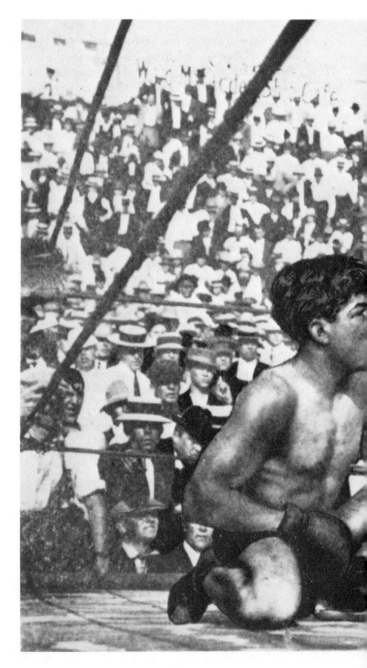

whereby Wolgast was to be given the victory no matter what the cost might be."

But there were those who supported Wolgast as the fouled fighter. One of those, Hector J. Streyckman, the man who edited the Keystone comedies for Mack Sennett, was at the fight with his boss and filmed all the action. He said his evidence supported Welch's decision because Rivers fouled Wolgast.

"I rushed the negative to the laboratory and made a print which I showed in slow motion to the reporters. The action was clearly shown as Wolgast dug his fist three times into Rivers' *midsection*. Then, Rivers' knee was seen coming up in a convulsive action. . . . Rivers was a foul fighter. He should have been disqualified."

By the time Ad's career had ended, he had fought over 130 contests, every one of which was a hard and brutal battle. He scored 38 knockouts, losing only 9, and, so the records indicate, was never down for the count. He lost his memory in 1920 and was confined to a sanatorium.

Indian Joe Rivers made $250,000 in the ring, but lost most of it to bad living and worse investments. When Wolgast was placed in confinement, his most frequent visitor was Indian Joe. An incredible, ironic ending to an even more incredible fight.

The world's most famous double knockout—both Wolgast and Rivers (left) went down at the same time. Here, Rivers claims a foul while the referee, Jack Welsh, plucks Wolgast from atop Rivers and counts the challenger out at the same time.

Jack Dempsey—Jess Willard

July 4, 1919

Jess Willard was a 6-foot 6-inch hulk of a man who had emerged from a grizzled ancestry of miners, cowpokes, gandy dancers, oil men, lumberjacks, and plowboys to lay claim to the ersatz title of "Great White Hope," a distinction given to any fighter of more than 175 pounds and the right complexion. Nicknamed "the Pottawatomie Giant," the cowboy-turned-fighter had established a respectable record in the ring and an aura of invincibility outside it, having killed another of the so-called White Hopes, Bull Young, with one punch. Matched with an out-of-shape and mentally weary 37-year-old Jack Johnson in Havana in 1915, Willard wore the champion down and knocked him out in the twenty-sixth round—the longest heavyweight championship bout in Queensberry history—to become heavyweight champion of the world.

With the title safely ensconced under his massive arm, Willard hit the obligatory vaudeville circuit, stopping just once to defend his crown, against Frank Moran in a lackluster no-decision fight in Madison Square Garden. Disposing of Moran, Willard found no other bona-fide challengers on the horizon. But just below the horizon and rising like the morning sun was a man named William Harrison Dempsey.

Dempsey—originally fighting under the name "Kid Blackie," in testimony to his penetratingly dark features, and then under the adoptive name of Jack, taken from the former middleweight "Nonpareil" Jack Dempsey—had blazed a path across the West with a string of one-round knockouts. Fighting out of a bobbing crouch that would become legendary, he approached every bout as a war. From his very first fight, against One-Punch Hancock in Salt Lake City in 1915, whom he prophetically dispatched with his first left hook following a feint, through his first four years of boxing, Dempsey had scored more first-round knockouts than any fighter in history: 26. Only once had the favor been returned, when the semistarved slugger had been taken out in the first round by Fireman Jim Flynn.

The boy-man who once had ridden the rails and lived in the hobo camps of the West now had a future and a manager, Jack ("Doc") Kearns. Dempsey and Kearns emerged on the scene in 1918 to challenge the giant Willard, who had gone underground after his defense against Moran, surfacing only three times in two years for exhibitions.

Together they had stepped over the prone bodies of up-and-coming—as well as down-and-going—heavyweights on the ladder to the heavyweight title, while Kearns invested the pronoun "I" with imperial importance, inserting himself into every situation, as in "I knocked out Gunboat Smith in two rounds." Carl Morris went in four rounds, six rounds, and in 14 seconds; Fireman Jim Flynn was returned the fa-

Opposite: *Jack Dempsey (left) sends Jess Willard into the ropes and onto the canvas for the first of seven trips*. Left (top to bottom): *Freeze-frame sequence of Dempsey's repeated assaults on Willard*.

Top: *A sea of straw hats protects the heads of the onlookers in the 100-degree-plus heat as Dempsey pounds on the unprotected Willard. Above: A mural by celebrated artist James Montgomery Flagg depicts Dempsey's knockout of Willard in their title bout.*

vor in kind in one round; Bill Brennan was disposed of in six; Fred Fulton was dispatched in 23 or 18 seconds depending upon which paper you read; Battling Levinsky went in three rounds, and so on. Now there remained only one challenger, and Doc Kearns had him.

The fight was set for July 4, 1919. The site was set for Toledo, Ohio. Toledo had been selected because it not only was "near the center of population," one of promoter Tex Rickard's underlying principles of promotion, but also because Ohio Governor James M. Cox guaranteed that, in the absence of any adverse boxing laws on the books of the Buckeye State, the fight would take place as promised.

The Dempsey-Willard bout generated more interest than any fight since Rickard's previous outdoor promotion, the Jeffries-Johnson match, nine years before to the day.

With the thermometer at the breaking point, so were Rickard's nerves. His whole future depended on the show's success. He found Dempsey alone in his dressing room, minutes before he was to depart for the ring. Pushing his straw hat back on his head and puzzling about how to begin, he dove in with, "Jack, this Willard's a big and tough fighter. He just might kill you. Remember what he did with a single punch of his to Bull Young." Dempsey broke into Rickard's soliloquy to say, "I know he did, Tex." Encouraged that Dempsey was paying attention, Tex took another puff on his

two-dollar cigar and hurried on, "Take my advice. If he hits you a good shot and hurts you, go down and stay down before he kills you. I don't want you killed." Wishing Dempsey good luck, he turned and walked quickly out of the room.

After a steady procession of preliminaries a half-hour apart, blimps and biplanes flying overhead, and a bayonet and dagger fighting exhibition, the two fighters came down the aisles more than 30 minutes late. Standing opposite each other to get the referee's instructions, the fighters' height differential was exaggerated. Willard looked even larger than his 6 feet 6 inches, 245 pounds, because of his obvious flab, and Dempsey looked smaller than his 6 feet 1 inch, 180 pounds, because of his tanned, intense look, magnified by a two-day growth of beard. Then the bell, and the fight started.

With the first punch, Dempsey's right to the heart, followed by a devastating left hook to the jaw, the fight was all but over. As Willard fell for the first time, his jaw had been broken. He staggered upright to face Dempsey, who stood above him like an avenging angel, ignoring all niceties. Dempsey dropped him again. Again he struggled upright and again Dempsey floored him. This was repeated again and again, with metronomic repetition, until finally the giant fell for the seventh and last time in the round, sitting in the corner like he was relaxing after a swim, his arms extended along the lower strands of rope supporting his huge body, which heaved and shook. The referee's arm swung down in rhythmic motion as those in the crowd who could— many were pinioned to their seats by the oozing green sap of the wood—stood and roared. It was over! Willard's jaw had been broken in seven places and Kearns, who had wagered between $10,000 and $100,000 that Dempsey would add yet another one-round knockout to his record, danced around the ring, hugging his warrior. Dempsey put on his sweater and made his way down the aisle, while everyone else looked around in confusion.

But unbelievably the fight was *not* over! The bell had rung while Willard was reposing in the corner, the turnbuckle as his backrest, the count unfinished. Willard was dragged back to his corner—his jaw broken, four teeth missing, his eyes closed, his nose smashed, and two ribs cracked—to do battle again. And Dempsey had now to fight his way back up the aisle to take his place in the corner for another round. But it was only a matter of time now, and after the third round, Willard sat on his stool unable to continue and sobbed, "I have a farm in Kansas and a hundred thousand dollars . . . I have a farm in Kansas and a hundred thousand dollars . . . I have a farm . . ." Jack Dempsey stood in the middle of the ring—the new heavyweight champion.

Benny Leonard—Richie Mitchell

January 14, 1921

The freelance world of boxing has one enormous plus going for it: its matchmakers are able to structure their offerings and provide audiences with all the trappings of melodrama and morality plays within the confines of the four ring posts.

The early club fights in New York always had the added element of match-ups which would make the modern wrestling matchmaker's typecasting pale by comparison. Local favorites from one section would invariably be pitted against the local favorites from another; Irishmen would fight Italians; Jews would fight Irishmen; the local 86th Street champion would fight the local 84th Street champion; or any one of dozens of other combinations from the potential variations available, all in the name of good match-ups, and good entertainment.

It was in that world of point-counterpoint that characterized the early days of boxing that the most sought-after performer was one who combined the boxing ingenuity of Young Griffo, the masterful technique of James J. Corbett, the punching power of Jack Dempsey, the alertness of Gene Tunney, and the speed of Mike Gibbons. That one man was the legendary lightweight champion Benny Leonard, "the Ghetto Wizard."

Leonard had grown up in a world of hyphenated Americanism, a world where street gangs on New York's Lower East Side sought to stake a claim to territorial and bragging rights with their fists. It was a day and age where, if roving members of gangs from the Irish, Italian, or Jewish sections wandered into the territory ruled by another, they had to fight their way out, in a throwback to the old donnybrook days of Ireland. The only difference was that the shillelagh had been replaced by the fist.

Leonard had had his share of fights, especially in that area which lay just beyond his street, the area known as "No Man's Land," Eighth Street and Avenue C. One Saturday afternoon Benny's gang and the members of the Sixth Street Club became entangled in a war of fists and a street fight ensued in which everyone, down to the smallest member, took part. When the smoke of battle had cleared, two emissaries arranged for a member from each gang to "duke it out" in a special fight for gang supremacy. Leonard was chosen to represent his faction. The Sixth Street Gang chose a freckle-faced Irish kid named Joey Fogarty, a tough whose fists had already become a permanent part of the face of many of the Jewish kids from Leonard's neighborhood. Operating under a flag of truce, the two emissaries agreed to hold the fight in an impromptu ring in a roomy backyard in the Dry Dock section, all the better to flee in case of police intervention.

Both sides came out in force to cheer for their rep-

resentative, paying one cent for admission, the so-called receipts to be divied up, 60–40. Four ash cans were laid about the yard, with a huge rope interconnecting them and forming a ring. The boys went at it, without benefit of referee. For the first round the heavier Fogarty, clad in a pair of green swimming trunks and a green gym shirt, stalked the smaller Leonard, who wore cutoff woolen underwear. But it wasn't their respective sartorial splendors that was to carry the day as much as Leonard's splendid ringsmanship, a trait he was to develop further later in his career. Leonard moved and feinted his opponent out of position time and again. Finally, in the third round, he nailed the onrushing Fogarty with a beautiful right, and Fogarty was carried from the ring as Leonard was carried out on his gang's shoulders.

It was the beginning of his ring career. And the beginning of his continually being cast as the "Jewish" boxer against opponents who were, more often than not, Irish. Changing his name from Leiner to "Leonard"—after the old minstrel performer Eddie Leonard so that his mother wouldn't discover his new pursuit—Leonard began his professional career as a 15-year-old stripling in 1911 against, you guessed it, Mickey Finnegan. This time, although Leonard was outpointing his Irish opponent, Finnegan landed a right squarely on Leonard's nose, bringing forth a red sea of blood that caused the referee to stop the fight and award it to Finnegan.

The following year saw Leonard, who had now participated in 21 fights—winning 11 of those by knockout in a day when most went to a nondecision—up against a heavy puncher from Jersey City named Joe Shugrue. Bill Brown of Brown's Gym sold the fight as one between the Irish puncher and the Jewish favorite. He was not disappointed in the turnout, as the two factions jammed the club to the doors to root for their favorite. From the outset of the fight, Shugrue, who affected the style of Jim Jeffries—fighting out of a crouch, left hand extended—forced the action, also forcing Leonard to backpedal to stay out of danger. In the third, the hard-hitting Shugrue crashed a left into Leonard's solar plexus, causing Leonard to fall to the floor gasping for breath. The bell saved him, but only for more damage. For, in the fourth, although Leonard got off first, catching Shugrue on the chin and flooring him, the Irishman got up and chased Leonard across the ring, first hitting him in the eye and nearly blinding Leonard, and then coming over with a crushing right to the chin which dropped Leonard to his knees. Leonard arose groggily, and ran into another right and then a left to the mouth. As the stricken Leonard fell into the ropes, the referee decided he had had enough and stopped the fight. Leonard had suffered his second loss. His second by knockout. And his second to an Irishman.

Lightweight champion Benny Leonard

As Leonard sat in his corner sobbing, the victorious Shugrue came over to console the near-fallen fighter with the words, "Kid, you've got it. Don't let that knockout bother you. Other fighters were kayoed and came back. You'll do the same."

Benny Leonard *was* to come back. Fighting as many as 19 fights a year for the next five years, he was to win the lightweight championship on May 28, 1917, from Freddie Welsh in a ninth-round knockout and go on to defend it against Johnny Kilbane, Charley White, and Joe Welling, before signing to fight the first title fight in the new Madison Square Garden under the new Walker Law, allowing for 15-round fights to a decision.

His opponent that January night in 1921 was another Irishman, Richie Mitchell, the leading lightweight contender. But he was no ordinary contender. Three inches taller than Leonard, he was a better boxer than Joe Welling and a harder puncher than even Leonard himself. He had more than held his own with some of the "greats" of his day, men like Joe Rivers, Charley White, Lew Tender, Ad Wolgast, and Johnny Kilbane. The only knockout loss in his nine-year career had come at the hands of the same man he was to face for the championship, Benny Leonard. And that had come in 1917, little more than a month before Leonard won the title. On that date Leonard had gone to Milwaukee to face the local pride, and had not observed the protocol of the no-decision era: that one does not try to knock out a "homer" whom he might fight again. In the seventh round Leonard had feinted Mitchell into an awkward lunge and nailed him with a short right, leaving Mitchell to be picked up by the local burghers. Now the confident Mitchell sought to avenge the sole blotch on his record, and Leonard's failure to observe boxing's "no-decision" amenities.

Madison Square Garden is at once a building and a symbol. Originally a New York, New Haven & Hartford Railroad freight yard and depot, the structure had been converted in 1874 by none other than P. T. Barnum into a magnificent hall that measured 425 feet by 200 feet, called Barnum's Monster Classical and Geological Hippodrome. In 1890 William Vanderbilt put together a syndicate of Ward McAllister's famed Four Hundred—including John Pierpont Morgan, Hiram Hitchcock, and William F. Wharton—to raise $1.5 million to build a new "pleasure palace" on the spot at Madison Square. Opening in June 1890 with a concert and two ballets, it was described by the *New York Times* as "one of the great institutions of the town, to be mentioned along with Central Park and the bridge of Brooklyn."

Now, some 31 years later, the famed old dowager hosted not only its first championship fight to a decision, but also many of New York's top debutantes and duennas. All were part of a sellout crowd, which included many of the celebrities who took part in a fund-raising event for devastated France, a charity benefit run by J. P. Morgan's daughter, Anne, whose centerpiece was the Leonard-Mitchell fight.

Almost before the 400—plus some 14,000 others—had taken their places, the action was on. And the fight was almost over. For, when the opening bell rang, Leonard, cool and contemptuous of his foe, walked out and stabbed the Milwaukee idol in the face, following with a hard right to the jaw. Another right missed the jaw, but landed with such force on the cheek that Mitchell went down. It looked like Leonard's offhand prediction to gambler Arnold Rothstein that "It ought to be an easy fight. I probably can knock him out in the first round," would prove correct. As Miss Morgan and her guests joined with the common man in screaming at the action in front of them, a groggy Mitchell tottered to his feet at the count of nine. Mitchell sought to fall into a clinch, but Leonard stayed far enough away to avoid his grasp and caught the challenger with a shower of lefts and rights, ending with a left hook to the point of the chin. The challenger was down for the second time.

Again up at the count of nine, Mitchell was visibly reeling. And visibly bleeding, a gash under his eye giving him a hideous mask unrivaled by any Lon Chaney wore. Leonard leaped in again for the finish, rocking Mitchell with a left to the jaw and a right to the chin. Mitchell fell like a tree, finally gathering his limbs together to rise a third time. Up at the count of eight, Mitchell ran into still another steady bombardment of solid smashes. Only this time, instead of falling, he fought back, landing several hard punches to Leonard's head. Leonard, brushing off what seemed to be the challenger's dying gasp, waded inside to finish his man off. But a funny thing happened to him on his way: he caught a left to the stomach that carried Richie's last ounce of effort, his glove buried wrist-deep into Leonard's midsection. Then, as Leonard stood shock still, trying to catch his breath, Mitchell followed up his momentary advantage with a right hand that landed on the "button." Leonard went down as if he were shot.

It was unbelievable. One minute New York's famed gladiator, the world lightweight king, the idol of the Empire State, had been standing over his fallen foe; now he was being counted out. Not only was his patent-leather hair mussed, but blood was trickling out of the corner of his mouth and his eyes were dimmed. He tried to shake his head back to consciousness as his fans shouted inaudible instructions for him to get up, instructions echoed by his corner, which was trying to reach him over the din, "Get up, Benny! Shake your head, Benny!"

Leonard pulled himself semierect with 28 seconds to

44

Leonard has been called "the greatest boxer, pound for pound," ever. "The Ghetto Wizard" was recently selected as the fifth-greatest fighter of all time by Ring *magazine.*

go in the first round, the quick mind that had taken him so far full of cobwebs. But even while Mitchell's father, Billy Mitchell, was leaning through the ropes exhorting his son to "Move in, move in, finish 'im!" and Richie himself stood only a split second away from becoming the ninth lightweight champion of the world, Benny Leonard possessed enough ring savvy to hold out both hands and motion to Mitchell to "come on." Mitchell fell for the trickery, unsure of his adversary's intent and not knowing that had Leonard taken one step toward him he would have pitched forward, the ex-lightweight champion of the world. Mitchell stood there. Then, after a precious few seconds, he started forward. But by then it was too late. Leonard had regained his senses in those few seconds, preserving his crown and asserting his ring mastery.

The next round found Mitchell pressuring Leonard. Indeed, he scored with a right to the jaw that again had Benny wobbly. But Leonard, retreating on his bicycle, stayed away from Mitchell, as he used all the defensive tactics that had enabled him to survive thousands of street fights on the Lower East Side and more than a hundred and fifty in the ring. By the end of the round he was talking to Mitchell, taunting him with, "Is that the best you can do? Look . . . I'll put my hands down, you can't hit me. . . . If you think you've got me hurt, why don't you fight?" It was enough to drive a grown man to tears. Or, if you were Richie Mitchell, to tears of frustration, as his quarry got away and his chance for a world title evaporated.

By round 3 Benny Leonard was Benny "the Great" again, his hair now combed straight back, his jab in Mitchell's face and his straight right coming over the top. *This* was what the crowd had come to see.

By round 6, with Mitchell tiring from his wild swings and Leonard completely in control, Benny went back on the attack, landing a right with such power that it sent Mitchell down on his back. Once more Mitchell was on his feet at the count of nine. Lefts and rights rained on Mitchell's unprotected face, a face that was now but a faint reminder of what he had looked like just six rounds before; his lips were smashed and his eyes were closed with deep gashes above and below. The crowd began to chant for the referee to stop the slaughter. A buzzsaw of punches came in on his unseeing face and down he went again, for the fifth time. But the brave Irishman did not know the meaning of the word "quit" and arose at the count of six with a sneer of defiance on his face—a look that almost said to Leonard, "You're going to have to kill me to beat me." Staggering around, Mitchell caught still another fusillade of punches and dropped for the sixth time.

Incredibly, he arose once more. Leonard, who had

been opportuning referee Billy Haukup to intervene and was not getting a response, now took it upon himself to end the carnage. It was a beautiful right that caught Mitchell on the chin and dropped him still one more time. It was to be the last. His heroic foe, try as he might, couldn't bestir himself

Poised for victory in the neutral corner, Leonard waits while the referee gives Mitchell the chance to get up one last time.

again. Benny Leonard had won the most thrilling battle in the history of the lightweight division, turning what appeared to be certain defeat into victory.

Ray Arcel, handler of 18 world champions, once said, "Benny Leonard, in my opinion, was the greatest boxer, pound for pound, that I ever saw. He was *the* champion of the best lightweight division anybody has ever seen. Any of the leading contenders of that period could have been champion if Benny was not there." Particularly Richie Mitchell!

Jack Dempsey—Georges Carpentier

July 2, 1921

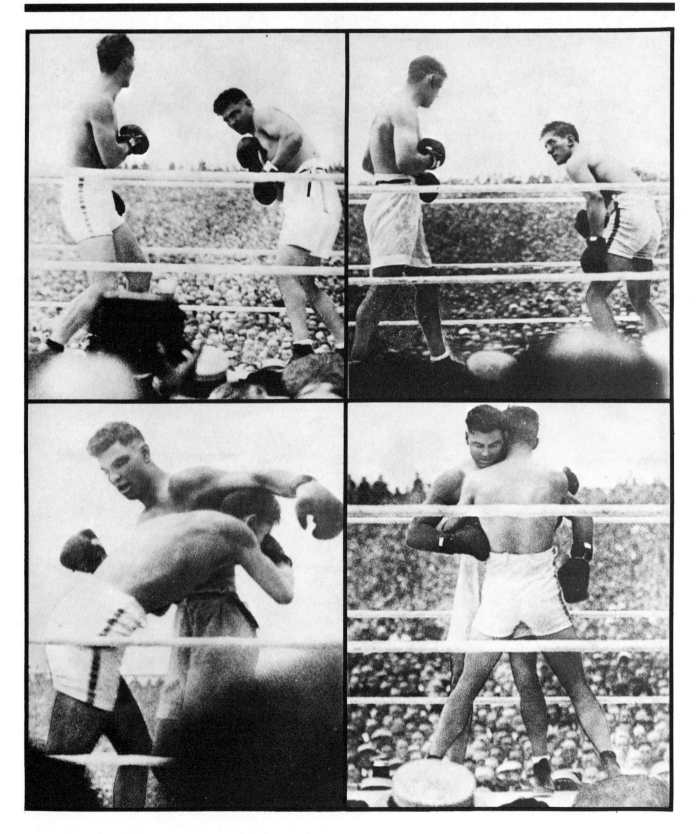

Although post–World War I America was hell-bent on pleasure-seeking, it still prided itself on its patriotic efforts in the recent conflict. It was the stated belief of many that the war had "knit us together," and an aroused America demanded conformity from its citizens. More than 6,000 persons were arrested for criticizing the government, the Constitution, and the flag. Americans paraded with signs identifying themselves as "100 percent patriots," and super-Americanism was in vogue. One thing that could not be tolerated by a proud and victorious America was anyone who had not "pulled his weight" in the war effort.

In February 1920, Jack Dempsey was indicted by a federal grand jury in San Francisco for draft evasion. He stood accused of violation of the Selective Service Act and making false statements to the district draft board in San Francisco. His first wife, Maxine Cates—a self-confessed "lady of loose morals"—initially testified against him. When she recanted, the jury brought in a verdict dismissing the charge. Nevertheless, the taint remained. Jack Dempsey had been a "slacker."

The charge and the resultant stigmata together with Dempsey's lackluster defense of his crown against Bill Brennan provided Tex Rickard with a matchmaker's dream and the opportunity to attain his goal of a million-dollar gate.

Rickard's announced philosophy was "Give the people what they want, the way they want it, and not the way you think best." Now he was prepared to give them what they wanted: a fight between Georges Carpentier and Jack Dempsey. Few professional judges of fighters agreed that it would be the best, but Rickard wasn't counting on them to buy many tickets.

At that moment in time, the light-heavyweight champion and one of the leading boxers in the world was a handsome French war hero named "Gorgeous" Georges Carpentier. Carpentier had been a professional boxer for 14 years, fighting in every division from bantamweight up as he matured. He had won all his six postwar fights by knockouts and had captured the light-heavyweight crown by knocking out Battling Levinsky in four rounds in October 1920. But what made Carpentier a "natural" opponent for Dempsey was not his ring record but his war record. While Dempsey was labeled a "slacker," Carpentier was a bona fide hero, having spent 18 months at the front flying a two-seater observation plane. He had been wounded twice and received the *croix de guerre* and *medaille militaire*. Rickard saw the fight not as an overgrown middleweight challenging for the heavyweight title but as a "hero" against a "villain." It was a classic match, a draw with a potential million-dollar gate.

Rickard put together a loose-fitting international consortium with British theatrical impresario Charles B. Cochran, who had an option on Carpentier's services and the money for the bout as well. Associated with Cochran was his American representative, William A. Brady, who had formerly managed both Corbett and Jeffries and had been associated with Cochran in some of his across-the-water theatrical productions.

Opposite: *Georges Carpentier (in striped trunks) tries to stay away from Jack Dempsey's vaunted power in the early rounds*. Above: *Dempsey begins to find the challenger in the third round*.

Still, Rickard was not prepared for the demands from the two participants. Doc Kearns demanded $300,000 and 25 percent of the film rights for the champion Dempsey. Carpentier, speaking through his French-speaking manager, Francois Descamps, who, in turn, spoke through his interpreter, crafty Jack Curley, demanded $200,000 plus one-quarter of the movie rights. Together, the two fighters were demanding more money than any fight had ever grossed.

Bluff and counterbluff followed, as each side played its hands for all they were worth. But Kearns' high-handed treatment of Cochran, Rickard, and Brady soon incited the wrath of the press. Kearns tried one more bluff, trotting out two waiters posing as Cuban millionaires to go through a ritualistic contract signing. It worked. The promoters gave in, hot on the scent of the elusive million-dollar gate.

The final articles of incorporation were signed November 5, 1920, one month before Dempsey stepped into the ring against Carpentier. Three days before, the country had had its first postwar election and, yearning to return to a nebulous state called "normalcy," it had swept out the Democrats. In the Harding landslide, New York State had elected Republican Nathan Miller governor. The new governor banned the Dempsey-Carpentier fight on the grounds

that half a million dollars was too much to pay a pair of prizefighters for a few minutes work at a time when thousands of men were out of work. That was enough for Cochran and Brady. Feigning headaches, they retired from the scene, leaving Rickard alone.

Rickard decided to do what came naturally: gamble. Short of funds—but not friends—Rickard posted the $100,000 promoter's bond and officially announced that he had taken over all other interests. The money came from a ticket speculator named Mike Jacobs, who had organized the leading Broadway ticket brokers for the purchase of preferred seats. They provided Rickard with $160,000, a sufficient grubstake to carry out his promotional plans.

With the money—and bout—in hand, Rickard searched close to New York for a site for the match. He found one on a desolate lot near Jersey City owned by a paper box manufacturer named Boyle and contracted for a massive bowl which would house over 90,000 fans. The press quickly named the site "Boyle's Thirty Acres."

Rickard had the right combination: a handsome war hero, the darling of society who had led a charmed life and was called "the Orchid Man" (the title of his movie then making the rounds) versus a forboding, animalistic former

50

Above: In fighting poses, Carpentier displays his readiness for his opponent, Dempsey. *Opposite:* Dempsey rounds into shape for his international battle against "the Orchid Man," Georges Carpentier.

Carpentier lands a right to Dempsey's jaw in the second round;
Dempsey recovers before the challenger, who broke his hand with
this punch.

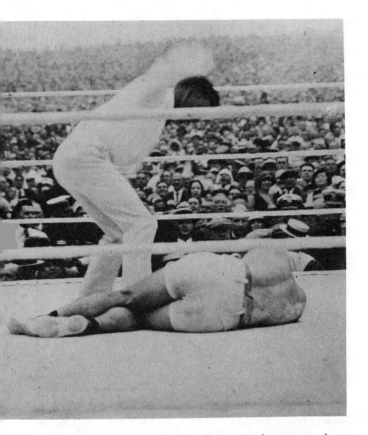

hobo with a dark stubble of beard, a man who possessed no charm and had been labeled a "slacker" by a federal grand jury. It was a classic match between hero and villain, and Rickard ballyhooed it for all it was worth, which was plenty.

The excitement was contagious. The first truly international fight in more than a decade attracted global attention. David Sarnoff arranged with Rickard to broadcast the fight on radio, making it the first major sporting event ever to grace the airwaves. Society in general—and ladies in particular—were planning to attend, lending tone, glamour, and the all-important element of celebrity to the event. Newspapers from around the world were sending correspondents. What was in actuality a mismatch between a second-rate fighter and a first-rate heavyweight champion was transcending the level of a mere sporting event; it was now an international event. Everything about the fight, even Carpentier's little poodle, Flip, was news. Weeks before the fight, Rickard was guaranteed his dream: a million-dollar gate.

On the afternoon of Saturday, July 2, 1921, 80,000 fans squeezed into the rickety stadium just outside Jersey City, paying $1,789,238—still a record. Rickard was not only amazed at the success of the ballyhoo, but at the appearance of so many of society's finest. "Did you ever see so many millionaires?" the impressionable Rickard asked

Womblike and lying on the canvas, Carpentier is counted out by the referee.

everyone within earshot, looking at the $50 ringside seats which contained more money per square foot than any event in the history of sports. And way out "there," somewhere east of Newark, the cheaper seats began to sway precariously under the excited movement of thousands of fans.

As the appointed time of 3:30 P.M. approached, and the last two preliminary fighters—AEF champion Gene Tunney and Soldier Jones—had left the ring, the sweatered Dempsey and the robed Carpentier began to make their way into the vast amphitheater. There they were greeted by the full-throated roars of the more than 80,000 spectators and the sounds of trumpets blaring forth "La Marseillaise." The far more popular Carpentier received the adulation of the crowd, while Dempsey merely got the ovation due a champion, co-mingled with more than a few shouts of "slacker."

A few prefight words from Rickard, admonishing Dempsey not "to spoil it," and the fight was on. At the bell, the challenger, looking smaller than his announced 172 pounds, came out jabbing. The champion answered with a left hook to the body followed by a straight right to the nose. In the second, the challenger attacked and nailed Dempsey with a hard right high on the head. He pursued his advantage, driving Dempsey to the ropes where he landed several more hard punches to the head of the obviously disturbed champion. As the bell sounded for the third round the real possibility existed that not only would Carpentier "make a fight of it," but that the championship might actually change hands. Dempsey decided he had had enough. Rickard and the crowd had gotten their money's worth. Now it was Carpentier's turn in the barrel. The 3–1 favorite landed punch after punch on the almost-defenseless Frenchman as he swayed in front of the oncoming champion in cadence with the swaying stands that rimmed the stadium. A full three minutes of pummeling closed one of the challenger's eyes and caused his body to turn bright red. Only the bell staved off the inevitable, as the wounded Frenchman barely made it back to his corner. Two short lefts accompanied by a crushing right put the challenger down. He dragged himself up, barely beating the count, and was met by yet another flurry of punches. He went down again and curled up womblike on the canvas. Major Andrew White screamed into his ringside microphone: "The Frenchman is down! . . . three . . . four . . . Carpentier makes no effort to rise . . . six . . . seven . . . he's lying there . . . nine . . . ten . . . he's out. The fight is over! Jack Dempsey remains the heavyweight champion of the world!"

Although one writer was to call it "an afternoon waltz," the Rickard flair for matchmaking and promotion had made boxing history. He was now indeed the King of Promoters.

Gene Tunney—Harry Greb

May 23, 1923

own inability to avoid them. Greb rushed Tunney and caught him with a right to the jaw seconds into the ninth round and then scored with a left hand that opened a cut over Gene's right eye. Tunney returned the courtesies extended by Greb, hitting in the clinches himself. But Greb won the ninth round, and the next two as well, even though Tunney proved in the eleventh that he could and would match Greb in what the writers called "longshoreman tactics."

Greb's fouling became more flagrant in round 12, so much so that Haley, the referee, stopped the action momentarily to lambaste the champ. Greb argued so vehemently that it seemed as if Haley might switch places with Tunney and start trading punches with the Wildcat himself.

Tunney began connecting again in the thirteenth, much as he had earlier in the fight. A Tunney punch during a clinch now had Haley warning Gene. Tunney was putting it together again, but it didn't look good as the fighters head-

ed to their corners at the close of the round. Greb's furious pace over the last eight rounds seemed to give the Pittsburgher a slight edge in the scoring, and neither man seemed capable of knocking the other out.

But Tunney, nicknamed the "Devil Dog," had no dog in him. There were still six minutes of boxing to go and six minutes was more than enough time to turn the fight around. The fighters began mixing it up in close as the fourteenth frame got underway. Both men landed right hands to the body. Then Greb threw another right to the body; but this time Tunney responded with a hard right to the face that shook Greb up. Gene went down to the breadbasket once more, bringing the champion's hands down. It was do-or-die for Tunney now, and seeing the opening he'd been waiting for he leaped in with a right-hand smash that caught Greb's jaw almost flush. The crowd rose to its feet as the Wildcat nearly fell off his. Tunney was all over him now, unleashing a fusillade of punches as the round wound down. But Greb, still swinging wildly, stayed up until the bell sounded, after which his cornermen threw him onto his stool and attempted to ready him for one more round. They dumped nearly a bucket of ice water on his head as he shook it from side-to-side in an attempt to clear the cobwebs. Greb came out for the final round in no condition to attack, but he stood up for the full three minutes. Tunney took the round; and when the decision was announced, he took that too.

Tunney was the American light-heavyweight champion once again. It was that right to the jaw in the fourteenth round that made the difference, though Greb and his manager were unconvinced of that fact. "Well, it can happen even in New York," Red Mason bawled to anyone who would listen. "They say that crime is abating in the big cities and that Broadway is exempt from robbers. Perhaps Broadway is, but Madison Avenue and Madison Square Garden evidently are not."

Though the newsmen generally agreed with the verdict, Greb's demand for a rematch and charges of robbery were given some credence the next day when Muldoon, chairman of the state athletic commission, inexplicably denounced his own officials and said that Greb should indeed have been declared the winner.

They fought again that December, with Tunney again taking a close decision over Greb. But by that time, Greb was the middleweight champion of the world, having beaten Johnny Wilson and taken that title in New York's Polo Grounds in August.

And Gene Tunney, following both Benny Leonard's advice and his own guiding star, had begun his climb to the top of the heavyweight division, toward his date with destiny—and Jack Dempsey.

Harry Greb, known as the "Pittsburgh Wildcat," came into the ring the American light-heavyweight champion, but surrendered his title to Tunney in a brutal fight.

Jack Dempsey—Luis Firpo

September 14, 1923

If they had been two bull moose, horns interlocked, fighting for their turf, they would have ground each other into fine dust; if they had been two Roman gladiators, replete with tridents and shields, they would have reduced each other into two puddles that could have been borne off by blotters; and if they had fought on a barge, Luis Angel Firpo would have beaten Jack Dempsey to become the heavyweight champion of the world.

Luis Angel Firpo was a great bull of a man. Dubbed by one writer, less than imaginative, "the Wild Bull of the Pampas," this Argentinian stood some 6 feet, 3 inches tall and weighed some 220 pounds in the days when heavyweights barely scaled 200. His idea of fighting was simple: hit your opponent with a bludgeoning right hand, period. But his skills, or lack thereof, had gotten noticeable results. He had taken on—and beaten—six men since he had landed on the shores of America some 18 months before, dispatching all of them in fewer than the scheduled number of rounds. His victims included among their number two whom the heavyweight champion of the world, Jack Dempsey, had also dispensed, Jess Willard and Bill Brennan. And Firpo had needed only four more rounds to do away with them than it had taken Dempsey.

So, it was no wonder that promoter Tex Rickard looked upon this walking version of the Andes as the next logical contender for Jack Dempsey. Especially since Dempsey had just practiced mayhem less on his opponent, Tommy Gibbons, than on the little town of Shelby, Montana, in his last fight. And, if memory served Rickard correctly, and it usually did, his last Dempsey fight was a million-dollar one, with another foreigner—in that case, Georges Carpentier—serving as the party of the second part. Rickard couldn't

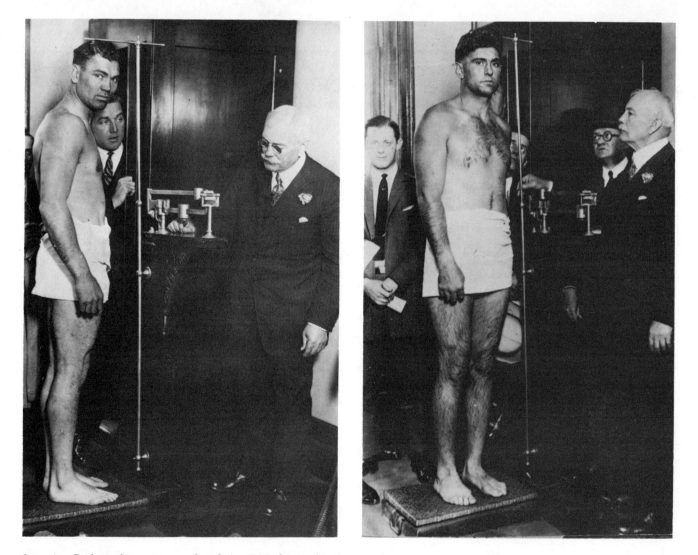

Opposite: *Perhaps the most-remembered moment in boxing history came in the first round when Luis Firpo (right) sent Jack Dempsey flailing out of the ring and into the press section.* Above (left and right): *At the traditional weigh-in before the fight, Dempsey (left) and Firpo appear fit.*

59

Dempsey (in white trunks) and Firpo are locked in a first-round clinch, one of the few times both were upright during the fight.

think of a better match than one between Dempsey and Firpo in early fall in New York. But the giant Firpo, who, like many immigrants, had come to America thinking the streets were paved with gold, and would break the fingers of anybody around him to get to an idle nickel lying on the sidewalk, knew the worth of a build-up almost as much as he knew the worth of a build. He wasn't about to be rushed into a match with Dempsey, preferring, as he told Rickard in his best English—which also was his worst English, almost nonexistent—that he wanted to wait another year before challenging anyone for the title. Rickard eyed the man before him, dressed in a rumpled $15 suit with a yellowed celluloid collar that would have been discarded months before if it hadn't cost another quarter to buy another, and said, "But next year you *may* get a lot of money fighting Dempsey. This year, you *will* get a lot of money." It took no interpreter to tell Firpo what to do. He signed, thereby becoming the first Latin American ever to challenge for a world's title.

But even if Luis Firpo had impressed his victims with his might, Rickard's move had not impressed the New York media as right. One columnist was moved to write, "Has Rickard run out of common sense, as well as contenders? Firpo, without question, is the clumsiest-looking oaf ever proposed as a challenger to a heavyweight champion." The oddsmakers concurred, installing Dempsey—in this, his fourth title defense—as an overwhelming 3–1 favorite.

However, a sports-starved public viewed the battle as a battle of giants and paid no heed to disproportionate odds or a disparaging press, thronging to the Polo Grounds the day of the fight for tickets. With a larger army on hand than Gallieni had led out of Paris to the first battle of the Marne, some 125,000 fans, believing that, like nature, Rickard abhorred a vacuum, tried to fill 82,000 seats. It was a classic case of demand far outstripping supply. In those pre-ERA days, a woman headed the long grey line of people pushing to get general admission tickets. However, despite her long vigil, when push came to shove and the line was broken up by a frantic mob seeking to get the bleacher seats, she lost her place. When the line was reassembled and the tickets actually were placed on sale the crush of the crowd was so great that she was somewhere on the outskirts of the crowd, unable to get within half a block of the ticket window.

Still, some 85,000 fans came in through the gates, over and under the turnstiles, and even over the fence, to fill the 82,000 seats and give Rickard another million-dollar-plus gate, paying $1,188,603 for the privilege of seeing two men beat the living whey out of each other. They overflowed the aisles, stood on seats and gave little ground to those seeking their rightful seats, especially up in the $50 ringside

section. The only time the sea of humanity parted was when the two combatants coursed down from their centerfield dressing rooms to be greated by rousing cheers. It was a crescendo that was never to subside.

Standing in the middle of the ring to receive their instructions from referee Jack Gallagher, the difference in size could be seen. There was a 24-pound difference in their weights, Firpo weighing in at 216½, Dempsey at 192½. But their size differential was measured in more than mere weight, for Firpo stood almost three inches taller than the champion, and his primitive musculature made the champion seem puny by comparison. As referee Gallagher intoned the instructions, an interpreter stood at Firpo's side. But even an interpreter couldn't have given voice to two instructions that never were uttered, two instructions which could have changed the course of the heavyweight division: that upon scoring a knockdown a man must go to the furthest neutral corner and that a man knocked from the ring must get back in within 10 seconds under his own power.

Then, there was the bell, seemingly lost in the continuous cataract of sound which 85,000 voices made. Firpo came out in an unusual stance, for him. It was the classic boxer stance, taught him by his American trainer, Jimmy DeForest, who had tried to instill in this South American ne-

Newspapermen eager to save their typewriters assist Dempsey back into the ring as Firpo stands ready to meet his fallen adversary.

61

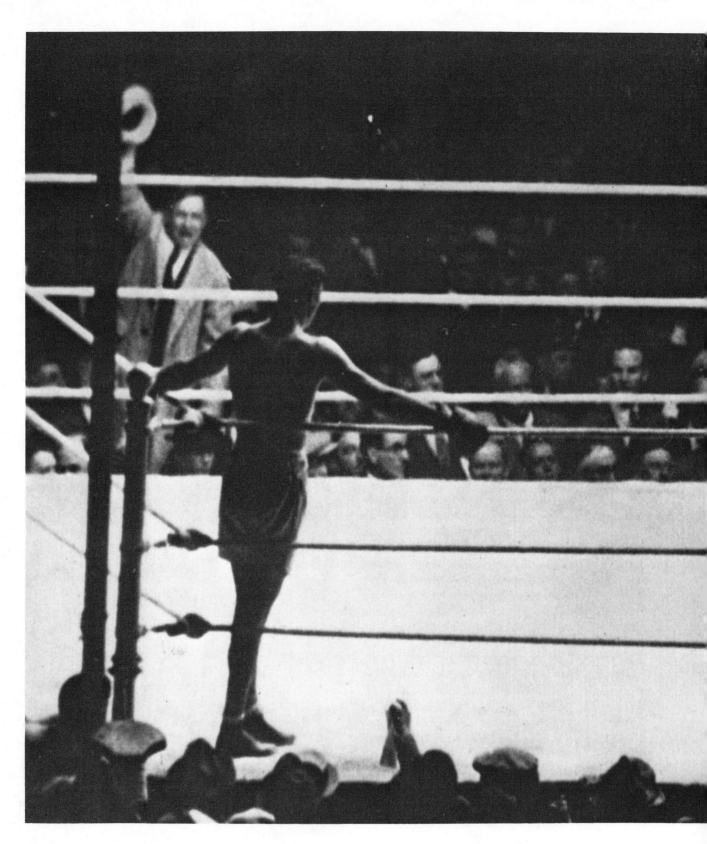

The final knockdown: As the referee counts out the felled Firpo, Dempsey watches from a neutral corner.

anderthal, who knew absolutely nothing about the science of self-defense—his only defense being his right fist—a modicum of science.

Dempsey crouched low, all the better to appraise the giant in front of him and minimize his target. The champion didn't get much of an opportunity to assess Firpo, or his moves. For Firpo's first punch was a thunderous—and ponderous—right, which caught Dempsey on the jaw, sending him to the canvas only 10 seconds into the fight.

Dempsey jumped off the canvas with no count, more embarrassed by being knocked off-balance than hurt, and went to the attack. As the two flailing behemoths' arms entangled, they fell into a clinch. The referee shouted "break" and, as the trusting Firpo dropped his hands and glanced inquiringly at the ref, Dempsey threw a left hook over Firpo's half held-up right. It landed on the jaw and now Firpo was down. He, too, was up without a count. The first two punches had produced two knockdowns. All within 20 seconds. It was to set a record, and a pattern. For as soon as Firpo had bounced up, he threw himself into the champion, connecting with a right to the only spot available to him, Dempsey's body. Dempsey continued to sacrifice his body, holding his hands high up, against his chin and against the chance that Firpo would land another of his lethal rights. But Firpo paid Dempsey no mind, just as he had paid no attention to advice from his handlers, and threw another looping right which came from somewhere out in right field. It caught the champion on the point of the jaw. But, this time, instead of finding refuge on the canvas—as he had from the first right—Dempsey, instead, found refuge in returning firepower with firepower, drilling a left uppercut through Firpo's haphazard defense. The Argentinian stood there wavering. Then he crashed, with a resounding thud, to the canvas for the second time.

As the entire crowd jumped to its feet, yelling, screaming, climbing up on the benches, falling down, clawing at each other, roaring forth a wild, tumultuous cascade of sound in the greatest sustained mass audience-hysteria ever witnessed, Firpo, too, tried to jump up. But Dempsey, like an avenging angel, stood over him, ready to jump on the man as soon as his hands left the resin of the canvas. As they did, Dempsey caught him with a left and a right. But instead of retreating, Firpo came on, throwing three devastating hammer rights into Dempsey's unguarded rib cage. Then, as he sought to bring off yet another booming right to the body, Dempsey stepped instead with his own bomb, a left hook to the chin. Firpo fell as if he had been poleaxed, flat on his face, arms surrounding his head.

Miraculously he arose, only to run into Dempsey who had positioned himself directly over the head of the fallen challenger. Dempsey was off target with a right, grazing Firpo's head. But Firpo was so groggy that its force brushed him back to the canvas for the fourth time. The referee tried to push Dempsey away. As he backed up, Firpo got up. Dempsey was back on him faster than you can say Luis Angel Firpo, and, after another left and right to the jaw, Luis Angel Firpo was back where he had begun that exchange—on the floor. This time, after righting himself, Firpo found Dempsey waiting for him the very second his hands had tentatively cleared the floor. Another right sent Firpo down for the sixth time in the round.

Somehow, from resolution or instinct, Firpo got to his feet, shaking but still trying to hurl just one of his rights at the onrushing Dempsey to turn the tide of battle. But before he wound up to throw it a left and a right from Dempsey floored the Argentine giant a seventh time. This time he looked like he was through, his head buried in the mat, his arms stretched out. But unbelievably the giant shook, shivered and then stood up, reaching a standing posture just before the fatal count of "10."

Now, calling on some superhuman effort, Firpo flung himself at Dempsey, bulling him away from him, across the ring. Then, with Dempsey on the retreat, the battle-blind and berserk Firpo threw a clubbing right which landed aside Dempsey's head, and the champion, impaled on the ropes, proved Newton's Law—that every action has an opposite and equal reaction—by falling through the ropes into the press section, feet flying and with his arms behind him to cushion his fall. It was the most famous moment in sports, captured for all time by George Bellows' equally famous portrait. In the words of Bugs Baer, Dempsey had "skipped three ropes at once." Somehow, in a stadium where Rickard had built the press benches higher than usual, fate conspired to have Dempsey fall on the typewriter of Jack Lawrence of the New York *Tribune*, who was more worried about protecting the 44 keys of his typewriter than the 192½ pounds of falling champion. But, whatever the reason, the result was the same; Lawrence hydraulically jacked the champ up onto the ring apron at the count of seven. By the count of eight Dempsey could be seen by a handful of people struggling up onto the ring apron. And by nine he had climbed through the middle and lower ropes and was back in the ring.

The rest of the round found Firpo literally hurling right hands at Dempsey, who instinctively rolled slightly under the punches, breaking their force. Had Firpo even had a hint of a left hand, the championship would have changed hands. But such was not the case, and he spent the remainder of round 1 taking aim at the bobbing head in front of him with an unvaried nonassortment of right-hand swings. The end of the round found Dempsey still on his feet, be-

64

ginning to throw punches of his own. Even after the bell he threw several punches at Firpo, all of which landed, leaving both men dazed and spent from their first-round efforts.

The bell for round 2 had scarcely sounded when Dempsey picked up where he had left off, throwing short inside punches and taking rights to the body. Dempsey, hurt slightly by one of Firpo's rib-crackers, fell into a clinch. Then, on the break, he stepped back in and began throwing combinations to Firpo's head. Two left hooks landed over Firpo's by-now limp guard. A left to the body, followed by two right uppercuts and another left to the body. Firpo tried to hold on, but Dempsey pulled away and caught the exhausted challenger with another left and right to the head. Firpo less fell than wilted to the ground, down for the eighth time. Once more he defied gravity and pulled himself erect

at the count of five. He pulled back and clouted Dempsey with a wild right to the neck. Dempsey moved in close and found Firpo with a left to the jaw and followed up with a right, literally lifting the Argentine from his feet and hurling him headlong to the floor with the crashing sound of a mighty oak falling from great heights. Firpo lay on the floor, full-length, his gloves covering his head. As the count progressed he shuddered and turned his body, trying once again to haul himself up—to get back into battle. But this time he was not to arise. This time it was over.

It had lasted exactly 3 minutes and 57 seconds, 237 seconds of mayhem, in which 11 knockdowns were scored in the shortest and wildest "great fight" in the history of boxing. It could hardly be called "the Sweet Science," but it was one helluva sweet quarrel.

Jack Dempsey emerged the champion in the shortest and wildest "great fight" in boxing history.

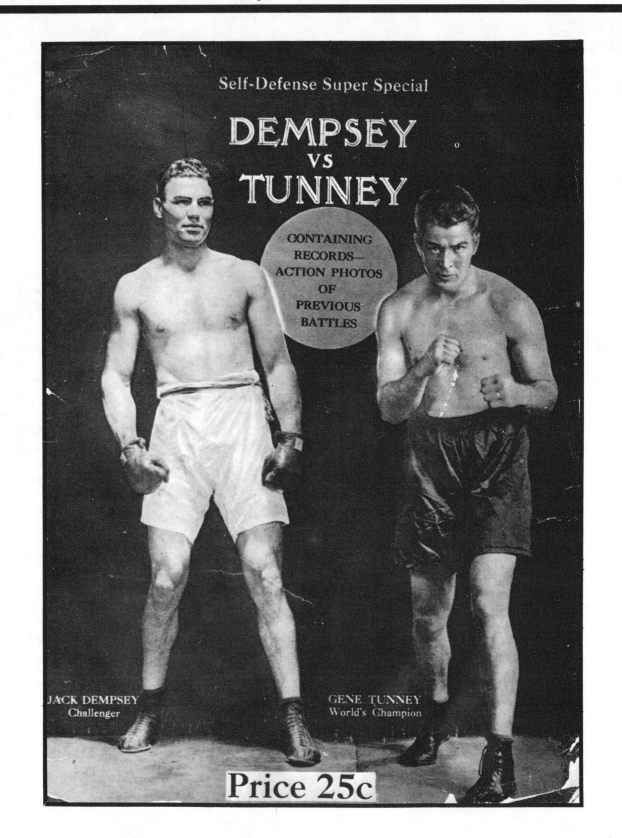

Self-Defense Super Special

DEMPSEY
VS
TUNNEY

CONTAINING
RECORDS—
ACTION PHOTOS
OF
PREVIOUS
BATTLES

JACK DEMPSEY
Challenger

GENE TUNNEY
World's Champion

Price 25c

The things one remembers about a big fight of long ago: the night of September 22, 1927, at Soldier's Field in Chicago, Illinois, and Gene Tunney was fighting Jack Dempsey for the heavyweight championship of the world.

To youngsters of today, hearing about Dempsey and Tunney must be like me listening to my old man tell about the dandified bank clerk from San Francisco, Jim Corbett, defeating the great John L. Sullivan for the heavyweight championship. And that happened only five years before I was born.

But the night Jack Dempsey had Gene Tunney on the deck I was there. I remember the dazed expression that came into Tunney's face as Dempsey slugged him with both hands over the ropes to the right of where I was sitting, and the film that clouded his eyes as he sank slowly to the ring floor, one leg crumpled beneath him.

How could I forget it? We were trying something new that year, something that had never been tried before at a big prize fight, a direct telephone connection between the working-press section at ringside and the composing room of a great metropolitan tabloid newspaper.

And so, for the big fight, we leased a telephone wire from ringside to composing room. Cost a pretty penny, too. But, there we were, I at ringside in Chicago, a rewrite man in New York, and our own private telephone line between us. Only we weren't alone, not by a long shot.

It started early in the seventh round with a sweeping left hook that Dempsey threw from the floor, knocking Tunney back into the ropes. It did more than knock him, it befuddled him, and Dempsey knew it. Dempsey was on him like a panther, slugging, hooking, crossing, left-right, left-right—every punch landing on Tunney's unprotected chin, causing his arms to drop and 105,000 souls to scream out of the darkness for the kill.

So Dempsey fanned him good, Tunney performed that slow fall to the floor, and Gallico, the boy editor, screamed into his telephone mouthpiece in a voice that had gone considerably falsetto from excitement. "Tunney is down from a series of lefts and rights to the head, for a count of . . ."

I stripped an earphone to pick up the count. Barry's arm fell and so help me he was saying "one" again. From there, he counted up to nine, at which point Tunney got off the floor. It did seem to me as though I couldn't have had all that intimate conversation with Nicholas in less than one second.

When the round was over, someone tapped me on the shoulder and I turned. There was a little man sitting there. He had graying hair, a gnarled ear, and a seamy face. He was holding one of those large, split-second stopwatches

with a dial like Big Ben, and he was looking at it with bewilderment. He said, "Hey, whadd'ya know about this? There's somethin' funny. I hit it when he went down and stopped it when he got up."

The hand showed that 14.5 seconds had elapsed. The little man and I stared at the watch. It kind of hypnotized us, because, as we both knew very well, if a stricken fighter isn't on his feet inside of 10 seconds he is presumed to be out, napoo, finished for the evening. I asked the little man who he was. He told me his name was Battling Nelson.

And I remember so vividly what happened in that round when Tunney got up and backtracked and backpedaled and skipped and retreated and faded away, always backward around the ring on his sturdy young legs. Dempsey chased and chased and chased on his aging and tiring dogs. And I recall that bitterly tragic moment when Dempsey could go no farther. He stopped and curled his dark-jowled visage into a sneer and made little pawing movements with his soggy, red-gloved, dynamite-laden hands, inviting Tunney to come to him and fight, knowing in his heart that

Opposite: *For a quarter anyone could read about Jack Dempsey and Gene Tunney, the participants in the famous fight known as the "Long Count."*
Right: *Heavyweight champion Gene Tunney was awarded this* Ring *magazine trophy for his sportsmanship, citizenship, and contributions to boxing.*

Tunney wouldn't because he was too smart. And I remember the first punch that was struck after the knockdown and the seemingly interminable chase, a right hand Tunney let go that landed on Dempsey's cheek and halted him in his tracks just before the bell.

But I remember other things, too, because it was more than just a prize fight. It was a climax to an epoch and a beginning of the end of an era when even the raindrops had seemed to be 14-karat—the golden decade of spending, pleasure, excitement, and sheer, exuberant, wasteful nonsense—10 crazy, wonderful, cockeyed years such as had never before been experienced.

All right, so this is 1981, and you feel pretty proud of the way we throw billions around like taxicab tips. But you haven't seen a prize fight in which the assembled customers coughed to the tune of $2,658,660 for the privilege of being there, a brawl in which the champion was paid a cool $1 million, an altercation where a single order for tickets amounted to $100,000.

All that happened upon the occasion of the second Dempsey-Tunney fight. Together, the two championship fights between Dempsey and Tunney in the consecutive years of 1926 and 1927 drew a little more than $4.5 million, and if you add the nonchampionship heavyweight fight staged in the summer of 1927, promoter Tex Rickard's total take for the three heavyweight fights was $5,637,823. And people were knocking one another down to get close enough to hand him the dough.

The notion for the big return match that was to draw the world-record gate was, of course, fermenting in Tex Rickard's mind a year earlier in Philadelphia, on the night of June 23, 1926, to be exact. That night, at the Sesquicentennial Stadium, Tunney battered the left side of Dempsey's face into jelly in 10 rounds and took his heavyweight title away from him.

But first there was the small matter of a Lithuanian sailor to be disposed of and the collection of another $1 million gate in the process. Jack Sharkey of Boston had soundly whipped Dempsey's nemesis, Harry Wills, the year before, and he had also knocked out or beaten every prominent heavyweight, including George Godfrey. A Dempsey-Sharkey match as a build-up for the second Dempsey-Tunney fight was a natural.

So the big fight wasn't officially on until the moment on the hot night of July 21 when sailor Sharkey, in the seventh round of an altercation he appeared to be winning on points, turned his countenance away from his opponent to protest to the referee that more than a few of Dempsey's shots were dropping below the Taylor-foulproof line.

The beautiful side view of the sailor's kisser, all

nude, unguarded, and inviting, was more than Dempsey could resist. He whipped over the old right hook, there was a "plock" followed by the usual thud, and Sharkey entered dreamland. The referee counted from 1 to 10, and Rickard had himself the biggest prize fight, with the most gate money, ever held anywhere, anytime.

Flynn let it be known that he believed that Maxie ("Boo Boo") Hoff, Philadelphia underworld king, and Abe Attell, New York gambler, had attempted to fix the Philadelphia fight in favor of Tunney by obtaining the appointment of a referee and one judge.

Gibson accused Dempsey of having fouled Sharkey and of planning to do the same thing to Tunney.

And then there was the hullabaloo over the referee!

There were three candidates who were supposed to be under consideration: Davey Miller of Chicago, Lou Magnolia of New York, and Walter Eckersall, the all-American football player who had become a sports writer on the *Chicago Tribune*.

Magnolia, a big-nosed, bald-headed fellow, was the best referee in New York, given to extravagant gestures in the ring, but honest and efficient. He was the choice of the Tunney camp. Of course, a New York referee had as much chance of pulling down that plum in Chicago as he would have had a chance of flying there, using his hands for wings.

In their first fight a year before, Tunney (right) took the fight to Dempsey and the championship from him.

Eckersall's honesty was not doubted, but he was an amateur, that is to say, not a licensed Illinois referee. The *Chicago Tribune* was plugging for his appointment.

In the newspapers on September 20, there appeared a brief item to the effect that the Illinois State Athletic Commission had granted Tunney's request for a 20-foot ring.

Flynn and Dempsey had been holding out for an 18-foot enclosure. Tunney wanted space to box, stab, and gallop. Dempsey was after a small ring where he could crowd, herd, and slug. Those extra two feet did it for Tunney.

The crowd was handled by 6,500 men, including 2,000 ushers, 400 ticket takers, 400 ticket inspectors (looking for the counterfeits distributed by those wags from New York), and 2,500 policemen. Sixteen selected police officers were detailed to guard Tunney before and after.

For those readers who have a real passion for figures, the attendance was 104,943, not as large as the crowd at Philadelphia where 120,757 had gathered; but the Chicago crowd rang up the world's largest prize-fight gate, still unsurpassed, of $2,658,660. Of this boodle, Tunney took down $1 million for the night's exercise, while Dempsey collected $450,000.

As a matter of fact, referee Dave Barry did not count to 14 at all. He tolled from 1 to 10; and before 10, at the count of 9, Tunney was on his feet and had embarked on his classic retreat.

That he was on the deck for an elapsed time of 14 seconds or so was wholly Dempsey's fault. Jack had that fight in his mitts and blew it because he had bad ring habits stemming from his bad temperament.

Top and above: *Despite being remembered for Dempsey's knockdown of Tunney, this fight was interesting because most of the punches landed during the ten-round bout were thrown by the champion, Tunney.*

69

Referee Barry starts the count after Dempsey finally obeys the command to go to a neutral corner.

Before the bell set them at one another's throats, it was completely understood by both contestants that in the case of a knockdown, the boxer who scored it should retire to the farthest neutral corner and, until he did so, the count of the fallen foe was not to begin.

When Tunney crumpled to the floor at the beginning of that fateful seventh round, Barry's arm came down for the count of one, as prescribed by the rules, as soon as Tunney's royal Francis made contact with the canvas. But, as the referee raised his arm to toll "two," he saw that Dempsey not only had failed to scamper to the farthest neutral corner but was hovering in the immediate vicinity, waiting for Tunney to get up so he could powder him again.

So the "one" business was all off. Barry stopped counting and motioned Dempsey to go to the neutral corner as agreed. Dempsey wasn't having any.

In the famous Firpo fight in New York, Dempsey stood over Firpo each time he knocked him down, and once he stood *behind* him, and got away with it. Firpo hadn't time to get his hands up before Jack was at him again. Jack kind of lost his noodle when he got the boys going.

Finally Dempsey made a concession and hied Barry to a corner. But it was the nearest corner, only a few feet from the prostrate and quivering Gene and right handy to him. Barry kept his head. He motioned Dempsey to the far corner and didn't return to his counting until the challenger started for it. Then, very properly and according to the agreement and the rules, he began again at "one."

When Dempsey and Tunney met for the second time, it was not just a boxing match, or prize fight, but the thrilling climax to a couple of true-life dramas. One couldn't stay away from it, any more than one could heave the conclusion

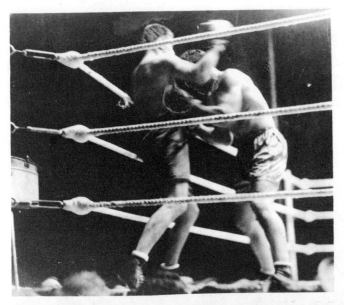

of a gripping serial into the wastebasket without reading it. What happened to these two men in the ring on the night of September 22, 1927, would not only determine the championship, but would vitally affect the lives of each.

You may take this as the firm belief of this eyewitness: had Dempsey immediately gone to the far corner, permitting the count to proceed as it had started, Gene Tunney would never have gotten up off the floor inside of 10 seconds. And if by some miracle Tunney had managed to haul himself aloft by 9, Dempsey would have pickled him.

Tunney won going away. He outpointed Dempsey in the first six rounds. In the eighth, he knocked Jack off his pins with a straight right. And in the ninth and tenth, with Dempsey exhausted from the bitter, fruitless chase in that heart-stopping seventh, Tunney gave him a solid thrashing.

When the fight was over, and ever after, Jack Dempsey was silent. *He* knew who was to blame for the "Long Count." That's how it was in the long, long ago.

Top: *Dempsey and Tunney in the throes of battle.* Above: *In the eighth round, Tunney turned the tables on Dempsey (left), flooring him in a knockdown remembered by few in the wake of the "long count"*

Henry Armstrong—Barney Ross

May 31, 1938

The elephants came to Madison Square Garden every spring with the Ringling Bros. and Barnum and Bailey Circus, stayed a few weeks, and moved along, but there was one—a great big white one—that moved in and stayed until the Garden's accounting department, losing more than peanuts, screamed bloody murder.

It was the Madison Square Garden Bowl, an idea which proved a super-dud in the days when New York was the unchallenged boxing capital of the world. The Garden was the center of global pugilism before World War II and frequently was hard-pressed to provide a stage for the many super-attractions in the world of fisticuffs it staged, so to speak. Why not provide a second stage in the outdoor months instead of cutting the management of the Yankee

Stadium and Polo Grounds in on the proceeds of big bouts, the promoters reasoned.

Land was cheap just across the Queensboro Bridge in the borough of Queens. Labor was even cheaper in the depths of the Great Depression. How about a "Bowl" out there in Long Island City, something that could handle almost twice the capacity of the indoor arena in midtown Manhattan? The Friday night swells could drive out or taxi it across the East River for a couple of bucks; the gallery gods could ride the subway direct to the site for five cents and be there in half an hour from midtown.

It was a great idea. And also one of the great failures. The fight fans just didn't feel right in the Madison Square Garden Bowl, a big wooden structure resting on an asphalt

Opposite: *Announcer Harry Balogh raises the arm of Henry Armstrong to signify his winning of the second of his soon-to-be three crowns.*
Above: *Prefight checkup certifies that champion Barney Ross (left) and challenger Henry Armstrong are fit and rarin' to go.*

base and exposed to the weather. Neither did the fighters. There was one streak where the title changed hands in seven straight fights.

One of these was Barney Ross's final defense of his welterweight crown. It was also Barney Ross's last fight. He had always said that if he was ever beaten badly that would be it! And Henry Armstrong, "Hammerin Henry," came out of the West, leather flailing like a threshing machine, to administer precisely such a beating.

The evening was May 31, 1938. Ross, true to his word, never fought again. Four years later he was in a bigger, more important, kind of a fight as a Marine on Guadalcanal, a Marine wounded and subsequently decorated.

But that's not a part of the story of the jinx of Madison Square Garden Bowl. Or the hop-skipping of Henry Armstrong from the featherweight to the welterweight crown, the first time (and last time) in history this feat was achieved. The lightweight crown, lifted off the brow of Lou Ambers, was to come a few months later, making Henry Armstrong the only fighter to hold the 127-, 135-, and 147-pound crowns simultaneously. Perhaps that is the story.

But first, the setting: Barney Ross, New York-born, Chicago-bred, won the welterweight title from Jimmy McLarnin in 1934, and lost it back to McLarnin in their rubber match the following year. The most popular Jewish fighter around New York since Benny Leonard, Ross's following was tremendous. He was polite, unassuming, and he could punch your head off. Rooting for him took your mind off worrying about the possibility that there might not be enough money at the end of the month to buy food. At least temporarily. He filled his fans' hearts with hope when they couldn't fill their stomachs.

Out on the West Coast, Armstrong, a transplanted St. Louisian three years Ross's junior, was struggling to keep alive battling for $50 and $100 purses among featherweights and lightweights equally as desperate. It was not the era of the easy buck, and fighters who didn't fight three minutes of every round weren't invited back the following week. No promoter ever had to worry about Henry Armstrong's enthusiasm.

Somewhere, maybe on the St. Louis streets, he had developed a style as deadly as it was peculiar. It utilized the idea of perpetual motion, and those who insisted that perpetual motion was scientifically impossible just never saw Armstrong in action.

He was precisely that, head bobbing, torso weaving, arms flailing, always moving forward. He fought that way until the other fellow dropped. In 175 fights, this happened 97 times.

While Henry Armstrong, chin virtually glued against his chest in a protective stance, was campaigning mostly through the Far West, the Madison Square Garden Bowl was working on its jinxed white-elephant record. If you had a little vegetable patch behind your house out on Long Island you could figure that the one day you wouldn't have to water would be the day a title fight was scheduled there. The rain would probably come late, along about 8 P.M., just in time to kill off the box office sales. And then it would rain in earnest around 10 P.M., just about the time the main event was scheduled to go on.

Among those who had felt the Bowl jinx had been McLarnin in that title loss to Ross; Primo Carnera, who lost his heavyweight crown to Max Baer; and Baer who in turn lost his crown to the "Cinderella Man," Jim Braddock. It was the sort of place calculated to make a champion think twice before he defended his title in "Omen, Sweet Omen."

In the mid-thirties the promotional battle between Mike Jacobs and Madison Square Garden was often a better spectacle than the one in the ring. The Garden had the money, the prestige, the political connections; and Jacobs, a graduate of selling peanuts on the Coney Island excursion boats and eventually a powerful ticket broker, had the brains. He set himself up as a rival to the entrenched Garden and had an unexpected ally in the emergence of Joe Louis. After a while he had beaten the Garden at its own game. Would Mike come over as the Garden's promoter, bringing his 20th Century Boxing Club along with him? Mike went. Armstrong-Ross was one of his promotions.

But even Mike, with the most impressive set of dental choppers since George Washington's carved ivory teeth, couldn't match the Bowl's weather jinx. Armstrong-Ross was scheduled for Thursday, May 26. At 4 P.M. it was postponed, and scheduled for the next night. Predictably it rained again and this time the out-of-towners flocked to the box office to get refunds.

The weekend was a disaster. A match race had been scheduled at Belmont between War Admiral and Seabiscuit but it too was called off. The weathermen indicated Saturday might be okay, but Mike wasn't going to buck the tradition of Saturday being a bad night for boxing. In those pre-TV days, you lived and died by the gate.

So on Tuesday night, May 31, with temperatures hovering around 50°F, they finally put the fight on, and the faithful came, but hardly flocked to the bowl, filling it to less than half its capacity.

Ross had trained down to 142. He had an 8½-pound edge. The contract said that 13 pounds would cancel. And Armstrong was suspected of cheating to make 133½, supposedly using plates fastened to the soles of his feet at the weigh-in; or so it was rumored. Was he trying to fool the slightly befuddled chairman of the New York State Boxing Commission, Major General John J. Phelan? After the weigh-in, with both fighters now dressed, someone "tipped" the General about the alleged contraband metal. "Take off your shoes and socks, Armstrong," demanded the General. Now Armstrong was almost as bewildered as the white-haired Dickensian character accosting him. He obliged the commissioner by partially disrobing.

The General bent down and ran his fingers along the bottom of Henry's bare feet. Armstrong was never much for showing emotions, but he was now struggling to keep from giggling. "General," he said, "you're tickling me." There was, of course, no sign of contraband. Or even athlete's foot.

That night, there was to be no tickling in the ring

when the two champions met. Ross, a deft workman, won the first two rounds, punching, sticking, and moving out of range of the onrushing Henry. He had worked secretly on an uppercut to get in at Armstrong's carefully protected chin. Once or twice he scored with it.

But those two rounds were the only ones he won on his own. He was awarded the seventh when Armstrong connected with a low blow, but by that time the issue was no longer in doubt.

Armstrong's swarming style, his merciless rain of punches at a superhuman rate, and his inexhaustible stamina was simply too much for Ross. Ross's right eye was damaged early, and closed by the seventh. His mouth was badly cut. He was bleeding from the nose. In short, he was a mess. But still he fought on.

In the second half of the fight it was no longer a question of who would win, but whether Ross would go down. Gasping, he tottered to his corner at the concluding bell for each round. The referee, Arthur Donovan, the best of his time, would come over and examine the damages between every round. Several times he asked Ross whether he wanted to continue. A proud Ross nodded assent.

Several times his cornermen, Art Winch and Sam Pian, suggested to Ross that he call it quits. But all they got was a determined shake of his battered head. And when the bell rang he came out, his soggy gloves held high in front of his face in a futile protective gesture, leaving Armstrong the unattractive task of trying to knock a brave man unconscious.

He failed, but he won the title. Donovan gave him 12 rounds, as did George Lecron, one of the judges. The other judge, Billy Cavanaugh, a prominent referee in that era, made it 10–4–1.

Ross, true to his promise, never fought again. But Armstrong did. He fought plenty. Two and a half months later he beat Lou Ambers for the lightweight title. Then, holder of the triple-crown for little men—the only other in history was Bob Fitzsimmons among the big men (middle, light-heavy, and heavy)—he gave up the featherweight crown. Making that limit had become too difficult. And, anyway, the money wasn't to be made in that class.

Henry Armstrong fought seven more years. He lost the lightweight crown back to Ambers and the welterweight crown to Fritzie Zivic. He never fought less than a dozen fights a year, during the years 1942 through 1944, but in 1945, he had only three, winning only one. He drew with someone named Chester Slider in January and lost to the same fighter the following month.

It was time to go. The scientists were right. There is no such thing as perpetual motion.

A relentless "Hurricane" Henry gets inside the defenses of Ross (right).

Joe Louis—Max Schmeling

June 22, 1938

The year was 1938. Europe was throbbing to the sound of goose-stepping boots and a demented paper-hanger's mad ravings. War was less than 15 months away and every arena was being used for propaganda purposes—even the sports arena.

It all started in 1936. That year, the Berlin Olympics had been used as a forum to promote Aryan superiority. Then, on June 22, 1938, it spread to the boxing arena, where Hitler's pride, Max Schmeling, took on the American *Schwartzer*, Joe Louis, for the heavyweight championship of the world.

No other fight in boxing history had such political and sociological overtones—not even the Jack Johnson-Jim Jeffries fight 28 years before. The Schmeling-Louis fight had more at stake than boxing supremacy; the winner could boast to the world of his racial might.

Louis and Schmeling had met two years before, on June 19, 1936, at Yankee Stadium, when Schmeling was the ex-heavyweight champion of the world and the undefeated Louis was the future heavyweight champion. Louis, the prohibitive favorite—with a record of 27 straight victories, 23 by knockout—began the fight by sticking his left in the black-browed German's face, winning rounds and closing Schmeling's left eye. But in round 4, eschewing his successful style, Louis changed from a jab to a left hook, and Schmeling, who claimed he had "seed something" in films of Louis' previous fights, proceeded to cross his straight right inside of Louis' hooks. One of Schmeling's overhand rights caught Louis on the head and drove him to the canvas. "The Brown Bomber" arose shakily at the count of two, but was obviously in trouble; he was so dazed he didn't even hear the bell for the end of the round. From that point on, it was only a matter of time until the end, which finally—and mercifully—came at 2:29 of the twelfth round when Schmeling clubbed Louis with two more overhand rights.

Suddenly, the supposedly invincible Louis was, in

Opposite: The Ring *magazine provides the vital statistics of both Max Schmeling (left) and Joe Louis before their first fight, later called "the Upset of the Century." Above: Billboard advertises the return bout, the political and boxing match-up of the pre-World War II era.*

the words of the New York *World-Telegram*, just an "ordinary boxer." And "Unser Max" was the toast of the totalitarian world. Dr. Paul Joseph Goebbels, the dreaded head of the Nazi propaganda machine, called Schmeling's wife to tell her the news, and offered his, and Der Fuehrer's, heartiest congratulations.

Now, two years later—and one year to the day after he had won the heavyweight championship of the world by knocking out Jim Braddock in eight rounds—Louis entered the ring at Yankee Stadium to defend his title for the fourth time. This time he was to fight against the only man who had ever beaten him, Max Schmeling.

With the betting crowd in Louis' corner, favoring him at 9–5, and Der Fuehrer in Schmeling's corner (Hitler called him personally before he left the dressing room), the two combatants came to the middle of the ring for the final instructions from referee Arthur Donovan. That would be the last time the outcome was in doubt.

Almost as soon as the bell for round 1 sounded, the champion was across the ring, swarming all over his former conqueror. As the crowd of 75,000 howled, Louis whipped a left hook to the German's chin and then rained rights and lefts to the body of the helpless challenger, sending him to his knees before the fight was 30 seconds old.

Louis drove Schmeling to the canvas three more times, with a vicious body attack. Schmeling staggered to his unsteady feet twice. The third time a towel fluttered in and Arthur Donovan called a finish to the fight at just 2:04 of the first round.

Even before the final knockdown, heavy-lidded Germans, gathered by their shortwave radio sets at three in the morning, had begun to turn them off and return to staring glumly into their half-empty beer steins. In black ghettos throughout America, celebrations were taking place, honoring the man who had brought honor to his people—and to America.

Above: *Referee Arthur Donovan circles a struggling Max Schmeling.* Right: *Dazed and beaten, Schmeling hangs onto the ropes for dear life as Louis continues his assault.*

Joe Louis—Billy Conn

June 18, 1941

HE WON'T GET AWAY
FROM ME WHEN HE'S HURT

DRAWN BY
Billy Conn

It was a scenario that had been repeated many times before, a good little man versus a good big man: Corbett versus Sullivan, Dempsey versus Willard, and the classic, David versus Goliath. Now it was to be Billy Conn, the former light-heavyweight champion who had renounced his claim to the lighter crown to take on the heavyweight champion of the world, Joe Louis. The fight was to be 174½ pounds against 200 pounds, boxer versus puncher, and machine gun versus howitzer.

Many believed that it was not merely a case of the dog in the fight, but the fight in the dog. They conceded that Conn had a chance; he had a greater one than any challenger since Max Schmeling, making him the shortest-priced underdog against Louis in three years, an 18–5 dog.

Conn had all the credentials to make this a fight, more so than any of Louis' previous 17 challengers, most of whom charitably fit into the disparaging class known as "bums of the month." Billy the Kid had gone into battle 67 times before, winning 58 and losing only 8, all by decision. One fight ended in a draw. And although he had only twelve

Preceding page: *Referee Eddie Joseph signals it's all over for Billy Conn in his valiant but futile effort to uncrown Joe Louis in what* The Ring *panel chose as "the greatest fight of all time."* Top: *Drawing by Conn of his fight plan.* Above: *Louis covers up to Conn's twelfth-round attack.*

knockouts to his credit, six of those had come in his last eight outings against the bigger boys—men like Bob Pastor and Gus Dorazio, both of whom were past victims of Louis.

Conn's adherents also pointed out that Louis was no longer the murderous puncher he had been a few years ago when he destroyed Max Schmeling in 124 seconds. His last three opponents—Buddy Baer, Tony Musto, and Abe Simon—had gone an average of almost 10 rounds. Louis' age, 27, and recent susceptibility to injury—he was cut under the left eye in his most recent fight, which took place just three weeks before against Baer—gave further proof of his "slippage." Or so it was argued.

Conn's consummate boxing skill, with his flashy left hand serving as the centerpiece, made him a lineal descendant of Jim Corbett, the first of the great scientific boxers. Conn could block punches with his arms, elbows, and gloves, and further nullified his opponents' punches by "rolling" with them. It was argued that even when hit, Conn had remarkable recuperative powers, having been knocked down only twice in his career, once by Oscar Rankin and once by Solly Krieger, and gotten up to finish both fights, beating Rankin in the process. Sweet William had always used his ring craftsmanship and speed to defuse his opponent's power, something his followers thought he could easily do against the more slow-moving Louis.

If there was any rap against Conn, it was that he was headstrong, often trading punches when stung rather than moving away. Against the powerful Louis, this was seen as Conn's potential Achilles' heel. However, he was determined not to let that happen.

"I know I have lost my temper in some fights," the strong-willed Irish challenger said before the fight, "but you can bet I won't this time." And bet they did, bringing the last-minute odds down to 11–5.

Many in the crowd of 54,487 who jammed into the Polo Grounds that Wednesday night, June 18, 1941, believed Conn could do it. Members of the press, outstanding writers such as Hype Igoe and Willard Mullin, had gone out on a limb for Conn. So had several members of the boxing fraternity, including champions like Jim Braddock, Fred Apostoli, Gus Lesnevich, Lew Jenkins, and Fritzie Zivic.

Of course, Zivic could be excused for his enthusiasm; he was a "homer" rooting for a fellow Pittsburgher. But he was just one of the more than 6,000 fight fans who had journeyed from the Steel City hoping that Conn could catch lightning in a bottle and do something four previous light-heavyweight champions had failed to do—win the heavyweight championship.

But most of those in attendance just wanted to see the much ballyhooed fight, including Pete Herman, the for-

Top to bottom: *Louis unleashes a flurry of punches in close quarters, sending Conn to the canvas in the thirteenth and final round.*

mer bantamweight champion, who was blind and yet had come all the way from New Orleans to "see" the action. Herman, like the other 54,486 fans in attendance, hoped the Louis-Conn fight would match the excitement of the last title bout held at the Polo Grounds, the Jack Dempsey-Luis Firpo classic. Neither group, Billy's fans nor boxing's faithful, would be disappointed.

After two rounds, both the Conn fans and the boxing fans were wondering if Billy's build-up wasn't merely the figment of some P.R. man's pipe dream, as Louis pursued him across the ring, landing some heavy punches without more than a token return. From the opening bell, when Louis advanced immediately over to Conn's corner to "get at" the challenger, through the next six minutes of fighting, it was all Louis as he kept up a steady tattoo on Conn's body, staggered him with two rights in the second, and controlled the action. Conn made a great effort to evade the oncoming Louis, and stay continually on the move.

The third round was different. Although retreating, Conn was able to connect several times with his left, even stopping to hook his left into Louis' face and follow up with a left-right that forced Louis to hold on, something he hadn't had to do in his previous 17 defenses. Conn's performance gave heart to his adherents and credence to the rumor that

Conn was a slow starter because of an unusually slow heartbeat which required a warm-up period.

Conn started round 4 with a characteristic retreat and then suddenly stopped and threw a straight left which connected with the oncoming Louis. Conn followed up with a solid right to the chin and another right to the jaw, buckling Louis' knees. On the attack for the first time, Conn threw several short shots at Louis, most of which connected. Then Conn landed a hard left to the head and a right to the jaw. This was the Conn everyone had been promised. It was also the fight they had come to see.

Just as the momentum had swung to Conn, however, it swung back again to Louis. The champion hurt Billy with a left to the stomach, then, in close quarters, landed a vicious left hook to the jaw which staggered the challenger, who fell against Louis. Louis followed up with a torrent of punches to the unprotected flanks of the challenger, who, at the bell, staggered to the wrong corner.

Revived with smelling salts, Conn resumed his dancing in round 6. But Louis, moving in on his target, dragging his back foot like he was wiping it on the canvas, found his elusive target and pounded his body, buckling the challenger's knees with a vicious left hook to the pit of the stomach. Miraculously, Conn came back to score with a flurry to Lou-

Joe Louis catches Conn with a straight left, setting up his final attack.

is' head, but Louis found Conn again to the body and the head, opening a small cut over Billy's right eye.

Conn continued his dancing in round 7, staying out of Louis' reach and even landing a few flurries of his own for good measure. Round 8 found Conn moving in for the first time since the fourth, jarring Louis with repeated one-two's, once when pinioned against the ropes. The round ended with Conn swarming all over a suddenly bewildered Louis, rattling rights and lefts to the vulnerable head of the champion.

Brimming with "Conn-fidence," the suddenly laughing challenger moved in on Louis, telling him as he pulled him into a clinch, "You've got a fight on your hands, Joe." Joe knew it as Conn banged both hands to the head, followed up with a left to the face, and then threw a right that landed squarely on Louis' jaw, which hung open in amazement and pain. Shuffling forward, a newly frustrated Louis resorted to pushing Conn into the ropes and throwing one right, as the quicker challenger retaliated with a right and a left to the head and a right to the body. Suddenly the fight was all Conn.

Unable to land any effective blows to Conn's continually bobbing head, Louis followed Sam Langford's old adage to "kill the body and the head will follow." He dug a left and a right into Conn's stomach, then followed with another left, which he sunk into the pit of the challenger's midsection, and a left hook to the head. All of a sudden the challenger was on the floor. But it was a slip, the second by Conn. And Louis, ever the sportsman, stepped back and allowed his momentarily defenseless foe to regain his footing.

Conn came back in the eleventh, dashing out of difficulty whenever the steadily oncoming champion forced him into the ropes. He also tied up Louis or held on whenever the "Brown Bomber" attempted to force the action. Then the handsome Irishman would launch his own attack to the head, forcing Louis to hold on to avoid Conn's seemingly endless stream of punches.

Round 12 saw Conn dance less and punch more as he connected time and again with rights and lefts to the head. He staggered Louis with a left hook to the jaw. The hunter had now become the hunted. Conn pursued Louis around the ring. The man who had had Primo Carnera cowering, Max Baer frozen with fear, and Max Schmeling screaming in pain was in desperate trouble for the first time since his loss to Schmeling five years earlier. At the bell, the crowd was on its feet, cheering frantically, assured now they were seeing the sequel to the Dempsey-Firpo bout.

With the reviving smell of ammonia stinging his nostrils and the words of his trainer, Jack Blackburn—that Louis had "to knock him out to win"—stinging his ears,

The thirteenth round saw Billy Conn knocked down for the count.

Louis came out of his corner for the thirteenth round hell-bent upon finding his quarry and bringing him to bay. Conn greeted the now purposeful champion with a right and a left to get his attention, the right cutting Louis' ear. As Conn waded in with a left to the stomach followed by a right that missed Louis' chin, the champion landed a hard right of his own. It caught Conn flush on the jaw, snapping his head violently back. Louis followed up with three more hard rights to the chin, but, untrue to his prefight prediction that he would run away to stay another day, Conn fought back, out-slugging the champion at close quarters in a savage exchange. A right uppercut by Louis staggered Conn. Louis, now sensing the moment he had been waiting the past 38 minutes for, landed a volley of rights and lefts to Conn's head. Another right to the head spun Conn part way around and he fell, as if he were filmed in slow motion. Referee Eddie Joseph picked up the count over the inert form that had

almost been the heavyweight champion of the world. Conn tried to regain his feet, leaving his haunches at the count of 10, but it was too late. Referee Joseph signaled "the end," 2:58 into the thirteenth round.

The fight itself was memorable. It was magic, and it was one of the best ever seen in this or any other era. Joe Louis, the man who had been just six minutes and two seconds away from losing his crown to the man he called "the slickest" he had ever fought, had come back to reclaim and retain his title. And his claim as "the greatest boxer of all time."

As he left the ring, Louis espied his manager, John Roxbury, smoking a cigar.

"How many of those you swallow tonight?" asked the Brown Bomber. He didn't need to ask. Roxbury, and everybody who had seen the fight, had swallowed—and swallowed hard. But Louis had bitten the bullet, and won.

Eight . . . nine . . . ten . . . and out!

84

Tony Zale—Rocky Graziano

September 27, 1946

When America went marching off to war on December 7, 1941, many of boxing's champions went marching off as well, their titles frozen for the duration. The heavyweight title was frozen for more than four years, the light-heavy crown for almost five, the middleweight championship for five, the welterweight for five, etc., etc., etc. Fans were starved for action. Any action.

With the end of the war and the promised millenium

of world peace still unfulfilled, disenchanted Americans began feeling that their privations and principles had failed to gain them anything. So they turned from the rigors of problem-solving to the rituals of pleasure-seeking, embracing, in their free-wheeling mood, any excitement and escapism they could find. And boxing headed the gigantic laundry list of diversions available.

Two bouts in particular were much awaited: Louis-

Preceding page: *Rocky Graziano is floored by a first-round left hook from middleweight champ Tony Zale (left)*. Above: *In the second round, Graziano sends Zale to the canvas, but the champion is saved by the bell*.

Conn and Zale-Graziano. The Louis-Conn match had generated excitement five years earlier, and there had been ballyhoo attached to it ever since; and the Zale-Graziano bout promised to duplicate in action what it possessed in electricity. One was to acquit itself admirably; the other was to fail dismally.

Thirty thousand fans poured through the gates at Yankee Stadium on September 27, 1946, to see their local hero, Rocky Graziano, the quintessential warrior, challenge middleweight champion Tony Zale, "the Man of Steel," for the middleweight championship. This was to be Zale's first defense of the title he had held since he defeated Georgie Abrams for the vacant title back in 1941. He had taken that title into the service with him when he enlisted in the U.S. Navy in 1942, effectively freezing it for the duration of the war.

Since his discharge from the colors of gold and blue, Zale had six times reenlisted in the ranks of the black and blue, fighting a total of 22 rounds in preparation for his first title defense.

His opponent, Rocky Graziano, "the Dead End Kid," was a man who would stop at nothing to win. And he rarely did—holding his opponents by the throat, clubbing them in the ribs, kidneys, back, anywhere. But he always won.

Zale's representative, Sol Gold, was so apprehensive of Rocky's propensity for the illegal that he suggested that "the referee sit outside the ring, just like it used to be in England. Then," challenged Gold, "if Rocky wants to play rough, Zale can show him just what rough and dirty fighting is all about."

Gold went on to cite three incidents in which he claimed Graziano had taken the name of the Marquis of Queensberry in vain: grabbing Freddie ("Red") Cochrane, who was the welterweight champion at that time, by the throat and choking him with his left hand while hitting him with his right; knocking down Al ("Bummy") Davis with a punch well after the bell, then hitting Davis while he was helpless on the floor; and failing to go to a neutral corner after flooring Marty Servo, standing over him, à la Jack Dempsey, and hitting the welterweight king as soon as his hands left the canvas.

"There hasn't been a fight in which Graziano has not broken one or more of the rules," Gold added, gratuitously, but hardly graciously. He might have added that whatever the madness, Graziano's method seemed to work, as his record showed.

The crowd, on the other hand, thirsted for action, saw it coming, and made the good-, albeit devilish-looking Graziano a local favorite. Forget that he had gone AWOL, that he had spent time in a reform school for an aborted slot machine heist ("I never stole anything that didn't begin with A," Rocky was to say. "A car, a truck, a purse . . ."). Here was a man who was full of piss and vinegar, and ferocity. And they loved him.

They loved him so much they installed him as a 13–5 favorite in the opening odds. And although late Zale money came in, the odds closed favoring the 24-year-old challenger at 7–5.

The day before the fight, Zale's manager, Art Winch, showed confidence his boy would have no trouble knocking Graziano silly. "Tony loves boxers who move in on him," Winch said. "Graziano's style is made for Zale. First he'll wear him down with body punches, then he'll finish him off to the head."

Winch's prediction almost came true in the first round. Tony came out throwing rib-crackers from the opening bell, and less than a minute into the fight, a haymaker left hook had Rocky rolling around on the floor, groping for the ropes, desperately trying to pull himself upright. The crowd was frantic. The short-end bettors jumped up and down on their chairs, and threw their hats into the air. But Graziano was up at the count of four, menacing Zale with his vaunted right. At the bell it was Rocky on the attack as Zale tasted some of the firepower he would inspect more closely in round 2.

In the second round, Rocky cornered Zale and fired his right, one, two, three times. No one could have stood up under that barrage, not even the Man of Steel, who dropped his left leg, tucking it under his body in a position that made him look like a broken doll. Referee Ruby Goldstein pulled away the maniacal Dead End Kid. Graziano's face was flushed a fiery red. In the heat of battle he had lost all self-control, and like a jungle animal who senses the kill, was intent on nothing short of totally annihilating his victim.

At the count of four the bell rang. It saved Zale, who needed help to reach his corner. Zale complained to his corner of a throbbing sensation in his right hand. "I must have busted something," Tony muttered to Winch. Winch put pressure on various points on his hand, and when he dug his finger into the base of Zale's right thumb, the fighter winced with pain. Winch pretended nothing was wrong, but when Zale was in mid-ring trying to keep the Animal at bay, Winch whispered to his partner Sam Pian, "The thumb is broken."

In the third the Rock picked up right where he had left off in the second. It was right, right, right, then a left, and Zale, now bloody and hurt, didn't seem to be able to last much longer. He tried to fend off the challenger with jabs. He tried to turn away from the punches. Gore dripped from his mouth, but before the bell, Zale fired a right that came from somewhere down Yankee Stadium's right-field foul line. It landed on Rocky's nose, and now Rocky became an entrant in the Dracula's victims look-alike contest.

In the fourth round Zale made a slight comeback as his body punches began to take their toll on Graziano. As the frenzied mob yelled for the Rock to finish the job, he suddenly became the party of the second part, the "hittee" instead of the hitter.

In the fifth round, Zale could hardly keep his balance. Late in the round, Rocky turned loose his right-handed murder for the last time. Tony's face became a bloody mess. Zale tottered drunkenly across the ring, and only Graziano's wildness permitted Zale to stay upright. Tony was so hurt he started toward Rocky's corner, instead of his own at the bell.

During the rest period between rounds, Tony's cornermen shoved smelling salts under his blood-smeared nose in a desperate effort to snap him back to sensibility. There was little hope in Mudville for the mighty Zale.

Then, in the sixth round, after landing a few rights, Rocky stopped to take a breath. That was what Zale had been waiting for. A right hand landed in Graziano's stomach, up to the elbow. The punch literally paralyzed Graziano, and the following left hook sent him into oblivion.

By the time Rocky picked up the count the fight was over, and an exhausted Zale, still wavering from the effects of the earlier beating, had kept his title. His crown was intact, if slightly askew.

But even with the count of ten ringing in his ears, Graziano was anything but a beaten man. He jumped to his feet and tried to break away from Goldstein and get at Zale. Cops jumped into the ring as his handlers pulled Graziano into his corner where he sulked and muttered, "The count crept up on me. I didn't know it had gone so far."

In the dressing room after the fight, Graziano didn't remember the left hook that finished the job. The right hand to the body was the more devastating punch. "It knocked the wind out of me," Rocky said, alluding to the right to the midsection. "It straightened me up, tightened me all over, so it even clogged up my ears. Then I heard 'eight . . . nine . . . ten,' it all came so fast."

The pain in Zale's right hand turned out to be a break just below the right thumb. After the second round Zale said he told his corner, "My right hand's gone."

Winch looked him in the eye and said, "Tony, your left is as good as your right. Hook him and jab him and save the right for the short ones inside."

After the fifth round Winch told Zale, "Tony, he's more tired than you are. He starting to wing 'em. Take a chance with him in this round." He did. And the rest is history.

Referee holds a bemused Graziano as he tries to figure out how he was knocked out by champion Zale.

Rocky Graziano—Tony Zale

July 16, 1947

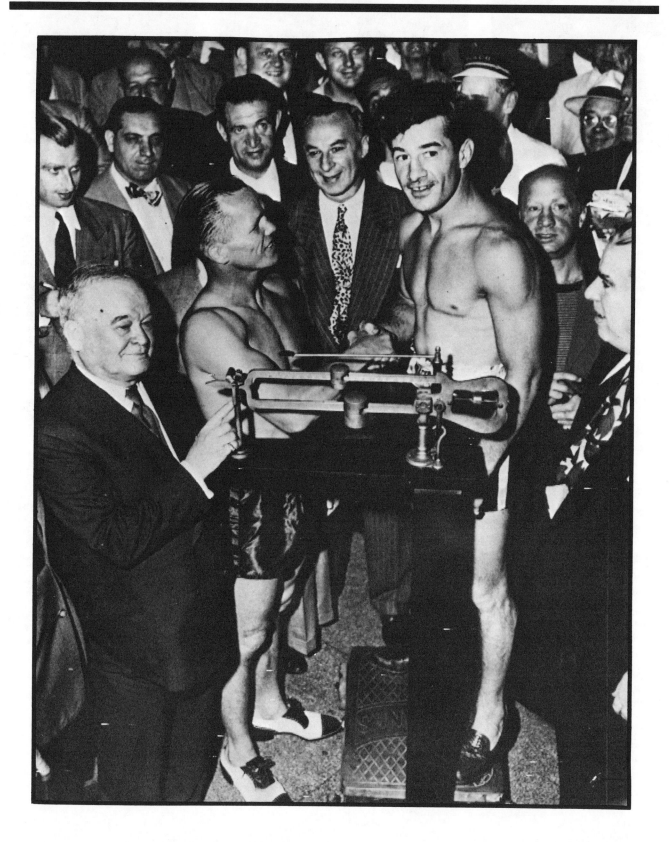

There have been twosomes throughout history that have gone together like salt and pepper. These twosomes have sprung up in many locales, and in every imaginable field: biblical, Cain and Abel; mythological, Damon and Pythias; musical, Gilbert and Sullivan; comical, Weber and Fields; athletic, Frick and Frack, etc. Boxing has its own twosomes. Perhaps one of its most famous pairings was that of Zale and Graziano. Like it says in the song "Love and Marriage," "You can't have one without the other."

For three years rivals Tony Zale and Rocky Graziano lit up the skies in the world of boxing with fireworks. And today, 33 years after their third battle, their fights are still legendary. They weren't fights, they were wars without survivors.

Their rivalry began the night of September 27, 1946, when Zale, "the Man of Steel" from Gary, Indiana, entered the ring with a record of 60 wins—36 by KO, 12 losses, and 1 draw, plus his 1941 middleweight crown—to do battle with Graziano. Rocky, a "Dead End Kid" from New York's Mulberry Bend ghetto, fought the way he lived, according to the rules of the street, alternately hitting and holding anyone who stood in his way. Graziano had compiled a record of 43 wins—32 by KO, 6 losses, and 5 draws, including sensational knockout victories over welterweight champion "Red" Cochrane and Marty Servo within the previous year.

In a battle that was more savage than scientific, Zale floored Graziano midway through the first round for a count of four. By the end of the round, however, Zale was on the receiving end of a Graziano bombardment and reeling under the attack. Round 2 saw "the Rock" batter the champion around the ring with rights and lefts to the head, splitting Zale's lip in the process, and finally toppling Tony with four

Preceding page: Although Tony Zale (left) and Rocky Graziano seem amiable enough at their weigh in, the Illinois boxing commission warned, "We want this fight clean...."

Top (left to right): Graziano hits Zale; Zale tries to keep his balance; he touches a glove down but staggers; Zale whirls around to keep his feet from moving from under his body. Above: Zale lands a hard right in the third round.

Classic picture of Graziano-Zale donneybrooks, with the "Rock" on the offensive.

successive rights. The bell saved Zale at the count of three and Zale was literally dragged to his corner. In the third round Graziano continued his attack with a maniacal fury, hammering the champion at will. However, Graziano could not finish him off. When Zale came out for round 4, he was amazingly refreshed and began his own attack, throwing lefts and rights to the body of Graziano, and forcing the challenger to retreat. Early in the fifth, Zale pressed his advantage, concentrating on the body with both hands. Suddenly, Graziano leaped at the champ with a tigerish attack and drove Zale back with rights and lefts to the head. But once again Zale weathered the round and came out for round 6 renewed in vigor and purpose. Graziano made a final furious attempt to finish off "the Man of Steel," and the tide turned once more as Zale crashed home a thunderous right under Graziano's heart, followed by a left hook to the jaw. Rocky sank to his haunches, there to be counted out for the first time in his career.

A rematch between the two warriors was a foregone conclusion. Ten months later, on July 16, 1947, the two took part in another seesaw slugfest, this time at Chicago Stadium. Zale immediately took the fight to Graziano, punishing him with a steady body barrage and closing his left eye by the end of round 1. Zale switched his attack to the head in round 2, attempting to inflict greater damage to Graziano's injured eye, but by the end of the round was in trouble himself, as Graziano connected with a right to the jaw that straightened up the champion and had him so bewildered that he went to the wrong corner at the bell. In round 3, Zale split open Graziano's left eye and floored him for no count with another right to the head; then he drove the temporarily blinded Graziano into the ropes for an unanswered volley. Round 4 was more of the same, as Graziano spent more time

91

wiping the blood out of his eye than trying to wipe out Zale, although Zale went to the canvas—more from a slip than a punch. By round 5, the flow of blood had been stemmed, and Graziano started swinging, connecting with a right to the head that seemed to take the steam out of Zale. The champion took the initiative in the opening seconds of the sixth, but it was short-lived as Graziano threw a right cross and then another right to the jaw, and sent Zale reeling. Three more rights sent the champion down for a count of three, and when he arose the challenger was all over him, draping him over the middle strand of the ropes and pounding him at will. The fight was halted at 2:10 of the sixth round, and Rocky Graziano was the new middleweight champion of the world. He won the title on his tremendous punching power, his heart, and, as he put it, because "somebody up there likes me."

The rubber match came 11 months later in Newark, New Jersey—the *only* one that was filmed. Graziano came in as the prohibitive 12–5 favorite. He went out as the champion. The product of the Gary steel mills came out first—and fast—hooking a left to Graziano's jaw and knocking him down with less than a minute gone. The rest of the first round was all Zale's as he banged home his awesome one-two (a right to the body and left to the jaw) several times. Round 2 was a carbon copy of round 1, with Zale pounding home his combination. Then, for a brief moment, Graziano flurried, cutting loose with some of his old furiousness and forcing Zale to retreat. The third round continued where the second had left off; and then the roof caved in on Rocky as Tony caught the champion with a left hook that floored him. As Graziano struggled to an unsteady position, using the ropes as a crutch, Zale was on him again, determined to end it. He caught Rocky with a rib-crunching right to the ribs and followed it up, in perfect tandem, with a left to the jaw. Graziano went down, pole-axed, and lay there as referee Paul Cavalier counted out "the Rock" at 1:08 of the third round.

Tony Zale became the first middleweight champion since Stanley Ketchel to regain his title. Somebody "up there" obviously liked him, too.

92

In the fatal sixth round, Graziano pummels a helpless Zale on his way to the championship.

Ike Williams—Bob Montgomery

August 4, 1947

Pennsylvania has been the scene of two battles which were to determine the course of two civil wars: Gettysburg determined the outcome of the Civil War, in 1863, and Philadelphia, in 1947, ended a civil war that had split the lightweight division for nearly five years.

In what promised to be a classic grudge match, two pretenders to the crown were to wage boxing's version of a civil war—a war in which one would emerge a king.

The princes were the two provisional champions of the division: Ike Williams, sanctioned by the National Boxing Association; and Bob Montgomery, representing the interests of the New York and Pennsylvania Athletic Commissions. The dual championships were the result of parallel descendencies of the crown once held by Sammy An-

gott. Eleven months after acquiring the title from Lew Jenkins in a 15-round decision, Angott announced his retirement claiming that a severe hand injury made it impossible for him to continue his career. He was, in his own words, "through with boxing."

In order to fill the vacancy left by Angott's retirement, Beau Jack was designated the new champion by the New York Boxing Commission. He lost that crown on May 21, 1943, to Bob ("Wildcat") Montgomery. Montgomery held the title for only six months before he once again relinquished it to Beau Jack in a rematch. The tables turned again in Montgomery's favor in their rubber match in March of the following year. Montgomery went on to successfully defend his title against Arnie Stolz in June 1946 and Wesley

Preceding page: *Ike Williams (left) wards off a left from Bob Montgomery and manages to land his own left on the jaw*. Above: *Montgomery (left) hangs groggily on the ropes as Williams measures him for another blow*.

Mouzon in November of the same year. Both bouts ended in knockouts, in the thirteenth and eighth rounds, respectively.

But this was only half the story. Back at the National Boxing Association, the history of the lightweight division was being written differently. Sammy Angott decided that his severe hand injury wasn't as bad as first thought. According to him, *he* was still the man who should wear the championship belt, and a fight was sanctioned with Slugger White to settle the claim. Angott won that battle, but lost to Juan Zurita the following March.

Zurita held the crown for roughly a year and a half until Ike Williams knocked him out in the second round of their Mexico City match. Williams strengthened his claim to be the "true world champion" by defeating British Empire king Ronnie James in the ninth round of their title bout in Wales.

Thus the stage was set for the cutting of the Gordian knot which had entangled the lightweight division for so long. Throughout the entire period, calls had been heard from all corners to hold a unification battle which would again clear the air and simplify the record books. Nat Fleischer, the editor of the *Ring* magazine, even went so far as to crown Bob Montgomery *Ring*'s champion for two years.

Getting two champions to unify the title was, at best, difficult, with each fearful of giving up the privileges that even a partial championship provided. Some thought it more probable that two parallel lines should converge, than the title be successfully welded. But Einstein has taught us that parallel lines do indeed, join, albeit in infinity, and the same was true of "split championships." But the two men who held the split championships were to meet not in infinity, but in Philadelphia. And they had more reasons for being there than just unifying the lightweight crown.

Ike Williams and Bob Montgomery shared more than just "titles." These two men shared an intense and public hatred stemming back to their first meeting in January 1944, three years before.

"Philadelphia" fighters have long held a special place in the annals of boxing. To quote a cliché, they "came to fight," staging wars—in the ring and in the gym as well. In fact, observers over the years have felt that many "Philadelphia boxers" have left their best fights in the gym. Williams and Montgomery were two of the exceptions to the rule, each saving themselves for each other. And their own private war.

Williams, an upstart, had thrashed a friend of Montgomery's. In revenge, Bob said that he was going to repay Ike by not only knocking him out, but knocking him out of the ring as well. Their fight was no picnic, and Ike complained that Montgomery had fouled him all through the contest. In the twelfth round, Wildcat did his best to keep his word, sending Williams down—and out—for the first time in his career. The dislike simmered for the next three years in charges and countercharges played out in the sports pages across the country. It all came to a head in Philadelphia on the night of August 4, 1947.

Both men came into the fight with similar records. Williams had won 80 of his previous bouts while losing 10 and drawing 4 times. Forty-one of his victories were by KO. Montgomery—with 10 more fights to his credit—had won 85 while losing 12 and drawing 3. He had sent his opponents to the floor for the count 45 times. Most of the spectators with enough knowledge to have an intelligent opinion thought that Williams, the younger man, would have a slight advantage. The bookies, too, favored Williams, installing him as *the* favorite.

The crowd was too excited about the main event to notice the preliminaries, or much else of the tinsel-plated ceremonies which accompany a "title" fight. About the only time they did pay attention was to register their extreme dissatisfaction at the absence of middleweight champion Rocky Graziano, whose presence had been promised. Their booing stopped only when the bell rang to start the first round.

Montgomery immediately went for the body, blasting Williams' middle with shots that sounded like they came from a .44 gauge shotgun until Williams almost doubled up. It looked like a repeat of their first fight, but Ike found his left and began to jab the Wildcat away. Montgomery kept

Montgomery tries to get up,
but has all the appearances of a beaten man.

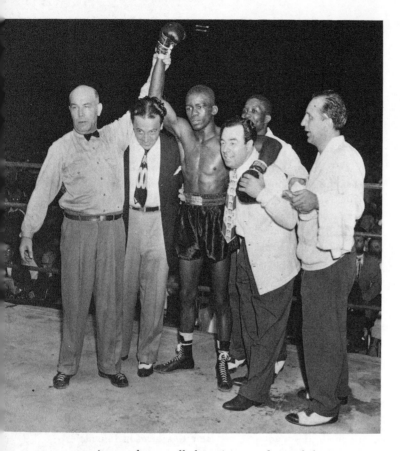

pressing, and soon all the science and art of the sport was forgotten as both men got caught in the web of their hatred. Oblivious to any potential danger his opponent might store in the dynamite carried in his gloves, they swung at each other with everything they had. The round ended with Williams, the left completely forgotten, shoving rights into Montgomery's face.

The second round was much the same with Williams again resorting first to his jab, but soon switched to trading punches with the ever-advancing Wildcat. There were some flashy blows, but most looked better than they were and none did any real damage.

In the third, Montgomery was lulled into believing that the NBA champion was wary of him, and he went in for the kill. Williams lashed out with looping uppercuts which drove Montgomery away, but not before Ike suffered a sizable cut over his right eye.

Jimmy Wilson, Williams' second, did his best to close the cut between rounds, but it would take six stitches after the battle to do that. For now, it was the bull's-eye Bob needed. He hacked away at it in the fourth as if he were more interested in further damaging Williams' impaired eye than in winning the fight. Now Ike wasn't jabbing at all, but

he *was* missing. And Montgomery didn't seem to care that he might connect. He didn't—or couldn't—stop. Neither man took any notice of the bell that ended the fourth round. They probably didn't even hear it.

The fifth round was like the fourth, and all those "knowledgeable people" began to wonder if they'd gotten it all wrong. It was still a fairly even fight, but the 28-year-old Montgomery wasn't showing the signs of age that had been so widely predicted.

That was all to change in the sixth. Somebody in his corner must have gotten through to Ike because he began working his left again—boxing Montgomery instead of merely slugging the air. Without warning, Williams rushed and let go at Montgomery with everything he had. Whenever Ike landed he did damage; and he landed just about wherever he liked on the Wildcat.

You could hear the cracking of the gloves as they struck flesh and see the red welts appear beneath the pounding leather. One instant Montgomery was standing there, throwing punches; the next, spinning, he had fallen on the middle strand of the ropes, and hung there, suspended like a sack of onions. Incredibly, he managed to beat the count.

Williams now had him where he wanted him and smashed Montgomery's head as if it were a punching bag. Bob held on, but it could only have been from instinct, or hatred, or both. After an eternity of punishment, the discipline dissolved and Montgomery dropped. Again the count began, and again, beyond all reasonable expectations, Bob made it up as the timekeeper tolled eight. But the referee had seen enough. He counted the standing fighter out at 2:37 of the sixth round. The civil war was over. Ike Williams was the undisputed lightweight champion of the world.

But the promoters wanted more. They always do. The contract for the bout had stipulated a rematch—whatever the circumstances. The group from Madison Square Garden wanted it to come off and set the date for early December.

Montgomery's friends urged him to take the $40,000 he'd earned for this fight and get out of the busted-beak business while he was still in one piece and able to enjoy the rest of his life. But he didn't retire; nor did he fight Williams again, either. He fought another six times without once winning and then retired.

Bob Montgomery was a beaten man.

Ike Williams was a winner. For him it was parties and pictures in the papers—a long career filled with 43 more wins loaded with heavy purses. Ike got the gravy.

Ike Williams was the king, and the lightweight champion of the world. The *only* lightweight champion of the world.

Williams, supported by manager Blinky Palermo, is acknowledged as the undisputed lightweight champion of the world.

Joe Louis—Jersey Joe Walcott

December 5, 1947

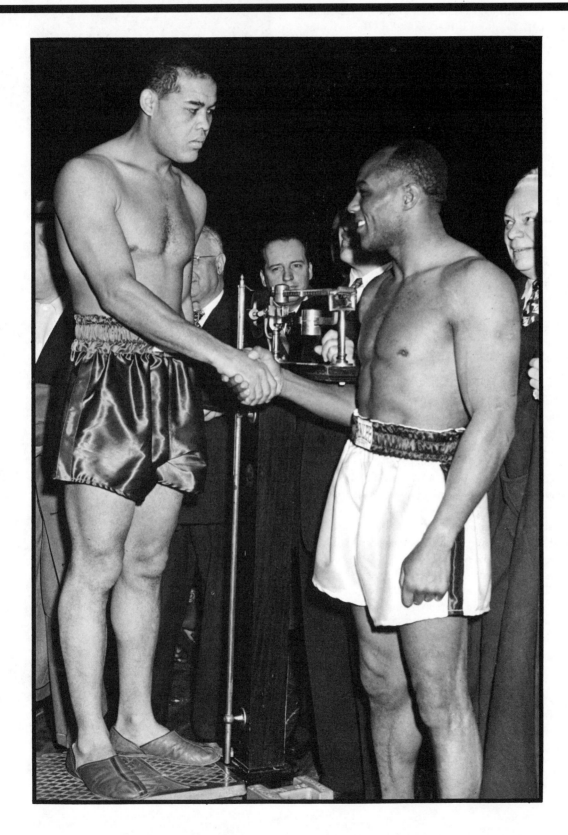

It was supposed to be a cakewalk for the great heavy-weight champion Joe Louis. Just another payday for the Brown Bomber. If you had read through the press clippings before the fight, you'd have thought Jersey Joe Walcott was even money not to show up.

Going into this fight, Walcott had had a spotty career at best. Christened Arnold Cream, Walcott had started fighting professionally in 1930 at the age of 16. He had won some, including knockout wins over Harold Johnson and his father in the same round, in the same arena, in the same city, 14 years apart. And he had lost some, knockouts at the hands of Al Etore in 1936, to Tiger Jack Fox in 1937, and to the hulking Abe Simon in 1940.

Although Joe Louis was 33 years old, he still maintained an aura of invincibility. Winning the heavyweight title from James J. Braddock in Chicago on June 22, 1937, Louis had successfully defended it 23 times, only twice going the full 15-round limit. The two survivors were Tommy Farr in 1937 and Arturo Godoy in 1940. In his last fight, Louis had knocked out Tami Mauriello in the very first round. Everyone figured Jersey Joe would go just as fast, if not faster.

The fight was originally scheduled to be a nontitle bout. A clipping from the New York *Daily Mirror* on September 16 read as follows:

> The 20th Century Club's announcement that the match, originally booked for November 14 as a 10-round nontitle affair, would be held in Madison Square Garden on December 5, as a 15-round championship fight, was regarded as (a) a reprieve for Walcott, and (b) strictly a technicality. The average fan can't see what difference it makes if Jersey Joe is flattened in the second round of a nontitle bout, or the first round of a championship fight.

On the day before the fight it was disclosed by Jim Jennings of the *Daily Mirror* that Louis, himself, did not consider Walcott a suitable opponent for Louis' twenty-fourth title defense.

Explaining a dispute between Louis and the promoters, the 20th Century Sports Club, Jennings wrote, "It is generally known that Louis was never keen about accepting Walcott as an opponent, and merely went through with what he considered a bad match, at the behest of the club."

Louis himself seemed supremely confident about his chances against the father of six, who, just three years before, had been on the Jersey welfare rolls. When asked on the day before the fight how he thought it would go Louis replied, "Well, I still plan to be champion, and I can tell you the fight won't go fifteen rounds."

For a fight that was imagined to be an open-and-shut

Preceding page: *Jersey Joe Walcott (right) greets champion Joe Louis during the weighing-in ceremony before the fight.* Above (top and bottom): *Stunned by a vicious right, Louis staggers and falls hurt to the canvas in the opening round of the fight.*

case, there was controversy, mostly emanating from the Walcott camp, on two very important subjects. The first problem concerned the selection of the referee. Both Walcott and his manager, Joe Webster, a Camden New Jersey cafe proprietor, petitioned the New York State Athletic Commission to use a referee other than Arthur Donovan.

"I am not questioning Donovan's ability," said Webster. "Neither am I questioning his honesty. But he has handled most of Louis' title fights, and I think the fans, as well as Walcott and myself, would welcome a change."

A check of the records shows that Donovan had, indeed, presided as third man on 12 of the 23 occasions Louis had defended his title since he knocked out Braddock in 1937. Donovan was the third man in the ring in Louis' last title defense, a KO of Tami Mauriello 25 months before.

"I have no man in mind to suggest to the athletic commission," Webster added. "Anyone besides Donovan would delight me. I think this is a sportsmanlike request and I hope the board will act favorably on it."

Louis was once asked if it were true he carried a "house referee"—meaning Donovan—with him. The champion replied with a deadpan expression, "Sure. Want to see it?" And he held up his huge right fist for inspection.

The other sore point was the selection of the boxing

Confident and sure, Walcott waits as Louis tries to clear the cobwebs.

gloves to be used. Louis wanted to use Everlast gloves, while Walcott preferred a pair manufactured by Ben Lee. Since the champ did not have the final choice, it remained the decision of the presiding athletic commissioner, Eddie Egan, who decided that Ben Lee models would do just fine.

The contract for the fight called for neither fighter to come in *over* 212 pounds. Louis never had weight problems before, winning the title from Braddock at 197 pounds. In his fight with Mauriello, Louis came in at 210. Yet, on the day before the fight, Louis was 214 pounds. He was faced with the task of drying out for the first time in his long career.

On Thursday, the day before the fight, Louis drank absolutely no fluids. On Friday morning, Louis drank one glass of orange juice, period. He took no solid foods. When he stepped on the scales, Louis weighed in at 211 pounds, 1 pound under the limit. Walcott easily made the prescribed weight, tipping the beam at 194½ pounds.

The betting odds on the day of the fight were overwhelmingly in favor of the champion, some places quoting a figure as high as 15–1. The Cleveland *Press* ran the headline, "Even Money Bet Walcott Won't Go Five Rounds," which was indicative of the combined opinion of the boxing community.

The referee finally agreed upon by all parties was veteran Ruby Goldstein. Although Goldstein had been a referee for many years, it was his first heavyweight championship bout.

On the night of December 5, 1947, a Madison Square Garden crowd of 18,194 people paid $216,477, a new Garden record, to watch the supposed mismatch. What they saw was anything but.

At the opening bell both fighters started slowly, probing with their left jabs. Then Louis backed Walcott into a corner and started lathering him with both hands. Suddenly Walcott walked away to his right and crossed over with a short overhand right, dropping Louis to his knees. Up at the count of two, Louis charged at Walcott and was staggered by another walk-away right hand. Louis fought back savagely, but could not land a punch effectively.

The next two rounds were nip and tuck, with Louis pursuing, and Walcott counter-punching. Both rounds were close and could have gone either way. But Walcott looked like anything but a 15–1 pushover.

Round 4 opened with Louis still coming forward, behind his left jab. Walcott was slipping side-to-side, when suddenly, Jersey Joe walked away, planted his left foot, and nailed Louis with a vicious right to the jaw. The champion went down, again. Louis, badly hurt this time, stayed down for the count of seven. Walcott swung wildly at him, but

Louis, who was still shaking the cobwebs out of his now-muddled head, managed to keep out of trouble for the rest of the round. The round ended with Louis, now fully recovered, chasing Walcott.

Round 5 began with Louis retreating. But Jersey Joe, the cutie that he was, declined to lead. Louis decided to come forward, and Walcott, getting cocky, clowned and slapped Louis backhanded with his right. Goldstein warned Walcott for his blatantly illegal manuever as the round ended.

In rounds 6 and 7 the pattern remained the same and Louis remained the aggressor, but Walcott scored the points.

As Louis came out for round 8, his face showed the wear and tear of the previous seven rounds; it was swollen on the left side. Walcott was clowning and feinting when suddenly, he got in a right hand squarely on Louis' left eye, and it started to close. Walcott scored with two more rights to the left side of the champion's face as the round ended. Between rounds, Louis' seconds held an ice bag to the champion's damaged eye.

Round 9 found Walcott jumping off his stool, and pumping in two more rights to the left side of Louis' face, obviously going after the damaged eye. Louis, in desperation, threw a left hook which cut Walcott over the left eye. Walcott, now in danger, began fighting back furiously, chopping Louis with short right hands. Louis suddenly jumped in with a right uppercut, and landed a right cross which hurt Walcott. Louis backed Walcott into the ropes and banged away at him with both hands as the round ended. The Garden was in bedlam; all 18,194 fans seemed to be on their feet.

Walcott, apparently recovered from the beating he took in the ninth, came out for the tenth and resumed his retreat. The tenth was uneventful, except for a long right by Walcott which landed high on Louis' head.

In round 11 Walcott regained his confidence and kept retreating behind his sharp left jab. Louis kept plodding in after Walcott, but couldn't do any damage, catching a savage right for his trouble. Louis spent the remainder of the round clearing his head.

Round 12 was more of the same, with Louis—his crown resting shakily on his head—moving forward, but Jersey Joe doing all the fistic damage. By the end of the round, Louis' eye was almost completely closed.

Round 13 was all Walcott's as he kept on his bicycle, landing his left jab at will. Louis continued to plod forward, hoping for the big punch which would turn the tide in his favor. Near the bell Walcott threw a long right hand, missed, and fell down to the canvas. He got up laughing. He could afford to, by now he was in complete control of the fight.

After the thirteenth round, Walcott's corner could be heard telling their charge that if he stayed away the last two rounds the fight was his. They didn't want Walcott making the same mistake Billy Conn had made six years earlier. In the Louis-Conn fight, Conn was ahead going into the thirteenth, and only had to last the fight on his feet to become the new champion. But in that round he tried to slug it out with Louis, and Louis deposited him on the canvas for the full count of ten. Now Walcott's corner implored him not to make the same mistake.

Walcott, heeding their advice, got on his superannuated bicycle, shuffling first one way, then the other, for the fourteenth and fifteenth rounds, like a moth always out of reach of Louis' firepower. By the fifteenth round the crowd could be heard hollering, "Keep running Walcott." And that's what he did. Others booed, but Walcott just kept dodg-

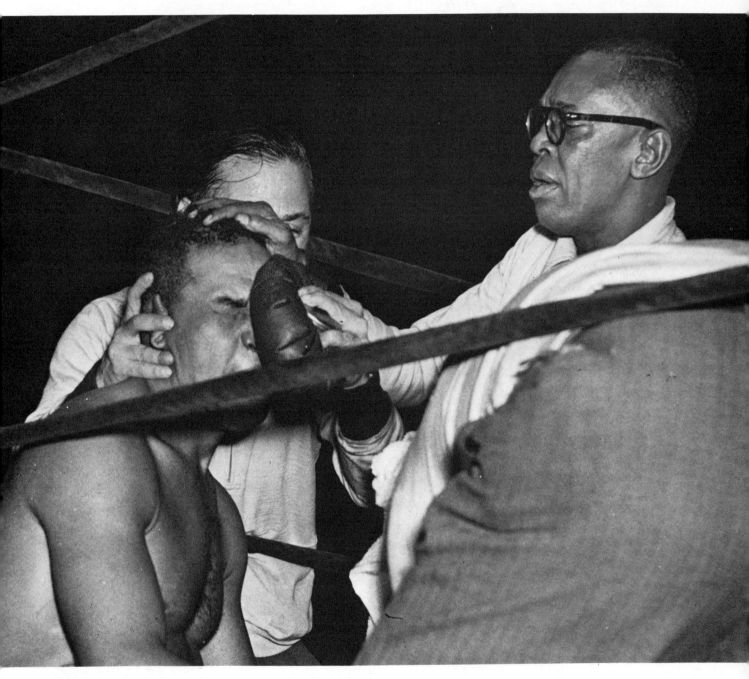

Joe Louis has a cold compress applied to his eye, injured during the first round.

101

ing Louis' weak advances. The final bell ended with the short-end bettors screaming with delight. It seemed to most a mere formality until the miracle was acknowledged: that Jersey Joe Walcott would be crowned the new heavyweight king.

In what seemed like an eternity without end, ring announcer Harry Balogh collected the ballots. Then he finally grabbed the mike in mid-ring. A regiment of special police surrounded the ring, pushing back fans who were trying to climb closer. A dejected Louis, looking equally defeated, started to climb through the ropes, but his handlers stopped him. Balogh read the scorecards in a steel voice: "Judge Frank Forbes scored the fight eight rounds for Louis, six for Walcott, one even." The crowd booed, and certainly, for the first time in his career, Louis heard them directed his way. Balogh continued, "Referee Ruby Goldstein had it seven rounds Walcott, six for Louis, two even." Cheers went up from the gallery. Then came the final tally, the makeweight: "Judge Marty Monroe, nine rounds Louis . . ." The rest was blotted out by the scream of the crowd. Joe Louis was still the champ.

No emotion crossed the badly battered face of Louis. Walcott looked like a little boy about to cry. Louis walked over to Walcott and said quietly, "I'm sorry," then quickly left the ring.

Don Florio, Walcott's trainer, led him toward midring and lifted his hand. Felix Bocchicchio, one of the other cornermen, clapped his hands feverishly, leading the crowd in applause. Walcott smiled and the crowd cheered. But he had gotten the fuzzy end of the lollipop and was, crowd emotions to the contrary, still the loser.

The newspapermen were kept waiting in the corridor outside Louis' dressing room for a full half hour before they were admitted.

"What's the matter, Joe?" someone asked.

One of Louis' handlers spoke up, "Joe hurt his hand in the fifth round. See!"

Louis held up his hand, a large bump across the back of it. Joe had an ugly swelling under his left eye, and his upper lip was swollen to twice its normal size.

Photographers rushed in the crowded room. "Give us a smile, Joe," they pleaded. Louis managed a small grimace.

"C'mon Joe, you can smile bigger than that," one said.

"I can't open my mouth any more," Joe answered, with a hurt look.

"Why did you start crawling through the ropes before the decision was announced?" one scribe yelled.

"I was mad at myself for fighting such a bad fight.

I was getting hit with all those sucker punches. I wanted to get out."

"Was Walcott a second-rate fighter tonight?" yelled one writer, alluding to Louis' statement before the fight.

Joe tapped his chest and said, "No, I was."

Walcott was despondent in his dressing room, weeping as the reporters entered. "I thought I won," Jersey Joe cried. "Louis' punches never hurt me. My corner told me I was ahead and to coast in that last round."

"Did he hurt you, Joe?"

"He never hit me like he must have hit some of the others," Joe replied. "I thought I won," he said again.

So did most everyone else. Out of the 33 writers who attended the fight, 22 had Walcott ahead, 10 had Louis ahead, and one called it a draw. It was small consolation for a man who was so close yet so far from wearing the heavyweight crown.

Four years later, at the age of 37, Jersey Joe Walcott landed a left hook on the jaw of champion Ezzard Charles in the seventh round, earning him the title he so justly deserved on the night of December 5, 1947. This time he didn't carry the three officials. This time, he carried his own judge in his fists.

Winner and still champion, Joe Louis wears the scars of battle.

Willie Pep—Sandy Saddler

February 11, 1949

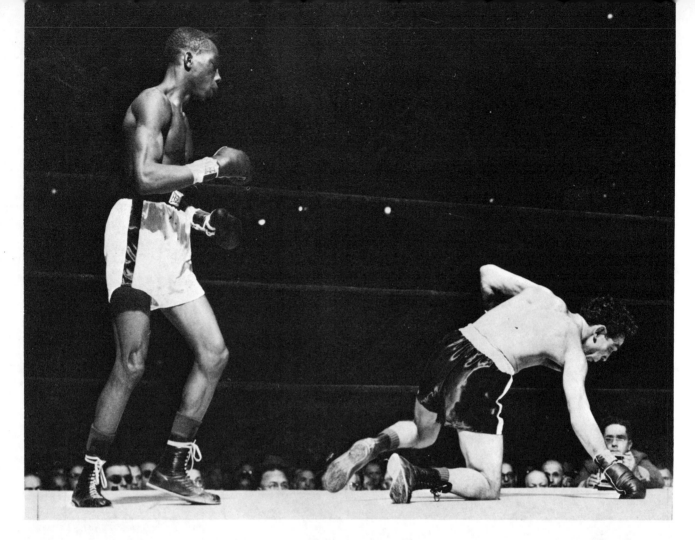

Willie Pep was up against "it" that night. And "it" was a lot to be up against. If he'd only been up against Sandy Saddler it would have been enough. Saddler had taken the title from Willie three and a half months before in a contest which ended in a fourth-round knockout. Pep was not just up against the embarrassment of that loss; he was also fighting the rumor which had circulated that it had been a fixed fight—that he'd taken a dive. Those who thought the fight had been on the level said that Willie Pep was washed-up, and too old to beat the younger boys. They said that he'd never really recovered from the injuries he'd sustained in a near-fatal plane crash in 1948. The miserable showing he'd made against Saddler was blamed on that accident and cited as proof that Willie just didn't have it any more. Nobody but a has-been finds himself on the floor for the count from one lonely little left jab. He didn't have a chance. And, if he did, somehow, someway, manage to win, it would just prove that he'd lain down in the first bout.

That's the way it was that night in New York when Willie Pep came to fight Sandy Saddler. But Willie didn't let any of that, or Saddler, stop him.

Pep wanted what was his, what he'd lost three and a half long months ago to Saddler's lucky punch. He wanted his self-respect. He wanted a chance to shine again in the minds and memories of fight fans, to be considered a ring immortal once more. People had begun to refer to him in those terms before that deadly left jab. The Pep legend had begun after Pep had beaten Jackie Graves four years earlier. In the third round of their fight, Pep told those at ringside that he wasn't going to throw a punch for the full three minutes.

"I moved around, feinted, picked off punches, made him miss, and I never threw a punch. All three officials gave me the round."

Willie Pep wanted his history and his destiny back, while all Sandy Saddler wanted was to keep his title. He didn't stand a chance.

Not that Saddler didn't have all the advantages on paper: he was taller, stronger, younger, and unanimously accepted as the far stronger puncher. In 99 starts, he'd won 91, 61 by knockout, losing only 5 times and drawing twice. He'd been knocked out only once in his career, by Jock Les-

Preceding page: *In this their second contest, Willie Pep (left) was seeking his destiny while Sandy Saddler was hoping to keep his title*. Above: *In their first meeting, Pep was knocked out in the fourth by Saddler.*

lie in three rounds, back in 1944. After putting Pep to sleep and taking his crown, Sandy went on to rack up four more knockouts and a 10-round victory.

Willie Pep had also won 91 times—but only 44 of these were by KO—with one draw. Pep had been floored only once in his career, by that infamous left jab of Sandy Saddler. Pep had a lot to say about that first fight as he trained for the rematch in a converted trolley barn in Hartford:

> He surprised me in every way. It's like I say, I licked Sierra and Sierra licked him, and Sierra kept telling me: "You'll lick him easy." All the time he was working with me he kept telling me what an easy fight I'd have. Even at the weigh-in he didn't look like much of a fighter. You know what I mean. . . . He's thin, a weak-looking guy. He looks like you could go poof and knock him over. I'm not trying to make excuses; I don't make excuses. But all of a sudden, he thumbs me two or three times, butts me under the mouth, he grabs me. . . . Friday night he won't hit me. I mean, sure, he'll hit me but he'll have his hands full Friday night.

Saddler's camp saw it differently: "Pep will run like a thief and when he gets tired, Sandy will knock him out."

To Saddler, it was to be a race, but one with Pep going backward. Race or not, it was an event the fans wanted to witness in person. Despite radio and television coverage, 19,000 people turned in over 87,000 hard-earned dollars for the privilege of "being" at Madison Square Garden for the classic confrontation between a boxer *par excellence* and a puncher. And they were still turning thousands away at the door. Three thousand general admission seats were sold in less than an hour on the afternoon before the fight. Gladys Gooding, the Garden organist, reflected the promoter's delight as she played "Happy Days Are Here Again" to open the program. Pep may have lost his title, but he still had his fans.

They came in droves from Pep's home state of Connecticut to prove that they didn't believe anything that was being said about Pep. A flow of Pep money drove Saddler from the favorite's position, with the odds leveling off just before the fight at 6–5 if you wanted to back Willie, and even money if you were backing Saddler. Both fighters looked fit as they waited for the ceremonies which dragged on—as they do at the beginning of any title fight—to end, and the action to begin.

Pep weighed in at 126 pounds, making the limit without an ounce to spare. Saddler was two pounds lighter. Pep's corner told the challenger to keep moving, never give Saddler a straight line, and never be the flat-footed target he was in their first encounter. Archie Moore, Sandy's stable-

mate, reminded Saddler to use the left hook to Pep's body to wear him down. The whistle blew, the bell rang, and the fight was on.

Pep was at it from the very beginning: dancing, jabbing, pushing his straight left into Saddler's face a full 37 times in the opening frame alone. Saddler pressed forward, but Pep just danced away, waiting till his opponent was off balance and coming in again, all the while piling up points.

By the third round, Pep was clinching Sandy, wrestling with Saddler whenever he threatened to deliver his heavy punches at close quarters. Breaking, Pep would dance away, only to return with another flurry whenever it suited him.

In the fourth Sandy found his target. Following Moore's advice, he went to the body and again almost upset Willie with a left jab. Pep seemed almost to be tapping a rhythm on Saddler's face as if it were a speed bag. It didn't seem possible that Pep would be able to keep up such a fast pace throughout the whole fight. Sooner or later, he would have to tire, and that's when Sandy would have his chance— or so it seemed to those at ringside.

There was a cut under Pep's eye by the fifth, but Willie ignored the injury, continuing to dance to his own

Referee Eddie Joseph vainly tries to pull apart Saddler (in white trunks) and Pep as all three fall against the ropes.

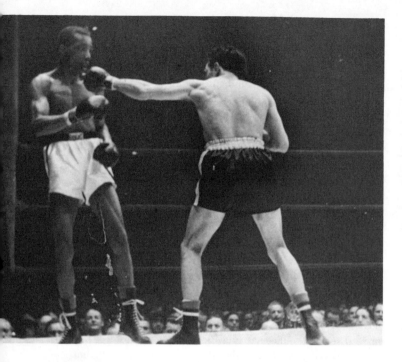

beat. Time and time again, Pep would reverse his backward steps, coming in to explode lefts and rights from all angles into Saddler's face. Pep kept it up in the sixth, but Saddler's rights were now beginning to find their mark, and Sandy scored his first winning round with head and body shots. Pep faded through the next two rounds and it looked as if age was beginning to catch up with the older man. Now, Pep was bleeding from a second cut, a fresher wound.

Saddler's best punch was a right cracked to Pep's jaw, which stunned the former champion. Now he was in trouble. But again he backpedaled out of danger, and came back to jab, jab, and jab again, continually unnerving Saddler with a glove which seemed to be permanently grafted to the champ's face.

Again, in the tenth, Saddler kept throwing combinations at Pep, but Willie refused to go down, he refused even to slow. Fighting back in flurries, using skill and art to keep the lean, hungry animal at bay, Pep denied Saddler the punches he so desperately needed to win. The wild, missed blows and the strength expended in missing them began to tell on Saddler. His arms began to have weight beyond their mass just as the little dancing master started to slow down enough to be found, But now, Sandy knew the price he had paid looking for the knockout blow. He could no longer hit cleanly, or with enough force to do damage. The sting was gone from his punches. And Pep was still throwing that crazing left as the bell ending the tenth sounded.

106

Saddler sagged against the rope between rounds with his head back and his long, skinny body limp in exhaustion as he watched and waited for the coming of the next round. From the bell for the seventh round it was clear that Pep had already taken control of the battle. Dancing and pressing, he made Saddler look like a drunken fool, keeping the champion pinned to the defensive with jabs and short rights, driving him back and cutting him down to his own size—inch by inch. It was hit and run. The instant Saddler was able to gather himself from the confusion and set himself up, preparing to attack Pep, the little man would be out of reach, beckoning from the other side of the ring. There was rarely a Willie Pep within reach when Sandy was ready to hit. There seemed to be several Peps, as Willie pedaled and gored at will.

In the fifteenth, knowing that all was lost if he couldn't score a knockout, Saddler found a reserve of strength. He almost pulled it out, rocking Willie with a hard right. But Pep was too close to his "Holy Grail" to lose it He outmaneuvered Saddler more by instinct than by any certain plan. But he finally saved the day and regained his crown, coming back to fight Sandy all around the ring, capping a fight with a skill that few thought he still had in him.

Pep proved himself to be perhaps the most intelligent, graceful, and artful fighter ever to have lived. He was a consummate artist and technician who sharpened and polished his skills, and won the world championship, again. He

Above (left to right): *Willie practices his "will-o'-the-whisp" treatment on Saddler to regain his crown.* Opposite: *An exhausted Pep is revived with ice bags.*

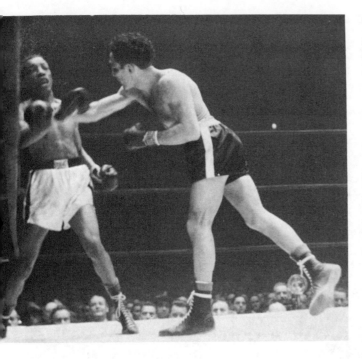 

showed he possessed the most valuable of all abilities—the ability to adapt.

Pep replaced strength with experience and youth with intelligence. He more than made up for his deficit in arm strength with the power of his legs. But more than any other part of his anatomy, Pep won this fight with his head—his brain—and not his brawn. For that, Willie Pep should stand as a model for all small schoolboys forced to face the inevitable bully. Pep may have been the finest master of the Western form of unarmed self-defense. That's what the judges were really declaring when they gave him the unanimous verdict that night. Lou Viscousi, Pep's manager, raised his charge high in the air in a celebration of victory. He held aloft a battered, bludgeoned man. The fight had been won, but Sandy Saddler had exacted a dear price, even in defeat: bruises, cuts, and a rich ceaseless flow of blood. But the true victor, Willie Pep's mind, lay untouched and safe.

It took seven stitches to close the cuts on Pep's face. Three over each eye, three on his left cheek, and two on his right cheek. It would be weeks before the bruises would disappear, and the scars would remain forever. The uncertainties and the rumors vanished instantly. There were no longer any questions of irregularities in the first fight. After this fight, it would be difficult to recall that there had been one before this. It would be impossible to remember that his career had been thought to be over. Willie Pep's talent and integrity were now facts, unquestionable certainties.

Sandy Saddler had questions as well as complaints. He was bitter about the way the referee, Eddie Joseph, had handled him in the clinches. Perhaps he had some justification. Articles appeared after the fight, repeatedly stating the views of both the English and other judges that they would not have permitted Pep such obvious advantages. Still, there were no protests lodged. Saddler had plainly been beaten and he knew it. Saddler had nothing to be ashamed of, and he only had to look at Pep's face to remind himself of that. He lost, but he lost to the best . . . the very best.

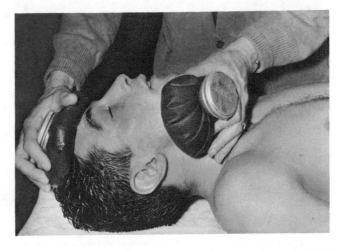

Sugar Ray Robinson—Kid Gavilan

July 11, 1949

Nothing replaces quality; nothing even comes close. It matters not how good you are or how much you try or how good you want to be. If you're not the best, you're second, and coming in second—to paraphrase one of sports' oldest clichés—is like kissing your sister.

Philadelphia, July 11, 1949. There's a ring staked near the closed section of the horseshoe arena called Municipal Stadium. It's a warm, near-perfect day and some 35,000 people—made all the larger by the fact that there will be no radio or television coverage of the event—are milling around the stands and onto the grass which leads to the ring where the welterweight championship bout between Sugar Ray Robinson and Kid Gavilan is to be fought later this evening. Confusion reigns everywhere: the parking lot has few attendants and even less order, if that is possible. Things

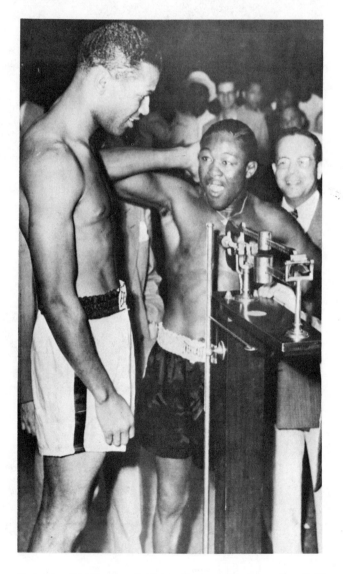

aren't much better inside the open coliseum. There, aisles are jammed and the press section is filled with people who literally have no "business" to conduct there. In total, $175,745 have flowed through the ticket windows and the lucky ticketholders are determined to make the most of every dime they have paid.

The bookmakers are there, too, taking more than dimes, as they install Robinson as the favorite to Gerardo Gonzalez, better known as "Kid Gavilan," translated from "the Hawk."

On paper, Robinson merited his 12–5 odds. Referred to as "pound for pound the greatest boxer in the world," Robinson had long ago proven that he was, losing only once in some 98 fights—and that to Jake LaMotta, whom he had since beaten four times—while scoring 62 knockouts, 15 in the first round. Gavilan, while no slouch—with a 52–6–3 record, and 17 knockouts, was viewed as "no match" for the Sugarman, who, rumor had it, had gotten down a little money on his chances to add yet another pelt to his collection.

Robinson's biggest battle was fought before the bout, as he strained to reach the class limit of 147 pounds. When the official declared him "in at the limit, to the ounce," Ray's pearly whites flashed. Others wondered if the strict regimen Robinson had followed to make the weight had sapped his stamina and staying power. Indeed, if it had, the younger "Kid" would have a chance—a good chance.

Perhaps that's why the Kid was smiling, later, after the preliminaries had come to an end and the fighters were entering the ring. The Hawk danced all over the ring to the beat of the "Kid Gavilan Rhumba," played by his supporters, who had flown in from Havana for the fight. They were backing their favorite with all their heart, as well as all their pesos. Kid Chocolate was fully behind him, as was Joe Louis, all predicting that Robinson would be mere "skin and bones" if he made the weight. Ray's answer was simple. He hoped, he said, that they "didn't bet on it."

As the two gladiators entered the ring, Gavilan's corner took on an aura of pure chaos. Everybody who had come from Havana to back him now seemed to want to be behind him, literally, wanting to be a second. It looked for a while as though another "Prelim" might suddenly erupt to settle the question, while push seemed to be turning into shove. Across the ring, in sharp contrast to the confusion that reigned in Gavilan's corner, the champion danced in his corner, all the while posing for photographers. He smiled wryly as the Cuban flag was unfurled in the ring and Gavilan wrapped himself within it. Through it all, a rhumba band's staccato beat filled the arena, creating a carnival atmosphere. But the fiesta was soon to come to an end.

Opposite: Kid Gavilan (left) attempts to crown Sugar Ray Robinson in their welterweight championship bout. Above: Challenger Gavilan (right) feigns amazement as Sugar Ray hits the weight squarely on the nose—147 pounds.

Waiting for the opening bell, both men sized up each other: the Kid looked anxious while the champ looked cool, his bones showing clearly through his skin like a three-dimensional anatomy model, his hair slicked back in the traditional Robinson style.

The bell sounded and neither man lost any time in coming out, moving close but staying cautious. The Kid took a left but came right back at Sugar. Ray threw a left to the body followed by a right cross to the chin and two stabbing lefts into Gavilan's face. They mixed eagerly, with Robinson taking a slight advantage in the scoring.

Sugar Ray was up before the bell, but round 2 started off slowly until the champion slammed a hook into his opponent's head followed by two quick shots to the body. Gavilan then took over, hooking to the head as Robinson answered with two short peppering left jabs. Gavilan came back, bobbing and weaving as he tried to move close. Ray made him pay for his insolence, landing left hooks to the body. The action roared on as punches flew in all directions. There was no question that Robinson was looking for a knockout, but Gavilan, rallying a body attack, reduced Sugar to mere counterpunching. Neither boxer landed a blow of any real power, but it was good, fast-paced action with both spectators and reporters splitting the score. Most gave the round to the champ.

Gavilan went right after Ray in the third with fast left hooks which had Sugar dancing the ring, relying on his jab to keep the Cuban off. The titleholder was kept on the defensive through most of the round as the Kid set the pace, punishing the body, forcing Robinson to hold. A good even flurry ended the session, which was generally given to Gavilan. The first three rounds set the pattern for the entire fight: Ray was boxing his opponent, hooking when he could and dancing when he had to. The Hawk was looking to bully the champion, digging heavy rights to the body in the clinches and moving him steadily into the corners and against the ropes.

The fourth was the challenger's best round. A piercing left hook split the skin over Robinson's right eye and Gavilan went for the wound like a shark in a frenzy. Robbie was thrown all over the ring, managing only a few counter body blows paid for with heavy Cuban punishment to his hurt eyebrow. The champ was in trouble as the Kid spun him around by the force of his punches as the clock ran down.

Robinson's corner worked furiously in the interim to close the cut which, if allowed to remain unchecked, could cause the title to change hands. This wasn't a time to take chances and the seconds made a crucial decision, applying Monsell solution, a coagulant banned in Pennsylvania be-

Sugar Ray Robinson delivers a stinging right to Gavilan's midsection during the hectic ninth round.

cause it contains iron and can be dangerous if used improperly. The desperate gamble worked: no protest was lodged and the heavy flow of blood into the eye ceased.

Ray began to answer the Cuban's challenge in the next round, dancing, looking for openings, and beating the Hawk on almost every exchange. Like an expert hunter, Robinson began to methodically attack the beast where he lived, slamming into the body with stiff hooks. This continued into the fifth when, after a quick flurry initiated by Gavilan, Robinson took control and hurt the Cuban as he pounded both his fists into the Kid's heart. Robinson not only took both rounds, but began to set the pace of the fight. The illusion that the Cuban would walk away from the ring with the title was fading fast.

Up until—and during—the sixth, the Kid gave as much as he took. Later, it was to become apparent that he was simply outclassed by a man whose skills were far superior. Before the middle rounds it could have been either man's fight. Then, barring a knockout, it became a battle with, as lawyers are wont to say, a conclusion certain.

Robinson slips a left from Cuba's Kid Gavilan in the fight's eleventh round. Robinson held on through fifteen—and held on to his crown in the face of Gavilan's challenge.

Gavilan tried to trap the champ on the ropes, but the price was high and the few times he managed to clinch and bully Ray into a corner, the champ easily boxed his way out. It was a magnificent demonstration of the art of self-defense, hardly wasted upon a younger and better-conditioned opponent.

The eighth round was the best. Gavilan found an opening and slipped a heavy hook into Robinson's face that had him reeling down the ropes and into the corner where the Kid had tried to put him all night. Gavilan came in sensing that he could end it all here and now. He was wrong. Robinson, though slowed, shot a left to the head which rattled the Cuban, and then delivered three more stunners. The tables suddenly were turned. And now it was the champion who was looking to finish it early. Yet, Gavilan was too good a fighter, too experienced, and too full of the dream of a championship, to do anything but his best. Though clearly beaten, he refused to go down or let up.

Sugar Ray was brilliant, but only because his challenger was equally so in his own right. If Gavilan had less heart, Robinson could never have given the crowd a display that since has classified this as one of the most memorable fights in boxing history. Great fighting, like great dancing, takes two.

That was the beauty of the remainder of the bout. For the next seven rounds, a man of perfection practiced his art with an opponent who, though he knew he was unlikely to win, refused to accept the inevitable. In the late rounds, Gavilan would try his best to take advantage of every Robinson lull—pushing in, bullying, hitting out with all he had as he tried for the knockout which could be the only salvation for the dream. Nothing had any effect on the master technician.

In round 14, Ray took a moment from peppering the Kid to turn and grin at Joe Louis, who was seated at ringside, in answer to the comment that he would be just "skin and bones" and, therefore, easily beaten. Gavilan pushed both of his gloves hard into that smiling face to the thundering cheers of his followers. Ray fell against the ropes and the Kid went at him for almost a full minute. The volley did little damage as most of the punches were taken on the shoulders, the head ducking, weaving, and evading by sheer grace the furious, but futile, best the Kid had to offer.

In the fifteenth Ray shook the Cuban, but he still refused to go down. Robinson was the one who was supposed to be in poor condition, but he was fresh enough to cap his tremendous display with a near-perfect finish which had the spectators standing in anticipation and appreciation. It was as if everything that had gone to create that night had been condensed and compressed into the last three minutes, a ta-

ble setting for the fast, unforgettable final round of a fast and unforgettable battle.

The scoring showed that, despite the action, it wasn't even a close fight. The referee, Charley Daggert, gave it to the champ nine rounds to six, as did another judge, Harry Lasky. Judge Frank Narsborough saw it even more one-sidedly, giving Gavilan the best of only three frames. The Cubans of course dissented, but the majority of onlookers couldn't deny that Sugar had dominated the preceedings.

If determination were recorded on the scoresheets, the Kid may have done better. The Hawk, who had never been knocked out, showed a courage and an aggressiveness which defied the mental conditions of a man who was being used as a demonstration piece for brilliance. No matter how often the Cuban was dazed, he came back—sometimes even managing to win the round with his flurries. Gavilan, with his reckless rushing and steady punching to the body, sought to wear down a champion he thought was nearing the end of his tenure. In truth, the plunges were responsible for the lopsided scoring, as it provided the champ with the perfect means to demonstrate his perfect skills. Robinson, the master matador, had what every bullfighter prays for, the perfect bull.

Neither fighter was really hurt in the brawl. Sugar Ray had that cut over his eye, and Gavilan was bleeding from the nose, and, of course, suffering from the decision. But there was ample compensation, with both men enjoying the best paydays of their careers—considerably more than the last time they had met when the outcome had been even more in favor of Sugar: "I paced myself for this fight and knew I was going to win although Gavilan fought a better fight tonight than he did the last time," said the victorious champion.

There was a lot of talk in the champ's dressing room about the future. It was said that he was looking to move up in class and take on the middleweight champion, Jake LaMotta.

The Hawk's quarters were noticeably quieter: "I not argue too much with the decision because in a close fight I figure judges give the decision to the champion but . . . I would like to make one more fight with him," said the challenger.

There was no other fight for him with Sugar Ray, but there were plenty of other fights. The Kid never lost that determination or that desire, and with the passing of time, acquired the skills necessary to be the best.

Gerardo Gonzalez, better known as "Kid Gavilan," became the welterweight champion of the world when he defeated Johnny Bratton two years after. The rhumba would go on.

Jake LaMotta—Laurent Dauthuille

September 13, 1950

Jake LaMotta's name evokes memories of a fighter who had no passing familiarity with the canvas; "the Bronx Bull," who brought the strategy of "playing possum" to life, charading as a beaten fighter one second and then, the trap sprung, coming back to life to catch a surprised opponent with a devastating fusillade the next; the only fighter to beat Sugar Ray Robinson in the Sugarman's first 132 fights; who went to the mat with Robinson five times; and the man who incensed some of the more sensitive fans by admitting to a Senate subcommittee that he had "thrown" a fight to Billy Fox.

Jake LaMotta was all these things—and more. He was a throwback to the barge fighter, one to whom every fight was a war with no survivors to be left; a rough-and-tumble fighter who gave every fan his money's worth; and a fighter whose name was never taken in vain when the words "art" or "science" were used to describe a boxer's style. He was *The Raging Bull*, and that was the basis of his fame.

LaMotta was born on July 10, 1921, in the teeming ghetto district of New York's Lower East Side, where he did what comes naturally to any street-smart youngster: he fought and fought and fought, becoming, in time, the toughest kid on the block and then the toughest kid in the neighborhood. Transferring his talents—the only ones he had—to the ring, LaMotta won 21 straight as a 185-pound amateur, and then looked for greater worlds to conquer.

Realizing that the greater world he was seeking to conquer lay in professional boxing, LaMotta trimmed his weight down to 170 pounds and entered the pro ranks as a full-fledged light-heavyweight with a four-round win over Charley Mackley on March 3, 1941. He ran off 14 more wins until his streak was stopped by Cleveland light-heavy Jimmy Reeves in late September of 1941. LaMotta alternated wins with losses for the remainder of the year—including another 10-round loss to Reeves—and then trimmed his weight down even further to campaign as a middleweight.

By the end of 1945 LaMotta had a record of 56–10–1, with 17 knockouts and was the class of the division. Still,

Opposite: *Laurent Dauthuille (left) the French challenger, avoids a left thrown by middleweight champion Jake LaMotta*. Above: *Far behind in points, LaMotta overcame Dauthuille's punches and knocked him out with thirteen seconds remaining in the fifteenth round*.

he was no closer to his goal: a championship fight.

Finally, with just three fights in 1947, including a dispirited loss to Cecil Hudson, LaMotta was mystifyingly stopped in the fourth round—although he never left his feet, thus preserving his perfect record—by "Blackjack" Billy Fox. Later testimony in front of the Kefauver Crime Subcommittee was to prove that Jake had worn his swim trunks for the fight with Fox in order to gain both Jim Norris' gratitude and a title bout with the winner of the third Zale-Graziano bout.

However, when Zale successfully regained his championship, he defended it not against LaMotta, but against Marcel Cerdan. And Jake was once again the middleweight bridesmaid.

LaMotta, attempting to perfect his number-three rating, took on all comers, including the unranked Laurent Dauthuille of France in a 10-rounder in Montreal on February 21, 1949. It was, as the Montreal *Herald* reported, "a savage fight." Wading in from the start, LaMotta had taken the fight to Dauthuille, who spent the first five rounds backing away, stabbing and jabbing at the ever-attacking LaMotta. Then, switching his tactics, Dauthuille fought LaMotta toe-to-toe, and, at the finish, had LaMotta in bad shape, spattered with his own blood. The decision, while close, was unanimous: Dauthuille.

LaMotta won his next fight against another Frenchman, Robert Villemain, then ranked as number eight, and won two more before being matched against yet another Frenchman, Marcel Cerdan, on June 16, 1949.

Above: *LaMotta (left) lands one on the face of Dauthuille in the fourth round*. Right (top to bottom): *With scant seconds remaining in the round—and the fight—a desperate LaMotta swarms all over the challenger.*

In a rough-and-tumble fight, LaMotta forced both the action and Cerdan to the canvas in the first round, using as pretty a hip roll as ever seen in a wrestling bout. Although the referee ruled it to be no "knockdown," it had done its damage; Cerdan had injured his left shoulder, rendering his left hand virtually useless. For five rounds he gave a good impression of a one-armed boxer, but it wasn't good enough to hold Jake and his patented bull rushes at bay; after the ninth round the gallant Frenchman was forced to retire. Jake LaMotta was now the forty-third claimant of the middleweight crown.

LaMotta almost immediately signed to defend his newly won crown against Cerdan on December 2. But the bout never happened; Cerdan was killed in an airplane crash coming over to the United States on October 27.

LaMotta then fought his first fight since winning the championship, losing a 10-round, nontitle decision to the "Second French Musketeer," Robert Villemain in mid-December 1949. After one more title defense—against Italy's Tiberior Mitri—LaMotta signed to fight the third Frenchman again, Laurent Dauthuille, on September 13, 1950 in Detroit.

If the Bronx was Jake's ancestral home, Detroit was his spiritual one. LaMotta had fought in "the Motor City" 17 times, losing only once, to Sugar Ray Robinson. And, although the verdict was unanimous, it was booed by the partisan crowd.

As LaMotta climbed into the ring, resplendent in his leopard skin robe, the 11,424 fans sensed that the only way

Dauthuille could win was to take the fight to the 11–5 favorite.

And that's exactly what his one-time conqueror did. Moving in and out with ease, the Frenchman piled up points on the slower-moving LaMotta in the first six rounds. Then, spurred on by warnings from referee Lou Handler in the sixth and seventh rounds, LaMotta momentarily came alive. He reverted back to his old pattern in round 9, continually rushing Dauthuille behind his outstretched left without throwing any additional blows and taking furious combinations from the challenger.

Far behind by round 12, Jake resorted to his old dodge, "playing possum." Stung by an overhand right to the head and floundering around the ring, he shook his head sadly, playing the role of a beaten man. When Dauthuille came closer to press home his advantage, he opened up with a wild flurry which lasted out the better part of 20 seconds and closed the round. It was his biggest rally of the fight.

However, it was short-lived. And when he began wobbling under an almost nonexistent barrage in the thirteenth, the crowd booed. But all of this was to serve as an appetizer for what was yet to come.

As the bell rang for the fifteenth and final round—and what looked like LaMotta's last three minutes as middleweight champion—the bruised and battered champion came off his stool squinting through the narrow split that remained of his swollen and cut left eye, mindful of his corner's final instructions that he'd "have to knock the Frog out."

Dauthuille, his face showing the effects of LaMotta's wild lefts, dripped blood. Inexplicably, although far ahead on everyone's scorecard, official and unofficial alike, he was told to "go in and fight."

Something had to give. What finally gave was Dauthuille. After taking the fight to LaMotta and landing a right atop the champ's head, Dauthuille stepped back to survey his handiwork. It was the last look he ever got.

For with fewer that 45 seconds remaining in the fight and his corner's shouted instructions ringing in his ears, LaMotta caught Dauthuille coming up to look for him with one deep-dish beauty of a left. Dauthuille staggered backward to the ropes with Jake in pursuit. Sensing the kill, LaMotta moved in, throwing a varied assortment of lefts and rights, all of which caught the reeling Frenchman. Finally, LaMotta felled him with one long, looping left, draping the challenger over the bottom rope, where referee Lou Handler counted him out with only 13 seconds left in the fight.

It was one of the many centerpieces in LaMotta's storied and stormy career, as well as the last time he was to successfully defend his championship. But what a defense!

LaMotta retains his title—barely—as Dauthuille goes down and out in the fifteenth round.

Sugar Ray Robinson—Jake LaMotta

February 14, 1951

February 14, 1951, was the anniversary of the St. Valentine's Day Massacre in Chicago; and just a few miles away from the infamous garage where it had taken place 22 years before, 14,802 paying customers packed Chicago Stadium to see what would soon become known as the "second edition." The attraction that Wednesday night was the much-ballyhooed matchup of two divisional champions, welterweight king Sugar Ray Robinson and middleweight titlist Jake LaMotta, fighting for LaMotta's crown. They did not leave disappointed, as more fireworks exploded on West Madison Street than had exploded over Clark Street 22 years before.

The combatants on this cold night were hardly strangers to one another. They had met no fewer than five times previously. ("I fought Sugar so many times," Jake would later crack, "that I'm lucky I didn't get diabetes.") Robinson had been the victor in all but one of the previous encounters, but the sole LaMotta win—in their second fight in Detroit eight years earlier—marked the only defeat to show up on Robinson's 123-bout professional career.

LaMotta, known as "the Bronx Bull," could boast that he hadn't once been knocked off his feet in 95 fights. He had in fact been stopped just once, by Billy Fox in 1947 while still standing erect, a loss which, even at the time, was regarded as highly suspicious. LaMotta would, years later, in sworn testimony before a Senate subcommittee, admit to having gone into the tank for the Fox fight.

While Robinson had campaigned actively, LaMotta, since lifting the title from Marcel Cerdan the previous June, when the Frenchman was forced to retire on his stool at the end of the tenth round because of a shoulder injury, had defended his crown only twice, and none too impressively. He had outpointed Tiberio Mitri of Italy, and the previous September had knocked out Cerdan's countryman, Laurent Dauthuille, with only 13 seconds left in the fight and the Frenchman ahead on all cards. LaMotta's indulgent lifestyle had also seen him balloon up to heavyweight proportions, and he had been forced to shed some 16 pounds in the weeks before the fight in order to make the middleweight limit. He just made it, finally coming in at an even 160, with Robinson a svelte 155½. Largely as a result of the fighters' head-to-head record, Sugar Ray had been installed as a heavy 3½–1 favorite.

By mutual consent, the fighters were equipped with six-ounce gloves for the Chicago match. "I got too much heart and stamina to be *his* valentine over the fifteen-round route," LaMotta allegedly said at the weigh-in. It turned out he was only half right. He showed plenty of heart; but his stamina proved to be his undoing.

Robinson came into the fight with a well-thought-out game plan, and stayed with it unwaveringly. He hoped to let the Bull exhaust himself early, and then take the fight from him in the later rounds. The execution of the strategy would lead New York *Mirror* reporter Dan Parker to later describe Robinson as "the greatest combination of brains, brawn, and boxing skill the modern prize ring has seen."

At the opening bell, LaMotta charged across the ring, a bull responding to the waving of a red flag. Dropping into a semicrouch, he tried to wrestle the challenger into the ropes, accompanying him with a relentless procession of lefts, and won the round handily. However, in the second, LaMotta was caught by a hard Robinson combination which left him holding on late in the round, and two jabs, followed by a hard-right uppercut in the third, sent him reeling.

Robinson appeared to be taking command in the early stages of the fourth round. But the Bronx Bull rallied in the closing minute, and sent Sugar Ray back to his corner bleeding from the nose. It was that kind of a battle: guile versus guts, head versus heart, combinations versus courage. LaMotta repeatedly charged back from cover, throwing caution to the wind—and punches to the head. His own lips already cut, he snarled out at Robinson, who still tried to keep LaMotta at a distance, backpedaling and counterpunching. Before the fifth ended, Robinson was also bleeding from the mouth.

Through the first eight rounds, the fans were getting more than their money's worth. They were witnessing one of boxing's greatest fights. It was still a close fight at that point—Referee Frank Sikora and Judge Spike McAdams both had it 4–3–1 for the champion after eight, while Judge Ed Klein saw it 6–2 for Sugar Ray. While action aplenty remained, it was to become one-sided, for LaMotta was not going to win another round on any of the three officials' cards.

Sugar Ray began to unleash his attack in the pivotal ninth round and in the tenth he countered a LaMotta hook with a smash to the right eye that left LaMotta taking on the look of a dark-eyed raccoon. In the eleventh, the Bull took his final shot. Trapping Robinson in a corner, LaMotta let fly with everything he had left in him. Robinson covered up and escaped, leaving the exhausted LaMotta all but out on his feet. The punishment he had absorbed in the twelfth had even Robinson's partisans crying out for mercy.

"Stop the fight," implored Robbie's manager George Gainford from his corner midway through the round. An unidentified man seated directly behind him demurred. "LaMotta's knocked out enough helpless guys in his time," argued the sadistic eavesdropper. "Let the bum take it himself for a while." Gainford apparently was persuaded by this logic. "Okay," he shrugged, "let him take it."

"Taking it," of course, was all that LaMotta could do

Jake LaMotta (right) scores a hard right to Sugar Ray Robinson's midsection in the first round of their middleweight championship fight, their sixth encounter of any kind.

at this point. One eye was closed, the other half-blinded by a torrent of blood gushing down his face in rivulets caused by the goring the Bull had taken. His face was further lacerated with open welts, and what hadn't been much of a nose before the fight was by now virtually nonexistent. Robinson seemed at times to be glancing toward the referee, Sikora, with a pleading look on his face. The only questions left were (a) would the Bronx Bull hit the canvas for the first time in his career? and (b) what was keeping him up?

But still, LaMotta stayed up. Hanging onto Robinson's trunks, grasping at the ring ropes, utterly unable to defend himself, LaMotta stood there helplessly, taking everything that was thrown at him: left hooks, right crosses to the face, shots to the ribs, uppercuts. A veteran reporter at ringside counted Robinson landing 56 punches in the thirteenth round alone.

Ringside observers were reminded of the Billy Fox fight; but this time it was for real. Beaten to a bloody pulp, and in his death throes, the final few moments of LaMotta's middleweight reign were his finest. Finally, with less than a minute left in round 13, and having witnessed more carnage than took place in the Clark Street garage 22 years earlier when seven members of Dion O'Banion's mob went down, Sikora mercifully stepped in and stopped the fight.

But, unbelievably, unlike the seven felled gangsters, LaMotta was still on his feet—in as amazing a display of sheer guts and bull-headed determination as has ever been seen in the ring.

While the new champion danced away to his dressing room, LaMotta collapsed on his stool and remained there for some 20 minutes before being led through the throng to his quarters. As Jake made his exit, the crowd rose to its feet and serenaded him with a chorus of "For He's a Jolly Good Fellow."

The postfight celebration in Robinson's room was attended by a minor controversy over whether Sugar Ray was in fact *still* the welterweight champ as well as king of the middleweights. Robinson and Gainford said "yes," and the World Boxing Council and the Illinois Commission disagreed. The issue ultimately became moot, anyway. Robinson went on to a long and storied career unequaled, perhaps, in the annals of the sport, while LaMotta's—after his brave last stand in Chicago—tumbled into mediocrity, obscurity, and, eventually, disrepute and disgrace.

LaMotta's legend might have been better served had he hung up his gloves right away after his own version of the St. Valentine's Day massacre. But this was obviously not to be.

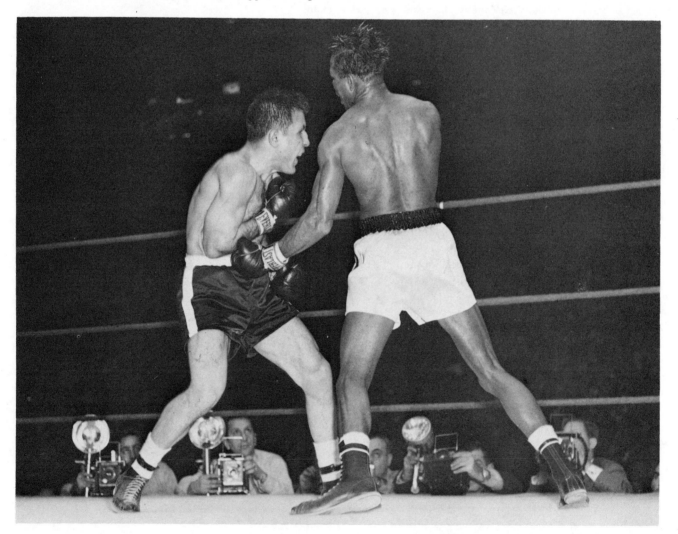

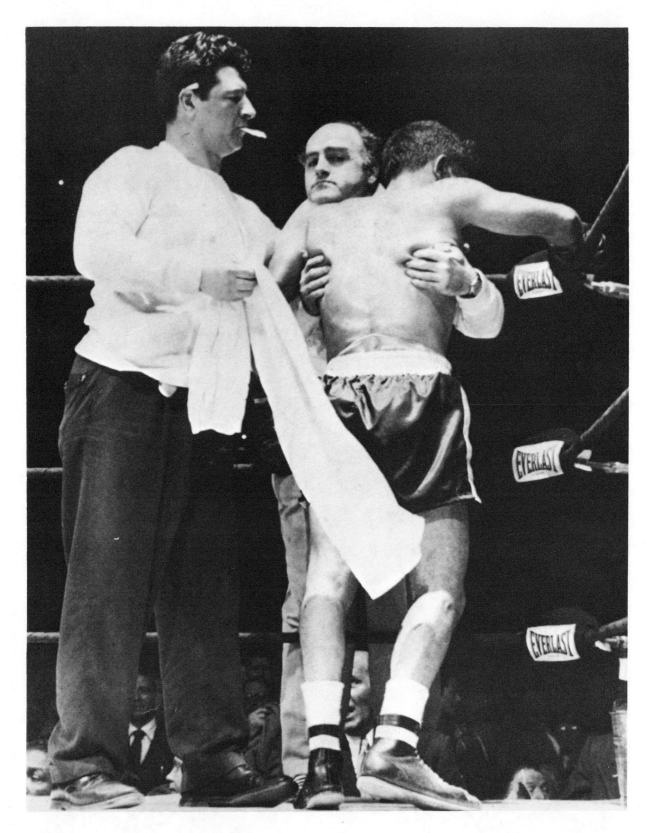

Opposite: *With sheer determination, LaMotta (left) withstood Sugar Ray's*
best. Above: *Although he had to be helped to his corner, the defeated*
LaMotta maintained his proud record of never having been knocked off his
feet.

Sugar Ray Robinson—Randy Turpin

September 12, 1951

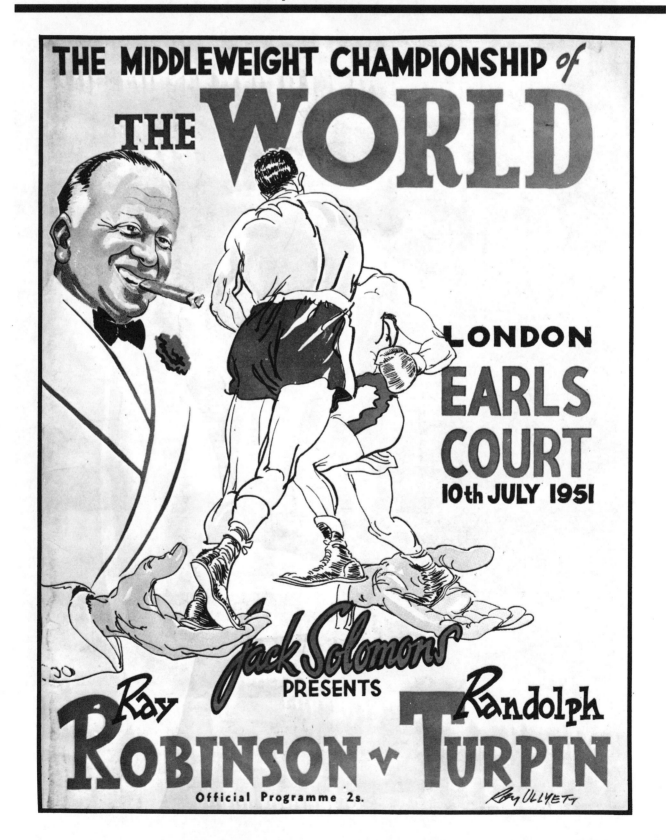

THE MIDDLEWEIGHT CHAMPIONSHIP of THE WORLD

LONDON
EARLS
COURT
10th JULY 1951

Jack Solomons
PRESENTS

Ray
ROBINSON v Randolph TURPIN

Official Programme 2s.

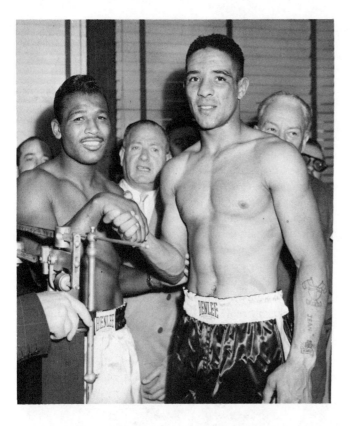

Sugar Ray Robinson did more living in slightly more than six months in 1951 than is usually alloted the average person in a lifetime. He won the middleweight title, he lost the middleweight title, he won the middleweight title, he caused a New York ballpark to sell out for a fight for the first time in almost three decades, and he put together his own version of a European Grand Tour.

First, the tour—or rather, first an explanation of the Grand Tour—something which has pretty much gone the way of $5.00 fancy dress shirts, $3.95 table d'hote French dinners with a choice of wine, and collegians wearing white buckskin shoes and celebrating their graduation with a tour of the continent. The Grand Tour was all very formal; one was always going and coming via either England or France, with visits to the Low Countries (Belgium, Luxembourg, and the Netherlands), Germany, and Switzerland. Today, graduation gifts usually come in more elaborate packages.

In 1951, Sugar Ray, who was moving into his thirties, beat Jake LaMotta for the 160-pound crown in February and decided to give himself a sort of graduation present, his own private Grand Tour, complete with entourage. There was a British fighter in Europe who eventually would be the party of the second part in a pretty fair payday. Meanwhile, let's have a look at Paris.

When Sugar Ray traveled it resembled a troop movement, complete with auxiliary transportation. There was usually his wife, his sister, his manager, George Gainford, and his wife, and half a dozen coat-holders, ranging from trainers to people who, if urged sufficiently, could run out and mail a letter.

And then there was the pink Cadillac, Sugar Ray's trademark around Harlem, where he had half a dozen enterprises. And which, not incidentally, gave him more visibility than an ad in the *Daily News*. "We're taking the pink Cadillac," announced Sugar Ray; "that'll shake 'em up on the Champs Elysees."

It did just a little more; it created massive traffic jams for the month *M. Sucre* was there. And it was from Gay Paree that he fanned out on his Grand Tour. He went to Switzerland to decision Jean Wanes, to Belgium to KO Jan DeBruin, and returned the following week to knock out Jean Walzack. Then it was on to Germany where he knocked out Gerhard Hecht in two rounds, but had to hide under the ring as the wrathful Berliners sought to dismember him for his "illegal" kidney punch. Then a big Italian automaker cajoled him into coming down to Turin to take Cyrille Delannoit in three. And then came Randy Turpin, whom Robinson had never seen.

The fee was an impressive $100,000, and why not? Robinson hadn't been beaten in eight years, his last and only setback coming at the hands of Jake LaMotta in 1943.

Turpin beat him, all right. He sliced his left eye in the seventh and outpunched Sugar Ray the rest of the way. In England the referee is the only one who votes on a decision, and it wasn't a hometown job.

"You were real good," said Robinson to Turpin after the latter's glove had been raised in victory, "just like everybody said you were. I have no alibis. I was beaten by a better man." Later Dr. Vincent Nardiello (Sugar Ray even traveled with his own doctor) took eight stitches in the wound.

The British Empire had its first middleweight champion since Bob Fitzsimmons, and Sugar Ray had a return bout coming up in New York in mid-September. It said so in the contract. Besides, British promoter Jack Solomons was currying favor with the World Boxing Council and was willing to offer up Turpin in a friendly hands-across-the-water gesture.

Robinson took a vacation on the Riviera, came home to a reception at City Hall as though he still had his middleweight title, then set about proving that the whole thing was a mistake.

It took him 10 rounds on a night few of those present will forget. The last time the capacity of the old Polo

Opposite: Official program from the first Robinson-Turpin encounter in July 1951, won easily by Randy Turpin. Above: The rematch between Sugar Ray Robinson (left) and Randy Turpin was a September night that few will forget.

Grounds had been tested was back in the early twenties for the Dempsey-Firpo fight. So great was the interest in the return Robinson-Turpin that 61,370 fans stormed into the Giants' ballpark, pouring a record middleweight take of $767,626 into the coffers of Madison Square Garden, which was promoting the fight in conjunction with WBC.

Despite his London setback Robinson was a 2–1 favorite. He was also ready to take on Turpin.

It was a fight which could have gone either way—up to the memorable tenth round. Robinson had a slight edge in the early going, fighting cleverly, forcing the pace, leading with lefts to keep the Britisher off balance, and exploding with two-fisted flurries from time to time. But rarely did Sugar Ray get through with a damaging blow. Turpin blocked well with his elbows and heavily-muscled arms ("He always looked more like a heavyweight than a middleweight to me," recalled Robinson) and his pull-back maneuvering kept the damages inflicted on him to a minimum.

Until the tenth round it was doubtful whether either got in a really telling blow. There was a good right cross by Robinson in the second that made Turpin's knees bend ever so slightly and there was another solid right that shook the champion somewhat in the third. But the crown wasn't going

to change brows on those brief flashes by the Sugarman.

But then the tenth rolled around, and after that Britannia no longer ruled the waves, or the middleweight division.

The round was almost half over when Turpin caught Robinson over the left eye (the eye that had required all that hemstitching after the first fight), and the blood gushed. Later Robinson was to say that Turpin had butted him, and that the blood had filled the eye, and absolutely blinded him. Whatever the circumstances, it drove him berserk, turning him into an avenging destroyer. When it was over, the middleweight crown had returned to the United States after its two-month sojourn in Merry Old England.

The final two minutes of ring action were all Robinson, and all nonstop. His usually carefully combed hair mussed and his eyes blazing, Robinson unloosed a violent barrage which included a right uppercut that caught Turpin's usually elusive chin. Turpin backed off, and landed a hook weakly in reply. It was to be his last punch and the calm before Robinson's relentless rain of blows which ended the fight.

Robinson blasted into Turpin with a left and right to the head. Then Sugar Ray unleashed a venomous right to

the jaw which caused Turpin to pitch forward, with Robinson backing off to let him fall. Turpin struggled to one knee, took the count of nine, then rose to face the whirlwind.

It was a right, and then an uppercut, that forced Turpin to the ropes. Seeking shelter from this onslaught, Turpin tried for the ropes near his corner. But Robinson followed. Head straight up, tucked uniquely between his hunched-up shoulders, Turpin sought to bob and weave to escape the searing fire. Then he ducked and tried to get under it, but there was no escape.

His legs turned to water; he could not move away. Robinson stepped back for the briefest of moments to survey his handiwork, then picked up where he had left off. And when he did, Turpin was finished. His knees gave out and he sagged against the ropes. It was at that precise moment that the referee, Ruby Goldstein, stepped in to stop it with only eight seconds left in the round.

In another time or another place. the round might have been permitted to end, but Goldstein wasn't taking any chances in the climate of that moment. Later, Goldstein's card was to show he had the fight even up to that time, but in the back of his mind was the tragic death of George Flores earlier in the month in a fight at Madison Square Garden.

Strangely, Turpin emerged from this maelstrom unmarked, with no bumps, and no lumps. "I was rolling with the punches, riding out the storm, and my head was clearing. There were only seven seconds remaining (eight). I didn't want to go down because I knew they would end it." Later Turpin said, just a little wryly, "Probably if I were the referee I'd have stopped it too."

It was Robinson's eighty-fifth knockout and one-hun-

Opposite: *Blood streams from Robinson's eye, but he gets off a stinging right to the jaw of Turpin (left)*. Above left: *Still another tenth-round right sends Turpin to the floor*. Right (top to bottom): *With Turpin pinned and weak against the ropes, Robinson (left) pulls back to deliver a crunching blow that sends his helpless victim into defeat*.

dred and twenty-ninth victory in 133 professional fights. And it was only the second time Turpin had been knocked out in five years of fighting. Sugar Ray was to fight for another 14 years during his amazing career, but never would he look so impressive in so little time.

New York hadn't been much of a town for Randy Turpin. But then, London hadn't been much of a town for Sugar Ray.

126

Surrounded by his trainers and his opponent, Sugar Ray has his arm raised in victory by announcer Johnny Addie (left).

Joey Maxim—Sugar Ray Robinson

June 25, 1952

As fights go, it was not one of the great ones. But the Battle of Champions will long be remembered for its dramatic—and ironic—ending. It was not a thrilling contest, and like the second Louis-Conn fight, the ending furnished the only sensational moment in a rather tame battle. The only sensational aspect, that is, other than the fact that the bout was fought in brutal heat registering 104°F under the Yankee Stadium lights on the hottest June 25 in New York history.

If Johnny Carson were to ask, in one of his rhetorical questions, "How hot *was* it," it could be answered, as one writer did, in the lead of his story, that the heat was "so terrific that green paint on the press box benches melted. . . ." The heat was so grueling that even the referee, Ruby Goldstein, collapsed between the tenth and eleventh rounds from a case of "typical heat prostration," marking the first time

in the history of championship fights that a referee was knocked out, too. It was *so* hot that it was to be the first, and only, time a thermometer ever won a title.

Goldstein, who recovered quickly after being helped from the boiling torture chamber, commented after the fight, "I felt myself going the round before when I asked for water and smelling salts. I could hardly see either Ray Robinson or Joey Maxim, and I couldn't keep track of the punches. I was cold and my legs felt numb. I can't understand feeling cold. At first I thought I was being roasted to death." Ray Miller, who substituted for Ruby, was asked what it felt like to get under the lights. "Just like the Sahara Desert," said Miller. "I'm surprised Ruby lasted as long as he did without benefit of adequate training."

But not even "adequate training" was enough to get Sugar Ray Robinson through 15 rounds in that sweltering hotbox. With an unbeatable lead over Joey Maxim, and a third world championship virtually under his belt, Robinson collapsed on his stool after the thirteenth round and could not come out for the fourteenth. Had it been a victory for Robinson—as it should have been, judging from the performance of the two fighters up until the abrupt and unthinkable ending—he would have joined the ranks of Henry Armstrong and Bob Fitzsimmons as the only pugilists to win three world crowns. But it was not to be. A victim of the terrific pace he set in the early going, Robinson became a victim not of Joey Maxim's punches, but of the intense heat.

Maxim, who did little to deserve this Christmas-in-June gift—except perhaps standing up in that furnace—retained his 175-pound crown in his second, and, as it turned out, last successful title defense. All Robinson had to do was last the limit, but the brilliant middleweight champion, who had made the fight for 13 rounds, outpunching and outboxing the plodding Maxim, exhausted himself by carrying the fighting load on this fire-and-brimstone evening.

Round 1 saw Robinson moving in, outdancing and outpunching the slower, heavier Maxim. From rounds 1 through 9, Robinson forced the action, pressing Maxim and landing at will. Here it was a jab, there it was a hook, and everywhere it was a steady staccato of leather as Maxim was reduced to clinching and wrestling with only an occasional attempt at a punch—most of which landed to Robinson's body. It was one of the greatest pitching and catching combinations since Ford and Berra, with Robinson doing the pitching.

It was almost as if they were on opposite electromagnetic currents. For, every time Maxim advanced, Robinson would quickly dance out of danger's way. And whenever Maxim retreated, Ray would move in on him.

By the end of round 9, the three judges' scorecards

Preceding page: *Light-heavyweight champ Joe Maxim (left) is driven back by a hard right from challenger Sugar Ray Robinson.* Above: *Robinson (left) ducks and tries to protect himself from the steady blows of Maxim.*

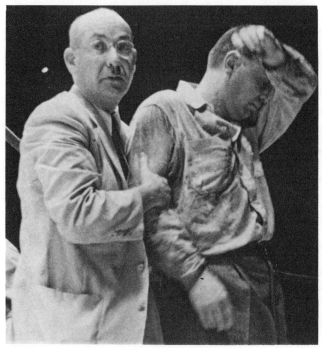

fight. The two exchanged jabs, fencing in mid-ring. Joey jabbed with a left to Robinson's head but missed his target with a left, while Robinson danced away only to come back at Maxim with a left to the body, followed by two rights. They clinched again and then Joey backed Ray up against the ropes with two hard left hooks. Ray countered with a right to the body. Maxim came back with a left and a left and a right at the bell ending the round—the first, and only, round that Maxim could clearly claim as his own.

It was also the last round for referee Ruby Goldstein, who was weaving beneath the bright lights and vicious heat. He was helped out of the ring by Dr. Alexander, in no shape to continue refereeing the fight. It was an omen of things to come.

Ray Miller replaced Goldstein in round 11 and Robinson came back to claim another round. This time, drawn together like metal and magnet, the two charged each other, scoring and grappling. Again it was Robinson who was the donor and Maxim the recipient of the bulk of the damaging punches.

But, by round 12, Robinson was visibly beginning to fade. Although he still had enough left in him to move in on Maxim with a barrage that caused the defender to trip and practically fall, by the end of the round the Sugarman was wilting, taking on the look of a flaccid waterhose after the faucet had been turned off. In point of fact, Robinson's faucet *had* been.

Round 13 found Robinson practically helpless in the ring, immobile and unsteady, and an inviting target for Maxim as he swayed under the bright klieg lights that were boiling the strength out of him. Yet Maxim, for some odd reason, failed to finish him off. As he tried to fight his way clear of the plodding champion, Robinson slipped to the canvas in the closing seconds of the round. The end of the round found Robinson weaving around the ring on the rubbery legs of a drunk, looking for his own personal lamppost, his corner; his handlers had to steady him and half-carry, half-drag their charge back to his stool.

There he stayed, unable to answer the bell for the fourteenth round. Maxim rushed across the ring to pick up where he left off when the bell announced the beginning of what should have been the fourteenth round. But there was to be none. The fight was over for Robinson. Joey Maxim was still the 175-pound champion.

Back in the dressing room, Ruby Goldstein had fallen asleep. When he awoke, the fight was over. When he asked which fighter had won, he was quite surprised.

"I had Robinson well ahead," he commented. And then the door opened and in came Robinson, a limp, dragging body supported by a couple of handlers. If you hadn't

showed Robinson not only well ahead, but—barring the unforeseen—unbeatable. Judge Barnes had it 8–1, Robinson; Judge Artie Aidala had Robinson ahead 7–1–1; and Referee Ruby Goldstein had the Sugarman up 5–2–2. It was a near shutout.

But during round 10 the two fighters reversed roles, with Maxim going on the offensive for the first time in the

Top: Robinson throws a left to Joey Maxim's head as Maxim returns with a right in cross-arm action during the bout. Above: Referee Ruby Goldstein (left) is helped from the ring by a doctor after being felled by the 104-degree heat.

seen him collapse in the fourteenth round and didn't hear the dressing room buzzing with, "the heat got him, just like the ref," you'd have sworn he was drunk. His eyes were rolling and there was no coordination in his body as they lifted him onto the dressing table.

Immediately the handlers began fanning Robinson's body, trying to extinguish the fire that burned within the sweating corpse. The first signs of life came back to him only after the commission doctor, Ira McCown, dug a needle into him.

In a few minutes he was sitting up, his eyes still glassy and gazing blankly into space. Through the haze, Robinson spotted New York Mayor Vincent Impellitteri. He eased off the table and, propping himself on someone's shoulders, staggered after him, pleading, "He didn't knock me out, did he?"

The Mayor spent a couple of minutes trying to convince Robinson that it wasn't Maxim who knocked him out, that it was, instead, the blistering heat. Then Sugar's handlers, who figured that a cold shower might bring him fully

to his senses, dragged Robinson—who had a headlock on the supporting Mayor—toward the showers. Robinson lurched into the shower, with the Mayor in tow.

Impellitteri didn't break away from Sugar until the cold water relaxed Robinson's strong grip. The water restored the bounce to Robinson's legs, and the life to his eyes, but his thinking was still as incoherent as before.

"The heat didn't get me," Robinson raved. "God willed it that way. You fellows think I'm crazy, but I'm not crazy."

By this time Robinson's friends decided that the heat had indeed driven him crazy, and requested he be taken to a hospital immediately. But when Dr. Nardiello approached Sugar, he defended himself, repeating, "I'm not crazy, you fellows may think I am, but God beat me!"

In the victorious dressing room of the champion, Joey Maxim confessed to visitors that he "wasn't sure what was happening when Robinson began to reel all over the place during the thirteenth round." But wily Jack Kearns, Maxim's manager, told the folks that it was "the way we

planned it. We had Joey lay back and let Robinson punch himself out. Somebody was bound to collapse in that heat. I didn't want it to be Maxim."

Joey, unmarked except for a slight swelling on his brow, went on, "I knew he was ahead. I'd have to be a dope not to know it. My corner kept yelling I'd have to come real fast to take it. . . . Well, I didn't have to, I guess. He couldn't take the heat so good. Maybe it was because he was the smaller guy."

Maxim, who had been tipped off by his corner as to Robinson's condition at the end of the eleventh round, explained his failure to earn a true knockout by saying that he wasn't sure Robinson was really suffering. "Robinson's smart," said Joey. "I figured he was just playing possum in the thirteenth, like Jake LaMotta, pulling the dead-man act. That's why I didn't move in on him more, but if he'd come up for the fourteenth, maybe I could have really been able to work on him and gotten a clean knockout."

Yet he admitted that it was harder fighting Robinson than heavyweights. "He's so fast, he's in and out. He made me think he was Maxim fighting those slow heavyweights."

But it was Maxim who was the slow heavyweight that night, and when asked why he hadn't thrown more punches at the dancing, jabbing Robinson, he grinned and replied, "I just couldn't get at him!"

Opposite: *A fresher Robinson (right) connects with Maxim's unprotected midsection.* Top: *Staggered by the sweltering heat, Robinson misses an open target.* Right: *A weary winner, Maxim was pronounced "still champion" when Robinson failed to come out for the fourteenth round.*

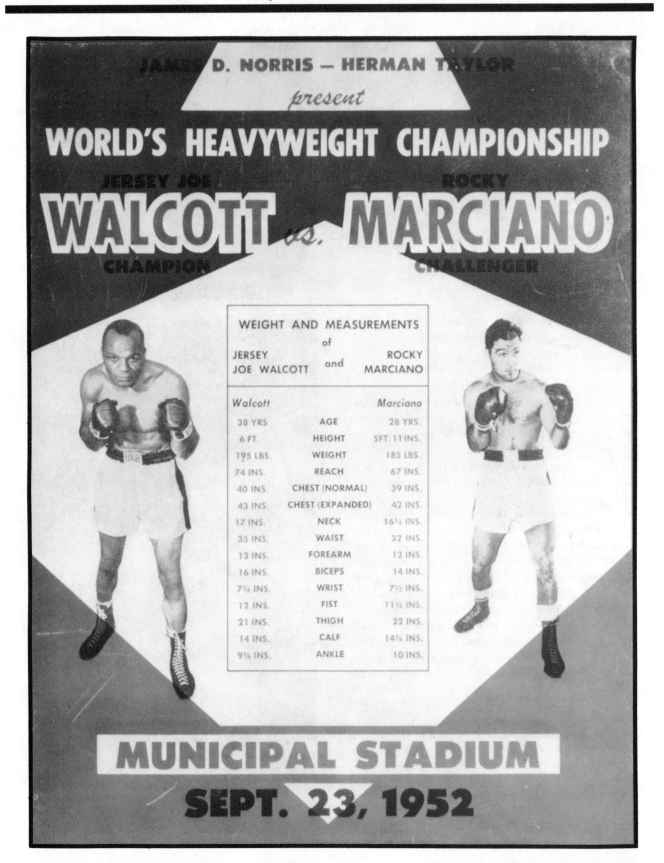

With one deep-dish beauty of a right at 43 seconds into the thirteenth round, Rocky Marciano almost tore the head off defending champion Jersey Joe Walcott, knocking off his crown in the process—a crown he had worn securely for the previous 12 rounds.

It was a right hand that traveled no more than six inches, and yet it reached back 70 years, to the first modern heavyweight, "Boston Strongboy" John L. Sullivan. And with it, Marciano became not only the first heavyweight champion to come from the same area as Sullivan, but the first man to ascend to the throne with a perfect record since Sullivan had accomplished the same feat seven decades before.

For 12 rounds the so-called Brockton Blockbuster had hardly seemed like the world-beater the betting society had thought he was when they made him a 9–5 favorite. The same firepower that had ended the career of Joe Louis, stopped Harry ("Kid") Matthews in two, and sent Carmen Vingo to the hospital, was totally ineffective in stopping Jersey Joe—or Father Time, Walcott's greatest ally.

Right from the opening bell, Walcott made a liar out of the naysayers who said that he was too old and "the Rock" was too much for the champ. Throwing his powerful left hook—the same left hook that had taken out Ezzard Charles just the previous year and decked Joe Louis three times—Walcott floored Marciano midway through the first round, the first time in his 43-fight professional career that Rocky had ever been down. Up at the count of four ("I got

up fast because I was more mad at myself than hurt," Marciano was to say later), he looked hurt. Eschewing his patented shuffle, the 198-pound Walcott went right back to the attack, swarming all over the 184-pound challenger who tried to swap punches with his adversary, staggering him again at the bell.

The second round was more of the same, with Walcott on the attack, even planting a left hook somewhere south of the border of Marciano's beltline, further adding to the challenger's discomfiture.

Rocky, trying to stem the tide of battle and turn the momentum, came out for round 3 in a deep crouch as his manager, Al Weill, kept up a staccato of "Keep down low, keep down low." But again Walcott found his way through the challenger's defense, landing another clean left to the chin. But despite repeated meetings of his chin with the champion's right, Marciano showed that even though he lacked polish and finesse, he possessed a chin of granite and a heart to match, as he came back to exchange shots with Walcott after the bell.

By round 6 "the Rock" had taken the battle to Walcott and made him fight his kind of fight, backing the champion to the ropes and blazing away with rights and lefts. During one of their heated exchanges, Marciano suffered a deep gash on his head and Walcott a cut eyelid. As the bell rang, blood flowed freely from Walcott's damaged left eye and the end looked imminent for the oldest champion ever to defend his crown.

But somehow, someway, somewhere, the solution

Opposite: *World's heavyweight championship participants Jersey Joe Walcott, champion, and Rocky Marciano, challenger.* Above: *Marciano (left) and Walcott happily shake hands before their fight.* Right: *Walcott's left misses Marciano's granite jaw.*

used to stem the flow of blood (and here the story gets clouded as to whether it was the solution used on Marciano's head or Walcott's eye) got into Marciano's eyes. By the end of round 7 Marciano came back to his corner hollering, "I have trouble with my left eye. I can't see."

He continued blind for three more rounds and Walcott made the most of them, using everything he knew to beat "the Rock." Marciano missed repeatedly and Walcott countered with his own lefts and rights, cutting Marciano between the eyes and on the forehead.

By the end of the twelfth round Walcott was in total

Above: *Rocky Marciano (right) unleashes the most devastating punch in boxing history—a solid right—to literally knock the crown off the head of Jersey Joe Walcott.* Bottom (left to right): *Walcott recoils from the impact of Marciano's punch, falling first against the ropes and then down.*

control. Ahead on all three officials' cards (7–4–1, 7–5, and 8–4), all he had to do was "last" nine more minutes. He missed by 8 minutes and 17 seconds.

With just 30 seconds gone in the thirteenth round, and with no punches thrown, Walcott unexplainably backed into the ropes. He was caught there with as hard a punch as had ever been seen in a fight—a short right hand that caught him coming off the ropes. As a grazing left (thrown for good measure and merely serving as a postscript) swept by him, Walcott slowly fell to the canvas, one arm hooked over the ring rope, a grotesque imitation of a religious fanatic in prayer. Referee Charley Daggert counted 10 over the inert form. He could have counted to 100; it would have made no difference.

Back in his dressing room, the thoroughly exhausted Marciano greeted his well-wishers—most of whom had had a piece of "the Rock"—while over in one corner his father, Peter Marchegiano, wept. "I'm proud," he said over and over again.

So were many other well-wishers who couldn't make it into the dressing room, but still crowded into the ring where their favorite son—26 years after Tunney had dethroned Dempsey in the very same ring—had won the title. They had all won. Everyone, that is, except Marciano, who had lost a new pair of trousers in the confusion to some souvenir hunter and had to leave Municipal Stadium with a bathrobe thrown over an incomplete suit.

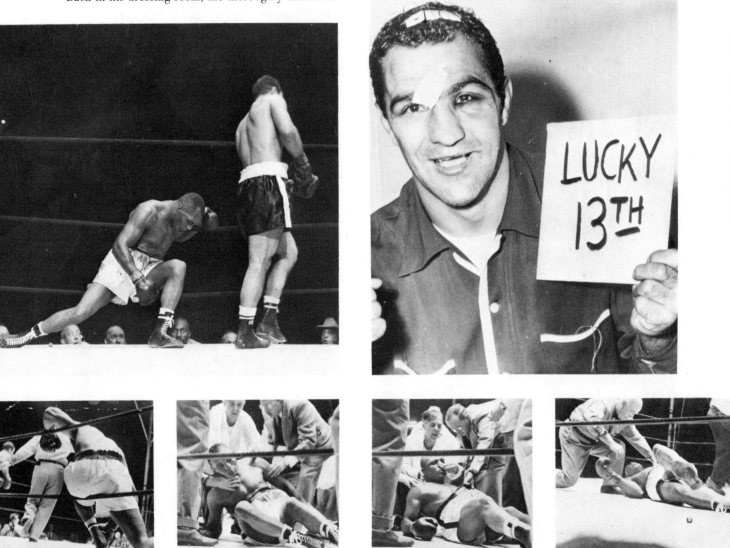

Top left: *The end for Jersey Joe*. Top right: *It was a lucky thirteenth round for "the Rock."*

135

Carmen Basilio—Tony DeMarco

November 30, 1955

	BASILIO		DeMARCO
AGE	28		23
HEIGHT	5 ft. 6½ in.		5 ft. 5½ in.
WEIGHT	147 lbs.		147 lbs.
REACH	67 in.		72½ in.
NECK	15 in.		16 in.
CHEST NORMAL	36½ in.		37¼ in.
CHEST EXPANDED	39 in.		39¼ in.
WAIST	29 in.		29¼ in.
FOREARM	15½ in.		15 in.
BICEPS	13½ in.		14¾ in.
FIST	11 in.		12¼ in.

Who said lightning never strikes twice in the same place? Certainly not Tony DeMarco. And definitely not the 13,373 who crowded into Boston Garden on the night of November 30, 1955, to see their hometown favorite attempt to do something no welterweight champ had done since Barney Ross did it 20 years before—recapture his welterweight crown.

Just 173 days earlier, DeMarco had lost his crown to Carmen Basilio, the ex-Marine with the craglike features that bore more than a slight resemblance to the Nantucket shoreline, in a 12-round throwback to the old barge fights. But now their local hero—called the "Miniature Marciano"—was fighting on his own turf, where he had lost just once in 33 outings. And, the local betting gentry was so sure that DeMarco would regain his crown that they had put their money where their faith was, bringing the prefight odds down to 6-5, pick 'em.

For, wasn't DeMarco the harder puncher with 30 of his 47 wins coming by KO—including his most recent win, a one-round knockout of tough Chico Vejar—as opposed to Basilio's record, with only 21 of his 47 wins by KO? And hadn't DeMarco taken the first fight to Basilio? Hadn't he battered him from proverbial pillar-to-post for the first seven rounds, only to run out of gas and lose the championship he had won just 70 days before from Johnny Saxton? And weren't they told that this time it would be a different De-Marco in there against Basilio; one who would stick and move and yet be able to take him out with one shot?

And damned if it didn't look like DeMarco would do it, as the boy from Boston's North End went after Basilio almost from the opening bell, jolting the champ with two hard left hooks to the head and a tremendous right to Basilio's well-worn features just before the bell. Round 2 saw both fighters banging away—Basilio to the body and DeMarco to

Opposite: *The tale of the tape for the Carmen Basilio-Tony DeMarco (right) match-up.* Above: *DeMarco (right) connects with Basilio's chin.*

the head. Basilio switched to the head just before the end of the round, cutting Tony's left eye, but also breaking his own left hand in the process.

Deprived of his best weapon, his left hook, Basilio went back out to do battle in the third, landing with his right to both the body and the head while DeMarco missed with wild lefts and rights to the head of the bobbing Basilio, only once reaching him with a solid four-punch barrage that shook the champ. The rest of the round belonged to Basilio.

That was to be Basilio's "last hurrah" in the land of last hurrahs for many a round, as DeMarco began landing his heavy artillery to the head of the champion in round 4, one of his rights driving Basilio back three feet into the ropes, another right stinging Basilio, who had to hold on.

Round 5 saw DeMarco stagger Basilio with a left-right combination and nail the champ with several hard rights. But the steel-chinned Basilio stayed upright, and answered with several good shots of his own. The torrid pace continued in round 5 as the challenger, totally without guile or deceit, aimed for and reached Carmen's head with a thunderous right-left combination, again staggering Basilio. The champion fought back, afterward saying, "I knew I had him in the fifth round. There wasn't any sting left in his punches."

But, looking back, Carmen may well have been whis-

Above (left to right): *Basilio (in white trunks) wins TKO from DeMarco in this stop-action fight sequence. The ref stepped in to stop the slaughter.*

Above: *Basilio is on his "rubber legs" after absorbing DeMarco's "best" punch.* Opposite: *A wide-open DeMarco takes a left to give one, a strategy that ultimately backfires.*

with an equally well-timed left hook. Suddenly the man who had been down only once in his previous 65 fights was doing a bandy-legged impression of Leon Errol, wobbling all over the ring as he literally took a standing knockdown. DeMarco was all over him. But even with a helpless victim half-standing and half-staggering in front of him, tottering on the brink of extinction, Tony couldn't land another, as he flailed away in animalistic style, throwing—and missing— more than 15 lethal punches in the last 20 seconds of the round.

Round 8 was more of the same, with a now-confident DeMarco hammering away at Basilio with savage hooks, overhand rights, and jolting right leads. He disdained any subtleties—no left jab, no movement, no anything, but bombs, bombs, and more bombs.

By the end of the eighth the three scorecards reflected the tide of the fight: 79–74, 78–67, and 79–73, all De-Marco. Basilio had to knock DeMarco out to win. And his corner echoed what everyone else in the Garden knew, hollering, "Carmen, that guy's got your title unless you go to the belly." And go to the belly he did, pounding DeMarco's unprotected middle with both hands from close quarters throughout most of the three minutes of round 9.

Suddenly DeMarco looked like he was fighting in slow motion as Basilio continued to work on his body in the tenth. Arm-weary and looking to land the one big blow, he was beaten time and again to the punch as the champion hit him where he lived, the belly.

By round 11 the tide had turned dramatically and the outcome was no longer in doubt. Basilio himself knew it when he hit him with a left and then a right cross to the body. "I could tell he was really groggy then. I didn't go for any knockouts—just wanted to work his body till then. Then I knew I could get him . . ."

The end came in the same round as before—the twelfth—as Basilio, by then a tired puncher himself, landed a tired right, followed by an equally tired left and another right. DeMarco, silly with fatigue, his fire out, fell under the ropes, his head on the apron. At the count of eight he somehow managed to stand up, and tottered forward to catch more of the same.

As Basilio caught DeMarco in a four-punch fusillade—left, right to the head, a left to the body, and a crushing right to the head—referee Mel Manning rushed in to grab the now-unconscious DeMarco by his right arm, ending the fight in a grotesque tableau, with DeMarco hanging straight down, arm suspended, in a modern-day crucifixion.

The time of the second "Boston Massacre"? It happened at 1:54 of the twelfth round, only two seconds more than it had taken Basilio to win their first brawl. Who says lightning never strikes twice in the same place?

tling past the graveyard, for DeMarco continued to land his haymakers on the unprotected chin of the champion in the sixth and seventh rounds. Immobile and unable to arrange his blows in combinations, DeMarco stood his ground and bombed away. And, with some 30 seconds left in the seventh, Basilio started a well-telegraphed right, but was caught

DeMarco is knocked down for the first time in the twelfth round.

Carmen Basilio—Sugar Ray Robinson

September 23, 1957

There is an old saying that no man walks so tall as the man who has accomplished something. And yet the man who walked the taller on the morning of Tuesday, September 24, 1957, was the shorter of the two men who had met the previous night in New York's Yankee Stadium to decide the middleweight championship of the world. In fact, he was perhaps the shortest middleweight champion of all time—Carmen Basilio.

Basilio *had* accomplished something. He had won the middleweight crown from the incomparable Sugar Ray Robinson in as grueling a contest as had ever been witnessed. And, he had become only the second welterweight champion ever to step up in class and win the middleweight title. But

Preceding page: *Official program cover for the September 23, 1957, match-up*. Top: *An autographed souvenir from the middleweight bout*. Above: *Carmen Basilio (right) ducks under a Robinson left*.

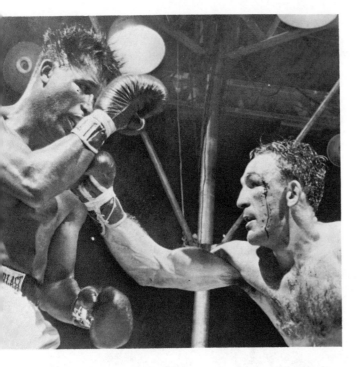

it wasn't Basilio's height—or lack of it—that decided the outcome of the fight. That was brought home to him when the two fighters were called to the center of the ring for their prefight instructions by referee Al Berl. Basilio, remembering the moment years later, recalled, "I was five-six and a half. I looked up at Sugar Ray. He was sneering at me, trying to scare me. So I started to laugh. I was laughing so hard that the ref had to stop to see if I was OK."

Carmen was not only OK, he was A-OK, and knew then that—to rephrase an old boxing adage—a good little man could beat a good big man if he had one other element to go with it. Determination. And that the Canastota, New York, onion farmer had, in abundance.

Basilio discovered early he needed that determination, for, almost from the sound of the opening bell, Robby began a steady ratta-tat-tat tattoo of left jabs into the readily available face of the challenger. By the time the crouching Basilio—whose crouch emphasized further the size differential even more than the five measured inches and six measured pounds, 160 to 154—was able to penetrate Robinson's defense for the first time, his craggy features had a slightly pink hue, the result of 13 direct hits by the champion's left jab.

Basilio was trying to go to the body, force the action, score on any part of Robinson that wasn't protected. But first he had to get past that jab, which kept coming at him with pistonlike efficiency. And when Basilio did get in, Rob-

Above: Robinson (left) draws first blood. Right (top to bottom): Eleventh-round action as Basilio and Robinson exchange lefts and rights.

143

inson tied him up, pulling his shorter arms in against his sides and holding on until the referee could part them and Sugar could escape back into mid-ring again, away from the bull-like charges of Basilio, away from the pressure Basilio was exerting. Far enough away to start the staccato of jabs all over again. But Robinson, who had gone in as the betting underdog—the fourth time in his last five fights he had been the underdog—looked like anything but an underdog for the first three rounds. This was the man they had called "the greatest pound-for-pound boxer" in the history of boxing, a phrase coined especially for him. And he was jabbing, stabbing, and even grabbing at the rough-hewed features of the man in front of him, beating him both with the punch and to the punch.

In the third round Robinson bloodied Basilio's nose with an uppercut. Then, in the fourth, Robby connected with a right uppercut that cut Basilio's left eye. But still the freshly stuck bull kept charging at his tormentor, throwing caution to the winds and lefts and rights to the body. Maybe it was his battle plan, or just maybe it was his cornerman, Angelo Dundee, who told the challenger before the start of the fourth round, "Go get him." Whatever it was, it worked. In the fifth, Basilio began to connect. Not that he hadn't before, but now it was more noticeable, attributable in part to the

144

Flurries like this gave Basilio (right) the split-decision victory.

fact that the 37-year-old Robinson was beginning to wind down, the clock in his elder statesman's body beginning to run on a different time. For the first time Basilio was able to rush Ray into the ropes and land a left-right combination, staying in close and beating the Sugar Man to the punch.

Round 6 was a momentary reprieve for Ray as he once again relied on his stock-in-trade, his left jab, catching the onrushing Basilio on the face with six beautifully timed jabs, moving under and over, countering, bobbing, and weaving. But that was Sugar's last draught of the eternal youth elixir, his last taste of what was. For the 37-year-old body trapped inside the 20-year-old mind was slowly taking over, slowly dictating the actions and reactions of its owner. And no amount of past greatness could will away the tiredness that now was—nor the determined challenger. Basilio was now pressing the suddenly slower champion, driving him and the body that had been through 157 ring wars through the hells of an intensive body attack.

Robinson continued to use his jab, but starting in round 7 he retreated behind it instead of using it as the first

Robinson was right on target—Basilio—in the twelfth round.

part of his vaunted one-two. And the shorter Basilio, disdainful of Robinson's left, kept coming in, throwing hooks, sweeping rights, and even straight right leads, catching Robinson with all of them.

As round 8 opened, Basilio, his eye now covered with grease coating the cut and looking more like a ghostly apparition than a gladiatorial aspirant, continued to press Robinson, landing with lefts and rights to the body and with left hooks to the head. Occasionally he would vary his attack with a left to the body and a right to the head or a right to the body and another right to the body. But no matter what variation Basilio tried it worked. Robinson, as was his trademark, would try to rally right before the bell in his traditional round-saving flurry, all the better to impress the judges, but to no avail. When he started to untrack, more in desperation than in deliberation, Basilio would beat him to the punch.

Rounds 9 and 10 were more of the same. By the tenth Robinson was on his bicycle, trying to move away, to rally his forces for one last-ditch attack. But he was paying for his backward flight as the ever-pressing ex-Marine kept atop him, wading in behind left-rights to the head and to the body.

The eleventh opened as the tenth had ended, with Robinson landing his left and Basilio his right. But this time the positions seemed reversed: it was Robinson landing the heavier blows, looking like he had gone to the well and found new life. Instead of waiting for a round-ending rally, he was carrying the action to Carmen from the beginning— a hard right to the body, another counter-right to the body, a left to the body, and rights and lefts to the body in close as Basilio failed to tie him up. Then, with less than a minute to go in the round, it was Basilio's turn. And what a turn it was. He nailed Sugar on the jaw with three rights, propelling him back to the ropes, and then proceeded to use the champion's head for fungo practice, connecting with a fusillade of punches to the head. It looked like Robinson might go down, but right before the bell he came off the ropes and held.

It was hard for even the most dedicated Robinson fan to see how Robby could come back. His legs were working on a different time basis. His body had been ravaged by Basilio's strafing punches. His best was probably not good enough to hold off the challenger. But in a bout that will be remembered for its eddies and tides, the twelfth was to take another turn, with Robinson turning back the clock, getting in two lefts and a right to the head of the challenger, followed by another left and right—all on target. Suddenly Basilio was on rubbery legs, his balance that of a marionette with its strings cut. One minute he was standing there erect,

145

if not tall, the next he was reeling around the ring, looking for a place to fall down. But his Leon Errol act was too good. He wouldn't go down. And at the bell he half-walked, half-staggered back to his corner. And the tired Robinson, having shot his bolt, went wearily back to his.

Still the fireworks weren't over. Robinson set out to finish up where he had left off in the thirteenth, landing an entire series of perfectly punctuated jabs to the now-bloody mess that had once been Basilio's face. It was Carmen who was throwing the desperation punches now; Robinson's were accurate and on target. But just as Robinson seemed to have stemmed the tide, back came Basilio with a vicious right to the jaw that shook Ray, followed by a left hook to the head. Then, as if in a kid's game of "now it's my turn," Robby came back with a right and two right uppercuts, again hurting Basilio. At the bell the 35,000 fans at Yankee Stadium were in bedlam, their voices as one, all cheering the two men who were putting on one of the greatest give-and-give battles in the history of boxing.

Robinson continued his assault in round 14, but no man—let alone a 37-year-old wonder—could maintain the pace. Although his left jab continued to work, his motions were slower, wearier, more tired. He hurt Basilio again, but couldn't follow it up. By the last round, he was circling and jabbing, experiencing trouble moving, as Basilio dictated the pace. Then came the bell, and the fight was over.

The decision was anticlimatic, a split decision. The referee called it 9–6 for Robinson, the two judges for Basilio, 9–5–1 and 8–6–1. Carmen Basilio was the new middleweight champion and Ray Robinson, for the fourth time, wore the title ex-middleweight champion of the world.

Afterward, each man, a winner in his own right, was to lose something. Basilio, the new middleweight king, automatically lost his welterweight crown, unable, by New York State law, to hold both crowns simultaneously. And Robinson lost his $500,000 purse, the IRS attaching it on "anticipated" income.

And yet whatever had happened, it couldn't be said, even by the heartiest of Robinson fans, that their man hadn't given his all. Nor that it wasn't the same old Robby that Basilio had beaten. It was. It was just that it wasn't the young Robinson whom Carmen had treated so indelicately. And therein lies the story of the fight, a great fight between two great fighters.

Above: The fifth round went to Robinson (right). Above right: *Newly crowned middleweight champion Basilio offers prayers of thanks.*

Archie Moore—Yvon Durelle

December 10, 1958

DURELLE		MOORE
30	AGE	43
175	WEIGHT	175
5ft.10½ in.	HEIGHT	5ft.11 in.
74 in.	REACH	75½ in.
	CHEST NORMAL	
39 in.		40 in.
	CHEST EXPANDED	
42½ in.		42 in.
	WAIST	
35 in.		35 in.
	THIGH	
24 in.		21 in.
	CALF	
16 in.		15 in.
	BICEPS	
16 in.		16 in.
	FOREARM	
13½ in.		12½ in.
	NECK	
16½ in.		17 in.

Throughout the ages, old men have been lionized in everything from literature *(The Old Man and the Sea),* to nursery rhymes ("Old King Cole") and song ("Ol' Man River"). But none of them held a candle to the old lion of the ring, Archie Lee Moore.

There was only one Archie Moore. He was glib, elegant, quick of wit and of hands, the possessor of more knockouts than any man in history, and holder of a world's championship for a longer period of time than any other champion except two. But the Methuselah of the ring will be remembered, not for any of those achievements, but instead for his performance on the night of December 10, 1958—the night he battled Yvon Durelle and proved that you can't keep a good man—old or young—down.

The road to that memorable night was paved with detours and plenty of hard rocks. Born in either Collinsville, Illinois, or Benoit, Mississippi, on either December 13, 1913, or December 13, 1916 (depending upon who was keeping score, Moore or his mother), Archie was either 42 or 45 years old the night of the fight. When asked about this discrepancy in his birthdate, the quick-thinking champion side-stepped and countered, "I have given this a lot of thought, and have decided that I must have been three when I was born."

Moore's first bout was in 1935 against Billy Simms, at Poplar Bluffs, Arkansas. It ended in a second-round knockout for Moore, his first of a record-setting 141. It also began his long career in "bootleg" fights and tanktowns on the so-called Chittlin' Circuit, which was open to "colored" fighters who couldn't break into the big time. By 1936, Moore hit the highways and byways of backwater America, fighting some 21 times, mostly in and around his adopted hometown of St. Louis. He won 18 fights, 16 by KO, and was ready to make the bridge to the next rung on the fistic ladder, the small town clubs.

However, there were so many gradations to boxing back in the thirties that one boxer once asked his manager, when he was booked for a fight in a town he had only a nodding acquaintance with, "Which one is it, small time, medium small-time, big small-time, little big-time, medium big-time, or The Bigtime?" And before Moore could even approach The Bigtime he had to pay his dues in more cities than anyone aside from Mssrs. Rand and McNally had ever heard of: cities like Keokuk, Quincy, and all points east, west, and south.

Moore fought 12 times in 1936 and won all 12, 10 by knockout, and the middleweight championships of Kansas, Oklahoma, and Missouri in the process. Now, it was on to the bigger time, if not The Bigtime, and Moore set sail for the more lucrative boxing pastures in California, where he

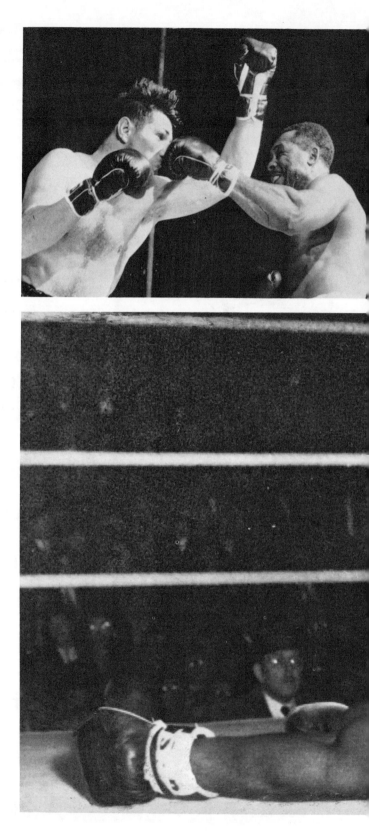

Preceding page: *The Yvon Durelle and Archie Moore tale of the tape.*
Above right: *The champion winces as Durelle connects with a crushing left in the first round.*

hoped to meet, and beat, the prominent middleweights fighting on the Coast and establish his credentials. However, as Moore's luck would have it, the day he arrived in San Diego was the day the boxing arena burned down.

This was the beginning of an unlucky streak that ran through Moore's early years: a severed tendon in the wrist here, a perforated ulcer that necessitated an operation to save his life there. If Moore had any luck, one wag suggested, it would "all be bad."

But Moore, who was to survive more hardships than Job ever endured (including acute appendicitis, organic heart disorder, etc., etc., etc.), clung to his dual dreams that he would somehow come back and someday become a world champion.

Through dedication and perseverance he accomplished his first goal, coming back in 1942 to win his first five fights by KO. His second goal, however, took longer, much longer. It took him more than 11 years and 58 knockouts to get a shot at a title.

And then, on December 17, 1953, in front of his hometown fans, Archie Moore finally achieved his second goal, beating Joey Maxim decisively for the light-heavyweight championship of the world. But even then Moore got the fuzzy end of the lollipop, earning only $800 for climbing to the pinnacle of his profession.

By now, Moore's rocket had flown too close to the moon for him to be content with mere hang-gliding. He sought something more. He had to have something more than the $800 he received for winning a world's title. And, in the strange and wondrous way boxing operates, he got it. For along with Maxim's championship belt came Maxim's manager, the wiley old Doc Kearns, the man who had guided Maxim—and, before him, Jack Dempsey—to the title.

It would be what Humphrey Bogart told Claude

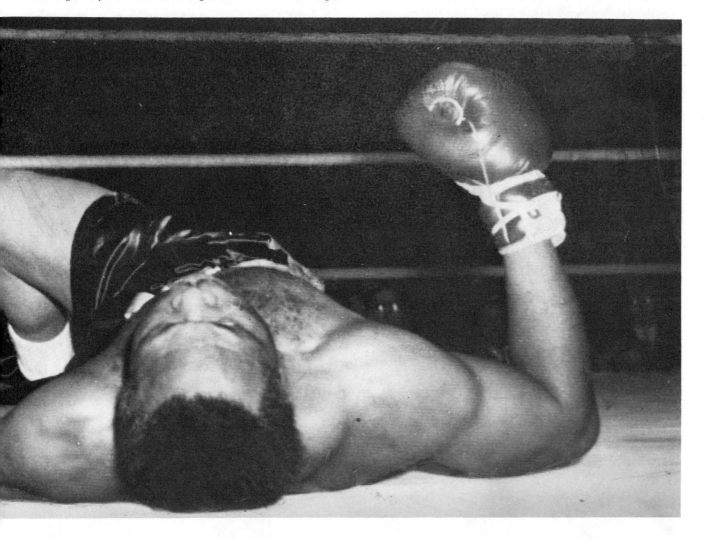

A seemingly beaten Moore finds himself on the floor one of three times in round 1.

149

Rains at the conclusion of the film *Casablanca*, "the beginning of a beautiful relationship." Together they would forge a new trail on the fistic horizon, stepping over prone bodies on their way to the top. Over the next six years Moore would go to the post 43 times, taking on all comers regardless of weight class, and dispatching 25 of them in fewer than the scheduled number of rounds. His victims began whizzing by with all the rapidity of signs on the San Diego freeway, with names almost as recognizable: Bob Baker, Joey Maxim, Harold Johnson, Bobo Olson, Nino Valdes, James J. Parker, Eddie Cotton, Willie Besmanoff, Charlie Norkus, and Howard King, among others too plentiful to enumerate.

Only twice during these six years was he to come up short. Both times in heavyweight championship fights. The first time he lost to Rocky Marciano in nine rounds after knocking down the Rock in the second with a short right uppercut. The second time he lost to Floyd Patterson in a fight for Marciano's vacated throne; it was a fight that has never been fully understood.

Beaten, but hardly vanquished, Moore returned to the more comfortable environs of the light-heavyweight division, defending his title about once a year. In 1957 he fought Tony Anthony, and in 1958 he fought Yvon Durelle. Therein lies the story of Moore's greatest comeback.

Yvon Durelle was a mightily muscled fisherman out of the Maritime provinces of Canada. The third-ranked light-heavyweight, he had brawled his way through 96 fights in 11 years, hammering out 38 of his opponents and outstaying another 36. Despite his record, which included six losses—six by KO—Durelle was thought to have two chances, little and none, of becoming the first Canadian to win a world's title since Jack Delaney had captured the light-heavyweight title some 32 years before. Many of the writers—and the betting gentry who had installed Moore as a 3–1 favorite—thought the fight a mismatch. In fact, the local correspondent from the Montreal *Gazette* thought so little of Durelle's chances that he wrote, "People snicker when the name of Yvon Durelle is placed alongside that of Archie Moore."

When Moore arrived at the prefight physical, resplendent in a midnight-blue tuxedo, a black homburg, and waving a silver-topped walking stick, he looked like he was snickering, too, if not laughing outright as he paraded around in what he called his "morning clothes." But the last laugh that night was almost on ol' Archie.

For that night, at the Montreal Forum, Archie had hardly had time to take off his gaudy red velvet dressing gown with the silver trimmings and show off his trim 173½-pound waistline before the "fit hit the shan." Work-

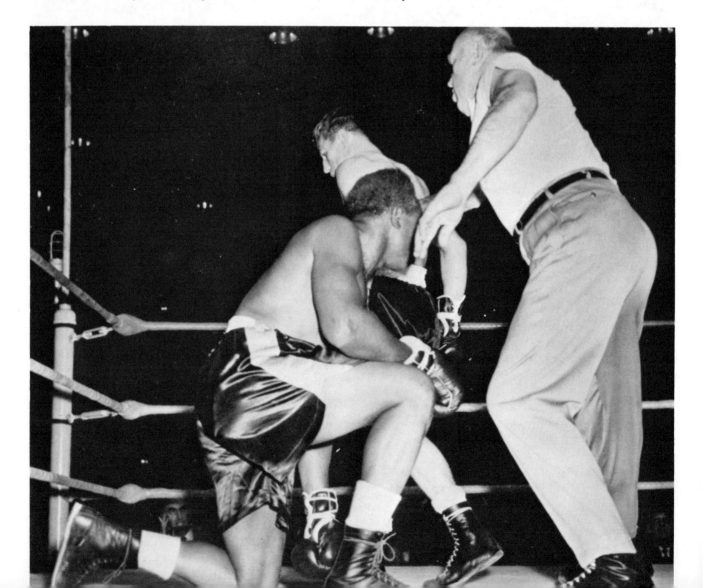

ing inside, Durelle delivered a right hand over the top to Moore's head. Moore dropped to the canvas as if he had been hit with a sledgehammer, which he might have been. The referee, former heavyweight champion Jack Sharkey, started tolling over the inert form of what appeared to be the soon-to-be-former light-heavyweight champion of the world.

After what seemed like an eternity—to Moore as well as to the 8,484 fans—the lifeless form beneath Sharkey stirred and righted itself on shakey legs at the count of nine. Durelle fairly flew from a neutral corner, cuffing the champion, and then, with another right, dropping him again. This time Moore was up without a count. Trying to hold on, to use every ounce of guile and mastery mustered in his 24-plus years in the ring, Moore attempted to weather the storm created by the fisherman in front of him. He hid behind his gloves, raised armadillo fashion, throwing out an occasional left. But Durelle was all over him, attempting to end the fight early.

As the seconds ticked off, and the sand in Moore's eternal hour glass slipped away, Durelle caught Moore with yet another right to the head, dropping him for the third time. Moore looked up at Sharkey as he tolled off the count, thinking, as he was to recall later, "Can this be me? Is this really happening to me?" (Later, much later, on the banquet circuit, he was to "remember" thinking to himself, "This is no place to be resting. I'd better get up and get with it.") And get up he did, at the count of nine, and somehow, someway, got through that first round, his longest round, fighting largely on instinct.

He was also able to take advantage of a mental lapse on the part of the challenger who later admitted that he didn't go for a knockout after the third knockdown because, "I forgot that this was a championship fight and that three knockdowns didn't halt the fight."

Round 2 found a totally different Moore coming out to face his challenger. No longer was he snickering. He was in a battle to the death. He started jabbing and hooking with his left, staying away from the lethal right hand in front of him. He not only managed to hold off the stronger challenger, he won the round on most of the unofficial cards at ringside. But Durelle came back in round 3, once again applying pressure and once spinning Moore around and catching him with a left and right that had the champion covering up.

Round 4 found both men flurrying, with Moore landing by far the flashier combinations and taking the play away from the challenger. So furious was the pace that their flurries continued far past the bell ending the round, angering both combatants. The fifth was a replay of the first with Durelle catching Moore with a wild left hook, sending him sprawling for the fourth time. Toward the end of the round,

Opposite: *In the first round Moore fought largely on instinct as Durelle attempted—and almost succeeded—to end the fight early by dropping Moore three times.* Right: *Ageless Archie stands over his fallen foe.*

Moore, unable to see much of anything, much less his wife, obediently waved, and Durelle, seated in the opposite corner, thought Moore was waving at him, scornfully.

Suddenly, out of the cloud that had enveloped him for the first fifteen minutes of the fight, Moore went on the attack, using his left as a battering ram, keeping it in the face of the challenger and trying to set up the one punch that would end it. Occasionally he would alter his attack, coming up with left hooks and combinations, as he did twice in the sixth when he staggered Durelle and bloodied his nose, and once in the seventh, when he floored the challenger for a count of three. But it was the left, and almost exclusively the left, that won Moore rounds six through nine. That and the fact that the 29-year-old challenger was running out of steam while the 42-going-on-45-year-old champion was coming on stronger.

Moore's systematic attack began to wear the challenger down, and he began to miss with wild punches as the obviously tired Moore reached back into his bag of tricks, if not into his memory, and staggered Durelle with a hard right.

It might have been at that exact moment that the momentum of the fight changed, when the fight went out of Durelle. Or, it might have been between rounds when Doc Kearns wouldn't let Moore sit down in his corner, but instructed him, instead, to wave to his wife in the audience.

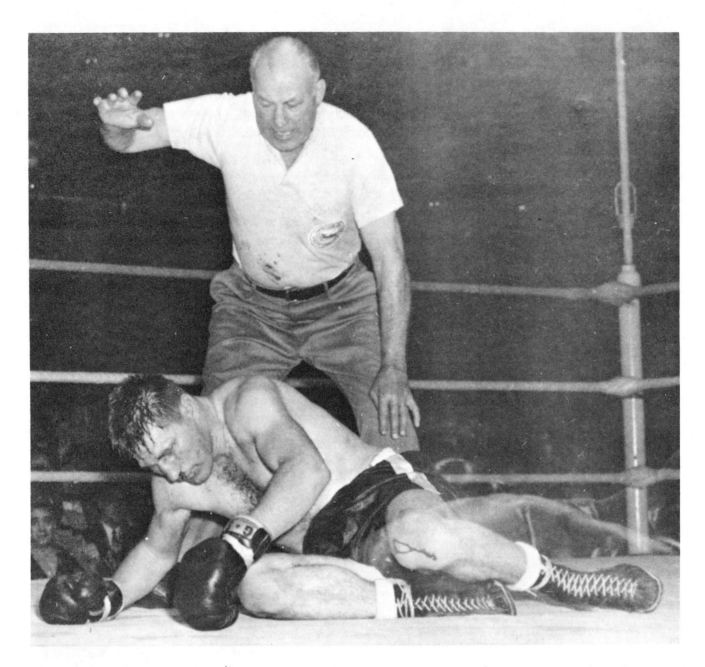

Moore continued to rake him with his left. And then, in the tenth, the bell began to toll for Durelle's Cinderella story as Moore carried the attack to his tired challenger, hitting Durelle with everything he threw—hooks, uppercuts, overhand shots, and right-hand chops. Near the end of the round Durelle collapsed under the cumulative weight of the fusillade, looking as far gone as Moore had nine rounds earlier. But the bell rang at eight, saving Durelle for one more round.

The eleventh was merely an extension of the tenth as an exhausted Durelle staggered out of his corner and fell down without being hit. Up at the count of nine, he ran into a short right to the chin and went down. And out.

Archie Moore had come back from the dead. The old man had done it again, adding another name to his list of KO victims, number 127 to be exact, breaking Young Stribling's record.

Archie Moore had retained his crown as king of the light-heavyweights and become in one night the all-time king of knockout artists. But he had done something else as well; he had seemingly found the secret of longevity.

152

Durelle lies dazed as referee Jack Sharkey counts him out. Durelle was Moore's 127th knockout victim, a feat that made Moore boxing's all-time KO king.

Floyd Patterson—Ingemar Johansson

March 13, 1961

If "Peanuts" cartoon character Charlie Brown had been a boxer, he would have been Floyd Patterson. Patterson's ring career was a tightrope walk across the chasm of his own introspective personality. He was a sensitive man, a perfectionist, and his own worst critic. The press admired Patterson the man, but doubted his credentials as a fighter. Floyd probably would have preferred it the other way around.

Patterson was born on January 4, 1935, in Waco, North Carolina. His family migrated to New York, and

young Floyd became embroiled in a life of petty juvenile crime. As with many ghetto youths, boxing became his salvation. His amateur career was spectacular, resulting in two New York and Eastern Golden Gloves championships in 1951 and 1952, and an Olympic gold medal in the middleweight division at the 1952 games in Helsinski. He turned pro on September 12, 1952, with none of the fanfare that accompanies the debut of today's Olympic champions.

Under the tutelage of his volatile, often-controversial manager Cus D'Amato, and trainer Dan Florio, Patterson managed to win 29 of his first 30 pro fights. (The lone loss was an eight-round decision to former world light-heavyweight champion, Joey Maxim.) His thirty-first outing was a 12-round points win over Tommy ("Hurricane") Jackson in 1956 which earned Floyd a match with world light-heavyweight champion Archie Moore for the newly vacant heavyweight title, a vacuum which had occurred just six weeks before when Rocky Marciano retired as the undefeated champion.

On November 30, 1956, in Chicago, Floyd dropped the 43—going on 50—year-old Moore with a leaping left hook in the fifth round and finished him off with a right-left combination. At 21 Patterson was the youngest man ever to wear the heavyweight crown, as well as the first Olympic medal winner to win the title.

Patterson might have been a great light-heavyweight. But at 182 pounds, he was as a mere child among men. Of the other heavyweight champions, only Rocky Marciano had a shorter reach. Worst of all, Floyd had a delicate chin and only an average defense. D'Amato exercised extreme caution in selecting his opponents, a strategy that probably added years to Floyd's reign as king of the heavyweights.

During his first two years as champion, Patterson successfully defended his title four times, knocking out four

Preceding page: *International souvenir program from the Johansson-Patterson fight*. Above: *Ingmar Johansson*. Above right: *Johansson (left) throws a closed-eye punch that fells Patterson in the first round*.

challengers who could be described as weak at best. However, they were hardly pushovers. Even Pete Radamacher, who had never fought professionally, managed to knock Floyd down; but his recuperative powers were extraordinary, and each time he managed to come back to whittle his opponent down to size—and to the floor.

Pressure from the media and the public began to build for Patterson to face one of the top contenders—Sonny Liston, Cleveland Williams, Zora Folley, Eddie Machen, or Nino Valdes. On September 14, 1958, less than a month after Patterson survived a knockdown and came back to stop Roy ("Cut and Shoot") Harris in his third title defense, number one heavyweight contender Eddie Machen traveled to Gothenburg, Sweden, to fight European heavyweight champion Ingemar Johansson. Johansson, undefeated in 20 fights, with 13 knockouts, was little-known outside of European boxing circles, where he had gained recognition by knocking out the likes of Henry Cooper and Joe Erskine. The handsome Swede pulverized the talented Machen with a ferocious right cross, stopping him in one quick, spectacular round. D'Amato was quick to accept him as Floyd's next challenger, assuming that like most European heavyweights, Ingemar would be "ready-made" for Patterson.

Patterson's and Johansson's fates were linked early on. Like Floyd, Ingemar represented his country at the 1952 Olympic games in Helsinki. While Patterson was earning international accolades, Johansson disgraced himself and his nation in front of a Scandinavian crowd. He reached the finals in the heavyweight division, only to be disqualified in the second round of his match with Ed Sanders of the United States for "not fighting."

Johansson turned pro on December 5, 1952, three months after Patterson. He stopped Franco Cavicchi in 13 rounds on September 30, 1956, to win the European heavyweight crown. He successfully defended that title twice, but prior to his upset of Machen there was no indication that he was destined to become the first fighter from outside the United States in 25 years, and the last white man to win the heavyweight championship of the world.

Of the 31 men who have laid claim to the heavyweight championship of the world during the gloved era, Patterson and Johansson are generally regarded as two of the least able. But the unique chemistry of their combined flaws and strengths produced one of the most exciting rival-

Above: *Champion Patterson scores a right to the side of Johansson's head, flooring the badly cut challenger.* Right: *Floyd Patterson.*

An overhead camera in the ring lights shows clearly Patterson's solidly placed left to the chin of Johansson (left).

ries in the history of boxing's glamour division.

Their protracted war was waged over a period of two years, in three pitched battles for the heavyweight title that consumed a total of only 14 rounds. All three fights ended in a knockout, with Johansson winning the first and Patterson the victor in the second and the third. Between them they made 12 trips to the canvas. And each fight was better than the one preceding it.

They met for the first time on June 26, 1959, at New York's Yankee Stadium. A small crowd of 18,215 filed into the 60,000-seat stadium—three thousand fewer people than had attended Patterson's previous defense against Roy Harris. But over $1 million was added to the $470,000 live gross by closed-circuit patrons—the largest gate of its kind in boxing history. Patterson was paid over $600,000—more money than Rocky Marciano ever made for one fight!

Patterson took the 4–1 underdog lightly and paid dearly for his contempt. A stand-up boxer with a basic jab right-hand offense in the classic European tradition, Ingemar controlled the action from the opening bell with his long, accurate jab as Patterson managed to get in one hard leaping left hook late in round 2—his only effective blow of the fight. The Swede, however, continued to keep the champion at arm's length with his persistent left, all the time ready with his right, the much-heralded—and just as often maligned—"hammer of Thor."

But with only 30 seconds gone in round 3, all hell broke loose. Johansson scored with a jab, and then took the wrappings off his right and threw a booming right cross that knocked Floyd down. The champion was up quickly, but was unconscious on his feet. Thinking he had knocked Ingemar down, he wandered toward a neutral corner. Johansson caught him with a left hook from behind that landed on the back of Patterson's head and a right which floored the champ for the second time. Patterson beat the count again, but two more awesome rights put him down yet a third time. He made it to his feet, but a right-left dropped him to the canvas again. By now Patterson was like a ghost, lifted up from the deck by some supernatural force and then made one with the canvas by Johansson's right. Now Johansson was on him, battering Patterson with both hands until he collapsed to the mat. Floyd arose for the fifth time, only to be flattened again, this time by a right uppercut, followed by a left and a right. The champion still refused to quit. Johansson walloped his now-helpless opponent with a left-right-left salvo until referee Ruby Goldstein mercifully stepped in and stopped the fight at 2:03 of round 3.

The new heavyweight champion of the world was an impishly handsome Romeo, who enjoyed night clubs more than fight clubs. The media loved him. "Ingo," as he was

called familiarly—and he was called frequently—lived up to his new title and lived up to the hilt; he was wined and dined at the most fashionable watering holes on two continents.

However the toast of the boxing world had a date with destiny, as well as one with Patterson. The original contract had guaranteed Patterson a rematch, and one was scheduled for June 20, 1960, at the Polo Grounds in New York. Johansson, never a dedicated athlete in any case, trained lightly for the second fight, believing that he only had to tap Floyd on the chin once with his vaunted right to retain the title. The Swede's right cross became a legend in its own time, alternately dubbed the "hammer of Thor" and "Ingo's Bingo." But, in fact, the blow was greatly overrated. Over the course of their series Johansson had Floyd down nine times, but was never able to put him away for the full count. Sonny Liston, who possessed a punch worthy of a legend, leveled Patterson twice for the 10 count in less time than it takes to drink one quick shot of Aquavit.

Patterson lived like a monk during his training for the second fight, avoiding the press while sharpening his tools to their finest edge. For the first time since winning the title, he was intensely motivated. He recognized that he had let Johansson control the pace of the first fight with his jab. To become the first man in history to regain the heavyweight championship he would have to be the constant aggressor,

Patterson's legs start to buckle after Johansson nailed him early in the first round, a round which saw Patterson hit the canvas twice.

and upset Ingemar's mechanical "one-and-a-two" rhythm, delivered like the beat of a Lawrence Welk tune.

Patterson was a changed fighter, physically and mentally. He came into the ring for the rematch weighing 190 pounds—a solid 8 pounds heavier than for the first fight. Johansson, for all of his laxity in training for the rematch, weighed in at a trim 194½—1½ pounds lighter than he had been a year before.

Following his fight plan, Floyd was the early aggressor. But with just a minute gone in round 2, Floyd encountered disaster in the form of a Johansson right that exploded against his head. This time instead of going down, he shook off the effect of the punch and backed away from Ingemar

for the remainder of the round. The blow had a salutary effect on Patterson. He discovered that he could take, and survive, the kind of blow that had felled him an incredible six times in the first fight.

Patterson's confidence grew with each passing round. In the fifth round he ripped a right to Ingemar's jaw that hurt the champion. Floyd followed up with a wild left hook which missed, but a second leaping left hook caught Johansson flush on the jaw, knocking him down. The Swede was up at nine, bleeding from his mouth and with a cut over his left eye. Patterson came roaring at him with one left hook after another. A final left hook—the hardest punch Patterson had unleashed in a career which spanned 64 fights

Stiffened by a Johansson left hook, Patterson is vulnerable to Ingemar's "toonder and lightning" right.

and 40 knockouts—came up from the floor and crashed into Ingemar's face. The champion went down like a sack of bricks, his head landing with a thud that was audible in the ringside section. His left foot twitched convulsively, and blood oozed from his mouth and nose as referee Arthur Mercante counted him out at 1:51 of the fifth round.

The rubber match was, if possible, more exciting, evoking memories of the Dempsey-Firpo fight. Staged at the Miami Beach Convention Hall on March 13, 1961, it drew a crowd of 31,892, and a gross of $3.3 million.

A third fight for the heavyweight championship between the same two men was almost unprecedented; only Ezzard Charles and Jersey Joe Walcott had duplicated the feat. The late Jimmy Cannon wrote that the two "are now experienced partners in violence, in the way a murderer and his victim are collaborators, each as important to the other in the act which destroys one of them. In some instances they resemble tragic Abbot and Costello . . . one has to be the straight man who degrades the other. The other must accept the humiliation. But the parts have not been assigned."

But, in a sense, the parts *were* assigned even before the first blow. Patterson had tasted humiliation in defeat and found it not to his liking. Johansson had also experienced defeat, but not the humiliation which attended it. Ingemar enjoyed being the heavyweight champion of the world, which is not the same thing as taking pleasure in winning fights. Winning was everything to Floyd; an end in itself. It was merely a means to Ingo.

Johansson, again the challenger, paid a heavy price

for his indifferent training methods. He carried 206½ pounds into the ring, 11¾ pounds more than he had weighed for the second fight. The excess baggage was arranged in soft folds around his midsection and thick rolls around his thighs. Patterson, at 194¾ pounds, was 12¾ pounds above his weight for the first fight, but he carried the additional bulk well.

Las Vegas oddsmakers, taking note of Ingemar's poor condition, made him a 4–1 underdog, in spite of the best efforts of his internationally respected trainer, Whitey Bimstein, who had worked long and hard to stiffen the Swede's jab and add a right uppercut to his limited repertoire.

Both fighters came out jabbing in round 1, Johansson with a long, straight left like a spear, and Patterson with a peculiar jab which unfolded like a jackknife. Ingemar tried a right, just grazing the champion's chin. They exchanged jabs, and Johansson followed up with a wicked right cross that caught Floyd flush on the chin. Patterson went down, jumping up at the count of three, as if he were merely going through the motions of genuflection. Referee Billy Regan continued the count, stopping at eight as Ingo waited in a neutral corner. The "mandatory eight count"—a relatively new innovation in professional boxing—had been adopted, with the consent of both fighters, for the first time in a heavyweight title fight. By the time Regan stopped counting, Patterson appeared to be completely recovered.

Johansson made haste to change all of that. He came straight at Floyd with an ineffectual jab, followed by another jolt from the "hammer of Thor" that stunned the champion. Johansson immediately launched yet another bolt of Swedish lightning, a sizzling right cross, followed by a left that knocked Patterson down a second time. This time the champion was hurt. "His eyes were glazed," referee Regan stated after the fight. Floyd took another mandatory eight count, just enough time for his remarkable powers of recovery to work their magic.

A replay of the first seemed to be unfolding. But wait! As Johansson waded in for the kill, Patterson reached down, somewhere deep inside, groping into the depths of his fractured confidence for a miracle. His hands—hands as fast as a middleweight's—flashed out with a right and a left. Johansson caught both punches with his face and went down; the first time since Dempsey fought Firpo, 40 years before, that both fighters had gone down in the first round of any heavyweight-title fight! The pro-Patterson crowd erupted as Ingo took a mandatory eight count. Floyd managed to get in one more hard left to the jaw before the bell sounded to conclude one of the wildest first rounds in heavyweight history.

Both fighers came out throwing lethal leather early

On all-fours, Johansson makes a vain effort to rise to meet Patterson's challenge.

in round 2, "Like two animals from another age," wrote John Underwood of the Miami *Herald.* They exchanged jabs. They traded hard rights to the head. Over-anxious, they both slipped to the canvas. Johansson jabbed as Floyd came at him from his unorthodox "peek-a-boo" stance. Patterson launched a right that grazed Ingo's ear and another right that slammed hard into the same ear. Johansson came right back with a swipe from "Thor's hammer" that caught Floyd on the jaw. The Swede began to find the range with his jab, scoring with it four times before Patterson rushed in to dig a brutal right to the body—the first effective body punch by either man in the entire three-fight series! They exchanged lefts and rights to the head, punishing punches calculated to end the fight, and Patterson ripped another right to Ingo's midsection and missed with a left at the bell.

Patterson came out jabbing hard in round 3. Twice he jolted Ingo with his left, absorbing a short right to the jaw in return. Floyd jabbed again, a sharp punch that opened a cut over the challenger's right eye. As Patterson rushed in to take advantage, the Swede picked him apart with a left-right combination and another right over Floyd's jab. Two more Johansson rights were on target, but lacked firepower. Patterson forced his way inside. Johansson unloaded a right to the champion's head. Patterson came right back with a punishing left hook to Ingo's chin, and Johansson retaliated with another big right. Now both fighters were absorbing the kind of punches which had dropped them in previous fights.

A cut appeared over Patterson's left eye early in round 4. Johansson was puffy under his left eye and bleeding from the gash over his right eye. Patterson opened fire with a right to the ear and another right behind it. He followed up with a ferocious combination—ripping a left hook and a right to the head that sent the challenger back into the ropes. They went back to exchanging jabs. Patterson stepped in with a brutal left to the belly. Johansson scored with a left and a right to the head, but they were arm punches lacking in real power. The champion dug another left to Ingo's ribs. They traded jabs and Johansson followed up with a tremendous right to the head. "Thor's hammer" had struck again and Patterson was hurt, but upright. He came roaring back, whipping punches with both hands to the body and the head. Johansson seemed overwhelmed, unable to establish his very methodical attack. Floyd slammed a final right into Ingemar's jaw at the bell.

The pace slowed noticeably in round 5. Johansson was beginning to tire, but Floyd failed to pursue either him or his advantage. They engaged in three minutes of jabbing, Ingo's game, leaving the champion wide open for the big follow-up right. But it never came. Patterson moved inside late

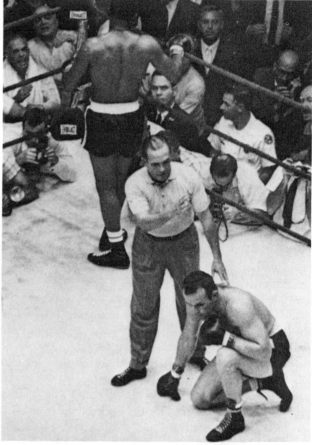

Top and above: *Referee Billie Regan counts out challenger Ingemar Johansson in the sixth round. Johansson was floored with a chopping right to the jaw. He started to rise midway through the count and at the count of nine started to rise again, but fell back to the canvas.*

in the round, with a hard left hook to the body and a short left-right salvo to the head.

Johansson was breathing heavily through his mouth at the start of round 6, his flabby body now soaked with perspiration. Patterson seemed fresh and confident. He was winning the rounds and controlling the pace of the fight. The round started slowly with an exchange of jabs. Twice Johansson found the mark with his left. A right came at Patterson's jaw, straight and hard. Ingo let another one go, a heavy punch that snapped Floyd's head back! Patterson's corner went wild, screaming at him to watch out for the right. The champion weathered the sudden squall and came back with a double jab. He missed with a right of his own, but quickly found the mark with a left to the body and a right to the head. Suddenly the Swede came alive, moving in behind his jab as Floyd backed off. A right flashed out at the champion's chin, but Floyd lessened its impact by backing away. Ingo unloaded his Sunday punch again, trying to knock Patterson into next week with another right. The blow was on target, but it lacked authority. Patterson retaliated with a left hook to the body, and missed with a right to the head. They squared off at ring center. You could see the power swelling in Patterson and draining from the fat, tired Swede. Floyd

lashed out with a leaping left hook that smacked into Ingo's forehead, just above the bridge of his nose, snapping his neck back. Two quick chopping rights to the temple followed it, knocking Ingemar to the deck. He struggled mightily and made it to his knees, balancing himself on his right glove as referee Billy Regan tolled the fatal digits. At the count of nine Johansson tried to rise, but he lost his balance. As Regan counted "10" Ingo was scrambling to get up with one glove still touching the canvas. Johansson later complained that he had received a quick count, but films of the fight revealed that he was, in fact, given *11* seconds to rise. The end came at 2:45 of the sixth round.

Floyd Patterson had retained his title, but his lofty achievement proved to be only a set-up for a great fall. Eighteen months later he was to climb into a ring in Comiskey Park, in Chicago, where he meekly surrendered his crown to a man who played on his wavering confidence like Joshua at the walls of Jericho. There were those among the naysayers who said Patterson lacked courage after Sonny Liston manhandled him. But such was not the case. Courage and confidence are not the same thing. And, in the final analysis, Floyd was a first-rate fighter, but a second-rate heavyweight champion.

Arms widespread, the ref proclaims, "It's all over!" for Johansson.

161

Cassius Clay—Sonny Liston

February 25, 1964

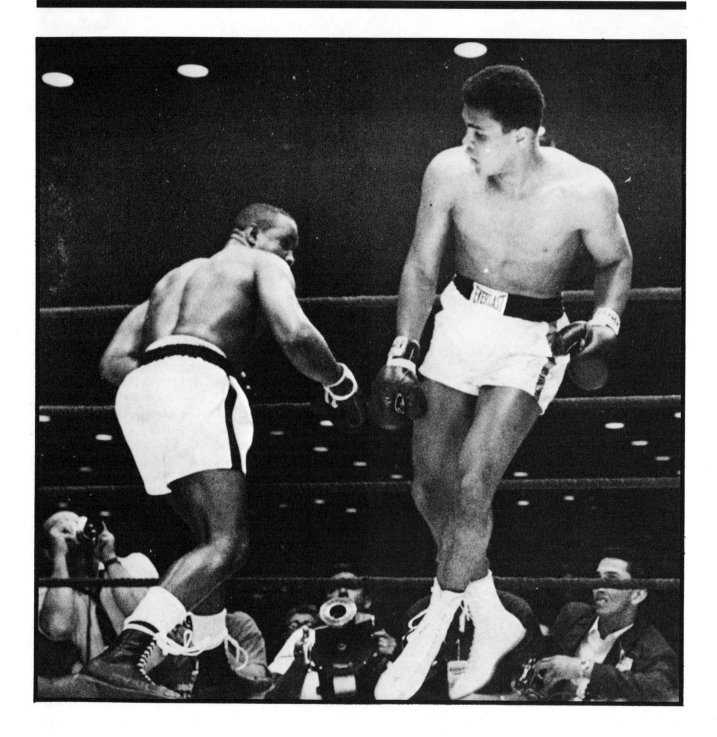

No event in recent American history, with the single exception of the assassination of President John F. Kennedy, is more shrouded in myth and mystery than the dethroning of heavyweight king Sonny Liston by Cassius Clay in Miami Beach on February 25, 1964.

Charles ("Sonny") Liston was a much-maligned and badly misunderstood man—one who devoted most of his adult life to a clumsy quest for respectability. Jose Torres, former light-heavyweight champion of the world and noted author, remembers Liston as "one of the most intelligent athletes I have ever met. He was so smart it wasn't even funny." But most of the world knew him as an ignorant, mean-tempered bully. This sharp difference between the man and his image may have had a great deal to do with his strange behavior on the night that he surrendered boxing's biggest prize.

Sonny was born into the family of an Arkansas sharecropper, a brutal drunkard who reportedly fathered 25 children. Sonny left home at the age of 13, after an argument with his father, to live with an aunt in St. Louis. There he drifted into a life of juvenile delinquency. At 16 he was already fighting with the local constabulary—their clubs against his fists. He eventually tried his hand at armed robbery. He was caught and sentenced to three concurrent five-year terms in the Jefferson City state penitentiary, an extremely harsh punishment for a young first offender.

A Roman Catholic prison chaplain had the foresight to suggest to inmate Liston that he channel his appetite for violence into boxing. Sonny agreed and quickly blossomed into a crude, but awesome talent. The authorities were sufficiently impressed to grant him a parole to pursue a career in the ring. In 1953, he captured the Chicago Golden Gloves heavyweight championship. A few months later he turned pro.

Blinkie Palermo, one of the mob figures who controlled professional boxing through the World Boxing Council, took an early interest in Liston's ring career. It was a Svengali-Trilby relationship that was at once Sonny's making and undoing. With Palermo's help, Liston was given every opportunity to climb up the heavyweight ladder. He began to peak in August 1958, with a first-round knockout of tough Wayne Bethea in Chicago. The fight lasted all of 69 seconds. Just long enough for Bethea to lose seven teeth.

Sonny's first win over a recognized contender came six months later in Miami Beach, where he annihilated huge Mike DeJohn, the hardest-punching white heavyweight around and a darling of "Friday Night Fight of the Week" fans, in six rounds.

During the next four years Sonny Liston marched through the heavyweight division like Sherman through Georgia, leaving few survivors. Cleveland Williams, a ferocious puncher in his own right, fell in three of the most brutal rounds ever fought by big men. Liston, seemingly immune to pain, absorbed a series of the Big Cat's best punches without flinching.

Four months later, in August 1959, Nino Valdes, a man who had beaten Ezzard Charles, was dispatched in three rounds. In March 1960, Williams and Liston clashed again in Houston. In another incredible match, it took Sonny only two rounds to finish the job. A month later Roy ("Cut and Shoot") Harris, who had gone 12 rounds in a title fight with Floyd Patterson, failed to survive three minutes with Liston. A third-round knockout of talented stylist Zora Folley in July 1960, and a 12-round decision over Eddie Machen in September of that year, entrenched Liston firmly in the number-one contender's slot, where he would languish for two long years.

The heavyweight division had never seen another man quite like him—a giant compressed into a 6-foot, 1-inch frame. His fists were 15 inches in circumference—bigger than Carnera's or Willard's. He had an 84-inch reach, 16 inches longer than Marciano's. He strengthened the muscles in his 17½-inch neck by standing on his head for a couple of hours a day. It was as if some futuristic geneticist had bred him in a test tube for the single purpose of beating up other men. His left jab knocked men out. It was in a class with Joe Louis'. His left hook was a lethal weapon, comparable to Joe Frazier's. He could go to the body with the ferocity of a Dempsey and launch a man toward the roof with an uppercut as powerful as George Foreman's. His right cross was a bit awkward, but he eventually perfected it into a deadly club.

But for all of his raw power and size, Liston's most remarkable attribute was psychological rather than physical. He made a science out of inspiring fear in the hearts and minds of his opponents, breaking their wills with a stony stare during the referee's instructions, and stuffing towels under his robe to make his enormous physique look even bigger and more intimidating. In short, he was the meanest "mother" on the block, and not only didn't he care who knew it, he *wanted* everyone to know it.

Liston's carefully crafted techniques of intimidation were never more effective than they were against Floyd Patterson on September 25, 1962, when Liston finally got his chance to fight for the heavyweight title.

Patterson's super-cautious manager Cus D'Amato had persuaded Floyd to stay clear of Liston for over two years, but pride and embarrassment finally got the better of the champion. Patterson was beaten before the first punch was thrown. He came to Comiskey Park in Chicago with a

Cassius Clay (right) "floats like a butterfly" away from the lethal right and impending left hook, as well as the intimidating hulk, of Sonny Liston.

163

*Locked arm in arm after missing jabs, Clay and Liston (right) proved equal
in size and ability—something Liston hadn't counted on.*

disguise hidden in a brown paper bag, making it easier to slink out of the stadium unnoticed if—or rather *when*—Sonny beat him. The fight lasted all of two minutes and six seconds. On July 22, 1963, Patterson tried again. This time he survived for two minutes and ten seconds. Both bouts could better be described as muggings than heavyweight-title bouts.

The new heavyweight champion was perhaps the least-liked man to hold the title since Jack Johnson. Newspaper editorials cried out for boxing commissions to strip him of his crown, because he had held up a gas station before he was old enough to vote. An anxious President Kennedy told Floyd Patterson that he had to beat Sonny. And the NAACP made haste to put distance between Liston and the "respectable" portion of the Negro race. The title that he had sought for so long, believing that it would magically make him as popular as his idol, Joe Louis, turned out to be an albatross. With a few contenders left in the division he had decimated, even Liston's chance to cash in on his crown seemed to be, at best, illusory. At worst, it was nonexistent.

A desperate search for a fresh face who could create box-office interest in a fight with the seemingly unbeatable Liston, turned up a 22-year-old youngster from Louisville, Kentucky, named Cassius Marcellus Clay. Clay first gained national recognition for himself in 1960 by winning a gold medal in the light-heavyweight division at the Olympic games in Rome. He turned pro in October 1960, under the tutelage of Angelo Dundee, who already had guided three other fighters to world titles.

Clay's early career proceeded apace, as he ran off a string of 17 victories—including 14 knockouts—against carefully chosen opponents. His style was a composite of extreme unorthodoxies in and out of the ring. He carried his hands low, some said dangerously low, as he cut wide circles around an opponent, stabbing out with a long, incredibly quick left jab, and delivering punches in dazzling bouquets of six, seven, and eight at a time. When a punch came at his head, he pulled back instead of slipping underneath it, or to the side as "the book" dictates.

Clay grabbed headlines for himself by stealing a page from a professional wrestler named Gorgeous George. He assumed an arrogant pose that insulted opponents and irritated the working press. To compound matters, beginning with his fight with Lamar Clark in April 1961, he began predicting, in amateurish verse, the exact round in which he would knock his opponent out. Incredibly, he made good on his predictions seven times, even disposing of contenders Alejandro Lavorante and 49-year-old Archie Moore in the promised round.

By March 13, 1963, while Sonny Liston was training for his rematch with Patterson, Cassius Clay, the punching poet, was big box-office news. An all-time-record crowd piled into Madison Square Garden, hoping to see an inflated light heavyweight named Doug Jones short-circuit Clay's prediction of a fourth-round knockout, and his career as well. They got more than they bargained for, as Jones, a notorious failure as a heavyweight, fought Cassius to a virtual standoff for 10 rounds, only to lose a hotly disputed decision.

Three months later Clay traveled to London to fight Henry Cooper, who was, like Jones, a fringe contender. Cooper possessed a heavy left hook and facial tissue as brittle as a 50-year-old coat of paint, tissue that gushed like a geyser when it broke under the impact of a punch.

Late in the fourth round "our 'Enery" unloaded an exquisite short left hook which exploded against Clay's chin and knocked him on the seat of his pants along the ropes. Cassius wobbled to his feet just as the bell sounded and before Cooper could follow up his momentary advantage. Between rounds Angelo Dundee miraculously "discovered" a tear in Clay's glove, manufacturing an excuse which delayed the beginning of round 5 and saving Cassius from the inevitability of a knockout. He answered the bell for round 5 and quickly turned Cooper's face into a real-life imitation of raw hamburger.

Even with his tarnished wins over Jones and Cooper, Clay found himself occupying the number-one contender's slot during a heavyweight-talent drought. He was eager for a fight with champion Sonny Liston, but few observers gave him the chance of the proverbial snowball in hell. Some gave him even less.

Liston's best punch was a left hook—the same blow that had twice sailed over Clay's low guard and knocked him to the canvas, once by Cooper and once by Sonny Banks.

Clay's chance at the title was the successful culmination of a two-year campaign to get Liston into the ring, a campaign that began moments after Sonny's enormous arm was raised by the referee on the night that he was crowned champion. That night Clay muscled his way through the crush in the ring at Comiskey Park, where he stood face to face with Liston and issued a loud challenge. And when Liston set up camp for his rematch with Floyd in Las Vegas, Clay was right there, needling him incessantly during his workouts.

Sonny's training sessions were calculated to inspire fear. He could break a heavy bag with one punch. He juggled a medicine ball as if it was a peanut, to the sultry tune of his favorite song, "Night Train." But Clay wasn't impressed. He taunted Liston in the gyms and haunted Liston in the casinos, issuing insulting challenge after insulting challenge.

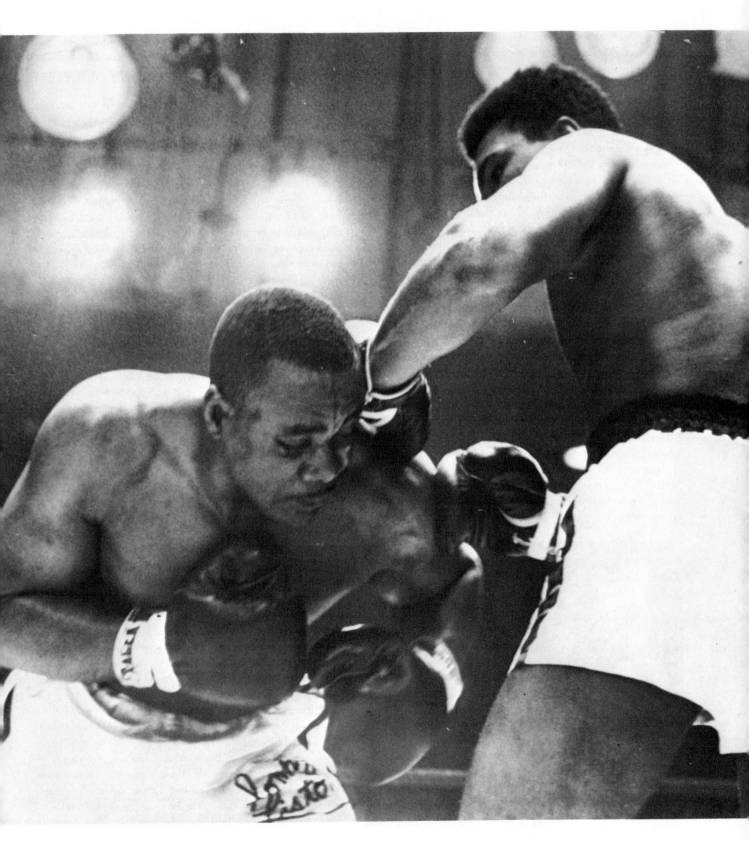

*Clay lands two simultaneous punches to Liston's shoulder, doing damage that
Liston later claimed rendered him unable to continue.*

By November 1963, Liston had had enough. He agreed to fight Clay in Miami Beach the following February.

The Sonny Liston who signed to fight Clay admitted to being almost 32 years of age, but no official record of his birth exists. Friends placed his age closer to 40. Dating back to his close 12-round decision over Eddie Machen in September 1964, Liston engaged in four fights that lasted a total of only six rounds. The fine edge that he had honed in his climb to the top had been dulled with ring rust. The one-sided nature of his two first-round knockouts of Patterson had disguised the fact that by the ordinary standards of the ring, Sonny was ready to be taken by the right opponent.

In compiling a 32–1 record, with 21 knockouts, Liston had traveled 10 rounds only three times and 12 rounds once. Virtually all his important wins were by quick knockouts. Even at his peak, when he was fighting regularly, he had never had to demonstrate great stamina.

Clay, an avid student of fight films, was endlessly curious about the particular strengths and weaknesses of his opponents. Dundee, his trainer, was perhaps the foremost analyzer of styles in the business. Together, they identified the obvious flaw in Liston's arsenal. Machen, a quick scientific boxer, adept at slipping punches and using the whole ring, had managed to last 12 rounds against Liston at his best, and come within a couple of points of beating him. The lone loss on Liston's record had been inflicted by a little-known journeyman named Marty Marshall, who subsequently lasted a full 10 rounds in another fight with Liston. Marshall, a defense-minded clown out of the Willie Meehan school, had frustrated Liston where better fighters had failed, because he employed lateral movement. If Cassius

Clay had mastered anything, it was lateral movement. If he could keep away from Liston until Sonny had depleted what had to be a limited supply of energy, anything might happen.

Clay was not content to rely on speed and strategy. He attacked Liston with a well-orchestrated psychological divertissement, coming to a rousing climax with the prefight weigh-in.

Weigh-ins are generally uneventful. Both fighters are usually anxious to get away from the press for a few final hours of rest and quiet contemplation of combat. With the moment of truth approaching for Clay, Sonny must have anticipated that he would confront a chastened challenger at the weigh-in, one who would be vulnerable to the usual Liston intimidation.

Clay and his entourage, including Drew ("Bundini") Brown, photographer Howard Bingham, Dr. Ferdie Pacheco, and Angelo Dundee, arrived first. They were wearing big cowboy hats and waving placards. Even Dundee, normally a conservative man, was wearing a hat. Clay and Brown, his court jester and resident witch doctor, were chanting like lunatics: "Float like a butterfly, sting like a bee! Rumble, young man, rumble!" The mob of reporters in the room pressed forward, trying to make some sense out of what was happening.

Liston walked into a madhouse. At first he couldn't even get close enough to Clay to fix his cold stare on him. When the two fighters were finally face to face, with the international media crowding around them to record the scene, Clay actually taunted Sonny, and Brown had to "restrain" him. When commission doctor Alex Robbins took the challenger's blood pressure it registered at 200/100—an alarmingly high reading.

A confused press rushed back to their typewriters, still trying to figure out exactly what had happened. Relying heavily on what turned out to be a case of self-induced high blood pressure, they reported that Clay was gripped by fear. The press might have been fooled, but Liston wasn't. He knew the look of fear on a fighter's face and this wasn't it. Madness, perhaps, but not fear.

Like most confirmed practical jokers, Liston hated nothing worse than being made a fool of himself. After the final travesty of the weigh-in, Sonny was determined to make Clay pay dearly for his fun, which was exactly what Cassius had hoped for.

That night, in front of a disappointing crowd of 8,297 fans rattling around Miami's spacious Convention Hall, a more composed Clay met Liston again. This time, face to face in the center of the ring for the prefight instructions, it became apparent that the two men were equal in

Champion Sonny Liston begins to show respect—and fear—when Clay begins to "sting like a bee."

size. This would be no confrontation between a Jack and a giant who lived at the top of the beanstalk—like the Liston-Patterson fights. And Clay, although outweighed by 8 pounds, 218 to 210, and giving away four inches in reach, stood a full two inches taller than Liston. It was a psychological victory for Clay, inasmuch as Liston had never fought anyone taller.

Liston tried once more with his famous death-ray eyes. *Six* towels had been stuffed under his robe, so that he looked like a wall of terrycloth. Clay met his gaze squarely. As referee Barney Felix gave his instructions, Clay hissed, "*Chump!* Now I got you, *chump!*" The shock must have hit Sonny harder than any punch he ever absorbed in the ring.

Liston was a somewhat mechanical fighter—a George Foreman trying to imitate Joe Louis. He had learned how to jab and feint and vary his punches. He knew how to cut off a ring. But his basic technique never changed: two steps forward, step again, and jab. Hook off the jab or follow it with a right. Two steps forward and so on. Clay had studied films of Sonny's fights, taking note of his ponderous, patterned footwork and the heavy jab that packed enough power to knock a man out.

As the bell sounded Liston lurched out of his corner, an energized Frankenstein coming to life. He nearly ran at Clay to begin the first exchange, but as soon as Sonny started his jab, Cassius slid gracefully to his own left, away from the punch. Clay also seemed to be running as he circled around the champion at a speed unheard of in a heavyweight contest. Liston jabbed and jabbed again, missing Clay's head by wide margins. The challenger's hands were almost dangling at his sides, leaving his head exposed to all kinds of mayhem. But each time Liston reached for it, it was gone, faster than you could say Cassius Marcellus Clay. As Clay moved to his left, Sonny made the correct adjustment, trying to decapitate him with a right hook. The punch missed. Liston kept shuffling forward, moving quickly enough for Sonny Liston, trying to maneuver Cassius into a corner, but not quickly enough to catch him. Clay didn't throw one punch in anger until the round was almost over. A left jab, like a switchblade knife pulled out from under a coat, snapped into Sonny's face. Clay stopped moving and unleashed a flurry of lefts and rights to the champion's face. Liston seemed frozen in time. By the time he woke up and surged forward, Clay was gone on his bicycle and the bell had sounded. Liston stomped back to his corner, snorting mad. By surviving the first round, Clay had already won an important psychological victory.

For all of his anger and anxiety, Liston still remembered what he had been taught by his trainer, Willie Reddish. After only one round of chasing Clay, he concluded that he would not be able to take him out early, with a single left hook to the head. First he would have to slow him down by clubbing his body, a process that Sonny was able to accomplish against most fighters in one or two rounds.

As the bell sounded to begin round 2, Liston charged out of his corner, throwing heavy punches with both hands. Quickly he forced Clay against the ropes, where he dug brutal blows to Clay's liver and kidneys before Cassius could wriggle out to ring center. Still moving, almost galloping, to his own left as Sonny came straight at him, Clay picked his openings with the care of a master craftsman. His jab never missed and he always followed up with a fast combination before gliding out of danger. Each time he was hit, Liston froze, unable to counter Clay's blows.

A tiny cut, barely perceptible, opened on the champion's left cheekbone, under his eye. It was the first time in 34 professional fights that Liston had shed even a drop of blood. Sonny retaliated with a long left that was like a 2×4 coming out of a basement window, catching Clay with a meaningful punch for the first time in the fight. The challenger recalls, "It rocked me back. But either he didn't realize how good I was hit, or he was already getting tired and he didn't press his chance." In fact, it would be many years before anyone would be able to tag Clay with *two* damaging blows to the head in quick succession, and his ability to absorb punishment to the body would become a legend.

Round 3 saw Liston still pressing forward, hacking away at air, and Clay revolving clockwise around him. Sonny was moving just a little bit more slowly now. Still he was able to jolt the challenger with punches to the body that appeared to be inconsequential, but were, in fact, painful. "After the fight Clay's ribs and flanks were one big angry red welt," remembers the challenger's physician, Ferdie Pacheco.

Midway through the third session Clay inflicted the first real damage of the fight. He feinted with his left and then drove a right uppercut into Sonny's cheek. The punch landed like an ice pick, and the once-tiny wound gaped open, spurting blood. Liston pawed at the cut, not completely believing what was happening. At the end of the third round he walked back to his corner, a wearier man. For the first time he sat down.

During training for the fight Liston had sustained a very minor injury to his left arm or shoulder—the kind of slight damage that athletes habitually ignore when there is a big payday at stake. Liston's handlers had prepared for a possible aggravation of this minor injury by including a solution of alcohol and oil of wintergreen in their corner kit. During the early rounds, Sonny unleashed dozens of full force punches at Clay's head that missed everything. Swinging at air is more fatiguing to the muscles than hitting a target. Inevitably Liston's sore shoulder began to ache under the strain. Between rounds 3 and 4 Sonny's corner was a busy place, as they worked to close the deep cut under his left eye and massaged his left shoulder with liniment.

Round 4 was the least eventful of the fight. Clay allowed Liston to work inside, sometimes covering up instead of moving laterally. The challenger, who had gone 10 rounds only three times, was pacing himself for a 15-round bout. And, as Cassius walked back to his corner at the end of the round, he was squinting and blinking. A bit of Liston's liniment had gotten into Clay's eye. As Dundee wiped the fighter's face with a sponge, more of the fiery substance went into both of his eyes, leaving him momentarily blind. He was frightened. No man, however brave, would willingly take on a wounded beast like Liston without full sight. In the challenger's corner they were unaware that the liniment had caused the problem. Clay wondered if Dundee hadn't put something in his sponge. He looked to Drew Brown and screamed, "Cut them off!" Referee Barney Felix came over to see what the confusion was about. Dundee, halfway down the steps that lead out of the ring, came back up, pushed Clay out into the ring with one hand, and snatched the stool out from under him with the other. "This is the big one, daddy!" he shouted as he launched his fighter into action.

All of this had not gone unnoticed in the champion's corner. Liston looked at Clay "like a kid looks at a new bike on Christmas," remembers Ferdie Pacheco. He came at Cassius with renewed energy, swinging his big fists like a pair of meat cleavers. How clearly Clay could see is still not certain. He walked out on unsteady legs, holding out his left hand like a blind man's cane. Sonny quickly backed him against the ropes. Clay leaned back, pushing his left glove into Sonny's face, slipping those punches he could see. Referee Barney Felix thought seriously about stopping the fight.

At first Liston's punches got through—agonizing wallops to the midsection and a couple of left hooks to the head. Clay began to move blindly around the ring on instinct, as his corner tried to guide him and Liston tried to tear his head off. Then his eyes began to clear, just as Sonny was slowing down and not throwing so many punches—and missing most of them. As the round drew to a close, Clay began lashing out with needle-sharp jabs, raising red welts under both of Liston's eyes.

Referee Barney Felix had the ring doctor take a precautionary look at Clay's eyes between rounds 5 and 6. On the other side of the ring, Liston's corner was a somber place. The champion was clearly tired now, having already boxed just one round less than he had fought in all of the preceding three and a half years.

Like a man trudging off to the guillotine, knowing what fate had in store for him, Sonny Liston shuffled out in the sixth round to face the fastest and perhaps the greatest heavyweight fighter in history. Quickly Clay went on the attack, missing with a left hook, but scoring with a wicked right-left combination to the head. When Liston failed to return the fire, Clay machine-gunned him with six consecutive unanswered punches—three lefts, followed by three rights. Sonny jabbed back listlessly and Clay ripped home a pair of lefts into the soon-to-be ex-champion's lumpy face. Clay then moved out to long range, circling and jabbing with surgical precision. The punches made a loud, painful thud as they wacked into Liston's sad face. There was a purple lump under the champion's right eye and a four-inch gash under his left one. Cassius missed with a big right that drew a rise from the crowd. He drilled holes in Sonny's head with his left, driving it into his face four times in succession. Sonny responded with a solid, short right that was his last hurrah, but Clay made him pay for his folly with two more razor-sharp lefts. The crowd roared its approval at the bell.

As Clay went back to his stool he shouted at the press section, "I'm gonna upset the world!"

Both corners worked feverishly on their fighters for 50 seconds of the allotted minute between rounds 6 and 7. At the 10-second buzzer Clay was on his feet, glaring across the ring at Liston, who was slumped on his stool, the sand slowly sifting out of his championship glass. Some observers claim that a tear coursed down his wounded cheek. Liston opened his mouth and spat out his mouthpiece onto the canvas, as if it had a bad taste. Suddenly, the fight was over! Liston's manager, Jack Nicon, had stopped it because of the severe pain in Liston's left shoulder.

Clay, looking like his feet were afire, leapt around the ring. "King!" he bellowed. "Eat! Eat! Eat your words! I am the king! I am the king!" he shouted to the 46 newspapermen at ringside, 43 of whom had picked Liston.

It is anyone's guess what really went through the bruised, confused head of Sonny Liston as he sat on his stool between the sixth and seventh rounds. His was a head that had been hit with policeman's clubs and filled with the strange paranoia of the underworld. Being the champion couldn't have been much fun for Sonny, not with the leaders of his own race, the press, and even the President of the United States lined up against him, and God knows what kind of creatures crawling out of his shady past to claim repayment for old favors.

You sensed that when Sonny Liston spat out his mouthpiece, he was spitting out the rotten, bitter fruits of a success that was really just one more disguised failure in the life of this unlucky man.

"I am the king," screamed Clay after being awarded a TKO and the world heavyweight title.

Muhammad Ali—Cleveland Williams

November 14, 1966

On Monday, November 14, 1966, two men out of Houston were making headlines around the world: Captain James Lovell and Major Buzz Aldrin, aboard the Gemini 12 spacecraft, were passing over the United States for the fourth time. But the eyes of the boxing world were focused instead on two other men in Houston: heavyweight champion Muhammad Ali (a.k.a. Cassius Clay) and challenger Cleveland Williams, who were fighting a 15-round title bout in the Astrodome.

The fight was Ali's seventh in defense of the crown, his first on American soil since he had made his famous "I ain't got no quarrel with them Viet Congs" remark earlier in the year. Caught in the patriotic backlash of angered politicians, Ali had been literally a man without a country, defending his title in Toronto, London, and Frankfurt, but not in the United States. This was to be, in effect, his "homecoming," although not a very popular one.

But Ali, who had once credited part of his success on the fact that he had stolen a page from the promotional guidebook of Gorgeous George ("I saw 15,000 people coming to see this man get beat. His talking did it. And I said,

'This is a g-o-o-o-o-o-o-d idea.' "), paid the boos and jeers no mind, certain they would be accompanied by bodies that would pay to see him get beat.

And they did pay to see him—whether it was to get "whupped" by their local hometown favorite, Cleveland ("Big Cat") Williams, or merely to see the first prizefight in what had been ballyhooed as the Eighth Wonder of the World, the Houston Astrodome—35,460 strong, setting an indoor record that had stood uneclipsed for 25 years, and paying in a near-record $461,290. When Ali entered the ring, the boos could be heard from all the way up to the $5 seats near the top of the ballpark's plastic crust down to the $100 ringside seats perched somewhere on the AstroTurf infield. And they were cheering, in one voice, for his opponent, challenger Cleveland Williams, who came into the ring weighing 212 pounds, a fraction of that weight a .357 magnum slug still lodged in his body, courtesy of a Texas State trooper who, two years before, had taken umbrage at something the Cat had said and now sat in the audience to root for the man who carried the souvenir of his handiwork.

But if Williams carried a slug into the ring with him

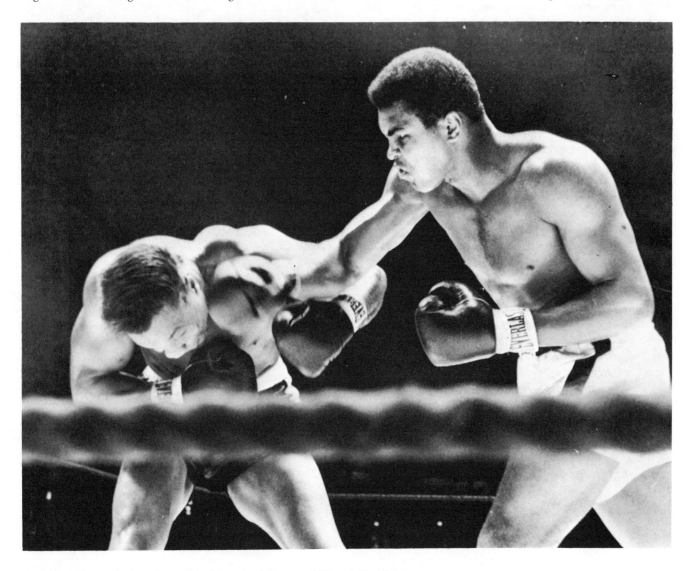

Opposite: *Houston's Astrodome played host to Muhammad Ali and Cleveland Williams.* Above: *Ali's stabbing right to the head of "Big Cat" Williams is right on the money.*

that night, he also carried an awesome record as well—the winner of 65 of 71 fights, 51 by knockout, 15 in the first round. His punching power was reputed to be the equal of any heavyweight in boxing—past or present—and there were those who believed that the Cat would triumph, including his voluble manager, Hugh Benbow, who said, "the Cat and me will take care of Clay in three."

But if Williams' punching power—compared to that of Liston and Bob Satterfield—was thought to be enough to turn the 5–1 underdog into a winner, on a percentage basis, Ali's was even better. Whereas Williams was batting .717, with his 51 knockouts in 71 fights, Ali was hitting .808, with 21 knockouts in 26 times at bat. Comparisons aside, one thing was sure: this fight would not go to a decision.

Ali-Clay, who came into the fight at 213½ pounds, the second highest weight of his career—up until that point—started off the fight in his usual manner, moving away from the ever-pursuing Cat, hands at his side, daring the 33-year-old (going on 40) Williams to "come and get him." Almost a minute passed as the two combatants went through their middle-of-the-ring charade. Finally, Williams threw a left at the ever-retreating Ali, but by the time he got there, the champ was gone, only to return scant seconds later to throw a flurry of punches off of his left jab.

Encouraged by his success, Ali shot a left to the body followed by three lefts to the head. Williams seemed paralyzed and unable to find his elusive tormentor, steadfastly standing like a tree while the champion flitted around him, picking his spots. Finally Williams got off first, cutting the

174

Top (left and right): *A picture-perfect right puts Williams back on his heels—and down.* Above: *Ali winces as he gets a taste of his challenger's medicine.*

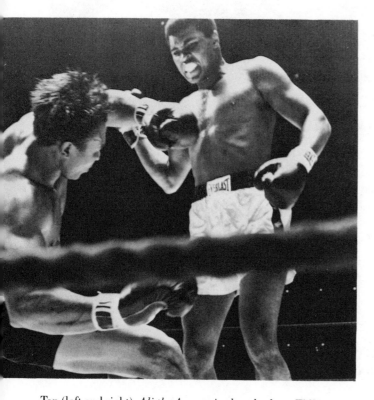

ring off on Ali and landing a stiff left to the head. It was a mistake, as Ali moved out of harm's way, and on his way threw a flurry of six punches, all landing to Williams' guarded but still unprotected head.

Williams, unable to find any gear but straight ahead, came in again, and for his trouble received a volley of eight more shots to the head, all landing. A trickle of blood could be seen on Williams' face as Ali began to play the role of a finger painter, smearing it across the whole of Williams' face with a jab, a straight right, a hook, and a right. The bell rang and a still fresh Ali skipped to his corner while Williams wearily trudged back to his.

The Cat came out of his corner for round two, the words of Benbow still ringing in his ear, "Jab ... jab ... jab." But jab at what? The will-o'-the-wisp who was in front of him just a second ago was long gone by the time he loaded up, and when he repositioned himself he was met by yet another volley of punches. Williams tried to put together a combination, landing a left to the body of the bobbing champion, but missing with his vaunted right to the head. He caught Ali-Clay with a left hook. And then it happened. Preceded by an accentuated five-step in-place tango maneuver he called "the Ali Shuffle," the champion threw a left and then a right reminiscent of the one he had caught the incom-

Top (left and right): *Ali the Aggressive knocks down Williams and celebrates his third-round TKO*. Above: *Williams was to go down three times in the second round and once more in the third*.

175

ing Sonny Liston with at Lewiston. Williams hung in midair momentarily and then fell to the canvas.

Painfully regaining his footing at the count of six— as referee Harry Kessler tolled off the mandatory eight— Williams was more like a lamb than a cat going back to the slaughter. A barrage of lefts and rights sent Williams spinning to the canvas again. This time he was up at five, but Kessler kept tolling the mandatory count of eight.

Once more Williams tried to go the only way he had ever learned to go—forward—and, for his efforts he caught more punches, this time a left and a right. He stood in mid-ring, looking like a puppet who had had his strings cut only recently, and then fell in as broad a fall as any Hollywood stuntman ever managed, down and apparently out. But as Kessler counted five over the spread-eagled form below him, the bell rang, saving Cleveland for yet another round. And another drubbing.

The third round was, in actuality, merely a continu-

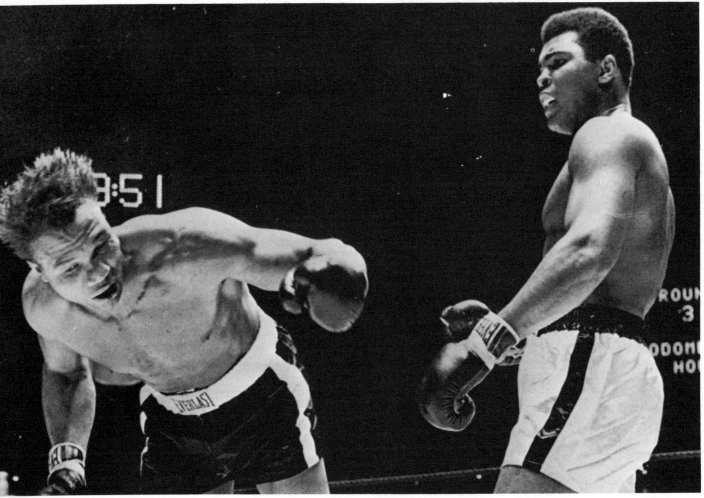

176

Top: Williams (left) starts down to the canvas in the third round as Ali defies him to get up. Above: Williams collapses like a puppet whose strings have been cut; Ali holds the scissors.

ation of the second. Ali, looking like he could take a man holding a .357 magnum as well as one with a .357 bullet lodged in him, went back on the attack, and found it difficult to miss the man in front of him. Then, as if he were remembering some promise unkept, he went back into his little five-step dance and threw another left-right combination. Williams did a two-and-a-half gainer to the canvas again. And again, incredibly, he climbed back to his feet.

The final scene was a tragic one. Cleveland Williams stood where he had arisen, making no attempt to defend himself—and unable to raise his hands—blood poured down from his nose while Ali savaged him with a left, a right, and another left. Referee Harry Kessler jumped in. He had had enough, even if the Big Cat hadn't.

It was over at 1:08 of the third round. And while it hadn't been a great fight, it had been Cassius Clay (a.k.a. Muhammad Ali)'s greatest, the night he had declawed the Cat.

Top: Ali pops another left off the jaw of Williams, who was to become all too familiar with them. Above: Williams went down four times during the fight before referee Harry Kessler decided the Big Cat had had enough.

Jose Napoles—Curtis Cokes

April 18, 1969

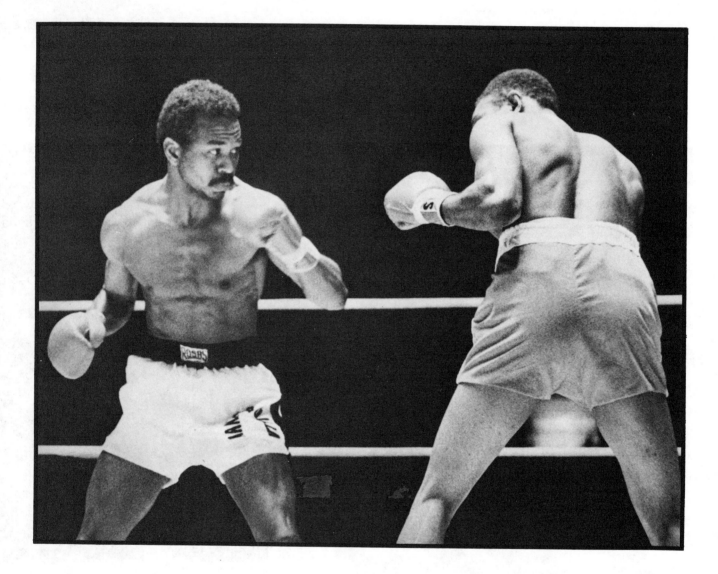

The lighted sphere descended slowly high above One Times Square in midtown Manhattan, and 1969 was underway. Nixon and Agnew were inaugurated as president and vice-president of the United States, both having pledged to return a high standard of morality to Washington, D.C. The Baltimore Colts thrashed the Cleveland Browns to win the National Football League championship and were eager to get on with the formality of doing the same or worse to the American Football League champion New York Jets in the third edition of something called the Super Bowl.

Curtis Cokes, the welterweight champion of the world, was as confident as the Colts. He was coming off an extremely successful year, his third consecutive one in which he scored seven victories, two in defense of his title, without getting into trouble even once.

Cokes, born in Dallas, Texas, in 1937, began fighting professionally in 1958, breaking into the welterweight top-ten in about four years. He lost a few bouts on points but was never hurt or knocked down until May 1964, when he took on Stan Hayward of Philadelphia in his forty-third pro fight. Cokes—by then the number-seven-ranked contender—dropped the Philadelphian with a left hook in the second round. But Hayward nailed Cokes solidly with a left hook of his own in the fourth frame, a shot from which Cokes never recovered. He went down three times, automatically ending the fight and putting the knockout loss on his record.

Cokes retired briefly after that loss but soon returned to the ring with a new style, one emphasizing his defense and counterpunching. The counterpunching, but not crowd-pleasing, Cokes won six of his next seven fights in the next two years, making him a prime contender for Emile Griffith's welterweight world title. When Griffith won the middleweight championship in 1966 the scramble to determine his successor in the welterweight ranks began. Cokes whipped Luis Rodriquez and Manuel Gonzalez to win the World Boxing Association title and then beat the European champion, Jean Josselin of France, to become the universally accepted welterweight champion.

Cokes was definitely a pragmatist. He boxed not out of some desire to be remembered through the ages as the greatest of all time, but because he realized that it was the best way to support himself and his family. He lived modestly in a house on a tree-lined block in the integrated Glen Oaks section of Dallas. His living standard was one that he could continue to maintain after his retirement from the ring when he would devote his time to the Dallas steakhouse in which he was a partner. Cokes was 31 years old in 1969 and had never been injured or cut in the ring. While his pinpoint counterpunching and defensive skills were beginning to at-

tract some followers, Cokes fully realized that his reluctance to move in on his opponents and bang away with both hands was hurting him at the gate. "People come out to see the sluggers," Cokes admitted. "But those who criticize me don't have to step in the ring and get hit. I want to win as badly as anyone, but it's just as important to me that I protect myself. When I'm through fighting I don't want my children to be ashamed of how I look."

But Cokes wasn't losing any sleep worrying about what his children would have to look at. For two years, no welterweight was able to mount a good fight against the champion, let alone beat him. He knocked out Francois Pavilla in 10 rounds, Charlie Shipes in 8, and blitzed the much-ballyhooed South African, Willie Ludick, in 5. After his last defense, a lopsided 15-round decision over Ramon LaCruz of Argentina, Cokes made his plans known. One, possibly two, more title defenses were on the agenda, after which Cokes would follow Emile Griffith's lead and invade the more glamorous, money-laden middleweight division.

In February, Cokes went to St. Louis for a tune-up

Opposite: *Jose Napoles (left) was the favorite in his world welterweight championship bout with champ Curtis Cokes.* Above right: *Champion Cokes steps on the scale as challenger Napoles smiles for photographers.*

179

and took less than a round to flatten Don Cobbs in a nontitle bout. But the welterweight championship was on the line when Cokes stepped into the Los Angeles Forum on April 18 to face the challenge of Jose Napoles. The 29-year-old Napoles held a record of 52 wins and 4 losses, was unbeaten for the last six years, and had 37 knockouts to his credit. But Cokes and his manager, Doug Lord, were confident of victory. Napoles, who fled Castro's Cuba in 1961 and now lived in Mexico—two fights in Los Angeles was the extent of his experience north of the border—made many suspect that the man known to his followers as "Mantequilla," because he was as smooth as butter, was afraid to face topnotch competition in the United States.

Promoter George Parnassus was paying the champion $80,000, the most ever paid for a welterweight up to that time. Eleven years later, welterweight champion Roberto Duran would throw up his hands in the middle of the ring and surrender his title to Sugar Ray Leonard, but would walk out with $8 million—100 times that purse. But Cokes was no Duran and $80,000 was more than appetizing for the steakhouse owner.

When the fighters entered the ring the predominantly Latin Forum crowd of 15,695 made it clear that they were rooting for the underdog, the challenger. But to win, Napoles had to beat Curtis Cokes, a champion who was at the top of his game.

Napoles came in low as the action commenced, throwing fast left hooks and popping short rights to the face and body as he bobbed and slipped the champion's constant jabs and infrequent right hands. The 145½-pound Cokes did not seem to benefit from the two-and-a-half-pound weight advantage, and the superior height and reach he had over the Cuban-Mexican challenger. Half of Napoles'

punches were missing, but the half that were not were taking their toll.

Cokes did what he had to do in the third round, landing his jabs consistently and avoiding Napoles' blows. But though he won the round, his punches did not slow Jose down, and when they came back for the next frame it was Napoles who was punching harder, and connecting.

The Mexican fans were ready to celebrate in the fifth round after Napoles caught the champion with a tremendous right to the head. But the experienced Cokes weathered that blow and dozens more like it that Napoles threw during the fifth, even coming back with a few of his own.

The challenger kept up the pressure, never letting up and landing the devastating hooks which had felled so many opponents in Havana, Mexico City, and Tijuana. Now he was landing them on the welterweight champion's desperate punches and landing repeatedly to Cokes' head. Mantequilla was smooth as butter all right, but he was also sharp—sharp as a stiletto. The blood was pouring from the champion's nose and his eyes were puffed and nearly shut. Cokes, who had prided himself on never having been cut, was now just fighting to survive.

As the fight moved into the double-digit rounds, the challenger began to slow down. He was still pressuring the champion and winning every round. But now he was also picking his shots. And his razorlike punches opened cuts over both of Cokes' eyes.

The ringside doctor and the referee examined Cokes' cuts in the thirteenth round and allowed the fight to continue. The champion gamely fought on, never going down as Napoles kept throwing leather. But when he returned to his corner at the conclusion of the round, he was an obviously beaten fighter. As the minute rest period wound down, Doug Lord informed the referee that his fighter could not continue.

The jubilant crowd surged toward the ring as referee George Latka signaled that Jose was the new welterweight champion. They put a sombrero on the champion's head and carried him out on their shoulders as the beaten Cokes was helped out of the ring.

Napoles made good on his pledge to grant the ex-champion first crack at the title. Cokes promised that he'd be a different fighter the next time around, but the Mexico City fans who showed up 72 days later to cheer their champion saw the same Curtis Cokes, and happily for them, the same Jose Napoles. After being battered once again into submission—this time after 10 rounds—Cokes said out loud what was apparent to all. "He's a very good fighter," said Cokes of his conqueror. "Sure as hell is a better fighter than Curtis Cokes."

Eyes battered closed, Cokes becomes a punching bag for the rights and lefts of Napoles.

Muhammad Ali—Joe Frazier

October 1, 1975

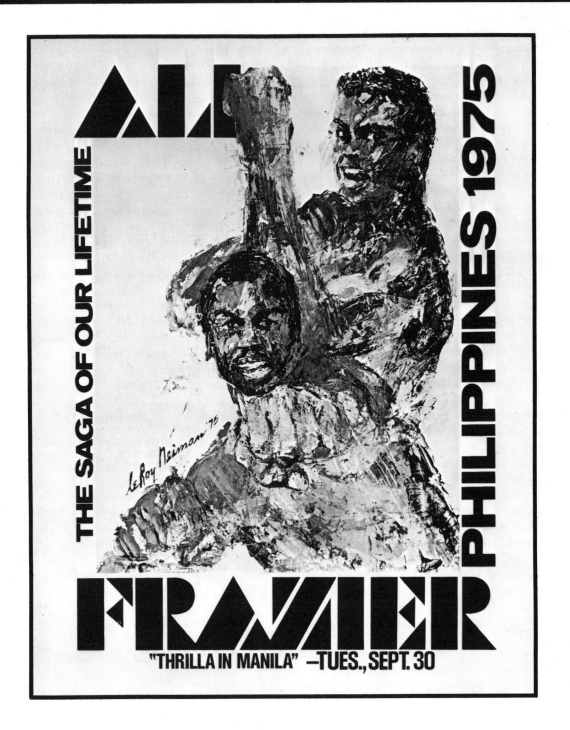

Promoter Don King had found plenty of willing investors in his hometown of Cleveland for the third Ali-Frazier bout, but then he and Ali, the man who made the ex-convict-turned-impresario a millionaire, trotted halfway around the world. The talkative pair traveled to exotic Kuala Lumpur, Malaysia, where Ali would waltz once again with Great Britain's pacifistic contender, Joe Bugner. Bugner was a man who, unlike most of the heavyweights representing the Union Jack (including some like Bruce Woodcock, of whom Red Smith once wrote, "Sleep came as it must come to all British heavyweights, midway in the fifth round"), finished the fight on his feet.

But it wasn't the prospect of Ali versus Bugner that aroused the wrath of fight fans. That came after Ali's announcement that he would retire after beating Bugner, a threat which led one wag to intimate that Ali had more retirements than the social security office.

King, ever the actor, told the press Ali's intentions were sincere.

"This is no publicity stunt," King said. "And Joe is upset. He has been eating, sleeping, and living for Ali. And I'm upset because I think Ali and Smokin' Joe should have a 'go' at it one more time. I think the public wants them to settle it once and for all."

This kind of talk made jaded observers feel that, indeed, the rubber match was almost certainly finalized. It sounded like the prehype hype for another of boxing's big bonanzas. And it was.

But King's remark about the public's interest rang true. Ali and Frazier, the punch and dance team who had already made two appearances together, were permanently interwoven in the consciousness of fight fans everywhere as an inseparable twosome. To mention one without the other would be like mentioning Burns without Allen, Gallagher without Sheen, or, closer to home, Pep without Saddler.

Their first meeting—an event so long awaited that it was properly billed as "The Fight"—had taken place at Madison Square Garden on March 8, 1971. Ali was still the preening butterfly, the majestic presence with swift lips, feet, and hands, then. He was 29 years old, but had had only two fights—against Jerry Quarry and Oscar Bonavena—after missing nearly three years due to his refusal to stand forward for the draft—and the righteous political chest-beating that took away his crown scant hours thereafter. But, despite his loss to the political powers that be, he was still undefeated inside the ring . . . until he stepped into the Garden ring.

Only Smokin' Joe left the fabled arena unbeaten that night. Forever pressing forward, his shoulders flapping and his head bobbing up and down, he came at Ali as one writer

182

described it, "like a wild beast caught in a thicket."

"It was like death. Closest thing to dyin' that I know of," said Muhammad Ali.

"Lawdy, Lawdy, he's a great champion," said Joe Frazier.

"Sit down, son. It's all over. No one will ever forget what you did here today," said trainer Eddie Futch, telling Frazier he was stopping the bout before round 15.

Eddie Futch's observation has proven to be as undeniably correct as was his decision to stop the aptly named "Thrilla in Manila," the third meeting between Muhammad Ali and Joe Frazier. It was an epic battle, an unforgettable fight between two unforgettable heavyweights—the final showdown between two great adversaries, the final glorious chapter in both of their magnificent careers.

These two great fighters, whose ring styles and personalities couldn't have been any more divergent, shared one final evening of greatness together. As Futch predicted, that night—October 1, 1975, at the air-conditioned Philippine Coliseum—is permanently etched in the history books, the hearts and minds of the people of 70 nations around the world who witnessed the fight, and in the memories of the millions who heard or read about it afterward.

It was a multimillion-dollar promotion which almost didn't come off.

Ali had regained the heavyweight title October 30, 1974, in the jungles of Zaire, when he cleverly used his "rope-a-dope" technique until the supposedly invincible George Foreman began to take on the look of a limp waterhose after the spigot had been turned off, tiring—and then

Preceding page: *LeRoy Neiman's flamboyant poster brought extra gl*. *the "Thrilla in Manila."* Opposite and above: *Legs up and on his bac* *Muhammad Ali was Joe Frazier's knockdown victim in the fifteenth r* *their first fight—called, justifiably, "The Fight."*

failing—in the eighth round. He began 1975, his thirteenth active year in the professional ring, with a final-round technical knockout over a game, but overmatched, New Jersey liquor salesman named Chuck Wepner.

Frazier, the 27-year-old son of a South Carolina sharecropper who had bulled his way to a 26–0 record with 23 knockouts and recognition as the new titleholder to succeed the defrocked Ali, saw his persistence pay off. One of his up-from-the-floor left hooks dumped Ali on his backside in the fifteenth round and Smokin' Joe took a unanimous decision.

But even in victory, Frazier suffered. For, although Ali went directly to a Manhattan hospital for a brief visit, the champion had to take a three-week rest in a Philadelphia hospital—and several rumors had him "dying."

Joe suffered further when, against the advice of manager-trainer Yank Durham, he defended his title against slugger Foreman in Jamaica on January 22, 1973. Seven knockdowns later, Foreman was the new champ. "My, my," Ali said upon hearing the news, "there goes five million dollars out the window."

But still their rematch was made—this one a non-

title, 12-round bout. They held a second Garden party in New York, but this time the men who previously had split $10 million worked for purses slightly below $1 million.

The sequel was marked by the 32-year-old Ali's holding, jabbing, and keeping Frazier outside where he could do little, or no, damage. Ali won a mildly debated unanimous decision and some assumed there would be no third fight. But Ali's destruction of Foreman in "the rumble in the jungle" was the perfect prelude to the final meeting. Twenty-seven rounds would now be followed by fourteen more.

"It'll be a killa, a chilla, a thrilla, when I get the gorilla in Manila," Ali spouted, adding Frazier's name to his rogue's gallery for opponents, alongside "Washerwoman" (Chuvalo), "Rabbit" (Patterson), and "Mummy" (Foreman). "I've got two punches for Frazier—the balloon punch and the needle punch. My left jab is the balloon and my right is the needle! I promise Joe Frazier will be in the hospital again!"

Above: *Joe Frazier covers up as Ali takes control in the first round of the "Thrilla in Manila." Above right: Ali connects with an overhand right to Frazier's head in early action.*

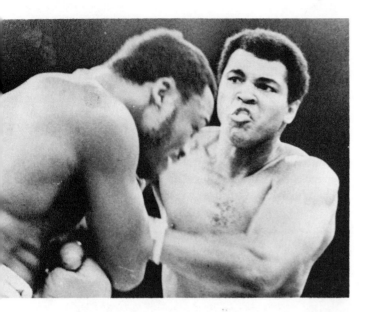

All of Ali's insults weren't laughed off by Frazier, despite their obvious intent to hype the gate. Inside those ropes, Frazier vowed, his dislike of Ali would be apparent.

"No question about it," Frazier said after Ali had whipped Bugner, "it's real hatred. I want to hurt him. If I knock him down, I'll stand back, give him breathing room. I don't want to knock him out in Manila, I want to take his heart out."

That last sentence had some meaning to Futch, who had replaced Durham when Yank died the previous year. He worried about Joe being overemotional.

"Joe was a little too emotional in the second fight," Futch said. "But he's not seething anymore . . . he's got quiet resolve."

An army of acupuncturists couldn't have applied more pressure than Joe would. Ali somehow survived and conquered his arch rival. But, as Ali was to admit later, "I wanted to quit. And you thought two old horses fightin' for

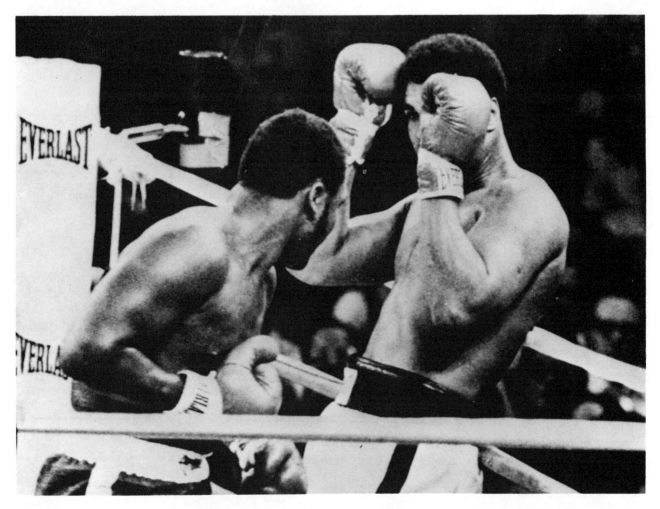

Top: *After exchanging insults before the fight, Frazier and Ali exchange blows in the ring*. Above: *In the middle rounds, Frazier backs Ali into the ropes, taking it to the champ as he drives him close to defeat and "death."*

185

the third time . . . you didn't expect to see that kind of fight, did you?"

No one could have or should have. But the two thoroughbreds exceeded all expectations. They ran one last great race, together.

Ali weighed in at 224½ pounds while Frazier came in at 215½ pounds during what, for Ali, turned out to be an uneventful weigh in. It was so uneventful that the two fighters didn't even exchange words. Perhaps Ali had a notion of what was to follow.

Frazier wound up making Ali eat a lot of his famous smoke, but not before Ali had fanned the flames early. Typi-

cally, the ring was a no-smoking area for the first round as Ali peppered Joe with jabs, snappy one-two's, and left hooks. The crowd of 25,000, which had fought its way through a three-hour traffic jam to get to the arena, gasped when Ali jarred Frazier with a hook in the opening round.

Ali had not come to perform any dance steps before President Ferdinand Marcos and his wife, Imelda. He had come to fight. And fight he did. Ali stood flat-footed in center ring in the opening moments of round 1. Referee Carlos Padilla Jr.—apparently a compromise choice after a disagreement by the opposing camps—quickly made it clear that Ali would not be allowed to get away with his customary

holding behind the opponent's head.

Ali stung Frazier with right-hand leads in round 2. Some began to think that Smokin' Joe might soon be extinguished. But Frazier kept coming back, fighting fire with fire, even though he was being bombed at will. Encouraged by his easy target, Ali tossed kisses to the crowd before the start of the third round.

After Ali rapped Frazier on the chin with two lead lefts, the two combatants went into the ropes where Ali began talking to his shorter opponent. Frazier scored with a left to Ali's chin but the champion went into a little "Ali-bi" charade to make the crowd and Frazier think it was only a

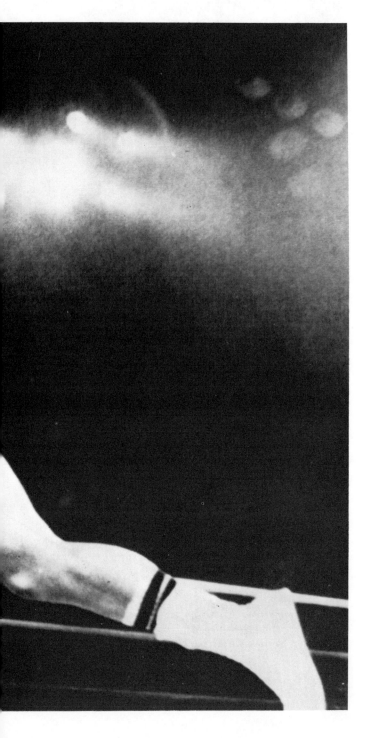

glancing blow. But it was in that fourth round that the tide started slowly turning in the other direction—toward Frazier.

Ali tagged Frazier with a left while Joe had one foot off the canvas. The force of that punch moved Joe sideways. Still, the human fireplug kept chasing the champion, withstanding the barrage and firing back.

Rounds 5, 6, and 7 were Frazier's rounds. Would Joe reclaim the crown he once held? Ali was back along the ropes, an inviting target for Frazier's smoke bombs. And Joe responded with those winging left hooks which had always been his professional calling card. A stiff left hand—perhaps Joe's single most powerful blow of the fight—was followed up in the sixth by a left-right-left. Any thoughts Ali had of a simple victory had vanished by now.

At the end of the sixth, Ali decided to rest on his stool for the first time. He knew he would have to go to his reserve tank to outdistance his opponent.

"We blew those rounds," Ali's trainer, Angelo Dundee, said. "You don't rest on the ropes against Joe Frazier . . . you take a licking."

Round 7 saw Ali, having tasted Frazier's power, get up on his toes. Ali snapped his jab. He tagged Joe with a three-punch combination in the next round but then reverted to tying him up whenever possible. The heat and the relentlessness of Frazier were both being felt by Ali's 33-year-old body. He knew how wrong his preconceptions had been. Coming out for the seventh, he told Joe, "Old Joe Frazier, why I thought you were washed up."

Frazier's reply was as pointed as one of his left hooks.

"Somebody told you all wrong, pretty boy," Frazier snapped, punctuating his remark with a bone-rattling left.

Frazier continued to take the measure of Muham-. mad, to search the depths of his ability and his will. Now, from the ninth through the twelfth rounds, Ali's rights were missing. His once-gossamer legs looked leaden. They were near the challenger's corner in round 11 when Frazier connected with a left-right-left salvo.

"I was getting him to do what I wanted him to," Frazier said. "Both of us did our duty."

That assessment showed typical Frazier modesty. They both continued to perform above and beyond the call of duty for their brutal trade.

But, in those middle rounds, Frazier kept boring in, trying to stick his head into Ali's chest. At this point, Ali was neither floating or stinging. He was surviving, barely. By the end of the tenth it was an even fight.

Frazier hammered away—hooks pounding Ali's kidneys, doubling up on hooks to body and head—as the champ

Legs and arms outstretched, Ali is clearly on the offensive as Frazier retreats, trying to see out of unseeing eyes as the end nears.

covered up along the ropes. Ali's spiritual cornerman, Drew ("Bundini") Brown, implored his boss to dig deep and turn things around.

"Force yourself, Champ!" Brown screamed. "Go down to the well once more! The world needs ya, Champ!"

While Brown's desperate coaching probably had little effect, Ali found something extra in his makeup, something which did much to reverse the now all-too-evident trend.

In round 12, Ali began an unmerciful assault which turned Frazier's head into a mass of lumps. It was a two-fisted attack which made blood trickle from the challenger's swollen mouth. Frazier's left eye was closing rapidly; the vacancy sign was going up. Ali landed five successive—and unanswered—punches at one point.

The stretch run was on and, heading for the wire, the sprinter forged ahead.

The thirteenth round saw Ali demonstrating his ability to finish a hurt foe. A solid left seemed to freeze Joe and then a less-than-overpowering right staggered him. Joe did a three-step retreat and, with his sight and his stamina now obviously limited, the outcome no longer seemed to be in doubt. Ali would be the winner unless Joe could reach even deeper than he had—unless Frazier had a home run punch left in his depleted arsenal.

Ali's slashing combinations ripped deeper and deeper into Frazier's flesh in the fourteenth round, but anyone who knew the man's record had to figure that Joe would not rescue himself, or look for help.

Ali scored with nine straight rights against his half-blind opponent. At the bell, referee Padilla helped guide Frazier back to the corner.

It was then that Futch, a 64-year-old wise man, outpointed his fighter. "Joe," Futch said, "I'm going to stop it."

Frazier, who could have retired earlier without any criticism, kept pleading. But Futch cut his gloves off. This evening, there was a sore winner and a sore loser, but there were also two self-satisfied men who undeniably had given it their best.

Left: *The impact of a Frazier punch to the midsection brings a grimace of pain across Ali's face.* Above: *Ali scores on the defenseless Frazier, the last punch of the fight.*

188

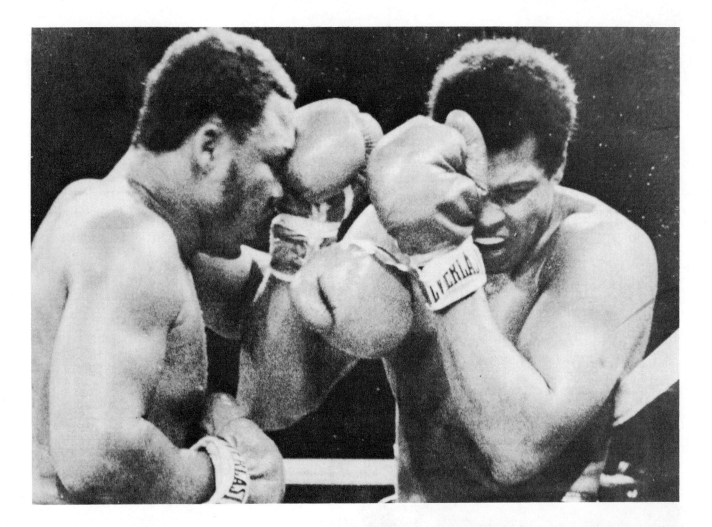

Ali spoke in whispers at a postfight news conference. There was no rhyming ridicule, only a respectful tone for the man who had made Muhammad feel he had come "next to death."

After directing his comments to Joe's 14-year-old son, Marvis—"Your father is a great man and a great fighter . . . never forget that"—Ali paid his respects to his foe, beaten but not fallen.

"I have nothing bad to say about Joe Frazier," he said hoarsely. "Without him I couldn't be who I am and without me he couldn't be who he is. We've been a pretty good team for four, five years."

The bouquet was returned in kind.

"I've seen walls tumble under shots like I gave him," Joe said. "He's a great champ."

Make that two great champs: Ali-Frazier. The hyphen belongs there. It fits. They are an historical entry. Boxing's quinella for the seventies.

Above: *Wearied by a seesaw flurry of punches, Frazier (left) and Ali protect and defend.* Right: *Surrounded by his fans, a happy but spent Ali is led to his dressing room following his successful defense of his title.*

189

George Foreman—Ron Lyle

January 24, 1976

It was, in the words of Red Smith, who had witnessed almost all of the heavyweight bouts in the more than 50 years of his career as a sportswriter, "the most two-sided battle of heavyweights in recent memory." It was the George Foreman-Ron Lyle heavyweight set-to.

The scheduled 12-round heavyweight-elimination fight between George Foreman, the former heavyweight champion, and Ron Lyle, the number-five-ranked contender, was reminiscent of a battle between two bull moose locked in heat, butting heads to protect their turf. A classic exhibition of the manly art of self-defense, it was not. It fell somewhere in between the manly art of self-destruction and a down-and-out bar fight, tempered, in part, by a hint of something right out of an old Laurel and Hardy film clip—Ollie hits Stanley in the face with a custard pie, Stanley reciprocates with a good, swift kick to the shins of the incredulous Ollie, who, in turn, plants a right to the top of the head of his willing foil, etc., etc., etc. It was, in short, a marvelous mélange of mayhem, and Foreman and Lyle played it to the hilt, turning it from a comedic sketch into a war, a war in which neither side was seeking survivors.

Foreman had not fought since he lost the heavyweight title to Muhammad Ali in "the Rumble in the Jungle" 15 months before in October 1974. That is, if you don't count his exhibition fights, including the afternoon in Toronto the previous April when he took on five different opponents in one afternoon. The "match" had all the trappings of low burlesque as Foreman "battled" a group of has-beens, never-weres, wrestlers, and even a "kissing bandit," parading around the ring as boxers. It was such a low blow to Foreman's already shaky psyche that he exited the ring, stage left, after his episode with the five dwarfs, and remained inactive for yet another nine months—a proper gestation period for him to put together a new fighting "family," including the veteran Gil Clancy and trainer Kid Rapidez, and embark upon a comeback in quest of the heavyweight championship he viewed as his.

"I think 1976 is going to be the year of George Fore-

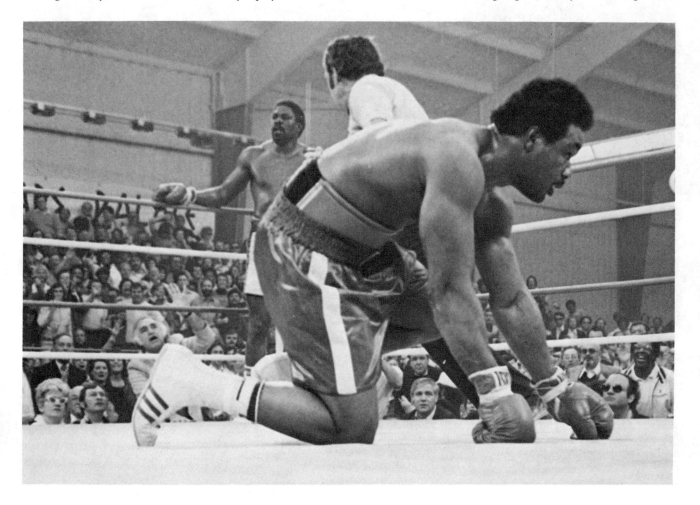

Opposite: *Former heavyweight champ George Foreman (right) goes down in the fourth round after a Ron Lyle assault.* Above: *Foreman regains his footing as the upright Lyle will soon become upright downright.*

man," the 27-year-old ex-champ intoned solemnly to those who were willing to listen. "I think with the bicentennial coming up, it's going to mean a lot to me. I feel I have a lot to do with the image of the United States," the man who had once carried America's colors around the Olympic ring immodestly continued. Now waving the flag again, he also admitted to having something to do with "the image of young people as well. And, if I can lose the title in one year, and win it back in 1976, it will inspire George Foreman to do a lot of other things."

George's reference to his self-perceived all-American image dated back to his glory days at the 1968 Olympics in Mexico City, when he held a tiny, American flag in his mas-sive hand—in contrast to other black athletes who chose, in-stead, to hold up a black-gloved black-power salute, after their victories.

Born in Marshall, Texas, on January 10, 1949, the fifth of seven children born to a railroad-construction work-er, George was somewhat of a delinquent as a youngster. A high school dropout, he spent two years hanging around street corners, contemplating wayward acts. In his own words, "You name it, I'd done it." George then joined America's Job Corps, and was sent to Fort Vannoy Conser-vation Center in Oregon, where he learned the trades of ma-sonry and carpentry.

There George learned the boxing trade as well. Doc

Broadus, Parks Job Corp Center vocational guidance director, noticed George's size and speed while watching him play football and persuaded him to try his hand at boxing. That was the start of something—something big.

In 1967, Foreman terminated this training in the Job Corps after winning the national Amateur Athletic Union heavyweight title in Toledo, Ohio, a victory which assured him a spot on the 10-man Olympic team selected to compete in Mexico.

His Gold Medal accomplishment at Mexico behind him, Foreman held back his pro debut until June 1969. George fought at regular intervals, winning most of his fights against nonentities in a few rounds, his most impor-

tant victory coming over durable and tough George Chuvalo, the perennial Canadian champion, whom he destroyed in fewer than three full rounds.

On January 22, 1973, in Kingston, Jamaica, Foreman challenged the undefeated heavyweight champion for the title. Frazier, a 3–1 favorite, was floored six times by Foreman, before referee Arthur Mercante mercifully stepped in to stop the slaughter at 1:35 of the second round.

Foreman's first title defense was in Tokyo on September 1, 1973, against someone called Joe ("King") Roman, the Puerto Rican heavyweight champion, a questionable designation, at best. The fight was over in two minutes of the first round. The powerful champ smashed the inept Roman to the canvas three times with devastating right-hand blows, one time even resorting to the unnecessary tactic of hitting Roman after he was down.

Foreman's second title defense came on March 26, 1974, in Caracas, Venezuela, and ended in two minutes of the second round, when he sent challenger Ken Norton to the canvas with such a thud that his trainer, Bill Slayton, personally jumped into the ring to halt the mismatch.

But Foreman, the indestructible, came tumbling down from his seemingly unassailable perch, on October 29, 1974, in Kinshasa, Zaire, when Muhammad Ali "rope-a-doped" his way to an eighth-round knockout, making Ali the second man in heavyweight history to recapture the heavyweight title.

Now George, having suffered the slings and arrows of his once-idolatrous public, was determined to make a serious comeback. His choice for an opponent was Ron Lyle. The sinister-looking Lyle had been, by his own admission, "to hell and back." The third of 19 children, Lyle spent 7½ years of a 15-25-year sentence for second degree murder at the Colorado State Penitentiary, in Canon City, where once, after a prison brawl, the seriously injured Lyle had been declared "clinically dead," only to survive.

His life in the ring was also one of survival, his career a series of comebacks. "I've made so many comebacks in and out of the ring that I've lost count," stated Lyle. "When I was twenty, I was cut up in a gang fight and pronounced dead, but I came back. All those years in a jail cell, and I came back, all the way to a title shot with Ali. I lost to Ali, but I came back to knock out Earnie Shavers. I lost to Jerry Quarry, and came back to beat Oscar Bonavena and Jimmy Ellis."

Ron Lyle began boxing professionally in 1971. After four years, he had won 29, while losing only 2 with 1 draw and 20 knockouts, good enough to earn him a title shot with Muhammad Ali. Lyle stunned the experts by outscoring Ali, and was leading on all cards through the first 10 rounds, be-

A benumbed Caesars Palace crowd watches as Lyle goes to the canvas in the fifth round, and stays.

193

fore succumbing to an Ali attack and being stopped on his feet in the eleventh round in his only fight since he had stopped dangerous Earnie Shavers in six. Thus, it was to be a "comeback" for both warriors.

The first round was very slow as the two dinosaurs circled, sizing up each other. Suddenly, a sneak right hit Foreman so hard that his pants almost fell off. As his trunks drooped dangerously low, Foreman staggered around the ring like a drunk on ice. The bell rang, saving George from further embarrassment. And harassment.

Rounds 2 and 3 were Foreman rounds, but just slightly, as Lyle spent a lot of time trapped in the corners, and not doing much about it. Foreman seemed to justify the 5–2 odds favoring him by popping away at Lyle, but not inflicting any apparent damage. By the end of the third round, Lyle's eye was getting a little puffy. But that was the extent of the damage done.

Incidentally, the second round lasted only two minutes, a development later confirmed by timekeeper John Worth. He said the round was shortened by a minute due to a malfunction of a timeclock used by ABC-TV, which he wrongly recognized instead of the official timer at the Sports Pavillion of the Caesars Palace Hotel.

The malfunction might have cost Foreman an earlier victory because at the two-minute mark of the second round Foreman had Lyle on the ropes and in apparent trouble. Another few monster right hands from the ex-champ and the afternoon might have ended earlier.

The fourth round was another story. Stunned by a right early in the round, Foreman went down like a sack of wheat, landing flat on his head, as if he were trying to get into a yoga position. He got up hurt and angry, and fired a roundhouse right that dislodged Lyle's mouthpiece. A left hook knocked Lyle under the lowest rope. Lyle got up with a look that said, "OK, now it's my turn." And it was! A wild left-right dropped Foreman on his shoulder. Everyone, including promoter Don King, who was in attendance—and hollering, "Now we won't have to deal with Foreman anymore"—thought it was over. But the bell saved the fallen Foreman.

Foreman's new manager, Gil Clancy, laid down the law to Foreman between rounds. "He's hurt and you're hurt," Clancy said. "The one that's gonna win is the one who wants it most." He thrust his rigid forefinger into Foreman's massive chest. "Do you want it most?"

"Sure I do, Gil," Foreman answered. But when he got off his stool for the fatal fifth, his knees quivered.

The two nearly spent beasts met, horns bared in midring, and commenced pummeling each other. A left hook drove Lyle's mouthpiece out of his mouth.

"When the mouthpiece went," Lyle said, "I lost control of my breathing for a while. That was the main thing. It split earlier in the week, and it was too late to have a new one made."

Thirty seconds later a barrage of blows from Foreman caught Lyle in his corner. Lyle seemed about to pitch forward on his face. When a man lands on his face he hardly ever gets up. Lyle didn't, and it was over at 2:28 of the fifth round.

"It was definitely the toughest fight I ever had," Foreman said afterward. "It could have gone either way. But I think I showed a lot of determination. I proved I have a little heart, and I could have gotten up in Africa too," alluding to the Ali knockout.

"But this time I got some instructions on what to do if I got hurt," said George, referring to Clancy, "and I didn't look in any corner. I knew I had to get up. When I went down I said, . . . please forgive me for saying this, 'I'll be God-damned if somebody is going to knock me out.'"

The referee, Charlie Roth, doubted if George would have beaten the count at the end of the fourth. "I thought he was done for," said Roth. "I didn't think George was going to get up the first time or the second time. He was out on his feet."

"When I got knocked down the second time," George continued, "I felt I paid my dues. I actually thought, I swear it, 'Joe Louis got knocked down sometimes, and he came back to win.' I felt embarrassed and angry, and it gave me more energy."

Foreman blamed his poor performance on inactivity. "I've got to stay more active. No doubt about it. I want to be champion again, but you can't be out fifteen months like I was. You have to be active to be in top-level form. I was rusty. Inactivity means you're this far from missing [taking] a punch, and when it doesn't miss you get hit."

Lyle appeared shaky when he walked to the platform for the news conference after the fight, stumbling up to take his position behind the microphones. But he said, "I'll keep fighting. This one could have gone either way. Like George said, 'You've got to get up.' I couldn't."

Foreman concluded, "I want to be champion again, and if it takes knocking everybody out, I will. I say the world loves a winner, and people are going to be kissing me for a long time." It was a long time—five more fights—before Foreman found himself being kissed-off, after losing to Jimmy Young, and kissing boxing goodbye forever. But it was all to be anticlimactic after his brawl with Lyle.

Writer Len Koppett was asked after the fight if he ever saw anyone fight like Foreman and Lyle just had. "Sure," said Len. "John Garfield, many times."

Larry Holmes—Ken Norton

June 9, 1978

Mention the name Ken Norton and trivia buffs will recall him as the only heavyweight champion in the long history of boxing who never won a title fight. His "tenure" came courtesy of a World Boxing Council edict, stripping the biggest prize in boxing from the shoulders of then-champion Leon Spinks, a ukase which elevated Norton to the top of the division—momentarily—and provided an opportunity for a little-known fighter from Easton, Pennsylvania, named Larry Holmes to emerge as the best of the big men in the post-Ali era.

In the more than 250 years of boxing history the heavyweight division has withstood all attempts at championship vivisection. Well, almost all. For even the most visible prize in all of sportsdom has experienced its "paper" champions before. Those synthetic champions—the ones who gained their version of the title without defeating the previous champion in the ring—were given the same credi-

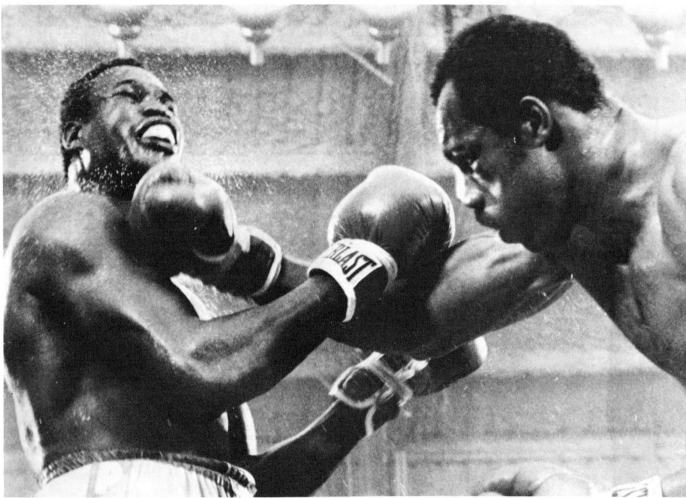

Preceding page: *In the first defense of the crown "given" him by the WBC, heavyweight Ken Norton (left) throws a left to the chest of Larry Holmes.* Top: *Challenger Holmes (left) backs away after having "eaten leather."* Above: *Holmes survived blows like this to win a split decision.*

bility as the Easter Bunny. Marvin Hart, Jimmy Ellis, and Ernie Terrell were virtually ignored by the public and the sporting press alike. They were champions created in vacuums, and on paper only. Ezzard Charles, who beat Jersey Joe Walcott for the vacant crown after Joe Louis retired as the undefeated champion, was not accepted until he defeated the Brown Bomber on his way to a comeback. And Jack Johnson had to do the same to Jim Jeffries before he gained universal recognition. The purists even regarded Floyd Patterson, who captured the vacant heavyweight title by beating Archie Moore after Rocky Marciano retired, as something less than the real thing.

But it wasn't until the 1970s—a decade of highly sophisticated fakery, when human beings were cloned, throwaway dishes became "in," and everyone became a hero for 10 seconds—that the public was willing to recognize two heavyweight champions of one world. Even at that, it took one of the most explosive ring wars ever waged in boxing's glamour division to transform the ersatz crown the WBC hastily conferred on Ken Norton into the genuine article; it took 15 rounds of marvelous mayhem between "champion"

Ken Norton and challenger Larry Holmes on June 9, 1978.

The first crack in the heavyweight crown came on September 28, 1976, when reigning champion Muhammad Ali barely retained his title on a highly controversial 15-round decision over Ken Norton in Yankee Stadium. It was the third meeting between these two warriors, and all three bouts had been decided by the most microscopic of margins. In spite of the fact that Ali had defeated Norton twice, the public and the press remained dissatisfied and began clamoring for a fourth fight.

Despite the increasing pressure, Ali bypassed Norton to fight pushover Alfredo Evangelista and the aging Earnie Shavers. Both times he won in an unimpressive fashion, and rather than risk his swiftly eroding skills again against Norton—who had pounded the previously undefeated Duane Bobick into plowshares the previous February in 59 seconds—Ali began looking for other worlds he could easily conquer, or slip by.

Recognized as the champion by both the World Boxing Association and the World Boxing Council (the two self-appointed governing bodies that sanction title bouts), Ali could do what he wanted with his crown, or so he thought. Then the WBC ordered Ali to fight the winner of the November 5, 1977, 15-round title elimination bout between Norton and Jimmy Young in Las Vegas. Ali reluctantly agreed and signed a letter of intent with the WBC powers-that-be. Norton decisioned Young in a close, controversial split verdict that put Ken in line for yet another crack at the heavyweight championship.

Both Norton and Jimmy Young were under contract to promoter Don King, who was waging a pitched battle against his arch rival Bob Arum for control of the most lucrative division in boxing. Control in this instance meant

Above: *Holmes misses a blow and Norton follows through in torrid fifteenth-round action.* Right: *Norton appears to have the upper hand—then the judges' decision came in.*

197

control of Ali, the biggest draw in professional sports. While King was licking his chops in anticipation of a second Ali-Norton title bout, Arum stepped forward with an offer for Muhammad to defend his crown against Leon Spinks, the 1976 Olympic gold medal winner in the light-heavyweight class who had only seven fights under his belt, including a draw with mediocre Scott Ledoux. Ali, who at this point was having great difficulty in maintaining his once-superb physique in the face of increasing age and decreasing regimen, opted for the less lucrative but supposedly easier match against the young and inexperienced Spinks.

On February 15, 1978, Spinks shocked the world by defeating the inflated ghost of the formerly great champion in Las Vegas and became universally recognized heavyweight champion.

The upset and the prospect of a multimillion-dollar rematch placed Arum on top of the heavyweight heap and left King holding a useless option on an Ali-Norton fight. It might have ended there, except for that letter of intent which Ali had signed for WBC president José Sulaiman to order Spinks, the now undisputed champion, to meet Ali's commitment; in other words, to force Spinks to make his first defense against Norton instead of giving Ali a rematch. The end result was that the WBC decided to withdraw its recognition of Spinks as the heavyweight champion because he

chose to give Ali, instead of Norton, an immediate rematch. This left Spinks as a demichampion, recognized only by the WBA, and left Sulaiman's group with the problem of what to do with the suddenly vacant WBC heavyweight championship. They elected to place their version of the crown on the head of Ken Norton, making him the champion on the basis of his win over Young.

Promoter King, still in possession of an option on "champion" Norton's services, immediately set up a "title" defense for Ken against one Larry Holmes, an undefeated contender and a loyal member of the King's court. The 28-year-old Holmes, who had been knocked out by Duane Bobick in the amateurs and done service as Ali's sparring partner, jumped toward the top of the heavyweight rankings one month after Spinks defeated Ali, when he totally dominated powerful veteran contender Earnie Shavers in Las Vegas, winning a near-shutout decision.

In spite of his perfect 27–0 record and the win over Shavers, the 6-foot 3-inch tall "Easton Assassin" was not highly regarded in boxing circles. For all of his 19 knockouts in 27 outings, Holmes was said to lack real power, and coming off his loss to Bobick—when he "retired" without hollering "*no más*"—he supposedly lacked courage as well.

Ken Norton, who admitted to being nearly 33 years old when he made his first and only title defense, was rated

a slight 7–5 favorite to defeat Holmes by the Las Vegas odds-makers. In a division where fighters mature late, Norton was probably at his peak, riding high after his important victories over Bobick and Young the year before. For all of his very real punching power—most of it concentrated in a lethal overhand right—Ken had a curious forward-moving crablike style, one which gave stylists like Ali trouble, but also made it difficult for Ken to back up, putting him in trouble with fighters who came straight at him, like George Foreman.

A capacity crowd of 4,500 was on hand at the Caesars Palace Sports Pavillion in Las Vegas on a warm spring night, with an additional 1,500 fans watching the fight on closed-circuit television in the hotel and millions more tuning in on network television. The requisite menagerie of celebrities and boxing luminaries was on hand, but a lot of the talk during the preliminary action focused on the upcoming September Ali-Spinks rematch in the New Orleans Superdome, for the *real* heavyweight championship of the world. From Norton and Holmes they expected a good heavyweight contest, a boxer-puncher confrontation that might produce some pleasing action, but promised little in the way of greatness. Besides, this was for the "paper" crown, not the real one.

The fight started slowly enough, with Holmes moving constantly around the ring behind a left jab that startled the *cognoscenti* with its accuracy and deadly force. Expectations of early fireworks from Norton, who had blown out Duane Bobick in less time than it takes to say "Great White Hope," were quickly dashed, as Ken employed extreme patience and caution in the opening heat.

Norton, an awesome physical specimen and a proven 15-round fighter, had a habit of electing to deliberately take it easy during certain portions of a fight. A weak finish cost him the third fight with Earnie Shavers. Against Holmes he chose to let Larry take the early lead, hoping for the inexperienced challenger to wear down during the final five frames.

The surprising potency of Holmes' left jab became apparent in the second frame. In quick succession he jolted Ken with a right-left thrown like a jab that was as hard as a hook. Norton's left eye began to swell up.

Norton trotted out his vaunted right in round 3. Holmes rattled his teeth with a triple jab—bing!—bing!—bam! The champion lurched at him, swinging a big right that Larry easily eluded. Again Norton unleashed his thunderous, ponderous right and missed the mark. The challenger made him pay dearly with a wicked right to the ear.

Norton began to pay more attention to the threat posed by Larry's long left hand by covering his face with his gloves in his patented crablike stance when he was not on the attack. He continued to move forward in low gear, dragging his right leg and using his peculiar crossed-arms guard, a technique copied crudely from Archie Moore. Occasionally he lashed out wildly with the right. All the while Holmes jabbed and jabbed, piling up points.

The action heated up a few degrees in the fifth frame. Norton finally hit the target with a heavy right. Holmes took the punch without blinking and responded with three rapier jabs. Then it happened: Holmes attacked for the first time with a left-right-left salvo and Norton came back with a wild right uppercut. The crowd applauded as Holmes did an Ali shuffle; and indeed, for that one moment, when he clipped Norton with three quick, hard punches, he looked like his idol had, stunning slow Sonny Liston with lightning volleys in their first meeting.

With five rounds gone Ken Norton began to realize that he was giving away the title that had been given to him as a gift. Holmes was pitching a shutout, winning every round with a left jab, or rather many left jabs and constant lateral movement.

Norton acted to alter the flow of the fight in round 6. He abandoned his overhand right lead, which had proven sterile, in favor of his own vastly underrated left jab. And he began to crowd Holmes against the ropes, backing him

Opposite: *Ken Norton (left) connects with Holmes' digestive tract.* Above: *Larry Holmes demonstrates the surprising potency of his punches, pounding out a close decision.*

Norton covers up in anticipation of Holmes' pumping jabs.

tant to try another attack on the injured Norton.

The momentum of the fight swung sharply in Norton's direction in round 8. The challenger's defense began to crumble as punches came at him in bunches: combinations, hooks off of the jab, a big overhand right, and a punishing straight left.

Holmes' great legs were still working in round 9, but his jab stopped pumping. Norton walked straight at him. A big right crashed into Larry's face like a bag of bricks dropped from a second-story window. Holmes was bleeding from the mouth and looked fatigued. In the tenth frame Norton delivered a left hook to the head that hurt Larry. Holmes' lead was melting like a stack of chips on one of the roulette tables at Caesars Palace.

After 10 rounds Ken Norton had the fight about where he wanted it, with the outcome to be decided in the final five frames—in the so-called "championship" rounds.

up with stiff jabs and double jabs and following up with vicious rights to the body when he had his quarry cornered. Holmes seemed to wilt under the first sign of pressure. Norton stepped up his pace another notch. He chased Larry all over the ring, scoring with a brutal left hook to the body, a right to the liver, and a left hook to the head as the challenger tried to hold him off with his jab.

After six rounds Larry Holmes had raised a grotesque swelling around Norton's left eye. Sensing that he might not last the distance, the "champion" tried to inflict some real damage in round 7. His punches were intelligently distributed, everything working off of the jab. Holmes' own jabbing offense was largely nullified, but he seemed reluc-

Top: *Recoiling from the impact, Norton seems vulnerable to Holmes' fifteenth-round artillery.* Above: *The fifteenth round was worthy of determining the outcome of the title fight.* Right: *Despite the beating he was taking, Norton rallied for an incredible fourteenth-round comeback.*

201

But Norton did not look like a happy warrior. Memories of too many close decisions—of a cold, wet autumn night in Yankee Stadium—haunted him. He wanted to knock Holmes out. And in the eleventh round he almost did. Norton ripped away with both hands. But somehow the challenger escaped. The bicycle that he had ridden for 11 rounds was traded in for a motorcycle. The crowd, which had thus far favored the underdog, Holmes, booed as they saw what they thought was simply the dog coming out in the challenger.

Ken Norton, born under the sign of Leo, with the astrological symbol of the lion emblazoned on his robe, was the king of the jungle in round 12, as Holmes tired rapidly. Two big rights collided with Larry's skull. Norton was also tired. His punches were wide and slow, but he was still dangerous as the round drew to a close. The champion had rallied to win five of the last six rounds.

In the thirteenth round Larry Holmes decided that he wanted to be a world champion. First came the jabs as he resumed pumping a steady stream of them at the oncoming Norton. The champion refused to back off. He walloped Larry to the body. As Ken rushed in, Holmes launched a rocket of a right hand! Quickly he followed up with a right, another right, and a left. They were hard punches to the head, but Norton shrugged them off. Holmes attacked again with a right uppercut and a straight right, then pumped both hands to the head. Norton staggered forward into the mouth of the beast. Holmes punished his audacity with a left-right combination to the head and a blinding flurry of punches. It was raining leather wherever Norton chose to stand, and he was barely able to do that.

In the wake of such a beating, it seemed unlikely that aging Ken Norton, a veteran of 11 years of legal violence, would have the strength to do much more than survive. Holmes, with youth and suddenly renewed confidence, seemed destined for victory.

Cus D'Amato's maxim, that "boxing is a contest of will and skill, with the will generally overcoming the skill, unless the skill of one man is much greater than the skill of the other," was never more true than in the final three rounds of this incredible heavyweight championship contest. It was willpower that fathered an unbelievable rally by Ken Norton in the fourteenth round.

The tornado that nearly blew Larry Holmes away began with a right lead that jarred the challenger. Twice Norton rattled Larry's teeth with right uppercuts. He doubled up a left hook—going to body and head—as Holmes beat a quick retreat. Norton stalked after him, trapping him in a neutral corner. Again and again the "champion" dug left hooks to the body, and lashed out with punches from both sides to the head. At the bell Norton unloaded a right up-

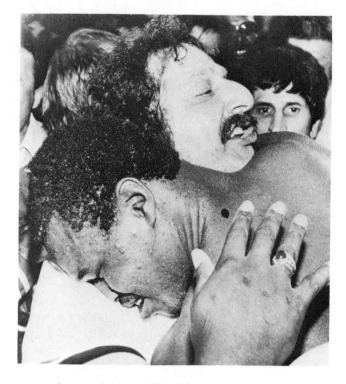

percut that nearly drove Holmes' teeth through the roof of his mouth.

The best, and the worst, was yet to come. Even those who had not bothered to keep a running score sensed that the fight would be decided in the final three minutes. Movie directors make films of fights that are merely bland facsimiles of the fifteenth round of the Norton-Holmes fight. It was, quite simply, the most violent finale in heavyweight title history. Skill and finesse were irrelevant. Both fighters were too weary and too damaged to do anything but stand in the center of the ring and take turns using each other's head as a tether ball, which is what they did for three full minutes. First it was Norton, still riding the crest of his fourteenth-round tidal wave. A right exploded under Holmes' jaw. Ken followed it with another bazooka that hurt the challenger. Norton jabbed at him, setting up a titanic right uppercut that might have launched Holmes' head into orbit, had it landed.

Now it was Larry's turn—Ken walloped the challenger's body. Holmes raged back at him, almost snarling as he whipped a left and a right into the champion's head. They stood head-to-head, lurching and leaning as they swapped punches. Holmes connected with a brutal right uppercut. Norton retaliated with a double hook to the body and head. Holmes found the strength for a final rally with 60 seconds left on the clock. In the final minute he battered the weary "champion" with both hands, snapping his head back and

Holmes, the champion, is embraced by his then-manager, Richie Giachetti, after Holmes won the fight.

buckling his knees. At the final gong Norton got in the last big lick—a right to the head. The crowd erupted in a standing ovation.

It was a fifteenth round worthy of determining the outcome of a heavyweight title fight, and it did. Judges Harold Buck and Joe Swessel had Larry Holmes on top by only one point after 15 seesaw rounds, 143–142. Judge Lou Tabot, the only official to give Norton the last round, saw it 144–143 for Ken. It was that close.

But if it proved anything, it proved that neither Norton nor Holmes should ever again be considered "paper" champs. Not after *that* fight.

Doused with water and thronged by well-wishers, Holmes celebrates his WBC world heavyweight title.

Roberto Duran—Sugar Ray Leonard

June 20, 1980

There are certain indicators which serve as scales of measurement, like barometers, which are based on scientific, or quasi-scientific techniques, just as the Richter is used for measuring seismographic tremors, the Dow-Jones average is used for measuring the stock market, and the Nielsen rating system is used for measuring the size of a television audience. The list goes on and on.

Then there are other indicators, every bit as reliable, if not as scientific. Every child remembers Uncle Wiggley's rheumatism which gauged the coming of a storm more often than not; political buffs can prognosticate the winner of the quadrennial election by the number of syllables in the candidates' last names, the winner being the candidate with the most syllables in all but two cases since 1900; and baseball-political followers can call the outcome of the fall election, for almost every time a Republican presidential candidate has won the national election, the American League has won that fall's World Series. And there is the "boxing-cum-economics" scale. It seems that whenever there is a financial downturn—whether it be a recession or a depression—the bout of the year is in the lighter divisions.

Sure, heavyweights dominate the scene. Especially in good times. During the Roaring Twenties, the heavyweight division was *the* focal point of boxing, just as it was during the "go-go" sixties and the early seventies. But the very day the stock market crashed, October 29, 1929—known forever after as "Black Tuesday"—there was a middleweight-title fight between Mickey Walker and Ace Hudkins. Not only was there no heavyweight title fight in 1929, there was not even a heavyweight champion—Gene Tunney had retired the previous year and no successor had taken his place for two more. In 1980, when all other indicators measured what the politicians would not tell us—that we were in the grips of another recession—the fight of the year was in the welterweight division: the Roberto Duran versus Sugar Ray Leonard welterweight championship battle.

On the one hand there was Sugar Ray Leonard, the darling of the electronic media, 25 years old, and the 1976 Olympic Gold Medal winner in the 140-pound class, coming home to Montreal where his fantastic career had started. The winner of 145 out of 150 amateur fights and 27 straight professional fights, the Sugarman was facing the legendary "Hands of Stone," Roberto Duran, who had won 70 out of 71 professional fights, ruled the lightweight division for nine years and had 55 knockouts, with 18 first-round knockouts, matching Sugar Ray's *entire* knockout total. It was the match for 1980, if not for the ages.

Vince Lombardi, sports' premier winner, was always so sure of his success that his strategy consisted of but one tactic: "I'll give the other team my game plan and plays. If

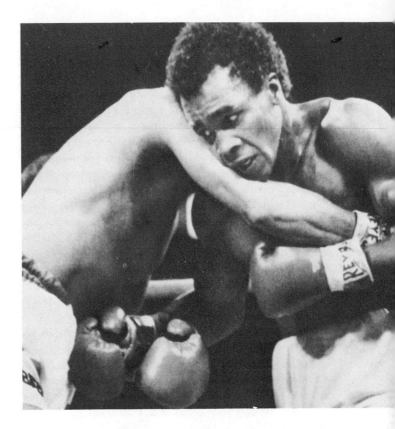

they can stop them, they'll win; if they can't, I'll win."

Sugar Ray Leonard tried the exact same approach in his first fight with Duran. Only this time, Roberto Duran stopped it and won.

The difference between Lombardi and Leonard was singlefold: Lombardi was talking about using *his* strengths, not the other guy's. He was challenging his opponent to make the mistakes, and taking advantage of him when he didn't respond correctly. Leonard, on the other hand, was determined to use his opponent's strength, not his own. Therein lies the underlying weakness in Sugar Ray's battle plan.

And so, he of the lightning fists and well-defined moves inexplicably took on the man with the hands of stone and the straightforward, but subtle, moves in a deadly game—a game of "machismo." And, as it seemed he must, Sugar Ray lost. He lost not only because the word "macho" is a Spanish word meaning "courage and aggressiveness," but because he was destined to lose playing another man's game: a game which played into Duran's hands "of stone."

The battle plan against Duran was Sugar Ray's idea. And his alone. "I surprised a lot of people with my tactics," he was to say after the fight. "I fought Duran in a way I thought I could beat him." Angelo Dundee concurred, say-

Opposite: Roberto Duran, on the offensive, pins the champion on the ropes.
Above right: Sugar Ray Leonard (right) shows the strain of nine rounds with Roberto Duran in their WBC welterweight title fight.

205

ing only that "it was his plan. He had it in his head that he was stronger than Duran." Even before the man with the plan entered the ring, Roberto Duran had scored the first punch, psychologically. Entering the ring a full two minutes before the World Boxing Council welterweight champion, Duran had beamed to the crowd and his handlers and followers had unfurled the Quebec liberation flag. It was to be his last smile of the night. He would waste none on the Sugarman, who entered the ring to the shouts of the patrons in the $20 seats, sitting somewhere North of Moose Jaw in the upper reaches of the same Olympic stadium where just four years before Leonard had become the darling of the 1976 Olympics. Now, in his best laid-back manner, he bowed respectfully to all four corners—*Nord, Est, Sud, et Ouest*—the sound of adulation drenching the ring, much like the cloudburst which had just drenched the 46,317 fight fans who had turned out to see what was billed as the "Fight of the Decade," just six months into the new decade. It was a build-up soon to be acquitted by the fight to follow.

But rain as it did on the more than 46,000 fans, it was not to rain on Roberto Duran's parade because very shortly after the first bell it became evident he intended to dominate the action, and Sugar Ray intended to allow him to do so. The man who had subordinated so many other fighters to his own purposes rushed, bulled, and grabbed inside, all the better to tie up the faster-moving Leonard and land his own body punches.

Before the fight, many had wondered about the selection of Carlos Padilla as the referee. His historic approach to a fight had been to break the two combatants whenever they got close enough to touch. Now, probably stemming from Ray Arcel's impassioned plea before the fight ("You're good . . . I only hope you let my boy fight his fight inside"), Padilla employed a hands-off policy, letting the bull and the matador get gored. It was Duran's kind of fight.

In the second round Duran bulled Leonard back to the ropes and landed one bonito right to Sugar's head. He then fell inside to follow up his advantage and his bulling.

Round 3 looked much the same: Duran inside and Leonard landing underneath. But Duran was the aggressor at all times, aggressor being the operative word in the definition of "macho."

By round 4 Leonard, for the first time, held his distance and forced Duran back to the ropes. But the rest of the round—if not the rest of the fight—found Duran crowding in, following Arcel's directive "not to let Leonard do anything, to keep him up against the ropes." Dundee's advice to Leonard ("Slip in and out, in and out") went unheeded.

As the middle rounds progressed, both battlers went

at it, toe-to-toe. And even though this was Duran's type of fight, now Leonard was landing more often and with more telling punches. The nonstop action—made even more nonstop by Padilla's refusal to break while there was anything resembling a loose hand showing—incited the fans to constant screaming, the Panamanian delegation shouting, "*Arriba, cholo.*" And the Leonard followers shouting, "Pour it on, Sugar."

Leonard was scoring. Sometimes heavily underneath as he caught Duran charging in. Several times he pulled his patented flurries and once even got away with an accentuated bolo. But it was Duran's aggressiveness that dictated—and, at times, even dominated—the fight, as he charged, pushed, punched, and even butted Leonard in the ninth round.

Coming down the stretch, Leonard fetched many a good right solidly on Duran's "macho"—and untrimmed—jaw. But all he got in return was a sneer from the Satanic-looking Panamanian, who then tore back into Leonard for more of the same. The pace and the noise continued unabated throughout the last two rounds, two rounds which Duran conceded to Leonard, so sure now of his imminent victory.

When the final bell sounded, Leonard extended his hands in friendship. Duran, macho to the end, did the only thing a macho man would: he walked past the man he hated with a passion that burned deep within him, and threw up his hands in exultation.

That exultation was premature, but correct. For when the decision was announced—148–147, 145–144, and 146–144, including 19 "draw" rounds amongst the three officials—Duran was the new *campeon del mundo* in as close, and exciting, a fight as boxing had ever seen.

Roberto Duran was, as always, proud in victory; he said after the fight, "I proved myself the better fighter." His interpreter, Louis Enriques, boastfully added, "Duran over Leonard, [General Omar] Torrijos over [President] Carter, and Panama over America."

And so, just as the Panama Canal passed to Panama in 1979, the welterweight title passed to Panama in 1980. Maybe that's what the two stars on the Panamanian flag truly symbolize: the blue for the waters of the Panama Canal and the red for the strength and skill of Roberto Duran.

For Leonard, there was another day, another fight with Duran—Montreal redux. And for that one he remembered another of Vince Lombardi's mottoes: "Winning isn't everything, it's the *only* thing." And he remembered again, five months later in New Orleans when he forced Roberto to throw up his hands in the eighth round more in frustration than hurt and yell, "*No más, no más.*"

Matthew Saad Muhammad-Yaqui Lopez

July 13, 1980

In one of the greatest fights a reporter could ever hope to cover, in one of the most spectacular fights a fan could ever dream of watching, Matthew Saad Muhammad retained his world light-heavyweight title for the fourth time, stopping fired-up challenger Alvaro ("Yaqui") Lopez in 2:03 of the fourteenth round after flooring him a total of four times during that round.

It was a dramatic ending to what had been a dramatic, seesaw, punch-filled, glorious fight at the Great Gorge Playboy Club.

Lopez, weighing 174¾ pounds, trained for a rough fight. He came to Great Gorge to take away Muhammad's title. To decision him. To knock him out. To cut him up. To win the title.

Muhammad, weighing 174¼ pounds, trained for his fight with an intensity he had never shown before, which was remarkable for a man who pushed himself in training all the time. It was as if he knew the fight would demand the best effort he had ever given, despite the fact he had stopped Lopez in October 1978.

For the first seven rounds, both fighters took turns punching the other around and being the aggressor. Early in the bout, Muhammad suffered a slight cut above his right eye. Lopez sustained a slice on the bridge of his nose in round 3. Neither cut determined the outcome of the fight—ferocity did.

The fierceness of the contest demanded three minutes of action in every round by both contestants. Three minutes per round is what they gave. For the first seven rounds, fans—and even hardened reporters—applauded the action. Then, unbelievably, the fight became even more exciting!

Going into round 8, judge Paul Cavaliere had Lopez in the lead, 4–2–1. Judge Emile Brunette and referee Waldemar Schmidt had Lopez leading 5–2. The *Ring* magazine card had it 4–3 Lopez at that point.

Round 8 must be written into the books as one of the most sensational, exciting rounds ever fought. Ever!

After being stung by a hook to the head early in the eighth, Lopez came back to nearly knock out the champion midway through the round, only to nearly get knocked out himself in the closing moments of the round.

Lopez hurt Muhammad with a hook flush on the chin, and began to taste a world title in this, his fourth attempt to win one.

Despite the pleas from his corner to "draw back and box," Lopez, 28, unloaded both hands against Muhammad. A left. A right. A left. A right. Every punch—nearly two dozen—crashed against the champion's jaw, the champion's head, the champion's face. The champion wavered, he staggered, he buckled. But the 26-year-old champion would not

fall. Not only did he remain on his feet, he came back punching with both hands to stagger and nearly drop the challenger. At the bell, the 1,300 fans in the Playboy Club Convention Center roared with the intensity of a crowd 10 times as large.

Round 9 saw the action slow, but only in comparison to the incredible pace both fighters had set through the first eight rounds. Both men were tired. Both men were hurt. But it was Muhammad—not Lopez—who recovered from the viciousness of round 8. Lopez won the round. He won that individual battle, but he lost the war in doing so. Lopez had punched himself out. His zip was gone. So was his long-burning hope of finally winning a title.

Lopez fought hard, but against this gritty, determined champion, he needed more. Much more. Like a child's windup toy, Lopez began to move more slowly. His legs lost their bounce, his punches their snap. Muhammad began to land with more frequency.

Approximately midway through round 14, Lopez was rocked by an overhand right. A right uppercut then dropped him. He was up at the count of eight, but went down again moments later from another right.

Again Lopez was up at eight, and again he ran into a right that sent him to the canvas. Referee Schmidt watched Lopez closely as the veteran contender rose at three. As the fight resumed—the three-knockdown rule had been waived—Schmidt continued to watch Lopez closely. Muhammad moved in; so did Schmidt. A sharp right to the chin dumped Lopez near the ropes. Again he arose, using the ropes to pull himself to his feet. But this time, Schmidt waved his arms. The fight was over at 2:03.

Afterward, Lopez said about the champion, "He is not a great fighter. He is a great puncher!"

When asked what happened in the eighth round, Lopez said, "I hit him [Muhammad] some good shots but he just didn't go down. That's why he's champion."

Muhammad—who did not appear before the press for 90 minutes after the fight—admitted he was in trouble during that eighth round, but "knew where I was." He said, "I knew I'd come back, and I did."

The victory upped the champion's record to 27–3–2. For Lopez, it was his tenth loss in 59 fights.

In New York's Gleason's Gym two days after the fight, Lopez put the championship bout in perspective better than anybody.

"It was a sensational fight," said the man who helped make it so. "You have no idea of how I wanted the title. But Saad Muhammad just wanted it more. It wasn't so much a case of me losing the fight as it was Saad Muhammad winning it."

Preceding page: *WBC light-heavyweight champion Matthew Saad Muhammad in typical victory pose.*

Yaqui Lopez sits on the mat after being knocked down by Saad Muhammad in the fourteenth round. Afterward Lopez said, "He is a great puncher."

Sugar Ray Leonard—Thomas Hearns

September 16, 1981

That blockbuster mentality that makes every fight sound like the Second Coming—and has given us enough "Fights of the Century" to take us through the era of Buck Rogers, 2400 A.D., has now given us a lesser celestial happening called The Showdown. But a recent performance was lesser in name only; not in magnitude. No matter what they called the Leonard-Hearns to-do, it was one helluva fight staged in front of almost 24,000 recently-released mental patients who seemed collectively dedicated to the deafening of America. And, in the end, Sugar Ray Leonard acquitted the hype by soundly thrashing the supposedly invincible Thomas Hearns in a fight with more twists and turns than could be found in an early O. Henry potboiler. In so doing he laid claim to the undisputed welterweight championship of the world. As well as to a place among the all-time greats.

Leonard won more than just the fight. He won what Rodney Dangerfield—for lack of a more descriptive phrase—would call respect. Not only from his hard-hitting opponent but from hard-boiled sportswriters as well, many of whom had discounted Leonard's stock, belittling his accomplishments as part of a media buildup.

For ever since Leonard exploded on the media scene and on the national screen he has been regarded by many doubting Thomases, Jims, and Larrys as a media phenomenon. Maybe Howard Cosell, who had hitched his braggin' to a star, was the reason for the press' downplaying of Ray's abilities. But Howie knows a winner when he sees one, and Ray always had the makings of one. Nonetheless, "Forget it!" said the rest of the media, who continued to view Leonard merely as the greatest boxer ever to come out of Palmer Park, Maryland. Nothing more. It seemed that most of the boxing writers could never bring themselves to acknowledge that Leonard was as good as he was because that other, unspeakable medium, TV, found him first.

Or maybe it was the fact that Leonard was denied the ultimate satisfaction of destroying the man who had beaten him previously—Roberto Duran. Such triumphs, of course, had served as the anchor of so many other legends—Sugar Ray Robinson, who turned the tables on Jake LaMotta, Randy Turpin, and Carmen Basilio; Muhammad Ali, who came back to "whup" Joe Frazier twice; Joe Louis, who destroyed Max Schmeling the second time around; Gene Tunney, who beat the only man who ever bettered him, Harry Greb; and Jack Dempsy, who almost came back to beat Tunney in the Battle of the Long Count. The centerpiece for each and every one of these ring worthies had been his comeback win over the man who had previously bedeviled him. All Leonard was remembered for was a desultory wave of a hand and the cry, "No más, no más." Of

such things are legends unmade.

Moreover, according to many old-timers, for whom boxing goes in one era and out the other, there was only one "Sugar" and that accolade was reserved for one man and one man alone—Ray Robinson. (In fact, Robinson himself had tried to preserve that title of respect for himself in the face of other Sugars. One time, so the story goes, when Robinson faced another of the pretenders to the Sugar crown, George Costner, he reputedly told Costner during the prefight instructions, "Now I'll show you who's the real Sugar," and proceeded to prove his point by laying out Costner in one round. Afterward, Robinson chided the artificial Sugar with, "Now go out and earn yourself the name.")

But it was not only the press and the old-timers who denied Ray Leonard his rightful place. He was thrice denied, this time by the betting fans, who made Hearns a 6½–5 favorite.

And so it was that Leonard, seeking to rid himself of so many dybbuks, came to an inferno called a ring that hot airless night in Vegas wearing a robe emblazoned with the solitary word, *Deliverance*. It was an eloquent message that should have tipped off those who were supposedly "in the know" that Leonard was driven to exorcise the many demons that possessed him.

Yet the task facing Leonard was monumental. As was his opponent, the 6'1"-going-on-6'1½" Hearns, a legitimate welterweight with a heavyweight wingspan of 78 inches—at least four inches longer than that of Leonard and longer still than many heavyweight champions. It was that reach, or so the reasoning went, that would allow Hearns to hold Leonard at bay, much as he had Pipino Cuevas, while setting up his lethal right hand. Hearns, however, was disabused of any such notions as Leonard slapped away his tentacle-like left time and again during the first two rounds. But while one of Hearns's favorite ploys was being negated by Leonard, Hearns was also defusing one of Leonard's, the tactic he had employed so successfully in the New Orleans fiasco—freaking out Duran with his mugging act.

For the first two rounds, the gladiators, who had apparently studied each other's playbooks, played with each other. Hearns, who chose to be introduced by the nickname the "Motor City Cobra," in preference to his more familiar moniker of "Hit Man," acted more like a cobra than a hit man. Leonard's game plan was to circle the stationary cobra, first one way and then the other, in the manner of a mongoose, attempting to tire out the man who had gone more than four rounds only eight times in his entire career. And so it went, Leonard darting back and forth, his eyes transfixed in a fierce determination not to blink, almost as if

Undisputed World Welterweight Champion Sugar Ray Leonard jubilates as a stunned Thomas Hearns, left, looks on after Leonard won the title with a 14th round TKO.

held by toothpicks, and Hearns resorting to long left jabs and an occasionally head-hunting right, most of which Ray avoided by pulling his head back Ali-style. The closest Hearns came to his tormentor was after the bell, when Leonard gave him a love-tap-cum-punch and Hearns clobbered him without turning the other cheek.

With Angelo Dundee's words, "Go out there and get him," ringing in his ears and a freshly minted mouse beginning to erupt under his left eye, Leonard went out in the third to take the fight to Hearns. The first thing he took was a right to the jaw. And, surprise of surprises, he didn't even blink. Now he knew he could catch anything Hearns threw. The insight was heady as Leonard stood his ground and swapped shots with Hearns, who was fighting in one-punch combinations. For the first time Leonard scored with his right and backed Hearns up; momentarily confused by Leonard's quick hand speed and agility, Hearns went on the retreat. At the bell, Leonard raised his hands in a victory salute. He now knew he would win, not merely that he could.

Rounds 4 and 5 mirrored the first two—sandwiched around Leonard's third—with Hearns pecking away at Leonard's angry-looking eye. But even in the face of Hearns's rapierlike left, Leonard was quietly moving inside with shots to the body. And, to the head, when he could reach the lanky WBA champion. Still, they were rounds for Hearns. Barely. But round 6 was to change the complexion for the fight.

For the first time, Leonard, having taken control of the fight despite Hearns's elongated left, was now crowding Hearns. Moving inside. And, what's more, beating Hearns to the punch. More correctly stated, he was beating him to many punches. First it was Leonard's right over Hearns's low left; then it was a left over Hearns's equally low right. Suddenly, a wild left hook to the head caught Hearns's attention. And turned his head. As Ray's corner screamed, "Speed, Ray, speed," Ray obliged with a rat-a-tat-tat staccato. Suddenly the Hit Man was the Hittee Man, wobbling under a barrage of blows almost too numerous to count. But numbered among them was one punch in particular— a hard left hook to Hearns's unprotected rib cage— which caused the cobra to grimace in pain. Its effects could not be appreciated then—it was one of a rapid-fire series of blows, as incapable of being severed from the rest as one pearl from a string—but one whose effects would be telling on Hearns. And, on the outcome of the fight.

Round 7 saw Leonard pick up right where he had left off, rattling more left hooks off Hearns's jaw than the Hit Man had experienced in his previous 32 fights. Over and over Leonard was to penetrate the would-be defenses of his spindly opponent , landing left hooks from in close as the crowd picked up the chant, Leo-nard, Leo-nard. . . ." Hearns, unable to stave off the swarming Leonard and unable to tie him up inside, merely grappled to keep him away, pushing at his tormentor. And yet, as Hearns began to take on the appearance of a pinball, ricocheting from pillar to rope, he evinced that intangible known as courage, a rare commodity in any fighter and one that separates the greats from the near-greats. It worked to keep his unsteady pins under him.

At the end of the round Hearns staggered off in the vague direction of his corner, much the worse for wear. But Leonard also looked weary from his prolonged fungo practice, breathing heavily as he plopped on his stool. Later Ray was to say, "I had him, but he didn't cooperate," which translated into, "I was arm-weary."

The eighth saw Leonard continue on the attack even as he wound down, with right leads and rights to the body in dutiful response to his corner's exhortations of "Body, Ray. . . Body, Ray. . . " Hearns, trying desperately to stem the seemingly inexorable tide that was all Leonard, attempted to catch Ray with a right. But, as the round came to a close with Leonard swarming in, he took off on his bicycle, throwing out his long left in a getaway manner. However, just as the fight had turned once, it was soon to turn again. Beginning with the bell for the ninth, Thomas Hearns reverted to the style that had seen him win 163 amateur fights, only 11 by knockout. Gone was the attempt to gain leverage by leaning in; gone was the low-held left and gone was the menacing Hit Man who instilled fear in the 32 opponents he had faced up to now. But gone too was the stationary target Ray had found so inviting. And, in its place, there suddenly appeared a masterful boxer, one who could finally take advantage of his 78-inch reach. It was the most startling role reversal since Edward G. Robinson played the leading man in *Woman in the Window*. The puncher had turned boxer and the boxer had turned puncher. And the puncher-boxer was clearly outpointing his supposedly faster opponent.

So it went through rounds 9, 10, and 11, with enough rights thrown to count on your right thumb. Hearns was clearly dominating the action—what little there was of it as the high rollers began clapping and whistling for more— and the fight. But he was always just one punch away from "Queer Street," the street he had come down before, the pavement barely beneath his feet. But Hearns's befogged condition was not apparent. Not apparent to anyone, that is, except trainer-manager Emanuel Steward, who spent his time between rounds doing anything and everything he could to snap Tommy out of his severe case of mal-de-ring— up to, and including, shouting at his charge, "If you're not

212

goin' to fight, damn it, I'm goin' to stop it!''

Somehow, Steward's shock treatment worked and Hearns came back. Strong. So, too, did his followers, and by round 12 they had worked themselves up into a frenzy, with Hearns himself leading their vocal exhortations as their hopes took flight and form in roars of "Tommee, Tommee...." No longer moving, Hearns came in on the one-eyed Cyclops who was stalking him, landing battering-ram lefts and rights to the body. It was Hearns's round. And his last hurrah, something even Hearns might have seen had he been able to analyze his right-hand haymaker at the half-blinded WBC champion, who somehow, someway, pulled his head back at the last instant.

Round 13, incredibly, saw still another turn in the tide of battle. Up off his stool came Ray, first pushing Hearns to the canvas as their legs entwined, then punishing Hearns with a right over a left and three left hooks to the head. Hearns tried mightily to hold Leonard off; unsure of how to clinch, he tried to throw a right. But Leonard beat Hearns to the punch, catching him and jarring him off balance. Another left by Ray, still another and a third, and suddenly Hearns was careening about the ring, his head rolling like a rag doll's, his motions uncoordinated. Leonard was atop Hearns as Hearns first leaned, then fell, into the ropes from a series of punches fired off too rapidly to count. Suffice it to say it was "Enough," as writer Vic Ziegel noted.

Finally, after a fusillade of rights the lanky Hearns, in his best imitation of an accordian, gently folded through the ropes. Referee Davey Pearl, who had ignored an obvious knockdown in the Larry Holmes-Earnie Shavers fight, deemed Hearns's exit from the ring more a fall than a knockdown—although they looked as if they were part of the same cause and effect—and told Hearns to "get up." As Hearns slowly reclaimed his feet and recollected his mind, trainer Angelo Dundee was up on the ring apron screaming, "Bullshit." Pearl motioned him down to his corner and looked back to find Leonard raking Hearns with another volley of punches, seemingly fired in a desire to prove something to somebody. This time he proved to Pearl that the Thomas Hearns leaning against the ropes on his haunches was knocked down by the collective force of his punches.

Pearl took up the count while Hearns tried to haul himself up to his 6′1″ height, no easy chore and one which had the appearance of a balloon slowly inflating. Finally, Prometheus was unbound and Hearns was unbound and Hearns was up, albeit unsteadily, as the count reached nine, just at the bell.

There seemed to be no doubt of the outcome now. At least not to 23,615 fans seated in the makeshift arena atop the tennis courts behind Caesars Palace. But three judges, who undoubtedly had been watching tennis instead of boxing, still had Hearns ahead. Leonard was to make sure that there would be no disputed verdict; he wanted the welterweight title and went out to do it himself. He leaped off his stool at the bell for the fourteenth round—the longest Thomas Hearns had ever gone in a fight—and went right at Hearns, throwing rights and lefts as Hearns tried to avert them by twisting his body back and forth from a right-handed stance to a southpaw style.

It was all to no avail as Leonard kept coming, throwing lefts to the body that made the exhausted Hearns wince and lefts to the head that made him blink. Finally Leonard landed his Mary Ann, a straight right to the chops, and threw up his hands in his traditional victory signal. But, miracle of miracles, Hearns wouldn't, or couldn't, fall and pitched backward into the ropes. Leonard wouldn't let him off the hook now and—between waving furiously to Referee Pearl to stop the fight—raked Hearns with right uppercuts, left hooks, and hard rights. Still, Hearns wouldn't go down. But even if Hearns hadn't had enough, Davey Pearl had. He pulled Leonard away as Hearns looked in his direction as if to quizzically ask, "Wha' happened?" and then reeled off in the direction of his corner, the *former* WBA welterweight champion of the world, at 1:45 of the fourteenth round.

At the press conference the next day, with both fighters sporting dark glasses and looking like Elwood and Jake Blues, Thomas Hearns was to show his respect for the "new champion, Sugar Ray Leonard...." It was a long time acomin', but maybe, just maybe, Sugar Ray Leonard will get the respect he deserves. And, yes, Virginia—and Maryland, and all points north, west, and south—there is a new Sugar Ray.

The Great Fights Record Book

Reprinted by permission from The Ring Record Book, *published annually by The Ring Publishing Corp.*

MUHAMMAD ALI
(CASSIUS CLAY)

Louisville, KY. Heavyweight
Born, Louisville, KY. Jan. 17, 1942. Height, 6 ft. 2½ inches.

1960 National AAU Light-Heavyweight Champion. 1960 National Golden Glove Heavyweight Champion. 1960 Olympic Games Light-Heavyweight Champion.

1960
Oct.   29—Tunney Hunsaker, Louisville ...... W 6
Dec.   27—Herb Siler, Miami Beach .... KO 4

1961
Jan.   17—Tony Esperti, Miami Beach .... KO 3
Feb.   7—Jim Robinson, Miami Beach ...... KO 1
Feb.   21—Donnie Fleeman, Miami Beach. ... KO 7
Apr.   19—Lamar Clark, Louisville .... KO 2
June   26—Duke Sabedong, Las Vegas ...... W 10
July   22—Alonzo Johnson, Louisville .... W 10
Oct.   7—Alex Miteff, Louisville .... KO 6
Nov.   29—Willi Besmanoff, Louisville ...... KO 7

1962
Feb.   10—Sonny Banks, New York .... KO 4
Feb.   28—Don Warner, Miami Beach ...... KO 4
Apr.   23—George Logan, Los Angeles ...... KO 4
May   19—Billy Daniels, New York .... KO 7
July   20—Alejandro Lavorante, Los Angeles . KO 5
Nov.   15—Archie Moore, Los Angeles .... KO 4

1963
Jan.   24—Charlie Powell, Pittsburgh ...... KO 3
Mar.   13—Doug Jones, New York .... W 10
June   18—Henry Cooper, London .... KO 5

1964
Feb.   25—Sonny Liston, Miami Beach ...... KO 7
(Won World Heavyweight Title)

1965
May   25—Sonny Liston, Lewiston, ME ..... KO 1
(Retained World Heavyweight Title)
July   31—Jimmy Ellis, San Juan .... Exh. 3
July   31—Cody Jones, San Juan .... Exh. 3
Aug.   16—Cody Jones, Goteborg, Sweden ... Exh. 2
Aug.   16—Jimmy Ellis, Goteborg, Sweden .. Exh. 2
Aug.   20—Jimmy Ellis, London .... Exh. 4
Aug.   20—Cody Jones, Paisley, Scotland .... Exh. 4
Nov.   22—Floyd Patterson, Las Vegas ...... KO 12
(Retained World Heavyweight Title)

1966
Mar.   29—George Chuvalo, Toronto .... W 15
(Retained World Heavyweight Title)
May   21—Henry Cooper, London .... KO 6
(Retained World Heavyweight Title)
Aug.   6—Brian London, London .... KO 3
(Retained World Heavyweight Title)
Sept. 10—Karl Mildenberger, Frankfurt,
Germany .... KO 12
(Retained World Heavyweight Title)
Nov.   14—Cleveland Williams, Houston ..... KO 3
(Retained World Heavyweight Title)

1967
Feb.   6—Ernie Terrell, Houston .... W 15
(Retained World Heavyweight Title)
Mar.   22—Zora Folley, New York .... KO 7
(Retained World Heavyweight Title)
June .15—Alvin Lewis, Detroit .... Exh. 3
June   15—Orvill Qualls, Detroit........... Exh. 3

1968
(Inactive)
1969
(Inactive)
1970

Clay announced his ring retirement at a special newsman's gathering he had called on February 3, 1970, at which he offered his belt to the winner of the Frazier-Quarry fight. His offer was turned down by Frazier.

On September 10, 1970, he announced his return to an active campaign in the ring and signed a contract to meet Jerry Quarry in Atlanta.

Oct.   26—Jerry Quarry, Atlanta .... KO 3
Dec.   7—Oscar Bonavena, New York ...... KO 15

1971
Mar.   8—Joe Frazier, New York .... L 15
(For World Heavyweight Title)
June   25—J. D. McCauley, Dayton .... Exh. 2
June   25—Eddie Brooks, Dayton .... Exh. 3
June   25—Rufus Brassell, Dayton .... Exh. 3
June   30—Alex Mack, Charleston .... Exh. 3
June   30—Eddie Brooks, Charleston .... Exh. 4
July   26—Jimmy Ellis, Houston .... KO 12
Aug.   21—Lancer Johnson, Caracas .... Exh. 4
Aug.   21—Eddie Brooks, Caracas .... Exh. 4
Aug.   23—Lancer Johnson, Port of Spain ... Exh. 4
Aug.   23—Eddie Brooks, Port of Spain ..... Exh. 2
Nov.   6—James Summerville, Buenos Aires . Exh. 5
Nov.   6—Miguel Paez, Buenos Aires ...... Exh. 5
Nov.   17—Buster Mathis, Houston.......... W 12
Dec.   26—Jurgen Blin, Zurich .... KO 7

1972
Apr.   1—Mac Foster, Tokyo .... W 15
May   1—George Chuvalo, Vancouver ...... W 12
June   27—Jerry Quarry, Las Vegas .... KO 7
July   1—Lonnie Bennett, Los Angeles .... Exh. 2
July   1—Eddie Jones, Los Angeles .... Exh. 2
July   1—Billy Ryan, Los Angeles .... Exh. 2
July   1—Charley James, Los Angeles .... Exh. 2
July   1—Rudy Clay, Los Angeles .... Exh. 2
July   19—Al Lewis, Dublin .... KO 11
Aug.   24—Obie English, Baltimore .... Exh. 4
Aug.   24—Ray Anderson, Baltimore .... Exh. 2
Aug.   24—Alonzo Johnson, Baltimore ...... Exh. 2
Aug.   24—George Hill, Baltimore .... Exh. 2
Aug.   28—Alonzo Johnson, Cleveland ...... Exh. 2
Aug.   28—Amos Johnson, Cleveland .... Exh. 2
Aug.   28—Terry Daniels, Cleveland........ Exh. 2
Sept. 20—Floyd Patterson, New York....... KO 7
Oct.   11—John Dennis, Boston .... Exh. 2
Oct.   11—Cliff McDonald, Boston .... Exh. 2
Oct.   11—Doug Kirk, Boston .... Exh. 2
Oct.   11—Ray Anderson, Boston........ Exh. 2
Oct.   11—Paul Raymond, Boston .... Exh. 2
Nov.   21—Bob Foster, Stateline........... KO 8

1973
Feb.   14—Joe Bugner, Las Vegas .... W 12
Mar.   31—Ken Norton, San Diego .... L 12
Sept. 10—Ken Norton, Los Angeles .... W 12
Oct.   20—Rudi Lubbers, Jakarta........... W 12

1974
Jan.   28—Joe Frazier, New York .... W 12
(Won American Heavyweight Title)

Oct.   30—George Foreman, Kinshasa .... KO 8
(Regained World Heavyweight Title)

1975
Mar.   24—Chuck Wepner, Cleveland........ KO 15
(Retained World Heavyweight Title)
May   16—Ron Lyle, Las Vegas .... KO 11
(Retained World Heavyweight Title)
July   1—Joe Bugner, Kuala Lumpur .... W 15
(Retained World Heavyweight Title)
Oct.   1—Joe Frazier, Manila .... KO 14
(Retained World Heavyweight Title)

1976
Feb.   20—Jean Pierre Coopman, San Juan ... KO 5
(Retained World Heavyweight Title)
Apr.   30—Jimmy Young, Landover .... W 15
(Retained World Heavyweight Title)
May   24—Richard Dunn, Munich .... KO 5
(Retained World Heavyweight Title)
June   25—Antonio Inoki, Tokyo .... Exh. D 15
(Above match was a boxer against a wrestler)
Sept. 28—Ken Norton, New York .... W 15
(Retained World Heavyweight Title)

1977
Jan.   29—Peter Fuller, Boston .... Exh. 4
Jan.   29—Walter Haines, Boston .... Exh. 1
Jan.   29—Jerry Houston, Boston .... Exh. 2
Jan.   29—Ron Drinkwater, Boston ...... Exh. 2
Jan.   29—Matt Ross, Boston .... Exh. 2
Jan.   29—Frank Smith, Boston .... Exh. 1
May   16—Alfredo Evangelista, Landover ..... W 15
(Retained World Heavyweight Title)
Sept. 29—Earnie Shavers, New York .... W 15
(Retained World Heavyweight Title)
Dec.   2—Scott LeDoux, Chicago .... Exh. 5

1978
Feb.   15—Leon Spinks, Las Vegas .... L 15
(Lost World Heavyweight Title)
Sept. 15—Leon Spinks, New Orleans .... W 15
(Regained World Heavyweight Title)

1980
Oct.   2—Larry Holmes, Las Vegas .... KO 11

1981
Dec.   11— Trevor Berbick, Nassau .... L 10

TB	KO	WD	WF	D	LD	LF	KO BY	ND	NC
61	37	19	0	0	4	0	1	0	0

ALEXIS ARGUELLO

Nicaraguan Junior Lightweight
Born, April 19, 1952, Managua

1968
Nov.   18—Israel Medina, Managua .... KO 1
Dec.   14—Miguel Espinosa, Managua .... W 4

1969
Jan.   23—Burrito Martinez, Managua ...... KO 3
Apr.   26—Miguel, Espinosa, Managua .... L 6

1970
Sept.   7—Marcelino Beckles, Managua...... KO 8
Oct.   17—Mario Bojorge, Managua .... KO 3
Nov.   14—Jose Urbina, Managua .... KO 1
Dec.   5—Julio Morales, Managua .... KO 3
Dec.   19—Armando Figueroa, Managua ..... KO 1

1971
Feb.   12—Tony Quiroz, Managua .... KO 6

Mar. 13—Raton Hernandez, Managua .... W 10
Apr. 17—Raton Hernandez, Managua ...... W 10
May 1—Halcon Buitrago, Managua .... KO 7
June 5—Kid Chapula, Managua .... KO 1
June 26—Marcial Loyola, Managua .... KO 2
July 17—Kid Clay, Managua .... KO 5
Aug. 14—Catalino Alvarado, Managua ..... KO 1
Sept. 4—Ray Mendoza, Managua .... KO 4
Oct. 2—Kid Clay, Managua .... W 10
Nov. 18—Vicente Worrel, Managua .... KO 2
Dec. 14—Jorge Reyes, Managua .... KO by 7

1972

Sept. —Jorge Benitez, Managua .... KO 1
Oct. 22—Memo Barrera, Managua .... KO 2
Nov. 17—Memo Ortiz, Managua .... KO 2
Dec. 12—Rafael Gonzalez, Managua ..... KO 7

1973

Mar. 30—Fernando Fernandez, Managua .. KO 2
Apr. 22—Magallo Lozada, Managua ...... W 10
May 26—Kid Pascualito, Managua ...... KO 3
June 30—Octavio Gomez, Managua ...... KO 2
Aug. 25—Nacho Lomeli, Managua ...... KO 1
Oct. 26—Sigfredo Rodriguez, Managua ..... KO 9
Nov. 24—Jose Legra, Managua .... KO 1

1974

Jan. 8—Raul Martinez, Managua ...... KO 1
Feb. 16—Ernest Marcel, Panama City .... L 15
(WBA Featherweight Title)
Apr. 27—Enrique Garcia, Managua ...... KO 3
May 20—Art Hafey, Managua .... KO 5
Aug. 29—Jose Aparico, Managua ...... W 12
Sept. 21—Otoniel Martinez, Managua ...... KO 1
Nov. 23—Ruben Olivares, Los Angeles ...-. KO 13
(WBA Featherweight Title)

1975

Feb. 8—Chico Apricio, San Salvador .... W 10
Mar. 15—Lionel Hernandez, Caracas ...... KO 8
(WBA Featherweight Title)
May 31—Rigoberto Riasco, Managua ..... KO 2
(Won vacant World Featherweight Title)
July 18—Rosalio Muro, San Francisco ..... KO 2
Oct. 12—Royal Kobayashi, Tokyo .... KO 5
(Retained World Featherweight Title)
Dec. 20—Saul Montano, Managua .... KO 3

1976

Feb. 1—Jose Torres, Mexicali............ W 10
Apr. 10—Modesto Concepcion, Managua .... KO 2
June 19—Salvatore Torres, Los Angeles..... KO 3
(Retained World Featherweight Title)

1977

Feb. 19—Godfrey Stevens, Managua .... KO 2
May 14—Alberto Herrera, Managua .... KO 1
June 20—Gave up the World Featherweight Title,
due to weight problems.
June 22—Ezequiel Sanchez, New York .... KO 4
Aug. 3—Jose Fernandez, New York ..... KO 1
Aug. 27—Ben Ortiz, San Juan .... W 10
Sept. 29—Jerome Artis, New York ...... KO 2
Dec. 18—Enrique Solis, Managua .... KO 5

1978

Jan. 28—Alfredo Escalera, San Juan .... KO 13
(Won WBC Junior Lightweight Title)
Mar. 25—Mario Mendez, Las Vegas .... KO 3
Apr. 29—Rey Tam, Los Angeles .... KO 5
(Retained WBC Junior Lightweight Title)
June 3—Diego Alcala, San Juan .... KO 1
(Retained WBC Junior Lightweight Title)
July 26—Vilomar Fernandez, New York ..... L 10
Nov. 10—Arturo Leon, Las Vegas .... W 15
(Retained WBC Junior Lightweight Title)

1979

Feb. 4—Alfredo Escalera, Rimini .... KO 13
(Retained WBC Junior Lightweight Title)
July 8—Rafael (Bazooka) Limon, New York KO 11
(Retained WBC Junior Lightweight Title)
Nov. 16—Bobby Chacon, Inglewood .... KO 7
(Retained WBC Junior Lightweight Title)

1980

Jan. 20—Ruben Castillo, Tucson .... KO 11
Mar. 30—Gerald Hayes, Las Vegas .... W 10
Apr. 27—Rolando Navarrete, San Juan ..... KO 5
Nov. 14—Jose Ramiz, Miami .... W 10

1980

Jan. 20— Ruben Castillo, Tucson...................KO 11
(Retained WBC Junior Lightweight Title)
Mar. 31—Gerald Hayes, Las Vegas..................W 10
Apr. 27— Rolando Navarrete, San Juan ....KO 5
(Retained WBC Junior Lightweight Title)
Aug. 9—Cornelius Boza-Edwards, Atlantic City...................................KO 8
—Relinquished WBC Junior Lightweight Title.
Nov. 14— Jose Luis Ramirez, Miami, Fla.......W 10

1981

Feb. 7— Roberto Vasquez, Miami Fla. ....KO 3
June 20—Jim Watt, London, England.............W 15
(Won WBC Lightweight Title)
Oct. 3—Ray Mancini, Atlantic City.............KO 14
(Retained WBC Lightweight Title)
Nov. 21—Robert Elizondo, Las Vegas...........KO 7
(Retained WBC Lightweight Title)

1982

Feb. 13—James (Bubba) Busceme, Beaumont ....KO 6
(Retained WBC Lightweight Title)
May 22— Andrew Ganigan, Las Vegas, Nev. KO 5
(Retained WBC Lightweight Title)
July 31—Kevin Rooney, Atlantic City...........KO 2
Nov. 12—Aaron Pryor, Miami, Fla........... KO by 14
(For WBA Junior Welterweight Title)

1983

Feb. 15—Relinquished WBC lightweight Title.
Feb. 26—Vilomar Fernandez, San Antonio ....W 10
Apr. 24—Claude Noel, Atlantic City.............KO 3

TB	KO	WD	WF	D	LD	LF	KO BY	ND	NC
83	63	15	0	0	3	0	2	0	0

HENRY ARMSTRONG

(Henry Jackson)
(Homicide Hank)
Born, December 12, 1912, Columbus, MI.
Weight, 145 pounds. Managed by Eddie Mead and Wirt Ross.

(Fought early in career as Melody Jackson)
Won 58 out of 62 amateur bouts.

1931

July 27—Al Iovino, No. Braddock, Pa....KO by 3
Aug. —Sammy Burns, Millville, PA .... W 6

1932

Won: Gene Espinoza, 4; Max Tarley, 4; Mickey Ryan, 6; Georgie Dundee, 6; Perfecto Lopez, 6; Steve Harky, 6; Perfecto Lopez, 8; Young Corpus, 6. Knockouts: Bobby Calmes, 3; Young Bud Taylor, 2; Vincente Torres, 3; Johnny De Foe, 4; Vince Trujillo, 7. Draw: Perfecto Lopez, 4; Perfecto Lopez, 4; Perfecto Lopez, 6. Lost: Eddie Trujillo, 4; Al Greenfield, 4; Baby Manuel, 6. No decision: Hoyt Jones, 4.

1933

Won: Kid Moro, 10; Baby Manuel, 10; Davey Abad, 10. Knockouts: Johnny Granone, 5; Gene Espinoza, 7; Max Tarley, 3; Joe Conde, 7; Ventura Arana, 5. Draw: Kid Moro, 10. Lost: Baby Arizmendi, 10.

1934

Won: Varias Milling, 10; Mark Diaz, 8; Midget Wolgast, 10. Knockouts: Sal Hernandez, 2; Baby Casanova, 3; Lester Marston, 7; Leo Lomelli, 5. Draw: Perfecto Lopez, 8. Lost: Baby Arizmendi, 12; Baby Manuel,

10.

1935

Won: Davey Abad, 10; Frankie Covelli, 8. Knockouts: Tully Corvo, 7; Alton Black, 7. Lost: Davey Abad, 10; Baby Arizmendi, 12.
Nov. 27—Midget Wolgast, Oakland .... W 10

1936

Jan. 1—Joe Conde, Mexico City ....L 10
Feb. 26—Ritchie Fontaine, Oakland ....L 10
Mar. 31—Ritchie Fontaine, Los Angeles ..... W 10
Apr. 17—Alton Black, Reno .... KO 8
May 19—Pancho Leyvas, Los Angeles .... KO 4
June 22—Johnny DeFoe, Butte .... W 10
Aug. 4—Baby Arizmendi, Los Angeles ...... W 10
Aug. 28—Juan Zurita, Los Angeles .... KO 4
Sept. 3—Buzz Brown, Portland .... W 10
Sept. 8—Dommy Ganzon, Sacramento ..... KO 1
Oct. 27—Mike Belloise, Los Angeles .... W 10
Nov. 2—Gene Espinoza, Los Angeles .... KO 1
Nov. 17—Joey Alcanter, St. Louis .... KO 6
Dec. 3—Tony Chavez, St. Louis .... LF 8

1937

Jan. 1—Baby Casanova, Mexico City ...... KO 3
Jan. 19—Tony Chavez, Los Angeles .... KO 10
Feb. 2—Moon Mullins, Los Angeles ...... KO 2
Feb. 19—Varias Milling, Hollywood ...... KO 4
Mar. 2—Joe Rivers, Los Angeles .... KO 4
Mar. 12—Mike Belloise, New York .... KO 4
Mar. 19—Aldo Spoldi, New York .... W 10
Apr. 6—Pete De Grasse, Los Angeles ..... KO 10
May 4—Frankie Klick, Los Angeles .... KO 4
May 28—Wally Hally, Los Angeles .... KO 4
June 9—Mark Diaz, Pasadena............. KO 4
June 15—Jackie Carter, Los Angeles .... KO 4
July 8—Alf Blatch, New York .... KO 3
July 19—Lew Massey, Brooklyn .... KO 4
July 27—Benny Bass, Philadelphia .... KO 4
Aug. 4—Eddie Brink, New York .... KO 4
Aug. 16—Johnny Cabello, Washington, DC .. KO 2
Aug. 31—Orville Drouillard, Detroit........ KO 5
Sept. 9—Charley Burns, Pittsburgh .... KO 4
Sept. 16—Johnny De Foe, New York ...... KO 4
Sept. 21—Bobby Dean, Youngstown .... KO 1
Oct. 18—Joe Marcienti, Philadelphia .... KO 3
Oct. 29—Petey Sarron, New York .... KO 6
(World Featherweight Championship)
Nov. 19—Billy Beautiful, New York ...... KO 5
Nov. 23—Joey Brown, Buffalo .... KO 2
Dec. 6—Tony Chavez, Cleveland .... KO 1
Dec. 12—Johnny Jones, New Orleans ...... KO 2

1938

Jan. 12—Enrico Venturi, New York ...... KO 6
Jan. 21—Frankie Castillo, Phoenix .... KO 3
Jan. 28—Tommy Brown, Tuscon .... KO 4
Feb. 1—Chalky Wright, Los Angeles ..... KO 3
Feb. 9—Al Citrino, San Francisco .... KO 4
Feb. 25—Everett Rightmire, Chicago ..... KO 4
Feb. 28—Charley Burns, Minneapolis ..... KO 2
Mar. 15—Baby Arizmendi, Los Angeles ...... W 10
Mar. 25—Eddie Zivic, Detroit .... KO 4
Mar. 30—Lew Feldman, New York .... KO 5
May 31—Barney Ross, New York .... W 15
(World Welterweight Championship)
Aug. 17—Lou Ambers, New York .... W 15
(World Lightweight Championship)
Nov. 25—*Ceferino Garcia, New York .... KO 15
Dec. 5—*Al Manfredo, Cleveland .... KO 3
(Armstrong relinquished Featherweight Championship)
*Welterweight Title Bout.

1939

Jan. 10—*Baby Arizmendi, Los Angeles ... W 10
Mar. 4—*Bobby Pacho, Havana .... KO 4
Mar. 16—*Lew Feldman, St. Louis .... KO 1
Mar. 31—*Davey Day, New York .... KO 12
May 25—*Ernie Roderick, London .... W 15
Aug. 22—Lou Ambers, New York .... L 15
(Lost World Lightweight Championship)

Oct. 9—*Al Manfredo, Des Moines ...... KO 4
Oct. 13—*Howard Scott, Minneapolis ...... KO 2
Oct. 20—*Ritchie Fontaine, Seattle .... KO 3
Oct. 24—*Jimmy Garrison, Los Angeles ..... W 10
Oct. 30—*Bobby Pacho, Denver .... KO 4
Dec. 31—*Jimmy Garrison, Cleveland ...... KO 7
*Welterweight Title Bout.
1940
Jan. 4—*Joe Ghnouly, St. Louis .... KO 5
Jan. 24—*Pedro Montanez, New York ...... KO 9
Mar. 1—Ceferino Garcia, Los Angeles .... D 10
(Middleweight Title Bout)
Apr. 26—*Paul Junior, Boston .... KO 7
May 24—*Ralph Zanelli, Boston .... KO 5
June 21—*Paul Junior, Portland .... KO 3
July 17—Lew Jenkins, New York .... KO 6
Sept. 23—*Phil Furr, Washington, DC ...... KO 4
Oct. 4—Fritzie Zivic, New York .... L 15
(Lost World Welterweight Championship)
*Welterweight Title Bout.
1941
Jan. 27—Fritzie Zivic, New York ......KO by 12
(World Welterweight Championship)
Oct. 1—Knocked out two men in two rounds each at Oklahoma City, OK, in exhibition bouts.
Oct. 12—Tried a comeback and knocked out two opponents in 2 exhibition rounds each.
1942
June 1—Johnny Taylor, San Jose .... KO 4
June 24—Sheik Rangel, Oakland .... W 10
July 3—Reuben Shank, Denver .... L 10
July 20—Joe Ybarra, Sacramento .... KO 3
Aug. 3—Aldo Spoldi, San Francisco .... KO 7
Aug. 13—Jackie Burke, Ogden UT .... W 10
Aug. 26—Rudolfo Ramirez, Oakland ...... KO 8
Sept. 7—Johnny Taylor, Pittman, NY ...... KO 3
Sept. 4—Leo Rodak, San Francisco .. KO 8
Sept. 30—Earl Turner, Oakland .... KO 4
Oct. 13—Juan Zurita, Los Angeles .... KO 2
Oct. 26—Fritzie Zivic, San Francisco ...... W 10
Dec. 4—Lew Jenkins, Portland, OR ...... KO 8
Dec. 14—Saverio Turiello, San Francisco ... KO 4
1943
Jan. 5—Jimmy McDaniels, Los Angeles...,. W 10
Mar. 2—Willie Joyce, Los Angeles .... L 10
Mar. 8—Tippy Larkin, San Francisco ...... KO 2
Mar. 22—Al Tribuani, Philadelphia .... W 10
Apr. 2—Beau Jack, New York .... L 10
Apr. 30—Saverio Turiello, Washington, DC . KO 5
May 7—Tommy Jessup, Boston .... KO 1
May 24—Maxie Shapiro, Philadelphia ..... KO 7
June 11—Sammy Angott, New York ...... W 10
July 24—Willie Joyce, Hollywood .... W 10
Aug. 6—Jimmy Garrison, Portland, OR ..... W 10
Aug. 14—Joey Silva, Spokane .... W 10
Aug. 27—Ray Robinson, New York .... L 10
1944
Jan. 14—Aldo Spoldi, Portland, OR .... KO 3
Jan. 26—Saverio Turiello, Kansas City .... KO 7
Feb. 7—Lew Hanbury, Washington, DC .. KO 3
Feb. 23—Jimmy Garrison, Kansas City ..... KO 5
Feb. 29—Jackie Byrd, Des Moines .... KO 4
Mar. 14—Johnny Jones, Miami .... KO 5

Mar. 20—Frankie Wills, Washington, DC .... W 10
Mar. 24—Ralph Zanelli, Boston .... W 10
Apr. 25—John Thomas, Los Angeles .... W 10
May 16—Ralph Zanelli, Boston .... W 10
May 22—Aaron Perry, Washington, DC .... KO 6
June 2—Willie Joyce, Chicago .... L 10
June 15—Al Davis, New York .... KO 2
June 21—Nick Latsios, Washington, DC ..... W 10
July 4—John Thomas, Los Angeles .... L 10
July 14—Slugger White, Hollywood .... D 10
Aug. 21—Willie Joyce, San Francisco ...... W 10
Sept. 15—Aldo Spoldi, St. Louis .... KO 2
Nov. 4—Mike Belloise, Portland, OR ...... KO 4
1945
Jan. 17—Chester Slider, Oakland .... D 10
Feb. 6—Genaro Rojo, Los Angeles....... W 10
Feb. 14—Chester Slider, Oakland .... L 10
1951
Ordained a minister of the Baptist church.

TB	KO	WD	WF	D	LD	LF	KO BY	ND	NC
175	97	47	0	8	19	1	2	1	0

Elected to Boxing Hall of Fame 1954.

CARMEN BASILIO
Born, April 2, 1927, Canastota, NY. Height, 5 ft. 6½ in. Managed by Johnny De John and Joe Netro.

1948
Nov. 24—Jimmy Evans, Binghamton .... KO 3
Nov. 29—Bruce Walters, Syracuse .... KO 1
Dec. 8—Eddie Thomas, Binghamton ...... KO 2
Dec. 16—Rollie Johns, Syracuse .... W 6
1949
Jan. 5—Johnny Cunningham, Binghamton .. D 6
Jan. 19—Jay Parlin, Binghamton .... D 6
Jan. 25—Ernie Hall, Syracuse .... KO 2
Feb. 19—Luke Jordan, Rochester.......... W 6
Apr. 20—Elliott Throop, Syracuse .... KO 1
May 2—Connie Thies, Rochester .... L 6
May 8—Jerry Drain, Syracuse .... KO 3
May 18—Johnny Clemmons, Syracuse .... KO 3
June 7—Johnny Cunningham, Syracuse .... KO 2
July 12—Jesse Bradshaw, Syracuse ...... KO 2
July 21—Sammy Daniels, Utica .... W 8
Aug. 2—Johnny Cunningham, Utica .... L 8
Aug. 17—Johnny Cunningham, Syracuse ..... W 8
Sept. 7—Tony DiPelino, Rochester .... W 8
Sept. 30—Jackie Parker, Syracuse .... KO 3
1950
Jan. 10—Sonny Hampton, Buffalo.......... W 8
Jan. 24—Casse Tate, Buffalo .... W 8
Feb. 7—Adrien Mogart, Buffalo .... KO 7
Mar. 6—Lew Jenkins, Syracuse .... W 10
Mar. 27—Mike Koballa, Brooklyn .... L 8
Apr. 12—Gaby Ferland, New Orleans ...... D 10
May 5—Gaby Ferland, New Orleans ...... KO 1
June 21—Guillermo Giminez, New Orleans .. KO 8
July 31—Guillermo Giminez, New Orleans .. KO 9
Aug. 28—Eddie Giosa, New Orleans .... L 10
Dec. 15—Vic Cardell, New York .... L 10

1951
Mar. 9—Flora Hita, Syracuse .... W 8
Apr. 12—Eddie Giosa, Syracuse .... W 10
May 29—Lester Felton, Syracuse .... L 10
June 18—Jonny Cesario, Utica .... L 10
Sept. 17—Shamus McCrae, Syracuse .... W 8
Sept. 26—Ross Virgo, New Orleans .... L 10
1952
Feb. 4—Emmett Norris, Wilkes-Barre ...... W 10
Feb. 28—Jimmy Cousins, Akron .... W 8
Mar. 31—Jackie O'Brien, Wilkes-Barre ..... W 10
May 29—Chuck Davey, Syracuse .... D 10
(Decision originally called a win then was changed.)
July 16—Chuck Davey, Chicago .... L 10
Aug. 20—Billy Graham, Chicago .... L 10
Sept. 22—Baby Williams, Miami Beach ..... W 10
Oct. 20—Sammy Giuliano, Syracuse .... KO 3
Nov. 18—Chuck Foster, Buffalo .... KO 5
1953
Jan. 12—Ike Williams, Syracuse .... W 10
Feb. 28—Vic Cardell, Toledo .... W 10
Apr. 11—Carmine Fiore, Syracuse .... KO 9
June 6—Billy Graham, Syracuse .... W 12
(Won NY State Welterweight Title)
July 25—Billy Graham, Syracuse.......... D 12
(For NY State Welterweight Title)
Sept. 18—Kid Gavilan, Syracuse .... L 15
(For World Welterweight Title)
Nov. 28—Johnny Cunningham, Toledo ...... KO 4
Dec. 19—Pierre Langlois, Syracuse .... D 10
1954
Jan. 16—Italo Scortichini, Miami .... D 10
Apr. 17—Pierre Langlois, Syracuse .... W 10
May 15—Italo Scortichini, Syracuse........ W 10
June 26—Al Andrews, Syracuse .... W 10
Aug. 17—Ronnie Harper, Ft. Wayne .... KO 2
Sept. 10—Carmine Fiore, New York .... W 10
Oct. 15—Allie Gronik, Syracuse .... W 10
Dec. 16—Ronnie Harper, Akron .... KO 4
1955
Jan. 21—Peter Muller, Syracuse .... W 10
June 10—Tony DeMarco, Syracuse......... KO 12
(Won World Welterweight Title)
Aug. 27—Italo Scortichini, New York .... W 10
Sept. 7—Gil Turner, Syracuse .... W 10
Nov. 30—Tony DeMarco, Boston .... KO 12
(Title Bout)
1956
Mar. 14—Johnny Saxton, Chicago .... L 15
(Lost World Welterweight Title)
Sept. 12—Johnny Saxton, Syracuse .... KO 9
(Regained Welterweight Title)
1957
Feb. 22—Johnny Saxton, Cleveland .... KO 2
(World Welterweight Title)
May 13—Leo Owens, Longview, OR .... Exh. 3
May 14—Leo Owens, Spokane .... Exh. 3
May 16—Harold Jones, Portland, OR ...... KO 4
June 27—Leo Owens, Jeannette, PA....... Exh. 3
Sept. 23—Ray Robinson, New York .... W 15
(Won World Middleweight Title)
Basilio relinquished World Welterweight Title.
1958
Mar. 25—Ray Robinson, Chicago............. L 15

(Lost World Middleweight Title)
Sept.   5—Art Aragon, Los Angeles .... KO 8
1959
Apr.   1—Arley Selfer, Augusta .... KO 3
Aug. 28—Gene Fullmer, San Francisco ...KO by 14
(For vacant NBA Middleweight Title)
1960
June 29—Gene Fullmer, Salt Lake City ...KO by 12
(For NBA Middleweight Title)
1961
Jan.   7—Gaspar Ortega, New York .... W 10
Mar. 11—Don Jordan, Syracuse .... W 10
Apr. 22—Paul Pender, Boston .... L 15
(For World Middleweight Title)
Apr. 25—Announced retirement.

TB	KO	WD	WF	D	LD	LF	KO BY	ND	NC
79	27	29	0	7	14	0	2	0	0

Elected to Boxing Hall of Fame 1969

GEORGES CARPENTIER
(The Orchid Man)
Born, January 12, 1894, Lens, France. Weight, 175 pounds. Height, 5 ft. 11½ in. Managed by Francois Descamps. Started as amateur flyweight in 1906. Had 11 amateur bouts.
1907
Feb. 24—C. Bourgois, Paris .... W 4
June 12—E. Vetinck, Paris .... W 4
Sept. 11—Mazoir, Paris .... L 4
1908
Nov.   1—Ed Salmon, Mais-Lafitte .... WF 13
Nov. 30—Ed Salmon, Mais-Lafitte ......KO by 18
—Moinereso .... KO 3
—Simon .... W 10
Dec.   7—Lepine, Paris .... W 6
Dec.   7—Charles Legrand, Paris .... D 6
Dec.   —Charles Legrand, Lens .... W 15
1909
Feb. 19—George Gloria, Paris .... KO by 6
Feb. 25—Simon, Paris .... W 10
Feb. 28—Charles Legrand, Lens .... D 20
Mar. 18—Achalme, Lens .... W 10
Apr.   6—Cheveau, Roubiax .... W 6
May 11—Aug. Relinger, Mauberge .... KO 6
May 11—Lampin, Mauberge .... KO 8
June 26—E. Vetinck, Lille .... KO 1
June 27—L. Dorgeuille, Lille .... KO 11
Oct. 15—Paul Til, Lille .... D 15
Oct. 23—L. Dorgeuille, Paris .... W 10
Nov.   —Lampin, Henin-Lietard .... KO 7
Nov. 24—Charles Ledoux, Paris .... W 15
Dec.   8—Georges Gaillard, Paris ...... W 6
Dec. 22—Paul Til, Paris .... W 10
1910
Jan.   5—Young Warner, Paris .... W-F 7
Jan.   8—Georges Gaillard, Lens .... W 10
Jan. 15—Wally Pickard, Brussels .... KO 8
Feb.   9—Lampin, Brussels .... KO 8
Mar. 12—Buck Shine, Brussels.......... L 10

Mar. 26—Fernand Cuny, Lyon .... W 10
Apr.   3—George Gloria, Lens .... KO 8
Apr.   9—Young Snowball, Paris .... KO by 4
July   6—Paul Til, Paris .... D 15
July 17—Hubert Baelen, Lille .... KO 2
Aug. 13—Fernand Cuny, Cabourg ......KO by 8
Sept.   5—Achille, Cambrai .... KO 5
Oct. 15—Percy Wilson, Paris .... W 10
Oct. 22—Jim Campbell, Paris .... KO 5
Nov.   6—Young Williams, Arras .... KO 7
Nov. 19—George Randall, Paris .... KO 10
Dec.   3—Henry Demlen, Brussels ...... W 10
Dec. 17—Jack Daniels, Paris .... W 10
1911
Jan.   8—Ed Brochet, Lens............. KO 7
Jan. 24—George Randall, Paris .... KO 5
Jan. 27—Henri Piet, Paris .... L 10
Feb. 17—Jack Daniels, Paris .... W 10
Mar.   1—Young Nipper, Paris .... W 8
Mar. 12—Harry Stassens, Lens .... KO 1
Mar. 15—Henrie Marchand, Liege ...... KO 6
Mar. 25—Jack Meekins, Paris .... W 10
Apr.   1—Sid Stagg, Roubiax .... W 10
Apr.   8—G. Colbourne, Brussels ...... W 10
Apr. 23—Henri Marchand, Arras .... KO 7
May 20—F. Loughrey, Paris .... W 15
June 15—R. Eutache.................... KO 16
(Welterweight Championship of France)
June 23—Jack Goldswain, Paris .... KO 4
Aug. 14—Arthur Evernden, Cabourg .... W 15
Aug. 29—Dixie Kid, Tourville ....KO by 5
Oct.   2—Sid Burns, London .... W 15
Oct. 23—Young Joseph, London .... KO 10
(Welterweight Championship of Europe)
Nov. 17—Theo. Cray, Boulogne .... KO 9
Dec. 13—Harry Lewis, Paris .... W 20
1912
Jan. 23—Battling Lacroix, Lille .... KO 9
Feb. 29—Jim Sullivan, Monte Carlo ..... KO 2
Apr.   —George Gunther, Paris .... W 20
May 10—Hubert Roc, Marseilles ...... KO 6
May 22—Willie Lewis, Paris .... W 20
June 24—Frank Klaus, Dieppe...........LF 19
Oct. 23—Billy Panke, Paris .... LF 17
1913
Jan. 10—Marcel Moreau, Paris .... W 8
Feb. 12—Bandsman Rice, Paris .... KO 2
Mar.   1—Cyclone Smith, Nice .... KO 3
Mar. 17—George Gunther, Nice .... KO 14
June   1—Bombardier Wells, Ghent ..... KO 4
June 29—Albert Lurie, Bordeaux .... KO 3
Aug.   6—Ashley Williams, Vichy ...... KO 4
Oct. 11—Jeff Smith, Paris .... W 20
Oct. 31—*M. Abott, Geneva .... KO 3
Dec.   8—Bombardier Wells, London .... KO 1
*Carpentier disciplined for alleged poor work.
1914
Jan. 19—Pat O'Keefe, Nice .... KO 2
Mar. 21—Joe Jeanette, Paris .... L 15
Apr. 14—George Mitchell, Paris........ KO 1
June   2—Hubert Roc, Valenciennes .... KO 3
June 14—Phillipe Robinson, Beziers ... KO 3
July 16—Gunboat Smith, London .... WF 6
(Claimed White Heavyweight Title)

1915–16
July 26—Kid Jackson, Bordeaux .... WF 4
Served in French army in world war as lieutenant in aviation corps.
1917
Jan. 27—Jean Bicot, Paris .... Exh. 4
1918
Jan.   1—Fernand Campagne, Paris ...... Exh. 4
Jan.   1—Jules Lanara, Paris .... Exh. 4
1919
July   1—Dick Smith, Paris .... KO 8
Sept. 29—C. Croiselles, St. Sebastian .... KO 2
Dec.   4—Joe Beckett, London .... KO 1
1920
Jan. 10—Blink McCloskey, Bordeaux ...... KO 2
Feb. 21—F. Grundhoven, Monte Carlo ..... KO 2
Oct. 12—Battling Levinsky, Jersey City .... KO 4
(Won Light-Heavyweight Title)
1921
July   2—Jack Dempsey, Boyle's Thirty Acres, Jersey City ....KO by 4
(For World Heavyweight Championship)
1922
Jan. 22—George Cook, London, Albert Hall . KO 4
May 11—Ted Kid Lewis, London.......... KO 1
Sept. 24—Battling Siki, Paris .... KO by 6
(Lost World Light-Heavyweight Title)
1923
May   6—Marcel Nilles, Paris .... KO 8
Oct.   1—Joe Beckett, London .... KO 1
1924
May   1—Arthur Townley, Vienna .... KO 2
May 31—Tom Gibbons, Michigan City ..... ND 10
July 24—Gene Tunney, New York........KO by 15
1926
May 21—Eddie Huffman, New York .... D 10
June 17—Tommy Loughran, Philadelphia .....L 10
July   7—Jack Burke, Denver........... KO 2
Sept. 15—Rocco Stragmalia, Alan, ID....... KO 3
1927
Jan. 11—Jack Walker, Paris .... Exh. 4

TB	KO	WD	WF	D	LD	LF	KO BY	ND	NC
106	51	30	4	5	6	1	8	1	0

Elected to Boxing Hall of Fame, 1964.
Died on Oct. 28, 1975, Paris, France.

BILLY CONN
(The Pittsburgh Kid)
Born, October 8, 1917. Pittsburgh, PA. Heavyweight. Managed by Johnny Ray.
1935
—Dick Woodwer, Fairmont, WV ......L 4
—John Lewis, Charleston .... KO 3
—Paddy Gray, Pittsburgh.......... W 4
—Bob Dorman, Clarksburg, WV ..... W 6
—Johnny Birek, Pittsburgh .... W 6
—Stan Nagey, Wheeling, WV .... W 4
Apr.   8—George Schley, Pittsburgh........ KO 6
Apr. 25—Ralph Gizzy, Pittsburgh .... L 4

217

June   3—Ray Eberle, Pittsburgh .... W 6
June   10—Ralph Gizzy, Pittsburgh .... L 6
July   9—Teddy Movan, Pittsburgh .... L 6
July   29—Ray Eberle, Pittsburgh .... W 4
Aug.   19—Teddy Movan, Pittsburgh .... L 4
Sept.   9—Georgie Leggins, Pittsburgh .... W 4
Oct.   7—Johnny Yurcini, Johnstown, PA ... W 6
Oct.   14—Teddy Movan, Pittsburgh .... D 6
Nov.   18—Steve Walters, Pittsburgh .... W 6

1936

Jan.   —Johnny Yurcini, Washington, PA ... W 6
Jan.   27—Johnny Yurcini, Pittsburgh .... KO 4
Feb.   3—Louis Kid Cook, Pittsburgh .... W 6
Feb.   17—Louis Kid, Cook, Pittsburgh ...... W 8
Mar.   16—Steve Nickleash, Pittsburgh ...... W 6
Apr.   13—Steve Nickleash, Pittsburgh ...... W 6
Apr.   27—General Burrows, Pittsburgh ...... W 6
May   19—Dick Ambrose, Pittsburgh .... W 6
May   27—Honeyboy Jones, Pittsburgh ...... W 8
June   3—Honeyboy Jones, Pittsburgh ...... W 10
June   15—General Burrows, Pittsburgh ...... W 8
July   30—Teddy Movan, Pittsburgh .... W 8
Aug.   10—Teddy Movan, Pittsburgh .... W 8
Sept.   8—Honeyboy Jones, Pittsburgh ...... W 10
Sept. 21—Roscoe Manning, Pittsburgh ..... KO 5
Oct.   19—Charlie Weise, Pittsburgh .... W 10
Oct.   22—Ralph Chong, Pittsburgh .... W 10
Dec.   2—Jimmy Brown, Pittsburgh .... KO 9
Dec.   28—Fritzie Zivic, Pittsburgh .... W 10

1937

Mar.   11—Babe Risko, Pittsburgh .... W 10
May   3—Vince Dundee, Pittsburgh .... W 10
May   27—Oscar Rankins, Pittsburgh .... W 10
June   30—Teddy Yarosz, Pittsburgh .... W 12
Aug.   13—Young Corbett, San Francisco ...... L 10
Sept. 30—Teddy Yarosz, Pittsburgh .... W 15
Nov.   8—Young Corbett, Pittsburgh .... W 10
Dec.   16—Solly Krieger, Pittsburgh .... L 12

1938

Jan.   24—Honeyboy Jones, Pittsburgh ...... W 12
Apr.   4—Domenic Ceccarelli, Pittsburgh ... W 10
May   10—Eric Seelig, Pittsburgh .... W 10
July   25—Teddy Yarosz, Pittsburgh .... L 12
Sept. 14—Ray Actis, San Francisco .... KO 8
Oct.   27—Honeyboy Jones, Pittsburgh ...... W 10
Nov.   28—Solly Krieger, Pittsburgh .... W 12

1939

Jan.   6—Fred Apostoli, New York .... W 10
Feb.   10—Fred Apostoli, New York .... W 15
May   12—Solly Krieger, New York .... W 12
July   13—Melio Bettina, New York .... W 15
(Won New York State
Light-Heavyweight Championship)
Aug.   14—Gus Dorazio, Philadelphia .... KO 8
Sept. 25—Melio Bettina, Pittsburgh .... W 15
(Title Bout)
Nov.   17—Gus Lesnevich, New York .... W 15
(Title Bout)
Jan.   10—Henry Cooper, New York .... W 12
June   5—Gus Lesnevich, Detroit .... W 15
(Title Bout)
Gave up his Light-Heavyweight crown to com-
pete as a heavyweight.
Sept.   6—Bob Pastor, New York .... KO 13

Oct.   18—Al McCoy, Boston .... W 10
Nov.   29—Lee Savold, New York .... W 12

1941

Feb.   27—Ira Hughes, Clarksburg, WV ..... KO 4
Mar.   6—Dan Hassett, Washington, DC..... KO 5
Apr.   4—Gunnar Barlund, Chicago .... KO 8
May   26—Buddy Knox, Pittsburgh .... KO 8
June   18—Joe Louis, New York ....KO by 13
(For Heavyweight Title)

1942

Jan.   12—Henry Cooper, Toledo .... W 12
Jan.   28—James D. Turner, St. Louis .... W 10
Feb.   13—Tony Zale, New York .... W 12
In U.S. Army

1944

Exhibition bouts for the Servicemen overseas, in
European theater of operations.

1945

Oct.   29—Bearcat Jones, Cleveland .... Exh. 3
Nov.   7—Bearcat Jones, Kansas City ..... Exh. 3

1946

June   19—Joe Louis, New York ....KO by 8
(For Heavyweight Title)

1948

Nov.   15—Mike O'Dowd, Macon .... KO 9
Nov.   25—Jackie Lyons, Dallas .... KO 9
Dec.   10—Joe Louis, Chicago............. Exh. 6

TB KO WD WF D LD LF KO BY ND NC
73 14 49   0 0   8   0   2   0   0
Elected to Boxing Hall of Fame in 1965

CURTIS COKES
Dallas, TX, Welterweight
Born, June 15, 1937

1958

Mar.   24—Manuel Gonzalez, Midland .... W 6
Apr.   8—Gil Tapia, Dallas .... W 4
Apr.   28—Jimmy Leach, Dallas .... W 6
May   12—Babe Vance, Waco.............. W 6
May   26—Cecil Courtney, Dallas .... W 6
June   30—Sammy Williams, Dallas .... KO 6
Oct.   27—Elmo Henderson, Dallas .... W 6
Nov.   22—Manuel Gonzales, Lubbock .... W 8
Dec.   1—Ruben Flores, Dallas............ W 6

1959

Jan.   20—George Carron, Lubbock .... KO 3
Apr.   1—Henry Watson, Dallas .... W 4
Apr.   27—Manuel Gonzales, Dallas .... L 10
May   18—Rip Randall, Dallas............ TD 3
July   27—Rip Randall, Dallas............. KO 1
Aug.   27—Reggie Williams, Baton Rouge .... KO 5
Sept. 14—Mel Ferguson, Dallas .... W 8
Dec.   2—Frankie Davis, Houston .... L 6
Dec.   14—Aman Peck, Dallas .... KO 5

1960

Mar.   1—Lovell Jenkins, Amarillo .... W 8
July   29—Pedro Ruiz, El Paso .... KO 3
Sept. 13—Joe Louis Hargrove, Dallas ...... KO 1
Oct.   24—Stefan Redl, Dallas .... KO 8

1961

Jan.   16—Joe Miceli, Dallas .... W 10
Feb.   13—Charlie Smith, Dallas .... W 10
Apr.   4—Hilario Morales, Juarez .... L 10
June   8—Kenny Lane, Dallas............. D 10
Aug.   3—Luis Rodriguez, Dallas .... W 10
Sept. 14—Manuel Gonzales, Dallas .... W 10
Dec.   2—Luis Rodriguez, Miami Beach ....L 10

1962

Jan.   23—Carlos Macias, Houston .... KO 4
Feb.   13—Kid Rayo, San Antonio .... W 10
Apr.   6—Hilario Morales, Dallas .... KO 5
May   11—Rudolph Bent, Dallas .... KO 8
Aug.   22—Joey Limas, Albuquerque .... W 10
Sept.   8—Manuel Alvarez, Monterrey.......L 10
Nov.   15—Hubert Jackson, Dallas .... KO 1
Dec.   10—Puno de Oro, Dallas .... KO 2

1963

Feb.   11—Johnny Newman, Hollywood ...... KO 2
Feb.   25—Joey Parks, Witchita Falls .... KO 5
Apr.   20—Joe Stable, New York ....L 10
May   21—Stan Harrington, Honolulu .... W 10
May   30—Flory Olguin, Albuquerque .... KO 5

1964

May   1—Stan Hayward, Philadelphia ....KO by 4
May   12—Tony Montano, Los Angeles .... W 10
June   9—Al Andrews, Las Vegas .... W 10
Aug.   10—Al Andrews, Fresno .... W 10
Aug.   27—Eddie Pace, Los Angeles...........L 10

1965

Mar.   15—Marshall Wells, Dallas .... KO 12
Apr.   23—Fortunato Manca, Rome .... W 10
Dec.   13—Billy Collins, New Orleans .... W 12

1966

July   6—Luis Rodriguez, New Orleans ..... KO 15
Aug.   24—Manuel Gonzalez, New Orleans..... W 15
(Won WBA Welterweight Title)
Sept. 27—Enrique Cruz, Corpus Christi ..... KO 7
Nov.   28—Jean Josselin, Dallas .... W 15
(Won vacant World Welterweight Title)

1967

Jan.   24—Francois Pavilla, Paris .... D 10
Feb.   20—Ted Whitfield, Dallas .... KO 3
Mar.   31—Joe Harris, New York ....L 10
May   19—Francois Pavilla, Dallas .... KO 10
(Retained World Welterweight Title)
Oct.   2—Charlie Shipes, Oakland .... KO 8
(Retained World Welterweight Title)

1968

Feb.   5—Jean Josselin, Paris .... W 10
Mar.   15—Jimmy Lester, Oakland .... W 10
Apr.   16—Willie Ludick, Dallas .... KO 5
(Retained World Welterweight Title)
June   15—Joe Ngidi, Johannesburg .... KO 4
June   28—Willie Ludick, Lourence Marques .. KO 3
July   5—Joseph Sishi, Durban .... KO 5
Oct.   21—Ramon LaCruz, New Orleans ...... W 15
(Retained World Welterweight Title)

1969

Feb.   10—Don Cobbs, St. Louis .... KO 1
Apr.   18—Jose Napoles, Los Angeles .....KO by 13
(Lost World Welterweight Title)
June   29—Jose Napoles, Mexico City......KO by 10
(World Welterweight Title)

1970

Jan. 28—Roberto Pena, Fort Worth .... KO 5
Mar. 3—Retired from the ring.
Aug. 11—Returned to ring as middleweight.
Aug. 11—Danny Perez, Dallas .... KO 7
Sept. 11—Fate Davis, Fort Worth .... W 10
Sept. 29—Harold Richardson, Dallas .... W 10
Nov. 3—Billy Braggs, Milwaukee .... KO 6

1971

Mar. 17—Fate Davis, Akron .... D 10
May 24—Rafael Gutierrez, San Francisco .....L 10
Dec. 2—Carlos Salinas, Sacramento ....L 10

1972

Sept. 9—Tap Tap Makathini, Durban .... L 10
Sept. 23—Joseph Hali, Port Elizabeth .... W 10
Oct. 5—Ezra Mzinyane, Capetown .... W 10

TB	KO	WD	WF	D	LD	LF	KO BY	ND	NC
80	30	32	0	4	11	0	3	0	0

JAMES J. CORBETT

(James John Corbett)
(Gentleman Jim)

Born, Sept. 1, 1866, San Francisco, CA. Height, 6 ft. 1 in. Managed by William A. Brady. His undated contests were:

Dave Eiseman, W.; Capt. J. H. Daly, W 2; Duncan McDonald, D; Mike Brennan, W 3; John Donaldson, W 4; Martin Costello, W 3; Prof. William Miller, W 6; Frank Smith, Salt Lake City, W; Joe Choynski, ND 1.

1886

—Billy Welch, champion amateur middleweight, Ariel RC, for gold medal, San Francisco ....L 4
—Billy Welch, Acme Club .... KO 1

1887

Aug. 27—Jack Burke, Olympic Club, San Francisco .... W 8

1888

June 30—Frank Glover, San Francisco ...... D 3

1889

May 30—Joe Choynski (police interfered) near Fairfax, 2-oz. gloves, $1,000 a side 4
June 5—Joe Choynski (180-172), barge, near Benecia, CA Choynski, skin gloves; Corbett, 5-oz. Referee, Patsy Hogan .... KO 27
July 15—Joe Choynski, San Francisco .... W 4
July 29—Dave Campbell, Portland, OR Corbett won, but agreed to a draw if he failed to score a knockout .... D 10

1890

Feb. 18—Jake Kilrain on points (183-201), 5-oz. gloves, $3,500, Southern ACNO. Referee, R. Violett .... W 6
Mar. 20—Sparred Mike Donovan, NYAC 3
Apr. 14—Dominick McCaffrey, gate, Casino Brooklyn, 12 min. 20 sec .... W 4

1891

May 21—Peter Jackson (182-198), $8,500 $1,500, California AC. Declared "no contest" and each received $2,500. Referee, Hiram Cook .... D 61

June 26—Sparred with John L. Sullivan, San Francisco .... Exh. 4
Aug. 5—Sparred with Jim Hall, Chicago 4
Oct. 8—Ed. Kinney, Milwaukee .... W 4

1892

Feb. 16—Bill Spilling of Rochester .... KO 1
—Bob Caffrey of Philadelphia ...... KO 1
—Joe Lannon, New York .... ND 3
Mar. 15—Match made with Sullivan, New York.
June 26—Appeared in "Sport McAllister," Bijou, New York ....
Sept. 7—John L. Sullivan (178-212), $25,000 purse and $20,000 stake money. Olympic Club, New Orleans; 5-oz. gloves, Marquis of Queensberry Rules. Referee, Prof. John Duffy. Corbett's seconds, Billy Delaney, Jim Daly, John Donaldson; bottle holder, Mike Donovan; timekeeper, Bat Masterson, Corbett got first blood in fifth round. Sullivan weighed 212, Corbett 178. Sullivan favorite 3 and 4 to 1 .... KO 21
(Won Heavyweight Title)
Oct. 3—Debut in "Gentleman Jack," Elizabeth, NJ ....

1893

Feb. 24—Posted money to fight Mitchell.
July 11—Signed articles to fight Jackson, $10,000 a side, Chicago. Match fell through.

1894

Jan. 25—Charley Mitchell, $20,000 purse, $5,000 a side. For championship, Duval Athletic Club, Jacksonville, FL. Referee, "Honest" John Kelly, Corbett's seconds, Billy Delaney, Jack Dempsey, John Donaldson, Wm. McMillan; timekeeper, Ted Foley, for club, "Snapper" Garrison .... KO 3
Apr. 12—Sailed for England on Feurst Bismark..
Sept. 7—Peter Courtney of Trenton, NJ ($4,750-$250). 2-minute rounds. For Kinetoscope, Orange, NJ (first motion picture of a fight). KO 6
Oct. 11—Matched with Bob Fitzsimmons for $10,000 a side in New York.

1895

Jan. 4—Jim McVey, New Orleans .... KO 3
June 3—Accepted $41,000 purse offered by Florida AC to fight Fitzsimmons.
June 27—Sparred with Sullivan at latter's benefit, New York.
Oct. 31—Contest with Fitzsimmons at Dallas, TX, for heavyweight championship, $41,000 purse and $10,000 a side declared off; cause, adverse legislation. Hot Springs AC offered $10,000 purse; Fitz arrested; Corbett surrendered and fight prevented Nov. 3.
Nov. 11—Announced retirement and presented championship to Maher, Maspeth, LI.
Nov. 25—Debut in "Naval Cadet," Lynn, MA.

1896

June 24—Tom Sharkey, San Francisco ...... D 4
Dec. 14—Jim McVey, New York .... Exh. 3

1897

Jan. 3—Ernest Roeber, Exhibition........ KO 1
Mar. 17—Bob Fitzsimmons, (183-167), Carson, NV, $15,000 purse, $5,000 a side. Referee, George Siler; timekeeper, Jim Colville KO by 14

1898

Nov. 22—Tom Sharkey, New York.........LF 9

1900

May 11—Jim Jeffries, Coney Island ......KO by 23
(Heavyweight Title Bout)
Aug. 30—Kid McCoy, New York .... KO 9

1903

Aug. 14—Jim Jeffries, San Francisco .....KO by 10
(Heavyweight Title Bout)

TB	KO	WD	WF	D	LD	LF	KO BY	ND	NC
33	9	11	0	6	1	1	3	2	0

Died Bayside, LI, Feb. 18, 1933. Buried Calvary Cemetery, Long Island City, N.Y.

Elected to Boxing Hall of Fame 1954.

LAURENT DAUTHUILLE

French Middleweight
Born, Chauny, France, Feb. 20, 1924.

1944

Sept. 17—Thiebault, Paris................ KO 2
Sept. 24—W. Mezergues, Paris .... KO 6
Oct. 15—M. Garcia, Paris............... KO 5
Nov. 12—L. Tassart, Paris .... W 10
Dec. 8—G. Corsin, Paris............... KO 5
Dec. 21—R. Thiebault, Nanterre .... KO 6

1945

Jan. 7—J. Dobiasch, Paris .... W 10
Feb. 4—J. Toniolo, Paris ....L 10
Mar. 18—E. Leclerc, Paris .... W 10
Apr. 22—Beneto, Paris................. KO 4
May 13—E. Marchand, Paris .... KO 9
Sept. 16—E. Leclerc, Paris .... W 10
Oct. 7—Kid Janas, Paris .... KO 8
Nov. 4—A. Diouf, Paris .... KO 8
Dec. 9—Joe Brun, Paris .... W 10

1946

Jan. 18—J. Despeaux, Paris .... KO 2
Feb. 22—Robert Charron, Paris .... W 10
Apr. 9—L. Van Dam, Paris............. KO 3
Apr. 21—T. Toniolo, Marseilles .... KO 1
May 25—Pankowiack, Paris .... W 10
July 13—A. Diouf, Paris .... W 10
Aug. 7—L. Van Dam, Amsterdam .... D 10
Oct. 28—Robert Charron, Paris .... W 10

1947

Feb. 1—Gus Degouve, Paris ....L 10
May 4—Widmer Milandri, Paris .... KO 2
June 15—Gus Degouve, Paris .... W 10
June 22—Manca, Marseilles .... D 10
Oct. 27—Robert Villemain, Paris...........L 10

1948

Jan. 24—Cyrille Delannoit, Brussels ....L 10
Feb. 28—Cyrille Delannoit, Brussels ....L 10
Apr. 12—Robert Charron, Paris .... W 10
May 14—Robert Villemain, Paris ....L 10
July 26—Mark Hart, London .... W 8
Sept. 11—Jean Stock, Geneva .... D 10
Oct. 22—Tiberio Mitri, Paris ....L 10
Dec. 6—Pete Zaduk, Montreal .... W 10

1949

Jan. 3—Ernie Forte, Holyoke .... KO 8

219

Jan. 17—Ralph Zanelli, Montreal .... W 10
Feb. 21—Jake LaMotta, Montreal .... W 10
Aug. 3—Johnny Greco, Montreal .... KO 5
Oct. 4—Sonny Horne, Montreal .... W 10
Nov. 21—Kid Gavilan, Montreal .... L 10
1950
Apr. 3—Charley Zivic, Pittsburgh .... KO 9
May 1—Steve Belloise, Montreal ...... KO 7
June 20—Tuzo Portuguez, Montreal ..... KO 6
July 19—Tuzo Portuguez, Montreal ..... KO 3
Sept. 13—Jake LeMotta, Detroit .... KO by 15
(World Middleweight Title)
Nov. 10—Paddy Young, New York .... W 10
Dec. 5—Otis Graham, Montreal .... W 10
1951
Feb. 12—Jean Walzack, Paris .... KO 8
Apr. 5—Claude Ritter, Paris............. KO 2
Apr. 30—Bobby Dawson, Paris .... KO 1
June 9—Robert Villemain, Paris.......... D 10
July 9—Tony Janiro, Montreal .... W 10
Aug. 22—Gene Hairston, Montreal .... W 10
Nov. 5—Gene Hairston, Montreal .... L 10
Dec. 5—Roy Wouters, Montreal .... KO 5
1952
Mar. 3—Jean Wanes, Caen .... KO 3
Mar. 17—Norman Hayes, Paris .... W 10
Apr. 21—Charley Humez, Paris .... L 10
July 28—Johnny Bratton, Montreal ..... KO by 3
Nov. 17—Mickey Laurent, Paris .... KO by 2

TONY DeMARCO
(Leonard Liotta)
Born, January 14, 1932. Height, 5 ft. 5½ in.
Managed by Bobby Agrippino.
1948
Oct. 21—Meetor Jones, Boston .... KO 1
Nov. 16—Meetor Jones, Salem .... KO 2
Dec. 10—Billy Shea, Boston .... KO 3
Dec. 14—George Silva, Salem .... W 6
1949
Jan. 14—Joe Palaza, Boston .... KO 2
Feb. 17—Ray Dulmaine, Boston .... KO 2
Sept. 12—Roger Lessard, Boston .... KO 5
Oct. 7—Edward White, Providence .... L 6
Oct. 21—Vic Young, Boston .... KO 1
Nov. 14—Frankie Steele, Boston .... W 4
Dec. 19—Frankie Steele, Boston .... KO 3
1950
Jan. 9—Art Suffolatta, New Haven ....KO by 5
Feb. 20—Bobby Veal, Boston .... KO 2
July 10—Roger Ringuette, Boston .... KO 1
Sept. 19—Ricky Ferreria, New Bedford ..... W 6
Sept. 25—Bobby Weaver, Holyoke .... KO 3
Oct. 9—Des Shanley, Holyoke .... W 4
Oct. 20—Joe Wright, Boston .... W 6
Dec. 11—Ken Murray, Boston .... W 6
1951
Jan. 11—Ken Murray, Portland .... KO 2
Jan. 18—Larry Griffin, Portland, ME .... W 8
Feb. 19—Reggie Martina, Boston .... KO 1

Mar. 12—Chick Boucher, Boston ....KO by 4
Oct. 1—Ferman King, Boston .... W 6
Nov. 27—Stanley Hilliard, Newark........ KO 4
Dec. 7—Joe Torrens, New York .... W 4
Dec. 17—Manny Santos, Trenton .... KO 2
1952
Jan. 15—Lewelyn Richardson, New York .... W 6
Jan. 26—Julie Colon, Brooklyn .... KO 3
Feb. 18—Ferman King, Providence .... W 8
Feb. 26—Abdul Ali, Newark .... KO 2
Mar. 1—Jackie O'Brien, Brooklyn .... W 8
Mar. 6—Puggy Brown, Newark.......... KO 4
May 1—Bryan Kelly, Montreal............L 8
May 15—Gene Poirer, Montreal............L 8
1953
June 13—Ken Parsley, Boston .... KO 6
June 25—Jimmy Redding, Boston .... KO 2
July 18—Pat Demers, Boston .... KO 7
Aug. 3—Terry Young, Boston .... KO 5
Sept. 10—Bertie Conn, Boston .... KO 1
Sept. 29—Chic Boucher, Boston .... KO 6
Oct. 10—Paddy DeMarco, Boston .... W 10
Dec. 12—Teddy Davis, Boston .... W 10
1954
Jan. 18—Wilbur Wilson, Boston .... W 10
Mar. 15—Wilbur Wilson, Boston .... KO 2
Apr. 24—Carlos Chavez, Boston .... W 10
May 22—Johnny Cesario, Boston .... W 10
July 2—George Araujo, Boston .... KO 5
Sept. 25—Chris Christensen, Boston ..... KO 6
Nov. 6—Pat Manzi, Boston .... KO 1
1955
Feb. 11—Jimmy Carter, Boston .... D 10
Apr. 1—Johnny Saxton, Boston .... KO 14
(Won World Welterweight Title)
June 10—Carmen Basilio, Syracuse ......KO by 12
(Lost World Welterweight Title)
Sept. 14—Chico Vejar, Boston .... KO 1
Nov. 30—Carmen Basilio, Boston ....KO by 12
(For World Welterweight Title)
1956
Mar. 5—Wallace (Bud) Smith, Boston ..... KO 9
Apr. 28—Arthur Persley, Boston .... W 10
June 16—Vince Martinez, Boston .... W 10
Oct. 13—Kid Gavilan, Boston .... W 10
Nov. 23—Gaspar Ortega, New York ...... L 10
Dec. 21—Gaspar Ortega, New York ...... L 10
1957
Feb. 9—Gaspar Ortega, Boston .... W 10
Mar. 30—Larry Boardman, Boston .... W 10
May 25—Walter Byars, Boston .... W 10
Oct. 29—Virgil Akins, Boston ....KO by 14
1958
Jan. 21—Virgil Akins, Boston ....KO by 12
1959
Mar. 11—George Monroe, Boston .... KO 8
Apr. 20—Eddie Connors, Boston .... W 10
1960
Feb. 10—Denny Moyer, Boston ....KO by 2
1961
Dec. 19—Don Jordan, Boston .... KO 2
1962
Feb. 6—Stefan Redi, Boston .... W 10
Mar. 1—DeMarco announced retirement.

TB	KO	WD	WF	D	LD	LF	KO BY	ND	NC
71	33	25	0	1	5	0	7	0	0

JACK DEMPSEY
(William Harrison Dempsey)
(Manassa Mauler)
Born, June 14, 1895. Manassa, CO. Weight, 189
lbs. Height, 6 ft. 1 in. Managed by Frank Price, Jack
Kearns.
(Early record unavailable. Started fighting in
1914 as Kid Blackie).
1914
—Fred Woods, Montrose .... KO 4
—Andy Malloy, Durango ....L 10
—Andy Malloy, Montrose .... KO 3
—Andy Malloy, Durango .... NC 10
Aug. 17—Young Herman, Ramona .... D 6
—George Copelin, Cripple Creek ... KO 7
Nov. 2—Young Hancock, Salt Lake City ... KO 1
Nov. 30—Billy Murphy, Salt Lake City ..... KO 1
—Johnny Person .... KO 7
1915
—Battling Johnson .... KO 1
—Joe Lions .... KO 9
Apr. 5—Jack Downey, Salt Lake City........L 4
Apr. 26—Anamas Campbell, Reno .... KO 3
June 13—Johnny Sudenberg, Tonopah .... W 10
July 3—Johnny Sudenberg, Goldfield ...... D 10
—Chief Gordon .... KO 6
Dec. 13—Jack Downey, Salt Lake City..... D 4
Dec. 20—Two-Round Gillian, Salt Lake City . KO 1
1916
Feb. —Johnny Sudenberg, Ely .... KO 2
Feb. 12—Jack Downey, Salt Lake City ..... KO 2
Feb. 23—Boston Bearcat, Ogden .... KO 1
Mar. 9—Cyril Kohn, Provo .... KO 4
Apr. 8—Joe Bonds, Ely .... W 10
May 3—Terry Kellar, Ogden .... W 10
May 17—Dan Ketchell, Provo .... KO 3
May —George Christian, Price .... KO 1
June —Bob York, Price .... KO 4
June 24—Andre Anderson, New York ...... ND 10
July 8—Wild Burt Kenny, New York ...... ND 10
July 14—John Lester Johnson, New York ... ND 10
Sept. 28—Young Hector, Salida .... KO 3
Oct. 7—Terry Kellar, Ely .... W 10
Oct. 16—Fighting Dick Gilbert, Salt Lake.... W 10
1917
Feb. 13—Fireman Jim Flynn, Murray ....KO by 1
Mar. 21—Al Norton, Oakland............. D 4
Mar. 28—Willie Meehan, Oakland .... L 4
Apr. 11—Al Norton, Oakland .... D 4
July 25—Willie Meehan, Emeryville, CA .... W 4
Aug. 1—Al Norton, Emeryville, CA .... KO 1
Aug. 10—Willie Meehan, San Francisco ..... D 4
Sept. 7—Willie Meehan, San Francisco ..... D 4
Sept. 19—Charley Miller, Oakland .... KO 1
Sept. 26—Bob McAllister, Emeryville, CA .... W 4
Oct. 2—Edward J. (Gunboat) Smith,
San Francisco .... W 4

Nov.　2—Carl Morris, San Francisco .... W　4

1918

Jan.　24—Homer Smith, Racine .... KO　1
Feb.　4—Carl Morris, Buffalo .... WF　6
Feb.　14—Fireman Jim Flynn, Sheridan ..... KO　1
Feb.　25—K.O. Bill Brennan, Milwaukee .... KO　6
Mar.　16—Fred Saddy, Memphis .... KO　1
Mar.　25—Tom Riley, Joplin .... KO　1
May　3—Billy Miske, St. Paul .... ND　10
May　22—Dan Ketchell, Excelsior Springs ... KO　2
May　29—Arthur Pelkey, Denver .... KO　1
July　1—Kid McCarthy, Tulsa .... KO　1
July　4—Bob Devere, Joplin .... KO　1
July　6—Dan (Porky) Flynn, Atlanta .... KO　1
July　27—Fred Fulton, Harrison .... KO　1
Aug.　17—Terry Kellar, Dayton .... KO　5
Sept.　13—Willie Meehan, San Francisco ..... L　4
Sept.　14—Jack Moran, Reno .... KO　1
Nov.　6—Battling Levinsky, Philadelphia .. KO　3
Nov.　18—Dan (Porky) Flynn, Philadelphia .. KO　1
Nov.　28—Billy Miske, Philadelphia .... ND　6
Dec.　16—Carl Morris, New Orleans .... KO　1
Dec.　20—Clay Turner, New York .... Exh.　4
Dec.　30—Edward J. (Gunboat) Smith, Buffalo KO　2

1919

Jan.　20—Big Jack Hickey, Harrisburg ...... KO　1
Jan.　23—Kid Harris, Reading .... KO　1
Jan.　29—Kid Henry, Easton .... KO　1
Feb.　13—Eddie Smith, Altoona .... KO　1
Mar.　1—Terry Kellar, Washington, DC ... Exh.　3
Apr.　2—Tony Drake, New Haven .... KO　1
July　4—Jess Willard, Toledo .... KO　3
　　　　(Won World Heavyweight Title)
Aug.　24—One-Round Harrison, St. Louis ... Exh.　4

1920

Mar.　5—Terry Kellar, Los Angeles ..... Exh.　3
Sept.　6—*Billy Miske, Benton Harbor ..... KO　3
July　2—Two spar. pards., Denver .... KO
Dec.　14—*Bill Brennan, New York ...... KO　12

1921

July　2—*Georges Carpentier, Jersey City .. KO　4
*Title Bout.

1922

July　18—†Elziar Rioux, Montreal, Exh. .... KO　1
July　19—Jack Renault, Ottawa .... Exh.　3
Sept.　4—Jack Thompson, Michigan City ... Exh.　2
Sept.　7—Andre Anderson, Michigan City ... Exh.　2
Oct.　7—Jack Thompson, Boston .... Exh.　3
†Dempsey stopped two other men in one round
each in the same ring.

1923

July　4—*Tommy Gribbons, Shelby, MT .... W　15
Sept.　14—*Luis Firpo, New York .... KO　2
*Title Bout.

1924

Feb.　10—Dutch Seifert, Memphis ..... Exh. KO　1
Feb.　11—Martin Burke, New Orleans ..... Exh.　2
Feb.　11—Tommy Marvin, New Orleans . Exh. KO　2
June　3—Rock Stragmalia, Los Angeles.. Exh.KO　3
June　3—Eli Stanton, Los Angeles ..... Exh.KO　1

1925

Engaged in 8 exhibitions.

1926

Feb. 8, knocked out Jack League, Tony Catalina,

Cowboy Warner and Marty Cuyler, 1 round each, Mem-
phis (exh.). Took on 6 opponents.
Feb.　12—Boxed six opponents, knocking out four
(exh.).
Sept.　23—Gene Tunney, Philadelphia .... L　10
　　　　(Lost Heavyweight Title)

1927

July　21—Jack Sharkey, New York .... KO　7
Sept.　22—Gene Tunney, Chicago .... L　10
　　　　(Heavyweight Title Bout)
　　The second Tunney fight ended Dempsey's active ring career.
　　From Aug. 20 to Dec. 20, 1931, Jack Dempsey
engaged in 34 exhibitions before a total attendance of
230,155 who paid $477,260 to see him perform. This
is a record.

1931

Aug.　19—Jack Beasley, Reno .... KO　2
Aug.　24—Big Bill Hartwell, Portland, OR ... KO　1
Aug.　24—Dave McRae, Portland, OR .... KO　1
Aug.　24—Denny Lenhart, Portland, OR .... Exh.　2
Aug.　24—Bob Mariels, Portland, OR ...... Exh.　2
Aug.　26—Denny Lenhart, Seattle .... Exh.　2
Aug.　26—Bob Frazier, Seattle............ Exh.　1
Aug.　26—Red Tingley, Seattle .... Exh.　1
Aug.　28—Big Tom Sawyer, Vancouver ...... KO　1
Aug.　28—Tiny Lamar, Vancouver......... Exh.　1
Aug.　28—Del Wolfe, Vancouver......... Exh.　1
Aug.　31—Elgin Taylor, Spokane .... KO　1
Aug.　31—Dee Richmond, Spokane .... KO　1
Aug.　31—Big Bill Neering, Spokane ...... KO　1
Aug.　31—Tony Talerico, Spokane .... KO　1
Aug.　31—Cyclone Thompson, Spokane .... Exh.　2
Sept.　2—Tom Moore, Aberdeen .... KO　1
Sept.　2—Al Devaney, Aberdeen .... KO　1
Sept.　2—Denny Lenhart, Aberdeen ...... Exh.　2
Sept.　4—Jimmy Byrnes, Eugene, OR ..... Exh.
Sept.　—Eddie Burns, Reno .... Exh.　2
Sept.　7—Sam Baker, Reno .... Exh.　1
Sept.　7—Red Tingley, Reno .... KO　2
Sept.　10—George Richard, Tacoma ...... Exh.　2
Sept.　10—Marine Ranierie, Tacoma ...... Exh.　1
Sept.　10—Cyclone Thompson, Tacoma ..... Exh.　1
Sept.　10—Wayne Potts, Tacoma......... Exh.　1
Sept.　14—Sailor Smith, Rock Springs, WY .. KO　1
Sept.　14—Joe Ferguson, Rock Springs, WY . Exh.　2
Sept.　14—Del Baxter, Rock Springs, WY ... Exh.　1
Sept.　14—Bud Doyle, Rock Springs, WY ... Exh.　1
Sept.　15—Jackie Silvers, Salt Lake City . Exh.KO　1
Sept.　15—Bill Longston, Salt Lake City . Exh.KO　1
Sept.　16—Del Baster, Logan, UT .... Exh.　1
Sept.　16—Batt. Lamoreaux, Logan,UT ..... Exh.　1
Sept.　16—Cyclone Workman, Logan, UT ... Exh.　1
Sept.　16—George Nelson, Logan, UT ...... Exh.　1
Sept.　17—Jack Smith, Boise, Idaho........ Exh.　1
Sept.　17—Hank Potter, Boise, ID .... Exh.　1
Sept.　17—Lewis O'Connely, Boise, ID .... Exh.　2
Sept.　17—Batt. Lamoreaux, Boise, ID ..... Exh.　1
Sept.　17—Mick. McCafferty, Boise, ID .... Exh.　1
Nov.　6—Jack Carroll, Provo .... Exh.
Nov.　6—Del Baxter, Provo .... Exh.
Nov.　6—Jack Carroll, Provo .... Exh.
Nov.　9—Tommy Davenport, Des Moines .... W　2
Nov.　9—Elijah Lee, Des Moines .... KO　1

Nov.　9—Happy Shade, Des Moines .... W　3
Nov.　11—Bearcat Wright, Omaha.......... W　4
Nov.　13—Pete Wistort, Moline .... W　2
Nov.　13—George Neron, Moline .... W　2
Nov.　18—Jack Roper, Kansas City, MO .... Exh.　2
Nov.　18—Charlie Belanger, Kansas City, MO Exh.　2
Nov.　20—Angus Snyder, Wichita .... KO　1
Nov.　23—Babe Hunt, Tulsa .... Exh.ND　4
Nov.　27—Rufino Alvarez, Phoenix .... KO　1
Nov.　27—Ernie Musick, Phoenix .... KO　1
Nov.　27—Jimmy Long, Phoenix .... KO　1
Dec.　4—Johnny Korando, Fargo .... KO　1
Dec.　4—Swede Grantsburg, Fargo ...... KO　1
Dec.　4—Charley Retzlaff, Fargo .... Exh.　1
Dec.　7—Szymka Zabuil, Duluth ...... Exh.W　1
Dec.　7—Charley Retzlaff, Duluth .... W
Dec.　12—Art Laskey, St. Paul .... W　2
Dec.　12—Jack Roper, St. Paul .... W　1
Dec.　12—Angus McDonald, St. Paul ..... W　1
Dec.　15—Charley Belanger, Winnipeg ..... Exh.　2
Dec.　15—Stan Trojack, Winnipeg .... Exh.　1
Dec.　15—Angus McDonald, Winnipeg ..... Exh.　1
Dec.　18—Herman Raschke, Sioux Falls..... KO　1
Dec.　18—Louis Zack, Sioux Falls.......... W　2
Dec.　18—Chas. Pailson, Sioux Falls........ KO　1

1932

Feb.　1—Bad News Johnson, Stockton, CA .. KO　3
Feb.　1—Wally Hunt, Stockton, CA .... KO　1
Feb.　8—Buck Everett, Milwaukee .... W　2
Feb.　8—Jack Roper, Milwaukee .... W　2
Feb.　11—K.O. Christner, Cleveland .... KO　3
Feb.　15—George Kohler, Flint .... KO　1
Feb.　15—Pat McLaughlin, Flint .... KO　1
Feb.　18—King Levinsky, Chicago .... Exh.　4
Feb.　23—Frankie Wine, Louisville ...... Exh.　4
Feb.　29—Jack Phillips, Dayton .... KO　1
Feb.　29—Pat Sullivan, Dayton .... KO　1
Mar.　3—George Trenkle, Cincinnati ..... Exh.　2
May　5—Ray Vanzke, Cincinnati .... Exh.　2
May　7—Johnny Chick, Columbus ...... KO　1
Mar.　7—Eddie Anderson, Columbus ..... KO　1
Mar.　10—Hank Hankinson, Akron ...... KO　2
Mar.　10—Tiny Powell, Akron .... KO　2
Mar.　12—Tim Charles, Toledo .... Exh.W　2
Mar.　12—Jack O'Dowd, Toledo .... Exh.W　2
Mar.　16—Big Ed Williams, Clarksburg, WV .. KO　1
Mar.　16—Freddie Taylor, Clarksburg, WV .. KO　1
Mar.　18—Billy Miles, Huntington, WV .... KO　1
Mar.　18—Jack Kearns, Huntington, WV ..... W　2
Mar.　1—Joe Doctor, Toronto............. W　4
Mar.　31—Babe Hunt, Detroit.......... Exh.　4

1940

July　1—Cowboy Luttrell, Atlanta .... KO　2
July　15—Bull Curry, Detroit .... KO　2
July　29—Ellis Bashara, Charlotte .... KO　2
　　Retired to referee boxing and wrestling.

1942

Enlisted in U.S. Coast Guard and was commissioned a
Lieutenant Commander.

TB	KO	WD	WF	D	LD	LF	KO BY	ND	ND
80	49	10	1	7	6	0	1	5	1

Elected to Boxing Hall of Fame 1954.

ROBERTO DURAN
Panamanian Welterweight
Born, June 16, 1951, Panama City
1967
Mar.	8—Carlos Mendoza, Colon	W 4
Apr.	4—Manuel Jimenez, Colon	KO 1
May	14—Juan Gondola, Colon	KO 1
May	30—Eduardo Morales, Panama City	KO 1
Aug.	10—Enrique Jacobo, Panama City	KO 1

1968
Jan.	12—Uche De Leon, Panama City	KO 2
Feb.	8—Leroy Cargill, Panama City	KO 2
Mar.	16—Cafe Howard, Panama City	KO 1
Apr.	2—Alberto Brands, Panama City	KO 4
Sept.	4—Eduardo Fruto, Panama City	W 9

1969
Mar.	12—Jacinto Garcia, Panama City	KO 5
May	3—Adolfo Osses, Panama City	KO 7
July	16—Serafin Garcia, Panama City	KO 5
Aug.	15—Luis Patino, Panama City	KO 7

1970
Apr.	5—Felipe Torres, Mexico City	W 10
May	16—Ernesto Marcel, Panama City	W 10
July	10—Clemente Mucino, Colon	KO 6
Sept.	5—Marvin Castanedas, Puerto Armuelles	KO 1

1971
Jan.	10—Nacho Castanedas, Panama City	KO 4
Mar.	5—Jose Angel Herrera, Mexico City	KO 6
Apr.	4—Jose Acosta, Panama City	KO 1
May	29—Lloyd Marshall, Panama City	KO 6
July	18—Fermin Soto, Monterrey	KO 3
Sept.	13—Benny Huertas, New York	KO 1
Oct.	1—Hiroshi Kokayashi, Panama City	KO 7

1972
Jan.	15—Angel Robinson Garcia, Panama City	W 10
Mar.	10—Francisco Munoz, Panama City	KO 1
	(Won World Lightweight Title)	
Sept.	2—Greg Potter, Panama City	KO 1
Oct.	29—Lupe Ramirez, Panama City	KO 1
Nov.	17—Esteban DeJesus, New York	L 10

1973
Jan.	20—Jimmy Robertson, Panama City	KO 5
	(Retained World Lightweight Title)	
Feb.	23—Juan Medina, Los Angeles	KO 7
Mar.	17—Javier Ayala, Los Angeles	W 10
Apr.	14—Gerardo Ferrat, Panama City	KO 2
June	2—Hector Thompson, Panama City	KO 8
	(Retained World Lightweight Title)	
Aug.	4—Doc McClendon, San Juan	W 10
Sept.	8—Ishimatsu Suzuki, Panama City	KO 10
	(Retained World Lightweight Title)	
Dec.	1—Tony Garcia, Santiago	KO 2

1974
Jan.	21—Leonard Tavarez, Paris	KO 4
Feb.	16—Armando Mendoza, Panama City	KO 3
Mar.	16—Esteban DeJesus, Panama City	KO 11
	(Retained World Lightweight Title)	
July	6—Flash Gallego, Panama City	KO 5
Sept.	2—Hector Matta, San Juan	W 10
Oct.	10—Alberto Vanegas, Panama City	KO 1
Oct.	31—Jose Vasquez, San Jose	KO 2
Dec.	21—Masataka Takayama, San Jose	KO 1
	(Retained World Lightweight Title)	

1975
Feb.	15—Andres Salgado, Panama City	KO 1
Mar.	2—Ray Lampkin, Panama City	KO 14
	(Retained World Lightweight Title)	
June	3—Jose Peterson, Miami Beach	KO 1
Aug.	2—Pedro Mendoza, Managua	KO 1
Sept.	13—Alirio Acuna, Chitre	KO 3

Sept.	30—Edwin Viruet, Uniondale	W 10
Dec.	14—Leonico Ortiz, San Juan	KO 15
	(Retained World Lightweight Title)	

1976
May	4—Saoul Mamby, Miami Beach	W 10
May	22—Lou Bizzarro, Erie	KO 14
	(Retained World Lightweight Title)	
July	31—Emilliano Villa, Panama City	KO 9
Oct.	15—Alvaro Rojas, Hollywood, FL	KO 1
	(Retained World Lightweight Title)	

1977
Jan.	29—Vilomar Fernandez, Miami Beach	KO 13
	(Retained World Lightweight Title)	
May	16—Javier Muniz, Landover	W 10
Aug.	6—Bernardo Diaz, Panama City	KO 1
Sept.	17—Edwin Viruet, Philadelphia	W 15
	(Retained World Lightweight Title)	

1978
Jan.	21—Esteban DeJesus, Las Vegas	KO 12
	(Retained World Lightweight Title)	
Apr.	27—Adolph Viruet, New York	W 10
Sept.	1—Ezequiel Obando, Panama City	KO 2
Dec.	8—Monroe Brooks, New York	KO 8

1979
Apr.	8—Jimmy Heair, Las Vegas	W 10
June	22—Carlos Palomino, New York	W 10
Sept.	28—Zeferino (Speedy) Gonzalez, Las Vegas	W 10

1980
Jan.	13—Josef Nsubugh, Las Vegas	KO 4
Feb.	24—Wellington Wheatley, Las Vegas	KO 6
June	20—Sugar Ray Leonard, Montreal	W 15
Nov.	25—Sugar Ray Leonard, New Orleans	KO 8

1981
June	10—Simon Smith, New York	Exh. 3
Aug.	9—Nino Gonzalez, Cleveland	W 10
Sept.	26—Luigi Minchillo, Las Vegas	W 10

1982
Jan	30—Wilfred Benitez, Las Vegas	L 15
	(For WBC Junior Middleweight Title)	
Sept	4—Kirkland Laing, Detroit	L 10
Nov.	12—Jimmy Batten, Miami, Fla.	W 10

1983
Jan.	29—Pipino Cuevas, Los Angeles	KO 4
June	16—Davey Moore, New York	KO 8

TB	KO	WD	WF	D	LD	LF	KO BY	ND	NC
81	58	19	0	0	3	0	1	0	0

YVON DURELLE
Baie Ste. Ann, NB, Canada
Light-Heavyweight
Born, Oct. 14, 1929. Height, 5 ft. 9 in.
1948
Aug.	—Sonny Ramsey, Chatham	KO 2
Aug.	—Al Fraser, Chatham	W 4
Sept.	—Al Fraser, Chatham	W 4
Sept.	—Percy Richards, Chatham	W 4
	—Billy Snowball, Chatham	LF 2
	—Al Batton, Chatham	KO 2
	—Sterling Adari, Chatham	KO 2
	—Irv Crosby, Chatham	KO 2
	—Harry Poulton, Newcastle	W 8
	—Harry Poulton, Newcastle	W 8
	—Manuel Leek, Frederickton	KO 6

1949
May	—Joe Tyles, Chatham	KO 1
June	—Jim Mooney, Chatham	W 8

July	—Bill McGlacklin, Frederickton	W 8
July	—Pat Davis, Newcastle	KO 2
July	—Kid Wolfe, Chatham	W 10
July	—Bill Landry, Newcastle	W 8
Sept.	—Ace McCluskey, Chatham	KO 5
Sept.	—Ossie Farrell, Chatham	KO 1

1950
May	10—Alvin Upshaw, Chatham	KO 7
	—Tiger Warrington, Moncton	W 10
	—Coo McRae, Bathurst	W 10
	—Cobey McCloskey, Charlottetown	W 8
July	1—Tiger Warrington, Montreal	W 10
Aug.	14—Coby McCloskey, Halifax	L 10
Aug.	21—Frankie Hamilton, Chatham	KO 3
Aug.	28—Ossie Farrell, Moncton	KO 1
Sept.	12—Cobey McCloskey, Chatham	W 12
Oct.	12—Cobey McCloskey, Nova Scotia	L 12
Dec.	7—Tiger Warrington, Yarmouth	W 10

1951
Jan.	—Roy Wouters, Halifax	L 10
May	23—Bob Stecher, Chatham	W 10
May	—Cobey McCluskey, Charlottetown	NC 9
June	—Arnold Fleiger, Chatham	KO 2
July	—Cobey McClusky, Moncton	KO 6

1952
May	—Eddie Zastre, Chatham	W 10
July	—Hurley Sanders, Chatham	L 10
Aug.	15—Bob Stecher, Chatham	W 10
Oct.	—Jimmy Nolan, Calgary	W 10
Oct.	—Hurley Sanders, Chatham	W 10

1953
May	2—George Ross, Glace Bay	KO 12
May	20—Tony Amato, Chatham	KO 6
June	25—Curtis Wade, Moncton	W 10
July	20—Joey Greco, Chatham	KO 4
July	—Archie Hannigan, Glace Bay	KO 5
Aug.	26—Wilfredo Miro, Logieville	KO 2
Sept.	2—Curtis Wade, Moncton	KO 7
Sept.	8—Gordon Wallace, Sydney	W 12
	(Won Canadian Light-Heavyweight Title)	
Oct.	1—Al Winn, New Brunswick	W 10
Oct.	15—Gordon Wallace, Moncton	W 12
Nov.	17—Doug Harper, Calgary	L 12
	(Lost Canadian Light-Heavyweight Title)	

1954
Jan.	20—Doug Harper, Calgary	D 12
Feb.	15—Floyd Patterson, Brooklyn	L 8
May	5—Waddell Hanna, Chatham	L 10
May	24—Billy Fifield, Glace Bay	KO 10
June	4—Charlie Chase, Moncton	W 10
June	9—Sampson Powell, Newcastle	W 10
June	23—Jerome Richardson, Moncton	W 10
July	7—Doug Harper, Newcastle	W 12
	(Won Canadian Light-Heavyweight Title)	
July	26—Paul Andrews, New York	KO by 5
Aug.	25—Bob Isler, Newcastle	W 10
Sept.	13—Bob Isler, Sydney	KO 1
Sept.	27—Gordon Wallace, Bathurst	W 12
	(Canadian Light-Heavyweight Title)	
Nov.	12—Gerhard Hecht, Berlin	L 10
Dec.	—Art Henri, Berlin	L 12

1955
May	24—Ron Barton, London	LF 3
June	16—Jimmy Garcia, Moncton	KO 8
June	23—Floyd Patterson, Newcastle	KO by 5
July	28—Billy Fifield, Moncton	KO 1
	(Canadian Light-Heavyweight Title)	
Sept.	3—Jimmy Slade, Glace Bay	KO by 7
Oct.	18—Yolande Pompey, London	KO by 7
Nov.	28—Artie Towne, Nottingham	L.Dis. 7

1956

May 20—Jerome Richardson, Hamilton, Bermuda .... W 10
June 19—Arthur Howard, London .... L 10
July 19—Tinker Picot, Moncton .... KO 4
Aug. 16—Alvin Williams, Moncton .... W 10
Sept. 6—Tinker Picot, St. John .... KO 4
Sept. 20—Gary Garafola, Moncton .... KO 1
Oct. 4—Chubby Wright, Moncton .... W 10
Oct. 27—Bobby King Frederickton .... KO 1

1957

Feb. 19—Clarence Hinnant, Miami Beach ... KO 8
Mar. 25—Clarence Floyd, New York .... KO 7
Apr. 22—Angelo DeFendis, New York ...... W 10
May 16—Leo Johnson, Moncton .... KO 5
May 30—Gordon Wallace, Moncton ...... KO 2
(Won British Empire Light-Heavyweight Title)
June 14—Tony Anthony, Detroit .... D 10
Aug. 15—Gunther Balzer, Chatham .... KO 8
Aug. 29—Tim Jones, Moncton .... KO 8
Sept. 25—Willi Besmanoff, Detroit .... W 10
Nov. 7—Floyd McCoy, Moncton .... KO 2
Nov. 22—Mario Nini, Edmunton .... KO 4
Dec. 11—Jerry Luedee, Tampa............ W 10

1958

Jan. 31—Clarence Hinnant, New York ..... KO 7
Mar. 14—Tony Anthony, New York ...... KO by 7
May 21—Germinal Ballarin, Montreal .... W 10
July 16—Mike Holt, Montreal .... KO 9
(British Empire Light-Heavyweight Title)
Aug. 28—Freddie Mack, Moncton .... W 10
Oct. 2—Louis Jones, Moncton .... KO 2
Dec. 10—Archie Moore, Montreal .... KO 11
(World Light-Heavyweight Title)

1959

May 12—Teddy Burns, Caribou .... KO 3
Aug. 12—Archie Moore, Montreal ....KO by 3
(World Light-Heavyweight Title)
Sept. 15—Al Anderson, Chatham .... KO 4
Sept. 28—Charlie Jones, Quebec City .... W 10
Oct. 22—Young Beau Jack, Moncton....... KO 9
Nov. 17—George Chuvalo, Toronto ......KO by 12
(For Canadian Heavyweight Title)
Nov. 18—Announced retirement.

ALFREDO ESCALERA
Puerto Rican Junior Lightweight
Born, Nov. 21, 1952

1970

Sept. 24—Bob Paysant, Portland, ME....... KO 3
Dec. 1—Rod Walsh, Scranton .... W 4

1971

Jan. 26—Don McClendon, New York ....L 6
Mar. 20—Willie Lugo, New York .... W 6
Mar. 24—Jimmy Jaynes, Boston .... W 6
July 26—Henry Ocasio, New York .... W 6
Sept. 2—Eddie James, Baltimore .... W 6
Sept. 7—Reynald Cantin, Sorel .... W 10
Sept. 23—Edwin Viruet, Paterson ....L 8
Oct. 25—Henry Ocasio, New York .... W 6

1972

Feb. 15—Diego Alcala, New York ....L 10
June 13—Alejandro Falcon, San Juan ...... KO 7
July 14—Carlos Penso, Ponce .... KO 1
Sept. 18—Miguel Morales, San Juan .... W 10

1973

Mar. 17—Miguel Montilla, Carolina .... L 10
Mar. 31—Rocky Orengo, Carolina .... W 10
Apr. 28—Gino Febus, Carolina .... L 10
July 14—Miguel Montilla, Caguas .... KO 8

July 21—Leo Randolph, San Juan .... KO 2
Aug. 21—Frankie Otero, San Juan .... KO 5
Sept. 15—Jose Luis Lopez, San Juan .... KO 6
Nov. 12—Antonio Amaya, San Juan .... W 10
Nov. 30—Mike Mayan, San Juan .... KO 4
Dec. 17—Johnny Copeland, San Juan ...... KO 5

1974

Feb. 4—Stanley Yanecheck, San Juan ..... KO 2
Mar. 3—Sigfredo Rodriguez, San Juan ..... KO 1
Apr. 1—Jorge Ramos, San Juan .... KO 3
May 30—Carlos Mendoza, San Juan .... KO 8
Aug. 3—Ricardo Arredondo, San Juan .. W disq 8
Sept. 9—Oscar Pitton, San Juan .... KO 5
Oct. 18—Eleuterio Hernandez, Pueblo ..... KO 8
Oct. 30—Memo Cruz, Oaxaca...............L 10
Nov. 15—Rodriguez Valdez, Pueblo .... KO 1
Dec. 14—Mario Roman, Mexico City .....KO by 2

1975

Feb. 24—Mario Roman, San Juan .... KO 3
Mar. 31—Francisco Villegas, San Juan....... D 10
July 5—Kuniaki Shibata, Tokyo .... KO 5
(WBC Junior Lightweight Title)
Sept. 20—Lionel Hernandez, Caracas .... D 15
(WBC Junior Lightweight Title)
Nov. 17—Gaetan Hart, San Juan .... KO 6
Dec. 12—Sven-Erik Paulsen, Oslo .... KO 9
(WBC Junior Lightweight Title)

1976

Feb. 20—Jose Fernandez, San Juan .... KO 13
(WBC Junior Lightweight Title)
Apr. 1—Buzzsaw Yamabe, Nara.......... KO 6
(WBC Junior Lightweight Title)
July 1—Buzzsaw Yamabe, Nara........... W 15
(WBC Junior Lightweight Title)
Sept. 18—Ray Lunny, San Juan .... KO 12
(WBC Junior Lightweight Title)
Nov. 30—Tyrone Everett, Philadelphia ...... W 15
(WBC Junior Lightweight Title)

1977

Mar. 17—Ronnie McGarvey, San Juan ...... KO 6
(WBC Junior Lightweight Title)
May 16—Carlos Becerril, Landover .... KO 8
(WBC Junior Lightweight Title)
Sept. 10—Sigfredo Rodriguez, San Juan ..... W 15
(WBC Junior Lightweight Title)

1978

Jan. 28—Alexis Arguello, San Juan ......KO by 13
(Lost WBC Junior Lightweight Title)
June 3—Rogelio Castaneda, San Juan ...... W 10
—Larry Stanton, New York .... KO 3
Oct. 27—Julio Valdez, New York.............L 10

1979

Feb. 4—Alexis Arguello, Rimini ....KO by 13
(For WBC Junior Lightweight Title)
Oct. 13—Antonio Cruz, San Juan..........D 10

1980

—Inactive

1981

Oct. 16—Ruby Ortiz, New York ....W 10
Nov. 21—Johnny Torres, Miami....................KO 8

1982

Jan. 9—Clemente Munoz, San Juan..............W 10
Jan. 22—Angel Cruz, New York.......................L 10
Apr. 9—Gene Hatcher, Fort Worth ....L 10
May 21—Jesus Nava, Miami Beach...............KO 7
July 2—Johnny Lira, Miami Beach.............W 10
Sept. 18—Guillermo Fernandez, Miami Beach
....W 10
Nov. 12—Maurice (Termite) Watkins, Miami.W 10

1983

Jan. 29—Sergio Medina, Los Angeles...............L 10

Mar. 25—Trad Thompson, Miami, Fla. ....KO 3
May 15—Martin Rojas, Miami, Fla. ....W 12
(Won American Inter-Continental Junior Welterweight Title)
July 8—Gene Hatcher, New York...................W 10

TB	KO	WD	WF	D	LD	LF	KO BY	ND	NC
67	29	21	1	3	10	0	3	0	0

LUIS ANGEL FIRPO
Born, October 21, 1895, Jujuy Province, Argentina. Weight, 216 lbs. Height, 6 ft. 3 in.

1917

Dec. 10—Frank Hagney, Buenos Aires ..... ND 6

1918

Jan. 12—Angel Rodriguez, Montevideo ...KO by 1
Sept. 28—William Daly, Chillan .... KO 7
Nov. 9—Ignacio Sepulveda, Santiago ..... KO 2
Dec. 14—Calvin Respress, Santiago .... WF 2

1919

Feb. 7—Calvin Respress, Santiago .... W 15
Apr. 12—Fernando Priano, Montevideo ... KO 4
Apr. 26—Arturo Manning, Montevideo .... KO 3
Nov. 1—Dave Mills, Santiago ....L 12
(For South American Heavyweight Title)

1920

Feb. 28—Andres Balsa, Valparaiso .... KO 6
Apr. 30—Dave Mills, Santiago .... KO 1
(Won South American Heavyweight Title)
July 2—Antonio Jirsa, Buenos Aires ..... KO 1
Dec. 11—Dave Wills, Buenos Aires .... KO 1
(Retained South American Heavyweight Title)

1921

Mar. 12—Gunboat Smith, Valparaiso ...... W 12
Apr. 23—Gunboat Smith, Buenos Aires .... KO 12
Sept. 27—Fernando Priano, Tucuman....... KO 2

1922

Mar. 20—Sailor Tom Maxted, Newark ...... KO 7
Apr. 4—Joe McCann, Newark............ KO 5
May 20—Italian Jack Herman, Brooklyn .... KO 4
Oct. 8—Jim Tracey, Buenos Aires .... KO 4

1923

Mar. 12—Bill Brennan, New York .... KO 12
May 12—Jack McAuliffe, New York .... KO 3
June 10—Italian Jack Herman, Havana .... KO 2
June 17—Jim Hibbard, Mexico City .... KO 2
July 12—Jess Willard, Jersey City .... KO 8
July 27—Joe Burke, Battle Creek .... KO 2
Aug. 2—Homer Smith, Omaha .... ND 10
Aug. 31—Charley Weinert, Philadelphia .... KO 2
Sept. 14—Jack Dempsey, New York ......KO by 2
(For World Heavyweight Title)

1924

Feb. 24—Farmer Lodge, Buenos Aires ..... KO 5
Mar. 7—Erminio Spalla, Buenos Aires ..... KO 14
Apr. 5—Al Reich, Barracas .... KO 1
Sept. 11—Harry Wills, Jersey City .... ND 12
Nov. 12—Charley Weinert, Newark .... ND 12

1925

(Inactive)

1926

Apr. 3—Erminio Spalla, Buenos Aires ...... W 12

1927–1935

(Inactive)

1936

May 9—Saverio Grizzo, Buenos Aires ..... KO 1
May 25—Siska Habarta, Rosario .... KO 3
July 11—Arturo Godoy, Buenos Aires ....KO by 3

TB	KO	WD	WF	D	LD	LF	KO BY	ND	NC
38	26	3	1	0	1	0	3	4	0

Died, August 7, 1960, Buenos Aires, Argentina.

ROBERT FITZSIMMONS
(Ruby Robert and Freckled Bob)

Born, May 26, 1863, Helston, Cornwall, England. Weight, 165 lbs. Height, 5 ft. 11¾ in. Managed by Martin Julian.

First appearance at Timaru, N.Z., in Jem Mace's competition, 1880, in which he defeated four men.

Next year, same competition, beat five men, among them Herbert Slade (the Maori).

Other not dated performances between 1882–1889 are as follows:

Jem Crawford, 3; Bill Slavin, 7; "Starlight," 9; Arthur Cooper, 3; Jack Murphy, 8; Brinsmead, 2; Jack Greentree, 3; Dick Sandall, 4, amateur championship of New Zealand; Conway, 2; Prof. West, 1; Pablo Frank, 2; Jack Riddle, 4; Eager, 2.

1889

Dec.   17—Dick Ellis of New Zealand, Sydney   W   3

1890

Feb.   10—Jem Hall, Sydney ....KO by   4
May   10—Arrived in San Francisco on Zealandia.
May   17—Tried out at California Athletic Club with Frank Allen, broke Allen's wrist.
May   29—Billy McCarthy, Australia, $1,250. California Athletic Club .... KO   9
June   28—Arthur O. Upham (154-lb. limit) $1,000 Audubon Athletic Club, New Orleans. Referee, Robert Lynd. Fitzsimmons' seconds, Jimmy Carroll, Tommy Danforth; Upham's, "Doc" O'Connell, John Duffy .... KO   5

1891

Jan   14—Jack Dempsey (150½–147½) $11,000-$1,000. Largest purse to date. Dempsey favorite in betting. Battle for world's championship, 3-oz. gloves, Queensberry rules; weighed five minutes before battle on scales in ring. Referee, Col. A. Brewster. Fitzsimmons' seconds, "Doc" O'Connell, Jimmy Carroll, Prof. Robertson; Dempsey's, Jack McAuliffe, Gus Tuthill, Mike Conley; Fitzsimmons' timekeeper, W. J. Crittenden; Dempsey's, Jimmy Colville. Fitzsimmons knocked Dempsey down in third round, got first blood in fifth. Fitzsimmons trained at Bay St. Louis, MS; Dempsey at Galveston, TX, New Orleans .... KO   13
Apr.   28—Abe Cougle, Chicago .... KO   2
May   1—"Black Pearl," Minneapolis .... W   4

1892

Mar.   2—Peter Maher, $9,000-$1,000. Olympic club, New Orleans, Fitzsimmons favorite in betting. Referee, Prof. John Duffy. Fitzsimmons' seconds, Jimmy Carroll, Joe Choynski, Alec Greggains; Maher's, Billy Madden, Gus Tuthill, Jack Fallon. Fitzsimmons' timekeeper, Geo. R. Clark, for Maher P. J. Donohue; for club, R. M. Frank. Fitzsimmons scored the first knockdown and blood in first round and won by a KO in 12.
Apr.   30—James Farrell, Newark .... KO   2
May   7—Joe Godfrey, Philadelphia .... KO   1
May   17—Jerry Slattery, New York .... KO   2
Sept.   3—Millard Zeuder, Anniston, AL..... KO   1

1893

Mar.   8—Jem Hall (167–163½) $40,000 prom-

ised. Crescent City Athletic Club, New Orleans. Referee, Prof. John Duffy, Fitzsimmons' seconds, Martin Julian, Frank Bosworth, Bill Fitzsimmons, Hall's, "Squire" Abingdon, Charley Mitchell, Jack McAuliffe, John Kline. Timekeeper for Fitzsimmons, Dominick O'Malley; for Hall, Bob Masterson; for club, R. M. Frank. Betting, 10 to 9 on Hall. Fitzsimmons won with a right half-arm upper cut .... KO   4
Mar.   25—Phil Mayo of Cleveland, Chicago .. KO   2
May   30—Warner, Baltimore .... KO   1
Sept.   5—Jack Hickey, Newark .... W   3

1894

June   17—Joe Choynski, catchweights, police interference, Boston. Referee, Cap. Bill Daly. Gate .... D   5
July   28—Frank Kellar of Michigan, Buffalo . KO   2
Sept.   26—Dan Creedon ($4,000–$1,000). Olympic Athletic Club, New Orleans. Referee, Prof. John Duffy .... KO   2
(Middleweight Title)
Oct.   11—Matched to fight Corbett, $10,000 a side.
Nov.   19—Con Riodan, Syracuse, N.Y. ..... Exh.   2
Riordan collapsed and died after bout. Fitzsimmons exonerated of blame for death.

1895

Toured with vaudeville company.
Apr.   16–19—Al Allich KO 3; M. Connors, New York .... KO   1

1896

Feb.   21—Peter Maher $10,000 and champ., Mexico, op. Langtry, TX. Fitz. about 163 lbs. Referee, George Siler, 5 oz., Im., 35s ..... KO   1
Feb.   29—Peter Maher, New York .... ND   3
Dec.   2—Tom Sharkey, San Francisco ......LF   8

1897

Jan.   3—Ernest Roeber, Exhibition........ KO   1
Mar.   17—James J. Corbett, Carson City ..... KO   14
(Won Heavyweight Title)
June   5—Leadvale Blacksmith, Exhibition ... KO   2

1899

June   9—Jim Jeffries, Coney Island ....KO by   11
(Lost Heavyweight Title)
Oct.   28—Jim Thorne, Chicago .... KO   1

1900

Mar.   27—Jim Daly, Philadelphia .... KO   1
Apr.   30—Ed Dunkhorst, Brooklyn .... KO   2
Aug.   10—Gus Ruhlin, Coney Island .... KO   6
Aug.   24—Tom Sharkey, Coney Island ..... KO   2

1902

July   25—Jim Jeffries, San Francisco .....KO by   8
(Heavyweight Title Bout)

1903

Oct.   14—Joe Grim, Philadelphia .... ND   6
Nov.   25—George Gardner, San Francisco .... W   20
(Won Light-Heavyweight Title)

1904

July   23—Phil. J. O'Brien, Philadelphia ..... ND   6

1905

Dec.   20—Jack O'Brien, San Francisco ....KO by   13
(Lost Light-Heavyweight Title)

1907

Mar.   7—Tony Ross, Newcastle, PA .... Exh.   4

July   17—John Johnson, Philadelphia.....KO by   2

1908

Sept.   21—Jim Paul, Benson Mines .... KO   1

1909

Dec.   27—Bill Lang, Sydney, New South Wales ....KO by   12

1914

Jan.   29—K. O. Sweeney, Williamsport, PA .. ND   6
Feb.   20—Jersey Bellow, Bethlehem, PA .... ND   6

Largest purse Fitzsimmons ever fought for was on March 8, 1893, in New Orleans, when he defeated Jem Hall in 4 rounds , purse $40,000. Bob received only part of the money.

TB	KO	WD	WF	D	LD	LF	KO BY	ND	NC
41	23	5	0	1	0	1	6	5	0

Oct. 22, 1917, died of pneumonia at Chicago, IL.

Elected to Boxing Hall of Fame 1954.

JOE FRAZIER

Born, January 12, 1944, Beaufort, SC
1964 Olympic Games Heavyweight Champion
Philadelphia, PA Heavyweight

1965

Aug.   16—Woody Goss, Philadelphia .... KO   1
Sept.   20—Mike Bruce, Philadelphia .... KO   3
Sept.   28—Ray Staples, Philadelphia .... KO   2
Nov.   11—Abe Davis, Philadelphia .... KO   1

1966

Jan.   17—Mel Turnbow, Philadelphia ...... KO   1
Mar.   4—Dick Wipperman, New York ..... KO   5
Apr.   4—Charley Polite, Philadelphia ...... KO   2
Apr.   28—Don Toro Smith, Pittsburgh ..... KO   3
May   19—Chuck Leslie, Los Angeles ...... KO   3
May   26—Al Jones, Los Angeles .... KO   1
July   25—Billy Daniels, Philadelphia ...... KO   6
Sept.   21—Oscar Bonavena, New York .... W   10
Nov.   21—Eddie Machen, Los Angeles ..... KO   10

1967

Feb.   21—Doug Jones, Philadelphia .... KO   6
Apr.   11—Jeff Davis, Miami Beach .... KO   5
May   4—George Johnson, Los Angeles ..... W   10
July   19—George Chuvalo, New York....... KO   4
Oct.   17—Tony Doyle, Philadelphia .... KO   2
Dec.   18—Marion Connor, Boston .... KO   3

1968

Mar.   4—Buster Mathis, New York .... KO   11
(New York State Heavyweight Title)
June   24—Manuel Ramos, New York ...... KO   2
(New York State Heavyweight Title)
Dec.   10—Oscar Bonavena, Philadelphia ... W   15
(New York State Heavyweight Title)

1969

Apr.   22—Dave Zyglewicz, Houston .... KO   1
(New York State Heavyweight Title)
June   23—Jerry Quarry, New York .... KO   7
(New York State Heavyweight Title)

1970

Feb.   16—Jimmy Ellis, New York .... KO   5
(Won World Heavyweight Title)
Nov.   18—Bob Foster, Detroit .... KO   2
(Retained World Heavyweight Title)

1971

Mar. 8—Muhammad Ali, New York .... W 15
(Retained World Heavyweight Title)

July 15—Cleveland Williams, Houston .... Exh. 3

July 15—James Helwig, Houston .... Exh. 3

1972

Jan. 15—Terry Daniels, New Orleans ...... KO 4
(Retained World Heavyweight Title)

May 25—Ton Stander, Omaha .... KO 5
(Retained World Heavyweight Title)

1973

Jan. 22—George Foreman, Kingston .....KO by 2
(Lost World Heavyweight Title)

July 2—Joe Bugner, London .... W 12

1974

Jan. 28—Muhammad Ali, New York .... L 12
(American Heavyweight Title)

June 17—Jerry Quarry, New York .... KO 5

1975

Mar. 1—Jimmy Ellis, Melbourne .... KO 9

Oct. 1—Muhammad Ali, Manila ....KO by 14
(World Heavyweight Title)

1976

June 15—George Foreman, Uniondale ....KO by 5
Retired from the ring after above bout.

TB	KO	WD	WF	D	LD	LF	KO BY	ND	NC
36	27	5	0	0	0	1	0	3	0

GEORGE FOREMAN
Born, Jan. 22, 1948, Marshall, TX

1968

Olympic Heavyweight
Champion

1969

June 23—Don Waldhelm, New York .... KO 3

July 1—Fred Ashew, Houston .... KO 1

July 14—Sylvester Dullaire,
Washington, D.C. .... KO 1

Aug. 18—Chuck Wepner, New York .... KO 3

Sept. 18—John Carroll, Seattle .... KO 1

Sept. 23—Cokkie Wallace, Houston .... KO 2

Oct. 7—Vernon Clay, Houston .... KO 2

Oct. 31—Roberto Davila, New York .... W 8

Nov. 5—Leo Peterson, Scranton .... KO 4

Nov. 18—Max Martinez, Houston .... KO 2

Dec. 6—Bob Hazelton, Las Vegas .... KO 1

Dec. 16—Levi Forte, Miami Beach .... W 10

Dec. 18—Gary Wiler, Seattle .... KO 1

1970

Jan. 6—Charlie Polite, Houston .... KO 4

Jan. 26—Jack O'Halloran, New York ...... KO 5

Feb. 16—Gregorio Peralta, New York ...... W 10

Mar. 31—Rufus Brassell, Houston .... KO 1

Apr. 17—James J. Woody, New York .... KO 3

Apr. 29—Aaron Eastling, Cleveland ...... KO 4

May 16—George Johnson, Los Angeles ..... KO 7

July 20—Roger Russell, Philadelphia ...... KO 1

Aug 4—George Chuvalo, Houston .... KO 3

Nov. 3—Lou Bailey, Oklahoma City .... KO 3

Nov. 18—Boone Kirkman, New York .... KO 2

Dec. 19—Mel Turnbow, Seattle .... KO 1

1971

Feb. 8—Charlie Boston, St. Paul .... KO 1

Apr. 3—Stamford Harris, Lake Geneva .... KO 2

May 10—Gregory Peralta, Oakland .... KO 10

Sept. 14—Vic Scott, El Paso .... KO 1

Sept. 21—Leroy Caldwell, Houston .... KO 3

Oct. 7—Ollie Wilson, San Antonio ...... KO 2

Oct. 29—Luis Pires, New York .... KO 4

1972

Feb. 29—Murphy Goodwin, Austin .... KO 2

Mar. 7—Clarence Boone, Beaumont ...... KO 2

Apr. 10—Ted Gullick, Los Angeles .... KO 2

May 11—Miguel Paez, Oakland .... KO 2

Oct. 10—Terry Sorrels, Salt Lake City ..... KO 2

1973

Jan. 22—Joe Frazier, Kingston .... KO 2
(Won World Heavyweight Title)

Sept. 1—Jose Roman, Tokyo .... KO 1
(Retained World Heavyweight Title)

1974

Mar. 26—Ken Norton, Caracas .... KO 2
(Retained World Heavyweight Title)

Oct. 30—Muhammad Ali, Kinshasa ......KO by 8
(Lost World Heavyweight Title)

1975

Apr. 26—Charley Polite, Toronto .... Exh. 3

Apr. 26—Boone Kirkman, Toronto .... Exh. 3

Apr. 26—Terry Daniels, Toronto .... Exh. 2

Apr. 26—Jerry Judge, Toronto .... Exh. 2

Apr. 26—Alonzo Johnson, Toronto .... Exh. 2

Nov. 26—Jody Ballard, Kianesha Lake .... Exh. 2

Dec. 17—Eddie Brooks, San Francisco .... Exh. 4

1976

Jan. 24—Ron Lyle, Las Vegas .... KO 4

June 15—Joe Frazier, Uniondale .... KO 5

Aug. 14—Scott LeDoux, Utica .... KO 3

Oct. 15—John Dennis, Hollywood, FL...... KO 4

1977

Jan. 22—Pedro Agosta, Pensacola .... KO 4

Mar. 17—Jimmy Young, San Juan .... L 12

TB	KO	WD	WF	D	LD	LF	KO BY	ND	NC
47	42	3	0	0	0	1	0	1	0

JOE GANS
(JOSEPH GAINES)
(Old Master)

Born, November 25, 1874, Baltimore, MD.
Weight, 133 lbs, Height, 5 ft. 6¼ in. Managed by Al
Herford.

Started his career in 1891. His bouts prior to
1895, of which there is any record, follow:

1891–1894

—Dave Armstrong, Baltimore .... KO 12

—Arthur Coates, Baltimore .... KO 22

—Tommy Harden, Baltimore .... KO 7

—George Evans, Baltimore .... KO 3

—Dave Armstrong, Baltimore .... KO 3

—Jack Daly, Pittsburgh .... KO 11

—Dave Horn, Baltimore .... KO 2

—Bud Brown, Baltimore........... KO 10

—John Ball, Baltimore .... W 6

—Jack McDonald, Newark .... W 7

—Dave Horn, Baltimore .... W 11

—Johnny Van Heest, Baltimore ...... W 9

1895

Feb. 6—Fred Sweigert, Baltimore .... W 10

Mar. 7—Sol English, Baltimore .... W 10

Mar. 16—Howard Wilson, Baltimore ...... W 10

Apr. 2—Kentucky Rosebud, Baltimore ...... W 7

Apr. 25—Kentucky Rosebud, Baltimore ..... W 6

May 4—Frank Peabody, Baltimore .... KO 3

May 20—Benny Peterson, Baltimore ...... KO 17

July 15—George Siddons, Baltimore .... D 20

Oct. 21—Joe Elliott, Baltimore........... KO 6

Nov. 18—Young Griffo, Baltimore .... D 10

Nov. 28—George Siddons, Baltimore ..... KO 7

1896

Jan. 11—Benny Peterson, Philadelphia ..... KO 3

Jan. 17—Joe Elliott, Baltimore........... KO 7

Jan. 28—Howard Wilson, Baltimore ...... W 8

Feb. 22—Jimmy Kennard, Boston .... KO 5

June 8—Jimmy Watson, Paterson .... KO 9

June 29—Tommy Butler, Brooklyn.......... W 12

Aug. 20—Jack Williams, Baltimore .... KO 2

Aug. 31—Danny McBride, Baltimore ...... D 20

Sept. 28—Jack Ball, Philadelphia .... W 4

Oct. 6—Dal Hawkins, New York .... L 15

Oct. 19—Jack Williams, Baltimore ...... W 2

Nov. 12—Jerry Marshall, Baltimore ...... W 20

Dec. 14—Charles Rochette, San Francisco... KO 12

1897

Apr. 3—H. Wilson, New York .... KO 9

May 19—Mike Leonard, San Francisco ...... W 10

Sept. 21—Young Griffo, Philadelphia ...... D 15

Sept. 27—Bobby Dobbs, Brooklyn .... L 20

Nov. 29—Stanton Abbot, Baltimore ...... W 5

—Jack Daly, Philadelphia........... ND 6

1898

Jan. 3—Billy Young, Baltimore .... W 2

Jan. 18—Frank Garrard, Cleveland ...... W 15

Mar. 11—Tom Shortell, Baltimore .... ND 6

Apr. 11—Young Starlight, Baltimore ...... KO 3

Apr. 11—Young Smyrna, Baltimore .... W 4

May 11—Steve Crosby, Louisville .... W 6

June 3—Kid Roberson, Chicago .... W 6

Aug. 8—Billy Ernst, Coney Island .... W 11

Aug. 26—Young Smyrna, Baltimore .... K 15

Aug. 31—Tom Jackson, Easton, PA .... KO 3

Sept. 26—Herman Miller, Baltimore ...... W 4

Nov. 4—Kid McPartland, New York ...... W 20

Dec. 27—Jack Daly, New York .... W 25

1899

Jan. 13—Young Smyrna, Baltimore .... KO 2

Jan. 28—Martin Judge, Toronto........ W 20

Feb. 6—Billy Ernst, Buffalo .... WF 10

Apr. 14—George McFadden, New York ...KO by 23

July 24—Jack Dobbs, Ocean City .... W 4

July 28—George McFadden, New York ..... D 25

Sept. 1—Eug. Bezenah, New York .... KO 10

Sept. 15—Martin Judge, Baltimore .... W 12

Oct. 3—Spider Kelly, New York .... W 25

Oct. 11—Martin Judge, Baltimore ...... W 20

Oct. 31—George McFadden, New York ..... W 25

Nov. 24—Steve Crosby, Chicago .... W 6

225

Dec. 11—Kid Ashe, Cincinnati . . . . W 15
Dec. 22—Kid McPartland, Chicago . . . . D 6

1900
Feb. 9—Spike Sullivan, New York . . . . W 14
Mar. 23—*Frank Erne, New York . . . . . . KO by 12
(For World Lightweight title)
*Gans refused to continue—asked to have the bout stopped.
Apr. 2—Chicago Jack Daly, Philadelphia . . . KO 5
May 25—Dal Hawkins, New York . . . . KO 2
June 26—Barney Furey, Cincinnati . . . . KO 9
July 10—Young Griffo, New York . . . . KO 8
July 12—Whitey Lester, Baltimore . . . . . . KO 4
Aug. 31—Dal Hawkins, New York . . . . KO 3
Sept. 7—George McFadden, Philadelphia . . ND 6
Oct. 2—George McFadden, Denver . . . . D 10
Oct. 6—Joe Young, Denver . . . . W 10
Oct. 16—Otto Sieloff, Denver . . . . KO 9
Oct. 19—Spider Kelly, Denver . . . . W 8
Nov. 16—Kid Parker, Denver . . . . KO 4
Dec. 13—Terry McGovern, Chicago . . . . . . KO by 2

1901
Feb. 15—Jack Daly, Baltimore . . . . WF 6
Apr. 1—Martin Flaherty, Baltimore . . . . W 4
May 31—Bobby Dobbs, Baltimore . . . . KO 7
July 15—Harry Berger, Baltimore . . . . ND 6
July 15—Jack Donahue, Baltimore . . . . W 2
July 15—Kid Thomas, Baltimore . . . . ND 6
Aug. 23—Steve Crosby, Louisville . . . . D 20
Sept. 20—Steve Crosby, Baltimore . . . . W 12
Sept. 30—Joe Handler, Trenton . . . . KO 1
Oct. 4—Dan McConnell, Baltimore . . . . KO 3
Nov. 15—Jack Hanlon, Baltimore . . . . KO 2
Nov. 22—Billy Moore, Baltimore . . . . KO 3
Dec. 13—Bobby Dobbs, Baltimore . . . . W 14
Dec. 30—Joe Youngs, Philadelphia . . . . W 4

1902
Jan. 3—Tom Broderick, Baltimore . . . . . . KO 6
Jan. 6—Eddie Connolly, Philadelphia . . . . KO 5
Feb. 17—George McFadden, Philadelphia . . . ND 6
Mar. 7—Jack Ryan, Allentown . . . . Stpd. 3
Mar. 27—Jack Bennett, Baltimore . . . . KO 5
May 12—Frank Erne, Fort Erie . . . . KO 1
(Won World Lightweight Title)
June 27—George McFadden, San Francisco . . KO 3
July 24—Rufe Turner, Oakland . . . . KO 15
Sept. 17—*Gus Gardner, Baltimore . . . . KO 5
Sept. 23—Jack Bennett, Philadelphia . . . . . . KO 2
Oct. 13—Kid McPartland, Fort Erie . . . . . . KO 5
Oct. 14—Dave Holly, Lancaster . . . . ND 10
Nov. 14—Charley Sieger, Baltimore . . . . . . KO 14
Dec. 4—Howard Wilson, Providence . . . . . . KO 9
Dec. 31—Charley Sieger, Boston . . . . W 10
*Title Bout

1903
Jan. 1—Gus Gardner, New Britain . . . . . . WF 11
Mar. 11—*Steve Crosby, Hot Springs . . . . . . KO 11
Mar. 23—Jack Bennett, Allegheny . . . . W 5
May 13—Tommy Tracey, Portland . . . . W 9
May 29—Willie Fitzgerald, San Francisco . . . KO 10
July 4—Buddy King, Butte . . . . KO 5
Oct. 19—Joe Grim, Philadelphia . . . . ND 6
Oct. 20—Ed Kennedy, Philadelphia . . . . ND 6
Oct. 23—Dave Holly, Philadelphia . . . . ND 6

Nov. 2—Jack Blackburn, Philadelphia . . . . . ND 6
Dec. 7—Dave Holly, Philadelphia . . . . ND 6
Dec. 8—Sam Langford, Boston . . . . L 15
*Title Bout

1904
Jan. 12—Willie Fitzgerald, Detroit . . . . W 10
Jan. 19—Clarence Connors, Mt. Clemens . . . . W 2
Jan. 22—Joe Grim, Baltimore . . . . W 10
Feb. 2—Mike Ward, Detroit . . . . W 10
Mar. 25—Jack Blackburn, Baltimore . . . . W 15
Mar. 28—*Gus Gardner, Saginaw . . . . W 10
Apr. 21—Sam Bolen, Baltimore . . . . W 15
May 27—Jewey Cooks, Baltimore . . . . W 8
June 3—Kid Griffo, Baltimore . . . . W 8
June 14—Sammy Smith, Philadelphia . . . . . . W 4
June 27—Dave Holly, Philadelphia . . . . ND 6
Sept. 30—Joe Walcott, San Francisco . . . . . . D 20
(For World Welterweight Title)
Oct. 31—*Jimmy Britt, San Francisco . . . . . WF 5
*Title Bout

1905
Mar. 27—Rufe Turner, Philadelphia . . . . ND 6
Sept. 16—Mike Sullivan, Baltimore . . . . D 15

1906
Jan. 19—Mike (Twin) Sullivan,
San Francisco . . . . KO 15
Mar. 17—Mike (Twin) Sullivan, Los Angeles . KO 10
May 18—Willie Lewis, New York . . . . ND 6
June 15—Harry Lewis, Philadelphia . . . . ND 6
June 29—Jack Blackburn, Philadelphia . . . . . ND 6
July 23—Dave Holly, Seattle . . . . W 20
Sept. 3—*Battling Nelson, Goldfield, NV . . WF 42
—George Kid Lavigne, Detroit . . . . . Exh. 3
*Title Bout

1907
Jan. 1—Kid Herman, Tonopha, NV . . . . . . KO 8
Sept. 9—*Jimmy Britt, San Francisco . . . . . . KO 6
Britt broke wrist in fourth round.
Sept. 27—*George Memsic, Los Angeles . . . . . W 20
*Title Bout

1908
Jan. 3—Bart Blackburn, Baltimore . . . . KO 3
Apr. 1—Spike Robson, Philadelphia . . . . . . KO 3
May 14—*Rudy Unholz, San Francisco . . . . . KO 11
July 4—Battling Nelson, San Francisco . . KO by 17
(Lost World Lightweight Title)
Sept. 9—Battling Nelson, Colma, CA . . . . KO by 21
(For Lightweight Title)
*Title Bout.

1909
Mar. 12—Jabez White, New York . . . . ND 10
Gans' biggest purse was in his match for lightweight title with Nelson at Goldfield, NV., Sept. 3, 1906, $34,000. Of this purse Gans received only $11,000 for winning, having agreed to give Nelson the balance, win, lose or draw, amounting to $23,000. Referee, George Siler.

TB	KO	WD	WF	D	LD	LF	KO BY	ND	NC
156	55	60	5	10	3	0	5	18	0

Gans died Aug. 10, 1910, Baltimore, MD.
Elected to Boxing Hall of Fame 1954.

KID GAVILAN
(Gerardo Gonzalez)
(The Hawk)
Born, January 6, 1926, Camaguey, Cuba. Managed by Fernando Balido, Angel Lopez and later by Yamil Chade. Height, 5 ft. 10½ in.

1943
June 5—Antonio Diaz, Havana . . . . W 4
June 12—Bartolo Molina, Havana . . . . W 4
Aug. 7—Nanito Kid, Havana . . . . D 6
Sept. 11—Sergio Prieto, Havana . . . . KO 5

1944
Oct. 1—Juan Villalba, Havana . . . . KO 9
Nov. 25—Kid Bombon, Havana . . . . W 10
Dec. 23—Miguel Acevedo, Havana . . . . W 10
Feb. 10—Kid Bombon, Havana . . . . W 10
Mar. 10—Jose Pedroso, Havana . . . . W 10
Apr. 21—Santiago Sosa, Havana . . . . KO 9
May 13—Kid Bebo, Cienfuegos . . . . KO 4
May 26—Julio Cesar Jimenez, Havana . . . . . . W 10
June 23—Pedro Ortega, Havana . . . . W 10
July 7—Jose Pedroso, Havana . . . . KO 4
Aug. 4—Julio Cesar Jimenez, Mexico . . . . . . W 10
Aug. 26—Pedro Ortega, Mexico . . . . KO 6
Sept. 22—Carlos Malacara, Mexico . . . . L 10
Nov. 3—Carlos Malacara, Havana . . . . W 10
Nov. 17—Johnny Suarez, Havana . . . . W 10

1946
Jan. 26—Kid Bururu, Havana . . . . W 10
Feb. 9—Kid Bururu, Havana . . . . W 10
Mar. 2—Jose R. Zorrilla, Bayamo . . . . KO 4
Mar. 9—Santiago Sosa, Havana . . . . W 10
Apr. 5—Tony Mar, Mexico . . . . L 10
June 22—Jesus Varona, Havana . . . . W 10
Aug. 4—Hankin Barrow, Havana . . . . KO 7
Aug. 24—Jack Larrimore, Havana . . . . KO 3
Sept. 7—Hankin Barrow, Havana . . . . W 10
Nov. 1—Johnny Ryan, New York . . . . KO 5
Dec. 7—Johnny Williams, New York . . . . . . W 10
Dec. 13—Johnny Williams, New York . . . . . . W 10

1947
Jan. 28—Julio Pedroso, Havana . . . . W 10
Feb. 7—Jose Garcia Alvarez, Havana . . . . . . W 10
Feb. 22—Baby Coullimber, Havana . . . . W 10
Mar. 12—Nick Moran, Havana . . . . W 10
Apr. 26—Vince Gambill, Havana . . . . KO 2
Aug. 11—Charlie Williams, Newark . . . . W 10
Aug. 18—Bobby Lee, Baltimore . . . . W 10
Sept. 2—Doug Ratford, Newark . . . . L 10
Sept. 15—Charley Millan, Baltimore . . . . . . KO 1
Sept. 15—Billy Justine, Philadelphia . . . . W 8
Oct. 23—Billy Nixon, Philadelphia . . . . W 8
Nov. 3—Beebee Wright, Baltimore . . . . . . KO 10
Dec. 29—Buster Tyler, New York . . . . D 10

1948
Jan. 12—Gene Burton, New York . . . . D 10
Jan. 23—Joe Curcio, New York . . . . KO 2
Feb. 13—Vinnie Rossano, New York . . . . W 10
Feb. 27—Ike Williams, New York . . . . L 10
Apr. 13—Doug Ratford, Brooklyn . . . . L 10
Apr. 26—Tommy Bell, Philadelphia . . . . W 10
May 28—Rocco Rossano, New York . . . . KO 1
July 22—Roman Alvarez, New York . . . . W 10
Aug. 12—Buster Tyler, New York . . . . W 10

Sept. 23—Ray Robinson, New York . . . . L 10
Oct. 21—Vinnie Rossano, Washington, DC . . KO 6
Nov. 12—Tony Pellone, New York . . . . W 10
Dec. 11—Ben Buker, Havana . . . . W 10
1949
Jan. 28—Ike Williams, New York . . . . W 10
Apr. 1—Ike Williams, New York . . . . W 10
May 2—Al Priest, Boston . . . . W 10
June 7—Cliff Hart, Syracuse . . . . KO 2
July 11—Ray Robinson, Philadelphia . . . . L 15
(World Welterweight Title Bout)
Sept. 9—Rocky Castellani, New York . . . . W 10
Oct. 14—Beau Jack, Chicago . . . . W 10
Oct. 21—Lester Felton, Detroit . . . . L 10
Nov. 21—Laurent Dauthuille, Montreal . . . . . . W 10
Dec. 17—Bobby Lee, Havana . . . . W 10
1950
Feb. 10—Billy Graham, New York . . . . L 10
Mar. 6—Otis Graham, Philadelphia . . . . W 10
Mar. 20—Robert Villemain, Montreal . . . . L 10
May 8—George Costner, Philadelphia . . . . . . L 10
May 26—George Small, New York . . . . W 10
June 8—Mike Koballa, Brooklyn . . . . W 10
June 19—Bobby Mann, Hartford . . . . W 10
July 7—Sonny Horne, Brooklyn . . . . W 10
July 13—Phil Burton, Omaha . . . . W 10
Aug. 15—Johnny Greco, Montreal . . . . KO 6
Oct. 23—Tommy Ciarlo, New Haven . . . . D 10
Oct. 30—Eugene Hairston, Scranton . . . . L 10
Nov. 17—Billy Graham, New York . . . . W 5
Dec. 4—Tony Janiro, Cleveland . . . . W 10
Dec. 22—Joe Micelli, New York . . . . W 10
1951
Jan. 26—Paddy Young, New York . . . . W 10
Feb. 19—Tommy Ciarlo, Caracas . . . . W 10
Mar. 10—Tommy Ciarlo, Havana . . . . KO 8
Mar. 30—Gene Hairston, New York . . . . W 10
Apr. 20—Aldo Minelli, New York . . . . W 10
May 18—Johnny Bratton, New York . . . . W 15
(Won American Welterweight Title)
July 16—Fitzie Pruden, Milwaukee . . . . W 10
Aug. 29—Billy Graham, New York . . . . W 5
(Gavilan gained international recognition)
Oct. 4—Bobby Rosado, Havana . . . . KO 7
Nov. 7—Tony Janiro, Detroit . . . . KO 4
Nov. 28—Johnny Bratton, Chicago . . . . D 10
Dec. 14—Walter Cartier, New York . . . . KO 10
1952
Feb. 4—Bobby Dykes, Miami . . . . W 15
(Won World Welterweight Title)
Feb. 28—Don Williams, Boston . . . . W 10
May 19—Ralph Zanelli, Providence . . . . W 10
May 28—Fitzie Pruden, Indianapolis . . . . . . KO 6
July 7—Gil Turner, Philadelphia . . . . KO 11
(Title Bout)
Aug. 16—Mario Diaz, Buenos Aires . . . . W 10
Sept. 6—Rafael Merentino, Buenos Aires . . . KO 9
Sept. 13—Eduardo Lausse, Buenos Aires . . . . . W 10
Oct. 5—Billy Graham, Havana . . . . W 15
(Title Bout)
1953
Jan. 13—Aman Peck, Tampa . . . . W 10
Jan. 21—Vic Cardell, Washington, D.C. . . . . . W 10
Feb. 11—Chuck Davey, Chicago . . . . KO 10
(Title Bout)

Apr. 14—Livio Minelli, Cleveland . . . . W 10
May 2—Danny Womber, Syracuse . . . . L 10
June 10—Italo Scortichini, Detroit . . . . W 10
July 15—Ramon Fuentes, Milwaukee . . . . W 10
Aug. 26—Ralph Jones, New York . . . . W 10
Sept. 18—Carmen Basilio, Syracuse . . . . W 15
(Title Bout)
Nov. 13—Johnny Bratton, Chicago . . . . W 15
(Title Bout)
1954
Feb. 23—Johnny Cunningham, Miami Beach . . W 10
Mar. 8—Livio Minelli, Boston . . . . W 10
Apr. 2—Carl (Bobo) Olson, Chicago . . . . L 15
(World Middleweight Title Bout)
Oct. 20—Johnny Saxton, Philadelphia . . . . L 15
(Lost World Welterweight Title)
1955
Feb. 4—Ernie Durando, New York . . . . W 10
Feb. 23—Hector Constance, Miami Beach . . . . . L 10
Mar. 16—Bobby Dykes, Miami . . . . L 10
June 2—Luigi Cemulini, Santa Clara . . . . . . NC 3
July 23—Cirilo Gil, Buenos Aires . . . . W 10
Aug. 13—Juan Bautista Burgues, Montevideo KO 7
Sept. 3—Eduardo Lausse, Buenos Aires . . . . . L 12
Dec. 3—Dogomar Martinez, Montevideo . . . . L 10
1956
Feb. 7—Peter Waterman, London . . . . L 10
Mar. 29—Germinal Ballarin, Paris . . . . L 10
Apr. 24—Peter Waterman, London . . . . W 10
May 13—Louis Trochon, Marseilles . . . . D 10
Aug. 18—Jimmy Beecham, Havana . . . . W 10
Oct. 13—Tony DeMarco, Boston . . . . L 10
Nov. 13—Chico Vejar, Los Angeles . . . . W 10
Dec. 4—Walter Byars, Boston . . . . L 10
Dec. 20—Ramon Fuentes, Los Angeles . . . . . . L 10
1957
Feb. 26—Vince Martinez, Newark . . . . L 10
Apr. 24—Del Flanagan, St. Paul . . . . L 10
June 17—Vince Martinez, Jersey City . . . . L 10
July 31—Gaspar Ortega, Miami Beach . . . . L 10
Oct. 22—Gaspar Ortega, Los Angeles . . . . L 12
Nov. 20—Walter Byars, Chicago . . . . W 10
1958
Feb. 19—Ralph (Tiger) Jones, Miami Beach . . L 10
Apr. 4—Ralph (Tiger) Jones, Philadelphia . . . W 10
June 18—Yama Bahama, Miami Beach . . . . L 10
Announced retirement from boxing, Sept. 11, 1958.

TB	KO	WD	WF	D	LD	LF	KO BY	ND	NC
143	27	79	0	6	30	0	0	0	1

ROCKY GRAZIANO
(Rocco Barbella)
Born, January 1, 1922, New York City. Middleweight. Height, 5 ft. 7 in. Managed by Irving Cohen.
1942
Mar. 31—Curtis Hightower, Brooklyn . . . . . . KO 2
Apr. 6—Mike Mastandrea, New York . . . . . KO 3
Apr. 14—Kenny Blackmar, Brooklyn . . . . . . KO 1
Apr. 20—Godfrey Howell, New York . . . . D 4
Apr. 28—Charley Ferguson, Brooklyn . . . . L 4

May 4—Ed Lee, New York . . . . KO 4
May 12—Godfrey Howell, Brooklyn . . . . . . KO 4
May 25—Lou Miller, New York . . . . D 6
In U.S. Army.
1943
June 11—Gilbert Vasquez, Brooklyn . . . . . . KO 1
June 16—Joe Curcio, Elizabeth, NJ . . . . . . KO 4
June 24—Frankie Falco, Brooklyn . . . . KO 5
July 8—Johnny Attelly, Brooklyn . . . . . . KO 2
July 22—Georgie Stevens, Brooklyn . . . . . . KO 1
July 27—Randy Drew, Long Island City . . . . KO 1
Aug. 12—Charley McPherson, Brooklyn . . . . . W 6
Aug. 20—Ted Apostoli, New York . . . . W 4
Aug. 24—Tony Grey, Long Island City . . . . . KO 6
Sept. 10—Joe Agosta, New York . . . . L 6
Sept. 21—Sonny Wilson, Brooklyn . . . . W 8
Oct. 5—Freddie Graham, Brooklyn . . . . . KO 1
Oct. 13—Jimmy Williams, Elizabeth, NJ . . . . KO 2
Oct. 27—Charley McPherson, Elizabeth, NJ . . D 6
Nov. 6—Steve Riggio, Brooklyn . . . . L 6
Nov. 30—Freddie Graham, Jersey City . . . . . W 8
Dec. 6—Charley McPherson, New York . . . . W 6
Dec. 27—Milo Theodorescu, Newark . . . . KO 1
1944
Jan. 4—Harry Gray, Jersey City . . . . W 8
Jan. 7—Baby Galento, New York . . . . KO 1
Jan. 18—Phil Enzenga, Brooklyn . . . . KO 5
Feb. 9—Steve Riggio, New York . . . . L 6
Feb. 14—Manny Morales, Highland Park . . . KO 4
Mar. 4—Leon Anthony, Brooklyn . . . . KO 1
Mar. 8—Harry Gray, Elizabeth . . . . W 6
Mar. 14—Ray Rovelli, Brooklyn . . . . W 8
Apr. 10—Bobby Brown, Washington . . . . . . KO 5
May 9—Freddie Graham, Washington . . . . KO 3
May 29—Tommy Mollis, Washington . . . . . . KO 7
June 2—Larney Moore, Brooklyn . . . . KO 2
June 27—Frankie Terry, Brooklyn . . . . KO 6
July 21—Tony Reno, Brooklyn . . . . W 8
Aug. 14—Jerry Fiorello, Long Island City . . . . W 8
Sept. 15—Frankie Terry, New York . . . . D 8
Oct. 6—Danny Kapilow, New York . . . . D 10
Oct. 24—Bernie Miller, Brooklyn . . . . KO 2
Nov. 3—Harold Green, New York . . . . L 10
Dec. 22—Harold Green, New York . . . . L 10
1945
Mar. 8—Billy Arnold, New York . . . . KO 3
Apr. 17—Solomon Stewart, Washington, DC . KO 4
May 25—Al Davis, New York . . . . KO 4
June 5—Freddie Cochrane, New York . . . . KO 10
Aug. 24—Freddie Cochrane, New York . . . . KO 10
Sept. 28—Harold Green, New York . . . . KO 3
1946
Jan. 18—George "Sonny" Horne, New York W 10
Mar. 29—Marty Servo, New York . . . . KO 2
Sept. 27—Tony Zale, New York . . . . KO by 6
(For World Middleweight Title)
1947
June 10—Eddie Finazzo, Memphis . . . . KO 1
June 16—Jerry Fiorello, Toledo . . . . KO 5
July 16—Tony Zale, Chicago . . . . KO 6
(Won World Middleweight Title)
1948
Apr. 5—Sonny Horne, Washington, DC . . . . . W 10
June 10—Tony Zale, Newark . . . . KO by 3
(Lost World Middleweight Title)

Oct.   10—Dom Youvella, Jersey City ...... Exh.   5
1949
June   21—Bobby Claus, Wilmington .... KO   2
July   18—Joey Agosta, West Springfield .... KO   2
Sept. 14—Charley Fusari, New York .... KO 10
Dec.   6—Sonny Horne, Cleveland .... W 10
1950
Mar.   6—Joe Curcio, Miami .... KO   1
Mar.   31—Tony Janiro, New York .... D 10
Apr.   24—Danny Williams, New Haven ..... KO   3
May   9—Vinnie Cidone, Milwaukee .... KO   3
May   16—Henry Brimm, Buffalo.......... KO   4
Oct.   4—Gene Burton, Chicago .... KO   7
Oct.   16—Pete Mead, Milwaukee .... KO   3
Oct.   27—Tony Janiro, New York .... W 10
Nov.   27—Honey Johnson, Philadelphia ..... KO   4
1951
Mar.   19—Reuben Jones, Miami .... KO   3
May   21—Johnny Greco, Montreal .... KO   3
June   18—Freddy Lott, Baltimore .... KO   5
July   10—Cecil Hudson, Kansas City .... KO   3
Aug.   6—Chuck Hunter, Boston..........WD   2
Sept. 19—Tony Janiro, Detroit .... KO 10
1952
Feb.   18—Eddie O'Neill, Louisville........ KO   4
Mar.   27—Roy Wouters, Minneapolis ...... KO   1
Apr.   16—Ray Robinson, Chicago........KO by   3
(For World Middleweight Title)
Sept. 17—Chuck Davey, Chicago .... L 10
Retired and became a television actor.

TB	KO	WD	WF	D	LD	LF	KO BY	ND	NC
83	52	14	1	6	7	0	3	0	0

Elected to Boxing Hall of Fame 1971

HARRY GREB
(Edward Henry Greb)
(Human Windmill)
Born, June 6, 1894, Pittsburgh, PA. Weight,
158 lbs. Height, 5 ft. 8 in. Managed by James M. (Red)
Mason and George Engel.

1913
Knockouts: Lloyd Crutcher, Punxsutawney, PA,
1; Red Cumpston, 2; Battling Murphy, 2; Terry Nelson,
3. Knockout by: Joe Chip, 2. Won: Buck Miller, 3; Al
Store, 4; Red Chumpston, 4; George Koch, 4. No decisions; Red Cumpston, 6; K. O. Kirkwood, 6; Hooks Evans 6; Mike Milko, 6; Mike Milko, 6; Young Sherbine,
6.

1914
Jan.   1—Whitey Wenzel, Pittsburgh ...... *ND   6
Jan.   7—Whitey Wenzel, Pittsburgh ...... *ND   6
Mar.   2—Mickey Rodgers, Steubenville, OH . WF   5
Apr.   14—Fay Kaiser, Pittsburgh .... *ND   6
May   13—Fay Kaiser, Pittsburgh .... *ND   6
May   25—George Lewis, Pittsburgh .... *ND   6
May   29—Whitey Wenzel, Pittsburgh ...... *ND   6
June   15—Walter Monoghan, Pittsburgh .... *ND   6
June   27—Irish Gargas, Pittsburgh .... ND   6
July   20—John Foley, Pittsburgh .... *ND   6
July   27—George Lewis, Steubenville, OH .. *ND 10
Aug.   10—Irish Gargas, Pittsburgh .... *ND   6

Aug.   24—Whitey Wenzel, Pittsburgh ...... *ND   6
Aug.   31—John Foley, Pittsburgh .... *ND   6
Sept. 26—Jack Fink, Philadelphia .... *ND   6
Nov.   14—Terry Martin, Philadelphia ...... *ND   6
Dec.   7—Joe Borrell, Philadelphia........ *ND   6
*No decision
1915
Jan.   1—Bill Donovan, Philadelphia ...... *ND   6
Jan.   8—Howard Truesdale, Philadelphia ... ND   6
Jan.   12—Bill Miske, Philadelphia .... *ND   6
Jan.   25—Jack Blackburn, Pittsburgh ..... *ND   6
Feb.   10—K. O. Baker, Pittsburgh .... *ND   6
Mar.   4—Whitey Wenzel, Pittsburgh ..... *ND   6
Mar.   6—Tommy Mack, Washington, PA .. *ND   6
Mar.   13—Jack Lavin, McKeesport, PA.... *ND   6
Mar.   25—Harry Baker, Pittsburgh .... *ND   6
Apr.   15—Whitey Wenzel, Pittsburgh ...... *ND   6
Apr.   22—Joe Borrell, Pittsburgh .... *ND   6
May   24—Whitey Wenzel, Pittsburgh ..... ND   6
May   31—Fay Kaiser, Connellsville .... *ND   6
June   25—Fay Kaiser, Cumberland, MD ... *ND 10
July   12—Tommy Gavigan, Pittsburg ..... *ND   6
July   21—George Hauser, Elwyn, PA ...... KO   6
July   22—Fay Kaiser, Cumberland, MD ... *ND 10
Aug.   23—Al Rogers, Pittsburgh .... *ND   6
Sept. 13—Al Rogers, Pittsburgh .... ND   6
Oct.   18—George Chip, Pittsburgh .... ND   6
Nov.   16—Tommy Gibbons, St. Paul ..... *ND 10
Dec.   16—Kid Graves, Pittsburgh ....KO by   2
(Greb broke arm)
*No Decision.
1916
Feb.   26—Walter Monoghan, Pittsburgh ..... ND   6
Apr.   1—Kid Manuel, Pittsburgh.......... ND   6
Apr.   27—Grant (Kid) Clark, Johnstown, PA . KO   7
May   6—Whitey Wenzel, Charleroi, PA .... ND   6
June   3—Kid Manuel, Pittsburgh.......... KO   1
June   17—Whitey Wenzel, New Kensington,
PA .... ND 10
June   26—George Chip, New Castle, PA ..... ND 10
Aug.   7—Al Grayber, Pittsburgh .... ND   6
Aug.   28—Jerry Cole, Pittsburgh .... ND   6
Sept.   4—Fay Kaiser, Cumberland, MD ...... W 10
Oct.   16—Jackie Clarke, Lonaconing, MD ... W 10
Oct.   21—K. O. Baker, Pittsburgh .... ND   6
Nov.   4—K. O. Sweeney, Pittsburgh ..... ND   6
Nov.   8—Knockout Brennan, Erie, PA ..... ND 10
Nov.   14—Jackie Clarke, Lonaconing, MD ... KO   3
Nov.   17—K. O. Brennan, Pittsburgh .... ND 10
Nov.   24—Tommy Burke, Buffalo .... KO 10
Nov.   27—K. O. Brown, Pittsburgh .... ND   6
Dec.   26—Bob Moha, Buffalo .... ND 10
1917
Jan.   1—Joe Borell, Pittsburgh .... ND   6
Jan.   13—Eddie Coleman, Charleroi, PA .... KO   2
Jan.   20—Jules Ritchie, Philadelphia .... KO   4
Jan.   29—Fay Kaiser, Lonaconing, MD ..... W 20
Feb.   10—Mike Gibbons, Philadelphia ...... ND 10
Feb.   12—K. O. Brennan, Buffalo .... ND 10
Mar.   5—Frank Brennan, Pittsburgh ..... ND   6
Mar.   20—Tommy Gavigan, McKeesport, PA . KO   5
Mar.   23—Young Herman Miller,
Johnstown, PA.............. KO   5
Apr.   2—Young Ahearn, Pittsburgh .... KO   1

Apr.   15—Zulu Kid, Pittsburgh .... ND   6
Apr.   16—Al Rogers, Charleroi, PA .... ND 10
Apr.   30—Al McCoy, Pittsburgh .... ND 10
May   5—Jackie Clark, Cumberland, MD..... D 20
May   9—K. O. Baker, Uniontown, PA ..... KO   5
May   19—Jeff Smith, Buffalo .... ND 10
May   22—George Chip, Pittsburgh .... ND 10
June   14—Frank Mantell, Uniontown, PA.... KO   1
July   2—Buck Crouse, Pittsburgh .... KO   6
July   30—Jack Dillon, Pittsburgh .... ND 10
Sept.   6—Battling Levinsky, Pittsburgh ... ND 10
Sept. 11—Jeff Smith, Milwaukee .... ND 10
Sept. 14—Jack London, New York .... KO   9
Sept. 17—Knockout Brown, Dayton .... KO   9
Sept. 22—*Battling Kopin, Charleroi, PA.... KO   3
Sept. 25—Johnny Howard, New York ...... KO   9
Oct.   5—Billy Kramer, Philadelphia .... ND   6
Oct.   11—Gus Christie, Buffalo........... ND 10
Oct.   19—Len Rowlands, Milwaukee ...... ND 10
Oct.   23—Gus Christie, Chattanooga .... W   8
Nov.   2—Soldier Bartfield, Buffalo .... ND 10
Nov.   19—George Chip, Cincinnati .... ND 10
*Kopin claimed broken wrist.
1918
Jan.   4—Terry Kellar, Pittsburgh .... ND 10
Jan.   14—Battling Kopin, Charleroi, PA.... KO   1
Jan.   21—Augie Ratner, New Orleans ...... W 20
Jan.   29—Zulu Kid, Bridgeport, CT .... W 13
Feb.   4—Jack Hubbard, Lonaconing ...... KO   3
Feb.   7—Frank Klaus, Pittsburgh .... ND   6
Feb.   16—Bob Moha, Cincinnati .... ND 10
Feb.   25—Mike O'Dowd, St. Paul .... ND 10
Mar.   4—Jack Dillon, Toledo .... ND 12
Mar.   11—Mike McTigue, Cleveland ...... ND 10
Mar.   18—Willie Langford, Buffalo .... ND   6
May   13—Al McCoy, Cincinnati .... ND 10
May   20—Soldier Bartfield, Pittsburgh ..... ND 10
May   29—Soldier Bartfield, Toledo .... ND 15
May   24—Gunboat Smith, New York .... ND   6
June   20—Zulu Kid, New York .... Exh. 6
June   24—Frank Carbone, Bridgeport .... W 15
July   4—Bob Moha, Rock Island, IL ..... ND 10
July   6—Harry Anderson, Cleveland ...... Exh. 4
July   16—Soldier Bartfield, Philadelphia .... ND   6
July   27—Eddy McGoorty, Ft. Sheridan ... ND 10
Aug.   6—Battling Levinsky, Philadelphia ... ND   6
Aug.   9—Clay Turner, Jersey City .... ND   8
Sept. 21—Billy Miske, Pittsburgh .... ND 10
Dec.   11—Sgt. Baker, London .... W   4
Dec.   12—Pvt. Ring, London .... W   4
1919
Jan.   4—Bob Moha, Buffalo .... ND 10
Jan.   15—Leo Houck, Boston .... W 12
Jan.   20—Young Fisher, Syracuse .... ND 10
Jan.   23—Paul Sampson, Pittsburgh .... ND 10
Jan.   27—Soldier Bartfield, Columbus ..... ND 12
Jan.   31—Tommy Robson, Cleveland ...... ND 10
Feb.   3—Len Rowlands, Pittsburgh ...... KO   3
Feb.   10—Bill Brennan, Syracuse .... ND 10
Feb.   17—Battling Levinsky, Buffalo .... ND 10
Feb.   28—Chuck Wiggins, Toledo .... ND 10
Mar.   3—Chuck Wiggins Detroit .... ND   8
Mar.   6—Leo Houck, Lancaster, PA ...... ND   6
Mar.   13—George K. O. Brown, Canton, OH ND 12

Mar. 17—Bill Brennan, Pittsburgh .... ND 10
Mar. 31—Billy Miske, Pittsburgh .... ND 10
Apr. 8—One Round Davis, Buffalo .... ND 10
Apr. 25—Leo Houck, Erie, PA .... ND 10
Apr. 28—Battling Levinsky, Canton, OH .... ND 10
May 6—Clay Turner, Boston .... W 12
May 8—Willie Meehan, Pittsburgh ...... ND 10
May 14—Bartley Madden, Buffalo .... ND 10
June 16—Joe Borrell, Philadelphia .... KO 5
June 23—Mike Gibbons, Pittsburgh ...... ND 10
July 4—Bill Brennan, Tulsa, OK .... W 15
July 14—Battling Levinsky, Philadelphia ... ND 6
July 16—K.O. Brown, Wheeling, WV ...... W 10
July 21—Yankee Gilbert, Wheeling, WV ... KO 3
July 24—Joe Chip, Youngstown, OH ...... W 12
Aug. 11—Terry Kellar, Dayton, OH .... W 15
Aug. 23—Bill Brennan, Pittsburgh .... ND 10
Sept. 1—Jeff Smith, Youngstown .... ND 12
Sept. 3—Battling Levinsky, Wheeling ..... ND 10
Sept. 18—Silent Martin, St. Louis .... ND 8
Oct. 13—Sailor Petroskey, Philadelphia ... ND 6
Nov. 17—George Brown, Canton, OH ..... ND 12
Nov. 24—Larry Williams, Pittsburgh ...... ND 10
Nov. 27—Zulu Kid, Beaver Falls .... ND 10
Nov. 29—Soldier Jones, Buffalo .... KO 5
Dec. 10—Clay Turner, Buffalo .... ND 10
Dec. 11—Clay Turner, Buffalo .... ND 10
Dec. 13—Mike McTigue, Binghamton ..... ND 10
—Happy Howard .... ND 10
Dec. 15—Billy Kramer, Pittsburgh .... ND 10
Dec. 22—Clay Turner, Philadelphia .... ND 6

1920
Feb. 6—Mike Lemair, Kalamazoo, MI ..... ND 10
Feb. 21—Bob Roper, Pittsburgh .... ND 10
Mar. 6—C. Chapman, New York .... W 4
Mar. 9—Clay Turner, Akron, OH .... ND 12
Mar. 15—Larry Williams, Pittsburgh ...... ND 10
Mar. 17—Tommy Robson, Dayton .... W 12
Mar. 25—K. O. Brown, Denver .... ND 12
Apr. 5—Bob Roper, Denver .... W 12
May 15—Tommy Gibbons, Pittsburgh ..... ND 10
June 2—Clay Turner, Pittsburgh .... ND 8
July 5—Bob Moha, Canton, OH .... ND 12
July 8—Larry Williams, Buffalo .... ND 10
July 31—Tom Gibbons, Pittsburgh .... ND 10
Aug. 14—Bob Moha, Cedar Point .... ND 10
Aug. 20—Chuck Wiggins, Kalamazoo ..... ND 10
Aug. 28—Ted Jamison, Grand Rapids ..... ND 10
Sept. 6—Chuck Wiggins, Benton Harbor ... ND 6
Sept. 22—Ted Jamison, Milwaukee ...... KO 6
Oct. 21—Gunboat Smith, South Bend ..... KO 1
Oct. 28—Mickey Shannon, Pittsburgh ..... ND 10
Nov. 10—Bartley Madden, Kalamazoo ..... ND 10
Nov. 22—Bob Moha, Milwaukee .... ND 10
Dec. 11—Jack Duffy, Pittsburgh .... KO 6
Dec. 21—Bob Roper, Boston .... W 10
Dec. —Mike McTigue, Pittsburgh ..... ND 10

1921
Jan. 20—Johnny Celmars, Dallas .... W 10
Jan. 29—Pal Reed, Boston .... W 10
Feb. 25—Jeff Smith, Boston .... W 10
Mar. 16—Jack Renault, Pittsburgh .... ND 10
Apr. 11—Soldier Jones, Toronto .... KO 4
May 5—Bartley Madden, Pittsburgh .... ND 10

May 13—Jimmy Darcy, Boston .... W 10
May 20—Jeff Smith, New Orleans .... D 15
May 29—Chuck Wiggins, South Bend ..... ND 10
Aug. 29—Kid Norfolk, Pittsburgh .... ND 10
Sept. 20—Joe Cox, New York .... ND 10
Nov. 4—Charles Weinert, New York ..... W 15
Nov. 11—Billy Shade, Pittsburgh .... ND 10
Nov. 25—Homer Smith, Newark .... KO 5
Dec. 6—Fay Kaiser, Philadelphia ...... ND 8

1922
Jan. 2—Chuck Wiggins, Cincinnati ...... ND 12
Feb. 1—Hugh Walker, Grand Rapids .... ND 10
Feb. 20—Jeff Smith, Cincinnati .... ND 10
Mar. 13—Tommy Gibbons, New York ..... W 15
May 12—Al Roberts, Boston .... KO 6
May 23—Gene Tunney, New York .... W 15
(Won vacant American Light-Heavyweight Title)
June 26—Hughey Walker, Pittsburgh ..... ND 10
July 10—Tommy Loughran, Philadelphia ... ND 8
Sept. 26—Al Benedict, Toronto .... KO 2
Sept. 29—Bob Roper, Grand Rapids ..... ND 10
Oct. 25—Larry Williams, Mariesville, RI ... KO 4
Nov. 10—Capt. Bob Roper, Buffalo ..... W 12
Dec. 25—Jeff Smith, Pittsburgh .... ND 10

1923
Jan. 1—Bob Roper, Pittsburgh .... ND 10
Jan. 15—Tommy Loughran, Pittsburgh ... ND 10
Jan. 22—Billy Shade, Jersey City .... ND 12
Jan. 30—Tommy Loughran, New York .... W 15
(For American Light-Heavyweight Title)
Feb. 5—Pal Reed, Newark .... ND 12
Feb. 16—Young Fisher, Syracuse .... W 12
Feb. 23—Gene Tunney, New York .... L 15
(For American Light-Heavyweight Title)
Aug. 31—Johnny Wilson, New York ..... W 15
(Won World Middleweight Title)
Oct. 4—Jimmy Darcy, Pittsburgh ...... ND 10
Oct. 11—Tommy Loughran, Boston ..... L 10
Oct. 22—Lou Bogash, Jersey City ...... ND 12
Nov. 5—Soldier Jones, Pittsburgh ..... ND 10
Nov. 15—Chuck Wiggins, Grand Rapids .. ND 10
Dec. 3—Bryan Downey, Pittsburgh ..... W 10
(Middleweight Title Bout)
Dec. 10—Gene Tunney, New York ...... L 15
(For American Light-Heavyweight Title)
Dec. 26—Tommy Loughran, Pittsburgh ... W 10

1924
Jan. 18—*Johnny Wilson, New York ..... W 15
Feb. 2—Jack Reeves, Oakland, CA ..... W 4
Mar. 24—*Fay Kaiser, Baltimore ...... KO 12
Apr. 19—Kid Norfolk, Boston .... LF 6
May 5—Jackie Clark, Kenilworth, MD .... KO 2
May 12—Pal Reed, Pittsburgh .... W 10
June 12—Martin Burke, Cleveland ...... ND 10
June 16—Frank Moody, Waterbury ..... KO 6
June 26—*Ted Moore, New York .... W 15
Aug. 21—Tiger Flowers, Fremont, OH ... ND 10
Sept. 4—Jimmy Slattery, Buffalo .... W 6
Sept. 15—Billy Hirsch, Steubenville, OH .. KO 2
Sept. 17—Gene Tunney, Cleveland ..... ND 10
Oct. 13—Tommy Loughran, Philadelphia .. D 10
Nov. 17—Jimmy Delaney, Pittsburgh .... W 10
Nov. 25—Frankie Ritz, Wheeling, WV .... KO 2
*Title Bout.

1925
Jan. 1—Augie Ratner, Pittsburgh .... W 10
Jan. 9—Bob Sage, Detroit .... W 10
Jan. 19—Johnny Papke, Zanesville, OH .... KO 7
Jan. 22—Kid Lewis, Pittsburgh .... KO 1
Jan. 30—Jimmy Delaney, St. Paul .... ND 10
Feb. 17—Billy Britton, Allentown .... W 10
Feb. 23—Young Fisher, Scranton .... NC 6
Mar. 27—Gene Tunney, St. Paul .... ND 10
Apr. 17—Johnny Wilson, Boston .... W 10
Apr. 24—Jack Reddick, Toronto .... W 10
May 1—Quintin Rojas, Detroit .... W 10
May 6—Billy Britton, Columbus, OH .... W 12
May 29—Tommy Burns, Indianapolis .... ND 10
June 1—Soldier Buck, Louisville .... W 10
June 5—Jimmy Nuss, Marquette, MI .... KO 4
July 2—*Mickey Walker, New York ..... W 15
July 16—Max Rosenbloom, Cleveland .... ND 10
July 23—Billy Britton, Columbus ...... ND 10
July 27—Ralph Bruucks, Wichita ...... ND 10
July 31—Otis Bryant, Tulsa .... KO 3
Aug. 4—Ed K. O. Smith, Kansas City .... KO 4
Aug. 12—Pat Walsh, Atlantic City ..... KO 2
Aug. 17—Tommy Burns, Detroit ...... W 10
Oct. 12—Tony Marullo, Pittsburgh .... W 10
Nov. 12—*Tony Marullo, New Orleans .. W 15
Dec. 14—Soldier Buck, Nashville ...... W 8
*Title Bout.

1926
Jan. 11—Roland Todd, Toronto .... W 12
Jan. 19—Joe Lohman, Omaha .... W 10
Jan. 26—Ted Moore, Los Angeles ..... W 10
Jan. 29—Buck Holly, Hollywood ..... KO 5
Feb. 3—Jimmy Delaney, Oakland, CA .. W 10
Feb. 12—Owen Phelps, Prescott, AZ ... W 10
Feb. 26—Tiger Flowers, New York ..... L 15
(Lost Middleweight Championship of World)
June 4—Art Wiegand, Buffalo .... W 10
June 15—Allen Joe Gans, Wilkes Barre .. W 10
Aug. 19—Tiger Flowers, New York ..... L 15
(For World Middleweight Title)

TB	KO	WD	WF	D	LD	LF	KO BY	ND	NC
294	47	64	1	3	5	1	2	170	1

Greb died Oct. 22, 1926, following operation on eye.

Elected to Boxing Hall of Fame 1955.

LARRY HOLMES
Easton, PA. Heavyweight
Born, Nov. 3, 1949, Cuthbert, GA.
1973
Mar. 21—Rodell Dupree, Scranton .... W 4
May 2—Art Savage, Scranton .... KO 3
June 20—Curtis Whitner, Scranton .... KO 1
Aug. 22—Don Branch, Scranton .... W 6
Sept. 10—Bob Bozic, New York .... W 6
Nov. 14—Jerry Judge, Scranton .... W 6
Nov. 28—Kevin Isaac, Cleveland .... KO 3
1974
Apr. 24—Howard Darlington, Scranton ..... KO 4

May 29—Bob Mashburn, Scranton........ KO 7
Dec. 11—Joe Hathaway, Scranton .... KO 1
1975
Mar. 24—Charley Green, Cleveland .... KO 2
Apr. 10—Oliver Wright, Honolulu .... KO 3
Apr. 26—Robert Yarborough, Toronto...... KO 3
May 16—Ernie Smith, Las Vegas .... KO 3
Aug. 16—Obie English, Scranton .... KO 7
Aug. 26—Charlie James, Honolulu .... W 10
Oct. 1—Rodney Bobick, Manila.......... KO 6
Dec. 9—Leon Shaw, Washington, DC ..... KO 1
Dec. 20—Billy Joiner, San Juan .... KO 3
1976
Jan. 29—Joe Gholston, Easton .... KO 8
Apr. 5—Fred Ashew, Landover .... KO 2
Apr. 30—Roy Williams, Landover .... W 10
1977
Jan. 16—Tom Prater, Pensacola .... W 8
  (U.S. Championship Tournament)
Mar. 17—Horacio Robinson, San Juan ..... KO 5
Sept. 14—Young Sanford Houpe, Las Vegas . KO 7
Nov. 5—Ibar Arrington, Las Vegas....... KO 10
1978
Mar. 25—Earnie Shavers, Las Vegas ...... W 12
June 9—Ken Norton, Las Vegas .... W 15
  (Won WBC Heavyweight Title)
Nov. 10—Alfredo Evangelista, Las Vegas.... KO 7
  (Retained WBC Heavyweight Title)
1979
Mar. 23—Osvaldo Ocasio, Las Vegas .... KO 7
  (Retained WBC Heavyweight Title)
June 22—Mike Weaver, New York......... KO 12
  (Retained WBC Heavyweight Title)
Sept. 28—Earnie Shavers, Las Vegas .... KO 11
  (Retained WBC Heavyweight Title)
1980
Feb. 3—Lonrenzo Zanon, Las Vegas..........KO 6
  (Retained WBC Heavyweight Title)
Mar. 31—Leroy Jones, Las Vegas ....KO 8
  (Retained WBC Heavyweight Title)
July 7—Scott LeDoux, Bloomington ....KO 7
  (Retained WBC Heavyweight Title)
Oct. 2—Muhammad Ali, Las Vegas.............KO 11
  (Retained WBC Heavyweight Title)
1981
Apr. 11—Trevor Berbick, Las Vegas...............W 15
  (Retained WBC Heavyweight Title)
June 12—Leon Spinks, Detroit ....KO 3
  (Retained WBC Heavyweight Title)
Nov. 6—Renaldo Snipes, Pittsburgh.............KO 11
  (Retained WBC Heavyweight Title)
1982
June 11—Gerry Cooney, Las Vegas ....KO 13
  (Retained WBC Heavyweight Title)
Nov. 26—Randall (Tex) Cobb, Houston..........W 15
  (Retained WBC Heavyweight Title)
1983
Mar. 27—Lucien Rodriguez, Easton, Pa..........W 12
  (Retained WBC Heavyweight Title)
May 20—Tim Witherspoon, Las Vegas..........W 12
  (Retained WBC Heavyweight Title)

TB	KO	WD	WF	D	LD	LF	KO BY	ND	NC
43	30	13	0	0	0	0	0	0	0

JAMES JACKSON JEFFRIES
(The Boilermaker)
Born, April 15, 1875, Carroll, OH. Weight, 220 lbs. Height, 6 ft. 2½ in. Managed by Bill Brady.
1896
  —Hank Griffin, Los Angeles .... KO 14
  —Jim Barber, Los Angeles .... KO 2

July 2—Dan Long, San Francisco .... KO 2
1897
Apr. 9—T. Van Buskirk, San Francisco .... KO 2
May 19—Henry Baker, San Francisco ..... KO 9
July 17—Gus Rublin, San Francisco .... D 20
Nov. 30—Joe Choynski, San Francisco...... D 20
1898
Feb. 28—Joe Goddard, Los Angeles........ KO 4
.Mar. 22—Peter Jackson, San Francisco .... KO 3
Apr. 22—Pete Everett, San Francisco ...... KO 3
May 6—Tom Sharkey, San Francisco ..... W 20
Aug. 5—Bob Armstrong, New York .... W 10
1899
June 9—Bob Fitzsimmons, Coney Island ... KO 11
  (Won Heavyweight Title)
Nov. 3—*Tom Sharkey, Coney Island ...... W 25
  *Title Bout.
1900
Apr. 6—Jack Finnegan, Detroit .... KO 1
May 11—*Jim Corbett, Coney Island ...... KO 23
  *Title Bout.
1901
Nov. 15—*Gus Ruhlin, San Francisco ..... KO 5
  *Title Bout.
1902
July 25—*Bob Fitzsimmons, San Francisco . KO 8
  *Title Bout.
Dec. 19—Jack Munroe, Butte .... Exh. 4
  *Title Bout
1903
Aug. 14—*Jim Corbett, San Francisco ..... KO 10
  *Title Bout.
1904
Aug. 26—*Jack Munroe, San Francisco ..... KO 2
  *Title Bout.
  Following his triumph over Jack Munroe in their return engagement, Jeffries finding that opponents were scarce for title matches, decided to retire. He induced Marvin Hart and Jack Root to fight for his vacated title, which they did on July 3, 1905, with Jeffries, the referee. Hart won and Jeff dubbed him the champion.
  After Tommy Burns had proved his right to the vacated title by eliminating all challengers Jack Johnson beat Burns for the title in Australia and then Jeffries came out of retirement in an effort to regain the throne.
1910
July 4—Jack Johnson, Reno........... KO by 15
  (Heavyweight Title Bout)
1921
May 3—Jack Jeffries, Los Angeles .... Exh. 3

TB	KO	WD	WF	D	LD	LF	KO BY	ND	NC
21	15	3	0	2	0	0	1	0	0

Died March 3, 1953, Burbank, CA.
Elected to Boxing Hall of Fame 1954.

INGEMAR JOHANSSON
European Heavyweight Champion
Born, Sweden, Sept. 22, 1932. 195 pounds, 6 ft. ½ in. As member of European team, competed against American Golden Gloves squad in Chicago, 1951; knocked out Ernest Fann in second round.
  Represented Sweden in 1952 Olympics in Helsinki; reached final in heavyweight class, but lost on second-round disqualification to Ed Sanders of the United States.
  Amateur record: 71 bouts, 11 losses.
1952
Dec. 5—Robert Masson, Gothenburg ...... KO 4
1953
Feb. 6—Emile Bentz, Gothenburg .... KO 2
Mar. 6—Lloyd Barnett, Gothenburg .... W 8
Mar. 12—Erik Jensen, Copenhagen .... W 6

  (Scandinavian Heavyweight Title)
Dec. 4—Raymond Degl'Innocenti,
  Stockholm .... KO 2
In Swedish Navy.
1954
Nov. 5—Werner Wiegand, Gothenburg .... KO 5
1955
Jan. 6—Ansel Adams, Gothenburg ...... W 8
Feb. 13—Kurt Schiegl, Stockholm .... KO 5
Mar. 5—Aldo Pellegrini, Gothenburg ..... WF 5
Apr. 3—Uber Bacilieri, Stockholm .... W 8
June 12—Gunter Nurmberg, Dortmundt..... KO 7
Aug. 28—Hein ten Hoff, Gothenburg .... KO 1
1956
Feb. 24—Joe Bygraves, Gothenburg........ W 10
Apr. 15—Jans Friedrich, Stockholm........ W 10
Sept. 30—Franco Cavicchi, Milan .... KO 13
  (European Heavyweight Title)
Dec. 28—Peter Bates, Gothenburg .... KO 2
1957
May 19—Henry Cooper, Stockholm .... KO 5
  (European Heavyweight Title)
Dec. 13—Archie McBride, Gothenburg ...... W 10
1958
Feb. 21—Joe Erskine, Gothenburg........ KO 13
  (European Heavyweight Title)
July 13—Heinz Neuhaus, Gothenberg ...... KO 4
Sept. 14—Eddie Machen, Gothenburg ...... KO 1
1959
June 26—Floyd Patterson, New York....... KO 3
  (Won World Heavyweight Title)
1960
June 20—Floyd Patterson, New York.....KO by 5
  (Lost World Heavyweight Title)
  Gothenburg is English spelling; Goteborg, Swedish, same city.
1961
Mar. 13—Floyd Patterson, Miami Beach ..KO by 6
  (For World Heavyweight Title)
1962
Feb. 9—Joe Bygraves, Gothenburg........ KO 7
Apr. 15—Wim Snoek, Stockholm .... KO 5
June 17—Dick Richardson, Gothenburg ..... KO 8
  (Won European Heavyweight Title)
1963
Apr. 21—Brian London, Stockholm .... W 12
  Retired to enter business.

TB	KO	WD	WF	D	LD	LF	KO BY	ND	NC
28	17	8	1	0	0	0	2	0	0

JACK JOHNSON
(John Arthur Johnson)
(Little Artha and the Galveston Giant)
Born, March 31, 1878, Galveston, TX. Weight, 195 lbs. Height, 6 ft. ¼ in. Managed by Morris Hart, Johnny Connors, Alec McLean, Sam Fitzpatrick, Abe Arends, George Little, Tom Flanagan, Sig Hart.
1897
  Knockout: Jim Rocks, 4; Won: Sam Smith, 10.
1898
  Knockout: Reddy Bremer, 3. Won: Jim Cole, 4. Draw: Henry Smith, 15.
1899
Feb. 11—Jim McCormick, Galveston .... D 7
Mar. 17—Jim McCormick, Galveston ...... WF 7
May 6—Klondike, Chicago .... KO by 5
Dec. 16—Pat Smith, Galveston............. D 12
1900
  Won: Josh Mills, 12.
1901
Feb. 25—Joe Choynski, Galveston .... KO by 3
Mar. 7—John Lee, Galveston .... W 15

Apr.	12—Charley Brooks, Galveston	KO	2
May	6—Jim McCormick, Galveston	KO	2
May	28—Jim McCormick, Galveston	KO	7
June	12—Horace Miles, Galveston	KO	3
June	20—George Lawler, Galveston	KO	10
June	28—Klondike, Galveston	D	20
	—Willie McNeal	KO	15
Nov.	4—Hank Griffin, Bakersfield, CA	L	20
Dec.	27—Hank Griffin, Oakland, CA	D	15

1902

Jan.	17—Frank Childs, Chicago	D	6
Feb.	7—Dan Murphy, Waterbury	KO	10
Feb.	22—Ed Johnson, Galveston	KO	4
Mar.	7—Joe Kennedy, Oakland	KO	4
Apr.	6—Bob White	W	15
May	1—Jim Scanlan	KO	7
May	16—Jack Jeffries, Los Angeles	KO	5
May	28—Klondike, Memphis	KO	13
June	4—Billy Stift, Denver	D	10
June	20—Hank Griffin, Los Angeles	D	20
Sept.	3—Pete Everett, Victor, CO	W	20
Oct.	21—Frank Childs, Los Angeles	W	12
Oct.	31—George Gardner, San Francisco	W	20
Dec.	5—Fred Russell, Los Angeles	WF	8

1903

Feb.	3—Denver E. Martin, Los Angeles	W	20
Feb.	27—Sam McVey, Los Angeles	W	20
Apr.	16—Sandy Ferguson, Boston	W	10
May	11—Joe Butler, Philadelphia	KO	3
July	31—Sandy Ferguson, Philadelphia	ND	6
Oct.	27—Sam McVey, Los Angeles	W	20
Dec.	11—Sandy Ferguson, Colma, CA	W	20

1904

Feb.	16—Black Bill, Philadelphia	ND	6
Apr.	22—Sam McVey, San Francisco	KO	20
June	2—Frank Childs, Chicago	W	6
Oct.	18—Denver Ed Martin, Los Angeles	KO	2

1905

Mar.	28—Marvin Hart, San Francisco	L	20
Apr.	25—Jim Jeffords, Philadelphia	KO	4
May	3—Black Bill, Philadelphia	KO	4
May	9—Walter Johnson, Philadelphia	KO	3
May	19—Joe Grim, Philadelphia	ND	6
June	26—Jack Monroe, Philadelphia	ND	6
July	13—Morris Harris, Philadelphia	KO	3
July	13—Black Bill, Philadelphia	ND	6
July	18—Sandy Ferguson, Chelsea	WF	7
July	24—Joe Grim, Philadelphia	ND	6
Nov.	25—Joe Jeannette, Philadelphia	LF	2
Dec.	1—Young P. Jackson, Baltimore	W	12
Dec.	2—Joe Jeannette, Philadelphia	ND	6

1906

Jan.	16—Joe Jeannette, New York	ND	3
Mar.	14—Joe Jeannette, Baltimore	W	15
Apr.	19—Black Bill, Wilkes-Barre	KO	7
Apr.	26—Sam Langford, Chelsea	W	15
June	18—Charlie Haghey, Gloucester	KO	2
Sept.	20—Joe Jeannette, Philadelphia	ND	6
Nov.	8—Jim Jeffords, Lancaster, PA	W	6
Nov.	26—Joe Jeannette, Portland, ME	D	10
Dec.	9—Joe Jeannette, New York	W	3
	—Billy Dunning	W	10

1907

Feb.	19—Peter Felix, Sydney	KO	1
Mar.	4—Jim J. Lang, Melbourne	KO	9

July	17—Bob Fitzsimmons, Philadelphia	KO	2
Aug.	28—Kid Cutler, Reading, PA	KO	1
Nov.	2—Jim Flynn, San Francisco	KO	11

1908

Jan.	3—Joe Jeannette, New York	D	3
June	11—Al. McNamara, Plymouth	W	4
July	31—Ben Taylor, Plymouth	KO	8
Dec.	26—Tommy Burns, Sydney	KO	14

(Won Heavyweight Title)

1909

Mar.	10—Victor McLaglen, Vancouver	ND	6
May	19—P. Jack O'Brien, Philadelphia	ND	6
June	30—Tony Ross, Pittsburgh	ND	6
Sept.	9—Al Kaufman, San Francisco	ND	10
Oct.	16—Stanley Ketchel, Colma, CA	KO	12
	—Frank Moran, Pittsburgh	Exh.	4

*Title Bout.

1910

July	4—*James J. Jeffries, Reno	KO	15

*Title Bout.

1912

July	4—*Jim Flynn, Las Vegas, NM	KO	9

Police ordered bout stopped. Johnson received
$30,000 for his end.
*Title Bout.

1913

Nov.	28—*Andre Sproul, Paris	KO	2
Dec.	19—*Jim Johnson, Paris	D	10

*Title Bout.

1914

June	27—*Frank Moran, Paris	W	20
Dec.	15—Jack Murray, Buenos Aires	KO	3

*Title Bout.

1915

Apr.	3—Sam McVey, Havana	Exh.	6
Apr.	5—Jess Willard, Havana	KO by	26

(Lost Heavyweight Title)
Bout was scheduled for 45 rounds. Referee, Jack
Welch.

1916

Mar.	10—Frank Crozier, Madrid	W	10
July	10—Arthur Craven, Barcelona	KO	1

1918

Apr.	3—Blink McCloskey, Madrid	W	4

1919

Feb.	12—Bill Flint, Madrid	KO	2
Apr.	7—Tom Cowler, Mexico City	D	10
June	2—Tom Cowler, Mexico City	KO	12
July	4—Paul Sampson, Mexico City	KO	6
Aug.	10—Marty Cutler, Mexico City	KO	4
Sept.	28—Bob Roper, Mexico City	W	10

1920

Apr.	18—Bob Wilson, Mexicali	KO	3
May	17—George Roberts, Tiajuana	KO	3
*Nov.	25—Frank Owens, Leavenworth	KO	6
*Nov.	25—Top Jk. Johnson, Leavenworth	W	5
Nov.	30—George Owens, Leavenworth	KO	6

*On same card

1921

Apr.	15—Jack Townsend, Leavenworth	KO	6
*May	28—John Allen, Leavenworth	Exh.	2
*May	28—Joe Boykin, Leavenworth	Exh.KO	5

1923

May	6—Farmer Lodge, Havana	KO	4
May	20—Jack Thompson, Havana	ND	15

Oct.	1—Battling Siki, Quebec	Exh.	6

1924

Feb.	22—Homer Smith, Montreal	W	10

1926

May	2—Pat Lester, Nogales, Mex.	W	15
May	30—Bob Lawson, Juarez, Mex.	WF	8

1928

Apr.	—Bearcat Wright, Topeka	KO by	2
May	15—Bill Hartwell, Kansas City	KO by	6

1930

	—Philadelphia Jack O'Brien	Exh.	3

1931

	—Chief White Horse	Exh.	3

1933

*Jan.	20—Maurice Griselle, Paris	Exh.	1
*Jan.	20—Ernest Guehring, Paris	Exh.	1

*On same card

1945

Nov.	27—Joe Jeannette, New York	Exh.	3
	—John Ballcort	*Exh.	3

*One-minute rounds.

TB	KO	WD	WF	D	LD	LF	KO BY	ND	NC
113	47	28	4	12	2	1	5	14	0

Killed in auto accident, June 10, 1946, Raleigh,
Buried in Graceland Cemetery, Chicago, IL.
Elected to Boxing Hall of Fame 1954.

JAKE KILRAIN

(John Joseph Killion)

Born, Feb. 9, 1859, Greenpoint, NY. Weight,
195 lbs. Height, 5 ft. 10½ in.

Began boxing in 1880, when he defeated "Dangerous Jack Burke," Boston, 3.

1883

George Godfrey, D 3; John Allen, W 4; Jem
Goode, D 6.

1884

Mar.	26—Charley Mitchell, Boston	D	4
May	8—William Sheriff, Cambridge	W	3
June	26—Mike Cleary, New York	D	4
July	3—Jem Goode, Chicago	D	5
Dec.	1—Jack Burke, Boston	D	5

1885

Apr.	16—John McGlynn, New Bedford	W	4
May	15—George Fryer, Boston	D	5
Oct.	29—Jerry Murphy, Bangor (Police)	D	2

1886

July	31—Jack Ashton, Brooklyn	W	8
Nov.	8—Frank Herald, Baltimore (Police)	W	8
Nov.	15—Joe Godfrey, Philadelphia	KO	2
Nov.	17—Tom Kelly, Philadelphia	KO	4
Nov.	19—Denny Killen, Philadelphia	W	4
Dec.	22—John P. Clow, Baltimore	W	4

1887

Mar.	8—Joe Lannon, Watertown, MA.		

($750-250) 2 oz .... NC 11

Dec.	19—Jem Smith for $5,000 a side and Championship of England Isle des Souverains, River Seine, France. Bare knuckles. London PR rules. Draw on account of darkness (2h. 30m) D106

231

1888

Jan. 7—Match with Sullivan made in Toronto.
July 8—John L. Sullivan, $10,000 a side and champ, at Richburg, MS. Bare knuckles. London PR rules. Referee, John Fitzpatrick of New Orleans. Seconds, Charley Mitchell and Mike Donovan; bottle-holder, Johnny Murphy, time-keeper, Bat Masterson. Afterward arrested and fined (2h.16m. 23s) . . . . KO by 75
Nov. 4—John F. Scholes, Toronto . . . . D 4

1890

Feb. 2—Felix Vacquelin, $2,000 New Orleans W 3
Feb. 18—Jim Corbett on points (201-183). 5 oz., $3,500 Southern Athletic Club, New Orleans. Referee. R. Violett . . . . L 6
June 10—Frank Bosworth, New York . . . . W 3
June 13—Tommy McManus, New York . . . . . . W 3
June 18—Dick Mayel, Cleveland . . . . W 3
Dec. 1—George Harris, New York . . . . W 2
Dec. 3—Mike Brenna, Montana, NY . . . . . . W 3
Dec. 4—G. Maguire, Utica, NY . . . . W 2

1891

Mar. 13—Geo. Godfrey (195-175) California Athletic Club . . . . KO 44
June 16—Frank Slavin of Australia (190-186), $5,000 each . . . . L 9

1895

Mar. 18—Steve O'Donnell, Boston . . . . D 8
May 6—Steve O'Donnell, Coney Island. KO by 21
Sept. 30—Abe Ulman, Baltimore . . . . ND 10

1898

Sept. 14—Frank Slavin, Baltimore (2 m.45s) KO by 1

TB	KO	WD	WF	D	LD	LF	KO BY	ND	NC
36	3	15	9	12	3	0	3	1	0

Died Dec. 22, 1937, Quincy, MA.

JAKE (JACOB) LA MOTTA
(Bronx Bull)

Born, July 10, 1921, New York, NY. Middle-weight. Height, 5 ft. 8 in. Managed by Mike Capriano and Joey LaMotta.

1941

Mar. 3—Charley Mackley, New York . . . . W 4
Mar. 14—Tony Gillon, Bridgeport, CT . . . . . . W 6
Apr. 1—Johnny Morris, White Plains . . . . . KO 6
Apr. 8—Joe Fredericks, White Plains . . . . KO 1
Apr. 15—Stanley Goisz, White Plains . . . . . . W 4
Apr. 22—Lorne McCarthy, White Plains . . . . . W 4
Apr. 26—Monroe Crewe, Brooklyn . . . . W 4
May 20—Johnny Cihlar, Brooklyn . . . . W 4
May 27—Johnny Morris, New York . . . . W 4
June 9—Lorenzo Strickland, Woodhaven, NY W 4
June 16—Lorenzo Strickland, New York . . . . . W 4
June 23—Johnny Morris, New York . . . . KO 3
July 15—Joe Baynes, Long Island City . . . . . W 6
Aug. 5—Joe Shikula, Long Island City . . . . . D 6
Aug. 11—Cliff Koerkle, New York . . . . W 6
Sept. 24—Jimmy Reeves . . . . L 10
Oct. 7—Lorenzo Strickland, White Plains . . . W 8
Oct. 20—Jimmy Reeves, Cleveland . . . . L 10

Nov. 14—Jimmy Casa, New York . . . . W 6
Dec. 22—Nate Bolden, Chicago . . . . L 10

1942

Jan. 27—Frankie Jamison, New York . . . . . . W 8
Mar. 3—Frankie Jamison, New York . . . . . . W 8
Mar. 18—Lorenzo Strickland, New York . . . . . W 10
Apr. 7—Lou Schwartz, New York . . . . KO 9
Apr. 21—Buddy O'Dell, New York . . . . W 10
May 12—Jose Basora, New York . . . . D 10
June 2—Vic Dellicurti, New York . . . . W 10
June 16—Jose Basora, New York . . . . L 10
July 28—Lorenzo Strickland, New York . . . . . W 8
Aug. 28—Jimmy Edgar, New York . . . . W 10
Sept. 8—Vic Dellicurti, New York . . . . W 10
Oct. 2—Ray Robinson, New York . . . . L 10
Oct. 20—Wild Bill McDowell, New York . . KO 5
Nov. 6—Henry Chmielewski, Boston . . . . . . W 10

1943

Jan. 2—Jimmy Edgar, Detroit . . . . W 10
Jan. 15—Jackie Wilson, Detroit . . . . W 10
Jan. 22—Charley Hayes, Detroit . . . . KO 6
Feb. 5—Ray Robinson, Detroit . . . . W 10
Feb. 26—Ray Robinson, Detroit . . . . L 10
Mar. 19—Jimmy Reeves, Detroit . . . . KO 6
Mar. 30—Ossie Harris, Pittsburgh . . . . W 10
May 12—Tony Ferrara, Cincinnati . . . . KO 6
June 10—Fritzie Zivic, Pittsburgh . . . . W 10
July 12—Fritzie Zivic, Pittsburgh . . . . L 15
Sept. 17—Jose Basora, Detroit . . . . W 10
Oct. 11—Johnny Walker, Philadelphia . . . . . KO 2
Nov. 12—Fritzie Zivic, New York . . . . W 10

1944

Jan. 14—Fritzie Zivic, Detroit . . . . W 10
Jan. 28—Ossie Harris, Detroit . . . . W 10
Feb. 25—Ossie Harris, Detroit . . . . W 10
Mar. 17—Coley Welch, Boston . . . . W 10
Mar. 31—Sgt. Lou Woods, Chicago . . . . W 10
Apr. 21—Lloyd Marshall, Cleveland . . . . L 10
Sept. 29—George Kochan, Detroit . . . . W 10
Nov. 3—George Kochan, Detroit . . . . KO 9

1945

Feb. 23—Ray Robinson, New York . . . . L 10
Mar. 19—Lou Schwartz, Norfolk . . . . KO 1
Mar. 28—George Costner, Chicago . . . . KO 6
Apr. 19—Vic Dellicurti, New York . . . . W 10
Apr. 27—Bert Lytell, Boston . . . . W 10
July 6—Tommy Bell, New York . . . . W 10
Aug. 10—Jose Basora, New York . . . . KO 9
Sept. 17—George Kochan, New York . . . . . . KO 9
Sept. 26—Ray Robinson, Chicago . . . . L 12
Nov. 13—Coolidge Miller, Bronx, NY . . . . . KO 3
Nov. 23—Walter Woods, Boston . . . . KO 8
Dec. 7—Charley Parham, Chicago . . . . . . KO 6

1946

Jan. 11—Tommy Bell, New York . . . . W 10
Mar. 29—Marcus Lockman, Boston . . . . W 10
May 24—Joe Reddick, Boston . . . . W 10
June 13—Jimmy Edgar, Detroit . . . . D 10
Sept. 12—Bob Satterfield, Chicago . . . . KO 7
Aug. 7—Holman Williams, Detroit . . . . W 10
Oct. 25—O'Neill Bell, Detroit . . . . KO 2
Dec. 6—Anton Raadik, Chicago . . . . W 10

1947

Mar. 14—Tommy Bell, New York . . . . W 10

June 6—Tony Janiro, New York . . . . W 10
Sept. 3—Cecil Hudson, Chicago . . . . L 10
Nov. 14—Billy Fox, New York . . . . KO by 4

1948

June 1—Ken Stribling, Washington, D.C. . . KO 5
Sept. 7—Burl Charity, New York . . . . KO 6
Oct. 1—Johnny Colan, New York . . . . KO 10
Oct. 18—Vern Lester, Brooklyn . . . . W 10
Dec. 3—Tommy Yarosz, New York . . . . W 10

1949

Feb. 21—Laurent Dauthuille, Montreal . . . . . L 10
Mar. 25—Robert Villemain, New York . . . . . . W 12
Apr. 18—O'Neill Bell, Detroit . . . . KO 4
May 18—Joey DeJohn, Syracuse . . . . KO 8
June 16—Marcel Cerdan, Detroit . . . . KO 10
        (Won World Middleweight Title)
Dec. 9—Robert Villemain, New York . . . . . L 10

1950

Feb. 3—Dick Wagner, Detroit . . . . KO 9
Mar. 28—Chuck Hunter, Cleveland . . . . KO 6
May 4—Joe Taylor, Syracuse . . . . W 10
July 12—Tiberio Mitri, New York . . . . W 15
        (Title Bout)
Sept. 13—Laurent Dauthuille, Detroit . . . . . . KO 15
        (Title Bout)

1951

Feb. 14—Ray Robinson, Chicago . . . . KO by 13
        (Lost World Middleweight Title)
June 27—Bob Murphy, New York . . . . . . KO by 7

1952

Jan. 28—Norman Hayes, Boston . . . . L 10
Mar. 5—Eugene Hairston, Detroit . . . . D 10
Apr. 9—Norman Hayes, Detroit . . . . W 10
May 21—Eugene Hairston, Detroit . . . . W 10
June 11—Bob Murphy, Detroit . . . . W 10
Dec. 31—Danny Nardico, Coral Gables . . . KO by 8

1953

(Inactive)

1954

Mar. 11—Johnny Pretzie, West Palm Beach . . KO 4
Apr. 3—Al McCoy, Charlotte . . . . KO 1
Apr. 14—Billy Kilgore, Miami Beach . . . . L 10

TB	KO	WD	WF	D	LD	LF	KO BY	ND	NC
106	30	53	0	4	15	0	4	0	0

BENNY LEONARD
(Benjamin Leiner)

Born, April 7, 1896, New York. Weight 130—133 lbs. Height, 5 ft 5 in. Managed by William (Buck) Areton, Billy Gibson and Jack Kearns.

1911

—Mickey Finnegan, New York . . . . KO by 3
—*Smiling Kemp, New York . . . . . . KO 1
—*Sammy Marino, New York . . . . . . ND 6
*Same night.

1912

—Johnny Falter . . . . ND 4
—Young Stanley . . . . KO 2
—Billy Meyers . . . . KO 1
Mar. 5—Joe Shugrue, New York . . . . . . KO by 4

232

—Battling Travis . . . . ND 6
—Battling Travis . . . . ND 6
—Youne Goldie . . . . KO 5
—Frankie Pass . . . . KO 3
—Young Cross . . . . ND 6
—Young Price . . . . KO 5
—Kid Goodman . . . . ND 6
—Young Goldie . . . . KO 5
—Kid Ghetto . . . . KO 6
—Kid Herman, New York . . . . ND 10
—Young McGowan . . . . KO 5
—Willie Singer . . . . KO 1
Nov. 2—Special Delivery Hirsch, New York ND 10
—Paddy Parker . . . . KO 2
—Jimmy McVeight . . . . ND 6

1913

—Johnny Carroll . . . . KO 1
—Eddie Powers . . . . ND 10
—Eddie Powers . . . . ND 6
Feb. 27—Frankie Fleming, New York . . . . KO by 5
—Dave Cronin . . . . ND 10
—Walter Brooks . . . . ND 10
—Frankie Fleming . . . . ND 10
—Tommy Houck . . . . ND 10
June 25—Young Lustig, New York . . . . . . ND 10
—Willie Jones . . . . ND 10
Aug. 2—Walter Hennessy, New York . . . . KO 3
Sept. 2—Ah Chung, New York . . . . KO 6
Oct. 4—Young Fitzsimmons, New York . . . ND 10
—Jack Sheppard . . . . ND 10
—Harry Tracey . . . . ND 10
Dec. 20—Danny Ridge, New York . . . . ND 10
Dec. 30—Special Delivery Hirsch, New York ND 10

1914

Jan. 3—Charlie Barry, Brooklyn . . . . ND 10
Jan. 6—Kid Black, New York . . . . ND 10
Jan. 20—Phil Bloom, New York . . . . ND 10
Jan. 24—Joe Stacy, New York . . . . ND 10
Mar. 3—Patsy Kline, New York . . . . ND 10
Apr. 3—Young Brown, New York . . . . ND 10
May 30—Willie Schaefer, New York . . . . . . ND 10
June 20—Teddy Hubbs, New York . . . . ND 10
July 18—Billy Kraemer, New York . . . . ND 10
Aug. 14—Tommy Houck, Elmsford . . . . . . KO 7
Aug. 22—Bobby Reynolds, New York . . . . . . ND 10
Aug. 25—Eddie Wallace, New York . . . . ND 10
Sept. 7—Pal Moore, Rockaway . . . . ND 10
Sept. 16—Joe Thomas, New York . . . . ND 10
Oct. 3—Phil Bloom, Brooklyn . . . . ND 10
Oct. 31—Young Driscoll, Brooklyn . . . . ND 10
Nov. 7—Harry Condon, New York . . . . ND 10
Nov. 26—Phil Bloom, New York . . . . ND 10
Dec. 12—Frankie Conifrey, New York . . . . . . ND 10

1915

Jan. 11—Jack Sheppard, New York . . . . KO 4
Jan. 16—Johnny Drummie, New York . . . . . . ND 10
Feb. 15—Tommy Langdon, Philadelphia . . . . ND 6
Feb. 18—Patsy Cline, New York . . . . ND 10
Mar. 12—Johnny Dundee, New York . . . . ND 10
Mar. 20—Jimmy Duffy, New York . . . . ND 10
Mar. 24—Joe Goldberg, New York . . . . ND 10
Apr. 29—Johnny Kilbane, New York . . . . . . ND 10
May 18—Franky Callahan, Brooklyn . . . . . . ND 10
June 19—Al Schumacher, New York . . . . . . KO 7

Aug. 13—Young Drummie, New York . . . . . . ND 10
Oct. 1—Al Thomas, New York . . . . ND 10
Nov. 8—Gene Moriarty, Brooklyn . . . . KO 3
Nov. 19—Joe Azevedo, New York . . . . ND 10
Dec. 17—Joe Mandot, New York . . . . KO 7

1916

Jan. 1—Joe Welsh, Philadelphia . . . . KO 5
Feb. 8—Phil Bloom, Boston . . . . KO 8
Feb. 11—Shamus O'Brien, Syracuse . . . . . . ND 10
Feb. 21—Jimmy Murphy, Philadelphia . . . . KO 6
Feb. 28—Rocky Kansas, Buffalo . . . . ND 10
Mar. 8—Johnny Dundee, New York . . . . . . ND 10
Mar. 13—Sam Robideau, Philadelphia . . . . ND 6
Mar. 17—Shamus O'Brien, New York . . . . . KO 7
Mar. 31—Freddie Welsh, New York . . . . . . ND 10
May 1—Charlie Thomas, Philadelphia . . . . ND 6
Apr. 19—Phil Bloom, New York . . . . ND 10
June 12—Johnny Dundee, New York . . . . . . ND 10
June 23—Vic Moran, New York . . . . ND 10
July 28—Freddie Welsh, Brooklyn . . . . ND 10
Aug. 18—Joe Azevedo, New York . . . . ND 10
Sept. 9—Eddy McAndrews, Philadelphia . . . KO 5
Sept. 14—Frankie Conifrey, New York . . . . . KO 7
Sept. 25—Johnny Tillman, Philadelphia . . . . ND 6
Oct. 10—Johnny Nelson, Philadelphia . . . . . ND 6
Oct. 18—Ever Hammer, Kansas City . . . . . . KO 12
Nov. 13—Banty Sharpe, New York . . . . ND 10
Nov. 15—Johnny Dundee, Philadelphia . . . . ND 6
Nov. 21—Harvey Thorpe, St. Louis . . . . . . KO 12
Nov. 28—Chick Simler, New York . . . . ND 10

1917

Jan. 23—Eddie Wallace, Philadelphia . . . . . . ND 6
Jan. 30—Phil Bloom, Brooklyn . . . . ND 10
Feb. 1—Frankie Callahan, Brooklyn . . . . . . ND 10
Feb. 28—Jimmy Regan, New York . . . . ND 10
Mar. 12—Johnny Tillman, Philadelphia . . . . ND 6
Mar. 22—Packey Hommey, New York . . . . . KO 9
Apr. 19—Richie Mitchell, Milwaukee . . . . . KO 7
May 7—Charley Thomas, Philadelphia . . . KO 6
May 10—Eddie Shannon, Brooklyn . . . . . . KO 6
May 28—Freddie Welsh, New York . . . . . . KO 9
(Won World Lightweight Title)
June 4—Joe Welsh, Philadelphia . . . . ND 6
June 18—Johnny Nelson, New York . . . . . . KO 3
July 25—*Johnny Kilbane, Philadelphia . . . KO 3
Sept. 3—Young Rector, Toronto . . . . KO 5
Sept. 12—Jimmy Paul, New York . . . . ND 6
Sept. 14—†Phil Bloom, Pittsburgh . . . . KO 2
Sept. 21—Leo Johnson, New York . . . . KO 1
Sept. 27—Eddie Dorsey, Buffalo . . . . KO 2
Oct. 5—Vic Moran, New York . . . . KO 2
Oct. 19—Jack Britton, New York . . . . ND 10
Oct. 22—Eddie Wagond, Philadelphia . . . . . . ND 6
Oct. 23—Young Erne, Buffalo . . . . ND 10
Oct. 24—Toughey Ramsey, Cleveland . . . . . KO 7
Nov. 12—Gene Delmont, St. Paul . . . . KO 8
Nov. 28—Frank Kirk, Denver . . . . KO 1
Dec. 12—Patsy Cline, Philadelphia . . . . ND 6
†Bloom broke his ankle.
*Title Bout.

1918

Apr. 8—Young Joe Borrell, Philadelphia . . . ND 6
Apr. 13—Jack Brazzo, Philadelphia . . . . KO 4
May 10—Young McCarthy, San Francisco . . . ND 4

May 14—Jimmy Ford, San Francisco . . . . . . Exh. 2
May 14—Joe Leopold, San Francisco . . . . . . Exh. 2
May 14—Johnny Arroussey, San Francisco . Exh. 2
May 20—Louie Rees, Los Angeles . . . . ND 4
May 25—Mike Golindo, San Diego . . . . W 4
June 6—Barney Adair, Buffalo . . . . ND 4
June 25—Jack Britton, Philadelphia . . . . ND 6
July 4—Jack Brazzo, Wildwood, NJ . . . . . . KO 8
July 16—Willie Jackson, New York . . . . . . Exh. 4
July 22—Young Gradwell, Jersey City . . . . KO 5
Sept. 16—Harry Pierce, Philadelphia . . . . ND 6
Sept. 23—Ted Lewis, Newark . . . . ND 8
Dec. 17—Chick Brown, New Haven . . . . KO 5

1919

Jan. 1—Paul Doyle, Philadelphia . . . . ND 6
Jan. 13—Eddy Kelly, Philadelphia . . . . ND 6
Jan. 20—Johnny Dundee, Newark . . . . ND 8
Jan. 31—Joe Benjamin, San Francisco . . . . . W 4
Feb. 5—Spider Roche, Oakland, CA . . . . . . ND 4
Feb. 7—Wildcat Leonard, Sacramento, CA . KO 4
Feb. 19—Willie Meehan, San Rafael, CA . . Exh. 3
Feb. 21—Willie Ritchie, San Francisco . . . . ND 4
Mar. 26—Harry Thorpe, Joplin, MO . . . . . . ND 10
Apr. 28—Willie Ritchie, Newark . . . . KO 8
May 21—Young Erne, Trenton . . . . KO 6
June 9—Charlie Pitts, Montreal . . . . ND 10
June 16—Johnny Dundee, Philadelphia . . . . ND 6
July 24—Joe Malone, Newport, RI . . . . . . KO 3
Aug. 11—Patsy Cline, Philadelphia . . . . . . ND 6
Sept. 4—Soldier Bartfield, Philadelphia . . . . ND 6
Sept. 8—Johnny Clinton, Syracuse . . . . . . ND 10
Sept. 17—Johnny Dundee, Newark . . . . ND 8
Oct. 1—Charlie Metrie, Detroit . . . . KO 7
Oct. 15—Phil Bloom, Detroit . . . . ND 10
Nov. 8—Soldier Bartfield, Jersey City . . . . ND 8
Nov. 17—Jimmy Duffy, Tulsa, OK . . . . KO 2
Nov. 27—Soldier Bartfield, Philadelphia . . . . ND 6
Dec. 6—Mel Coogan, Jersey City . . . . KO 2
Dec. 19—Red Herring, Memphis . . . . KO 6
Dec. 22—Jack Abel, Atlanta . . . . ND 10

1920

Feb. 9—Johnny Dundee, Jersey City . . . . . . ND 8
July 5—*Charley White, Benton Harbor . . . KO 9
Sept. 10—K. O. Loughlin, Camden . . . . KO 9
Sept. 25—Pal Moran, E. Chicago, IN . . . . . . ND 10
Oct. 4—Frankie Britt, Hartford, CT . . . . . . KO 5
Oct. 7—Johnny Sheppard, Paterson . . . . . . KO 3
Oct. 18—Johnny Tillman, Akron . . . . W 10
Nov. 11—K. O. Loughlin, Camden . . . . ND 10
Nov. 17—Eddie Kelly, New York . . . . KO 5
Nov. 26—*Joe Welling, New York . . . . KO 14
*Title Bout.

1921

Jan. 14—*Richie Mitchell, New York . . . . . . KO 6
Feb. 21—Eddie Moy, Dayton . . . . KO 3
Feb. 25—Joe Welling, St. Louis . . . . ND 8
June 6—Rocky Kansas, Harrison, NJ . . . . . . ND 12
Nov. 22—Sailor Friedman, Philadelphia . . . . ND 8
Nov. 29—George Ward, New York . . . . W 6
Dec. 20—Tim Droney, Philadelphia . . . . ND 8
*Title Bout.

1922

Feb. 10—*Rocky Kansas, New York . . . . W 15
Feb. 25—Pal Moran, New Orleans . . . . ND 10

233

Mar. 20—Johnny Clinton, Boston .... Exh. 10
May 19—Soldier Bartfield, New York .... W 4
June 26—Jack Britton, New York........... LF 13
     (For World Welterweight Title)
July 4—*Rocky Kansas, Michigan City .... KO 8
July 27—Lew Tendler, Jersey City .... ND 12
Aug. 5—Ever Hammer, Michigan City ..... ND 10
     *Title Bout.

1923
May 29—Pinkie Mitchell, Chicago .... KO 10
July 9—Alex Hart, Philadelphia .... ND 8
July 24—*Lew Tendler, New York .... W 15
Sept. 7—J. Mendelsohn, Philadelphia ...... ND 8
     *Title Bout.

1924
Aug. 1—Pal Moran, Cleveland .... ND 10
     Retired undefeated Jan. 15, Made comback as
welterweight in 1931.

1931
Sept. 9—Karl Lautchlager and Mickey Terry,
     Exhs., New Haven, 2 rounds each.
Sept. 16—Eddie Murray, Manuel Madera, Exhs.,
     KO, 1 rd. each; Teddy Hayes, KO, Exh.,
     Newark, 1 rd.
Oct. 6—Pal Silvers, Long Island City ..... KO 2
Oct. 27—Vittorio Livan, Boston .... KO 3
Nov. 6—Kayo Casper, Burlington, VT ...... D 10
Nov. 23—Buster Brown, Baltimore .... W 10

1932
Feb. 29—Billy McMahon, New York .... W 10
Apr. 11—Buster Brown, New York .... W 10
Apr. 19—Mike Sarko, New York .... KO 6
May 2—Willie Garafola, New York ...... KO 4
May 16—Marty Goldman, New York ...... KO 2
May 23—Jimmy Abbott, Paterson .... KO 6
June 8—Andy Saviola, New York .... W 10
June 16—Yg. Billy Angelo, Philadelphia ..... W 10
July 22—Eddie Shapiro, New York .... W 10
July 28—Billy Townsend, New York .... W 10
Aug. 11—Paulie Walker, New York .... W 10
Aug. 19—Mike Sarko, New York .... W 6
Sept. 2—Phil Rafferty, Long Beach, NY .... W 6
Sept. 8—Jimmy Abbott, Fort Hamilton, NY . KO 3
Sept. 12—Mike Sarko, New York .... W 6
Oct. 7—Jimmy McLarnin, New York .... KO by 6

1942
     Lieutenant in U.S. Merchant Marine.
     Became licensed referee on staff of New York
State Athletic Commission, 1943.

TB	KO	WD	WF	D	LD	LF	KO BY	ND	NC
210	71	18	0	1	0	1	4	115	0

Died April 18, 1947, New York.
Elected to Boxing Hall of Fame 1955.

(SUGAR) RAY LEONARD
Palmer Park, MD Welterweight
Born, May 17, 1956, Wilmington, NC
1976 Olympic Games
Light-Welterweight Gold Medalist

1977
Feb. 5—Luis Vega, Baltimore .... W 6

234

May 14—Willie Rodriguez, Baltimore .... W 6
June 10—Vinnie DeBarros, Hartford .... KO 3
Sept. 24—Frank Santore, Baltimore .... KO 5
Nov. 5—Augustin Estrada, Las Vegas ..... KO 5
Dec. 17—Hector Diaz, Washington DC...... KO 2

1978
Feb. 4—Rocky Ramon, Baltimore .... W 8
Mar. 1—Art McKnight, Dayton.......... KO 7
Mar. 19—Javier Muniz, New Haven .... KO 1
Apr. 13—Bobby Haymon, Landover........ KO 3
May 13—Randy Milton, Utica .... KO 8
June 3—Rafael Rodriguez, Baltimore ..... W 10
July 18—Dick Eckland, Boston .... W 10
Sept. 9—Floyd Mayweather, Providence .... KO 9
Oct. 6—Randy Shields, Baltimore .... W 10
Nov. 3—Bernardo Prada, Portland .... W 10
Dec. 9—Armando Muniz, Springfield ..... KO 6

1979
Jan. 11—Johnny Gant, Landover .... KO 8
Feb. 11—Fernand Marcotte, Miami Beach ... KO 8
Mar. 24—Daniel Gonzales, Tucson .... KO 1
Apr. 21—Adolfo Viruet, Las Vegas .... W 10
May 20—Marcos Geraldo, New Orleans...... W 10
June 24—Tony Chiaverini, Las Vegas ...... KO 4
Aug. 12—Pete Ranzany, Las Vegas .... KO 4
Sept. 28—Andy Price, Las Vegas .... KO 1
Nov. 30—Wilfred Benitez, Las Vegas ...... KO 15
     (Won World Welterweight Title)

1980
Mar. 31—Dave Green, Landover .... KO 4
June 20—Roberto Duran, Montreal .... L 15
Nov. 25—Roberto Duran, New Orleans ..... KO 8

1981
Mar. 28—Larry Bonds, Syracuse .... KO 10
     (Retained World Welterweight Title)
June 25—Ayub Kalube, Houston..................... KO 9
     (Won World Junior Middleweight
     Title)
Sept. 16—Thomas Hearns, Las Vegas............. KO 14
     (Retained World Welterweight Title)

1982
Feb. 15— Bruce Finch, Reno, Nev. .... KO 3
     (Retained World Welterweight Title)
Nov. 9—Announced retirement.

TB	KO	WD	WF	D	LD	LF	KO BY	ND	NC
33	23	9	0	0	1	0	0	0	0

CHARLES (SONNY) LISTON
Las Vegas, NV. Heavyweight
Born, St. Francis County, near Forest City,
Arkansas, May 8, 1932, Height, 6 ft. 1 in.

1953
Sept. 2—Don Smith, St. Louis .... KO 1
Sept. 17—Ponce DeLeon, St. Louis .... W 4
Nov. 21—Benny Thomas, St. Louis .... W 6

1954
Jan. 25—Martin Lee, St. Louis .... KO 6
Mar. 32—Stan Howlett, St. Louis .... W 6
June 29—John Summerlin, Detroit .... W 8
Aug. 10—John Summerflin, Detroit .... W 8
Sept. 7—Marty Marshall, Detroit.......... L 8

1955
Mar. 1—Neil Welch, St. Louis .... W 8
Apr. 21—Marty Marshall, St. Louis .... KO 6
May 5—Emil Brtko, Pittsburgh .... KO 5
May 25—Calvin Butler, St. Louis .... KO 2
Sept. 13—Johnny Gray, Indianapolis .... KO 6
Dec. 13—Larry Watson, East St. Louis ..... KO 4

1956
Mar. 6—Marty Marshall, Pittsburgh .... W 10

1957
(Inactive)

1958
Jan. 29—Bill Hunter, Chicago .... KO 2
Mar. 11—Ben Wise, Chicago .... KO 4
Apr. 3—Bert Whitehurst, St. Louis .... W 10
May 14—Julio Mederos, Chicago .... KO 3
Aug. 6—Wayne Bethea, Chicago......... KO 1
Oct. 7—Frankie Daniels, Miami Beach .... KO 1
Oct. 24—Bert Whitehurst, St. Louis ...... W 10
Nov. 18—Ernie Cab, Miami Beach .... KO 8

1959
Feb. 18—Mike DeJohn, Miami Beach ...... KO 6
Apr. 15—Cleveland Williams, Miami Beach . KO 3
Aug. 5—Nino Valdes, Chicago .... KO 3
Dec. 9—Willi Besmanoff, Cleveland....... KO 7

1960
Feb. 23—Howard King, Miami Beach ...... KO 8
Mar. 21—Cleveland Williams, Houston ..... KO 2
Apr. 25—Roy Harris, Houston .... KO 1
July 18—Zora Folley, Denver .... KO 3
Sept. 7—Eddie Machen, Seattle........... W 12

1961
Mar. 8—Howard King, Miami Beach ...... KO 3
Dec. 4—Albert Westphal, Philadelphia .... KO 1

1962
Sept. 25—Floyd Patterson, Chicago .... KO 1
     (Won World Heavyweight Title)

1963
July 22—Floyd Patterson, Las Vegas....... KO 1
     (World Heavyweight Title)
Aug.-Sept.–Exhibition Tour in Europe

1964
Feb. 25—Cassius Clay, Miami Beach .....KO by 7
     (Lost World Heavyweight Title)
Liston failed to come out for the seventh round.

1965
May 25—Muhammed Ali, Lewiston, ME ..KO by 1

1966
June 29—Gerhard Zech, Stockholm .... KO 7
Aug. 19—Amos Johnson, Goteborg......... KO 3

1967
Mar. 30—Dave Bailey, Goteborg .... KO 1
Apr. 28—Elmer Rush, Stockholm .... KO 6

1968
Mar. 16—Bill McMurray, Reno .... KO 4
May 23—Billy Joiner, Los Angeles .... KO 7
July 6—Henry Clark, San Francisco ..... KO 7
Oct. 14—Sonny Moore, Phoenix .... KO 3
Nov. 3—Willis Earls, Juarez .... KO 2
Nov. 12—Roger Rischer, Pittsburgh .... KO 3
Dec. 12—Amos Lincoln, Baltimore........ KO 2

1969
Mar. 28—Billy Joiner, St. Louis .... W 10
May 19—George Johnson, Las Vegas....... KO 7
Sep. 23—Sonny Moore, Houston .... KO 3
Dec. 6—Leotis Martin, Las Vegas......KO by 9

1970
June 29—Chuck Wepner, Jersey City .... KO 10
Dec. 30—Died in his Las Vegas, NV, home. His
     wife found him a week later, Jan. 5, 1971.

TB	KO	WD	WF	D	LD	LF	KO BY	ND	NC
54	39	11	0	0	1	0	3	0	0

ALVARO (YAQUI) LOPEZ
Stockton, CA Light-Heavyweight
Born, May 21, 1951

1972
Apr. 24—Herman Hampton, Stockton .... W 6
June 2—Herman Hampton, Carson City .... KO 3
June 16—Cisco Solorio, Stockton .... KO 6
July 1—Jesse Burnett, Stockton .... L 8
Oct. 24—King Henry Tavako, San Carlos .... W 6
Nov. 6—Mack Hearn, Eugene .... KO 6
Nov. 29—Herman Hampton, Stockton ...... KO 7
Dec. 11—Van Sahib, Eugene .... KO 2

1973
Feb. 8—Polo Ramirez, Stockton .... KO 7
Mar. 15—Al Bolden, Seattle .... L 10
Apr. 21—Hildo Silva, Santa Rosa .... W 10
June 9—Ron Wilson, Santa Rosa .... W 10
July 6—Dave Rogers, Gardnerville .... KO 5
Aug. 3—Ron Wilson, Reno .... KO 6
Aug. 22—Herman Hampton, Tacoma ...... KO 6
Sept. 20—Budda Brooks, Stockton .... KO 5
Nov. 1—Alfonso Gonzalez, Portland ...... KO 2
Dec. 6—Al Bolden, Portland .... W 10

1974
Feb. 14—Andy Kendall, Portland .... KO 5
Mar. 7—Willie Warren, Reno .... W 10
May 10—Hildo Silva, Stockton .... W 12
July 7—Joe Cokes, Gardnerville .... W 12
Oct. 11—Bobby Rascon, Portland .... KO 6
Nov. 13—Hildo Silva, Stockton .... W 10

1975
Mar. 4—Terry Lee, Sacramento .... KO 9
Apr. 8—Lee Mitchell, Sacramento .... W 6
May 14—Mike Quarry, Stockton .... W 10
July 3—Gary Summerhays, Gardnerville .... W 10
July 31—Jesse Burnett, Stockton .... L 12
Sept. 24—Jesse Burnett, Stockton .... W 12

1976
Feb. 12—Terry Lee, Portland .... W 10
May 3—David Smith, Stockton .... W 10
June 30—Karl Zurheide, Stockton .... KO 6
July 17—Larry Castaneda, Stockton ...... KO 9
Oct. 9—John Conteh, Copenhagen ..... L 15
(WBC Light-Heavyweight Title)
Dec. 8—Pete McIntyre, Stockton .... KO 6

1977
Mar. 7—Larry Castaneda, Stockton ..... KO 8
Apr. 22—Lonnie Bennett, Indianapolis ...KO by 3
June 17—Bobby Lloyd, Miami Beach .... KO 5
July 20—Manuel Fierro, Stockton .... KO 3
Sept. 17—Victor Galindez, Rome .... L 15
(WBA Light-Heavyweight Title)
Oct. 27—Chuck Warfield, Stockton ...... KO 4
Nov. —Clarence Geigger, Stateline .... KO 6
Dec. 15—Clarence Geigger, Stockton ...... KO 4

1978
Jan. 12—Fabian Falconette, Los Angeles ... KO 2
Mar. 2—Mike Rossman, New York .... KO 6
Mar. 17—Ned Hallacy, Las Vegas .... W 10
May 6—Victor Galindez, Lido DiCamaiore ... L 15
(WBA Light-Heavyweight Title)
July 2—Jesse Burnett, Stockton .... W 15
(U.S. Light-Heavyweight Title)
Oct. 24—Matt Franklin, Philadelphia ....KO by 11

(U.S. Light-Heavyweight Title)
1979
Jan. 17—Junior Albers, Stockton .... KO 3
Feb. 27—Ivy Brown, Sacramento .... KO 3
Sept. 12—Ernie Barr, Stockton .... KO 3
Oct. 4—Bashiru Ali, Redwood City .... W 10
Dec. 1—James Scott, Rahway .... L 10

1980
Apr. 16—Pete McIntyre, Fresno ....KO 8
May 20—Bobby Lloyd, Fresno .... KO 8
July 13—M. Saad Muhammad, McAllen.KO by 14
(For WBC Light Heavyweight Title)
Oct. 18—Michael Spinks, Atlantic City... KO by 7
Nov. 29—Carl Ivy, Lake Tahoe ....KO 3

1981
Feb. 14—Grover Robinson, Lake Tahoe ....KO 4
Mar. 18—George O'Mara, San Carlos ....KO 10
May 27—Willie Taylor, Stockton ....KO 7
July 24—S.T. Gordon, Reno, Nev. .... KO by 7
Nov. 27—Tony Mundine, Surfers Paradise ...KO 3

1982
Jan. 14—John Davis, Atlantic City...................L 10
May 5—Alvin Dominey, Stockton ....KO 6
June 1—King David, Sacramento...................W 12
July 31—Ken Arlt, Lake Tahoe ....W 10
Sept. 9—Roger Braxton, Stateline ....W 10
Nov. 27—James Williams, Incline Village.......W 10

JOE LOUIS
(Joe Louis Barrow)
(Brown Bomber)
Born, May 13, 1914, Lafayette, AL. Weight, 200
lbs. Height, 6 ft. 1½ in. Managed by Julian Black and
John Roxborough, and later by Marshall Miles.

1934
July 4—Jack Kracken, Chicago .... KO 1
July 11—Willie Davis, Chicago .... KO 3
July 29—Larry Udell, Chicago............ KO 2
Aug. 13—Jack Kranz, Chicago .... W 8
Aug. 27—Buck Everett, Chicago .... KO 2
Sept. 11—Alex Borchuk, Detroit .... KO 4
Sept. 25—Adolph Wiater, Chicago .... W 10
Oct. 24—Art Sykes, Chicago .... KO 8
Oct. 30—Jack O'Dowd, Detroit .... KO 2
Nov. 14—Stanley Poreda, Chicago .... KO 1
Nov. 30—Charley Massera, Chicago ...... KO 3
Dec. 14—Lee Ramage, Chicago .... KO 8

1935
Jan. 4—Patsy Perroni, Detroit .... W 10
Jan. 11—Hans Birkie, Pittsburgh .... KO 10
Feb. 21—Lee Ramage, Los Angeles .... KO 2
Mar. 8—Donald "Reds" Barry,
San Francisco .... KO 3
Mar. 28—Natie Brown, Detroit .... W 10
Apr. 12—Roy Lazer, Chicago .... KO 3
Apr. 22—Biff Benton, Dayton .... KO 2
Apr. 27—Roscoe Toles, Flint .... KO 6
May 3—Willie Davis, Peoria .... KO 2
May 7—Gene Stanton, Kalamazoo ...... KO 3
June 25—Primo Carnera, New York ...... KO 6
Aug. 7—King Levinsky, Chicago .... KO 1
Sept. 24—Max Baer, New York .... KO 4
Dec. 13—Paolino Uzcudun, New York ...... KO 4

1936
Jan. 17—Charley Retzlaff, Chicago .... KO 1
June 19—Max Schmeling New York .....KO by 12
Aug. 18—Jack Sharkey, New York......... KO 3
Sept. 22—Al Ettore, Philadelphia .... KO 5
Oct. 9—Jorge Brescia, New York .... KO 3
Oct. 14—Willie Davis, South Bend ....Exh. KO 3
Oct. 14—K.O. Brown, South Bend ....Exh. KO 3
Nov. 20—Paul Williams, New Orleans ....Exh. KO 2
Nov. 20—Tom Jones, New Orleans .....Exh. KO 3
Dec. 14—Eddie Simms, Cleveland .... KO 1

1937
Jan. 11—Steve Ketchel, Buffalo........... KO 2
Jan. 29—Bob Pastor, New York .... W 10
Feb. 17—Natie Brown, Kansas City .... KO 4

June 22—James J. Braddock, Chicago ...... KO 8
(Won World Heavyweight Title)
Aug. 30—Tommy Farr, New York .... W 15
(Title Bout)

1938
Feb. 23—Nathan Mann, New York .... KO 3
(Title Bout)
Apr. 1—Harry Thomas Chicago .... KO 5
(Title Bout)
June 22—Max Schmeling, New York .... KO 1
(Title Bout)

1939
Jan. 25—John Henry Lewis, New York ..... KO 1
(Title Bout)
Apr. 17—Jack Roper, Los Angeles .... KO 1
(Title Bout)
June 28—Tony Galento, New York .... KO 4
(Title Bout)
Sept. 20—Bob Pastor, Detroit .... KO 11
(Title Bout)

1940
Feb. 9—Arturo Godoy, New York .... W 15
(Title Bout)
Mar. 29—Johnny Paychek, New York ..... KO 2
(Title Bout)
June 20—Arturo Godoy, New York .... KO 8
(Title Bout)
Dec. 16—Al McCoy, Boston .... KO 6
(Title Bout)

1941
Jan. 31—Red Burman, New York .... KO 5
(Title Bout)
Feb. 17—Gus Dorazio, Philadelphia........ KO 2
(Title Bout)
Mar. 21—Abe Simon, Detroit .... KO 13
(Title Bout)
Apr. 8—Tony Musto, St. Louis........... KO 9
(Title Bout)
May 23—Buddy Baer, Washington, DC . Wdisq. 7
(Title Bout)
June 18—Billy Conn, New York .... KO 13
(Title Bout)
July 11—Jim Robinson, Minneapolis . . . Exh. KO 1
Sept. 29—Lou Nova, New York .... KO 6
(Title Bout)
Nov. 25—George Giambastiani, Los Angeles Exh. 4

1942
Jan. 9—Buddy Baer, New York .... KO 1
(Title Bout)
(Donated Purse to Naval Relief Fund)
Mar. 27—Abe Simon, New York .... KO 6
(Title Bout)
(Donated Purse to Army Relief Fund)
June 5—George Nicholson, Fort Hamilton . Exh. 3
Joined U.S. Army.

1944
Nov. 3—Johnny Denson, Detroit...... Exh. KO 2
Nov. 6—Charley Crump, Baltimore ....Exh. W 3
Nov. 9—Dee Amos, Hartford .... Exh.W 3
Nov. 13—Jimmy Bell, Washington, DC . . Exh. W 3
Nov. 14—Johnny Davis, Buffalo .... Exh.KO 1
Nov. 15—Dee Amos, Elizabeth .... Exh. W 3
Nov. 17—Dee Amos, Camden .... Exh. W 3
Nov. 24—Dan Merritt, Chicago......... Exh. W 3

1945

Nov. 15—Sugarlip Anderson, San Francisco Exh. 2
Nov. 15—Big Boy Brown, San Francisco ... Exh. 2
Nov. 29—Big Boy Brown, Sacramento ..... Exh. 2
Nov. 29—Bobby Lee, Sacramento .... Exh. 2
Dec. 10—Bob Frazier, Victoria .... Exh. 3
Dec. 11—Big Boy Brown, Portland ...... Exh. 2
Dec. 11—Dave Johnson, Portland .... Exh. 2
Dec. 12—Big Boy Brown, Eugene OR ..... Exh. 3
Dec. 13—Big Boy Brown, Vancouver ...... Exh. 3

1946

June 19—Billy Conn, New York .... KO 8
(Title Bout)
Sept. 18—Tami Mauriello, New York .... KO 1
(Title Bout)
Nov. 11—Cleo Everett, Honolulu .... Exh. 4
Nov. 11—Wayne Powell, Honolulu....... Exh. 2
Nov. 25—Perk Daniels, Mexicali, Mexico... Exh. 4

1947

Feb. 7—Arturo Godoy, Mexico City ...... Exh. 10
Feb. 10—Art Ramsey, San Salvador ...... Exh. 3
Feb. 10—Walter Hafer, San Salvador .... Exh. 3
Feb. 12—Art Ramsey, Panama City .... Exh. 3
Feb. 12—Walter Hafer, Panama City .... Exh. 3
Feb. 19—Arturo Godoy, Santiago, Chile ... Exh. 6
Feb. 27—Art Ramsey, Medellin, Colombia . Exh. 2
Feb. 27—Walter·Hafer, Medellin, Colombia Exh. 2
Mar. 10—Walter Hafer, Havana .... Exh. 2
Mar. 10—Art Ramsey, Havana .... Exh. 2
June 6—Rusty Payne, San Diego .... Exh. 2
June 6—Dick Underwood, San Diego ..... Exh. 2
June 13—Tiger Jack Fox, Spokane .... Exh. 4
June 23—Harry Wills, Los Angeles .... Exh. 4
Dec. 5—Jersey Joe Walcott, New York..... W 15
(Title Bout)

1948

Jan. 29—Bob Foxworth, Chicago .... Exh. 4
Feb. 9—Leo Matriccianni .... Exh. 4
June 25—Jersey Joe Walcott, New York..... KO 11
(Title Bout)
Sept. 30—Pat Comiskey, Washington, DC .. Exh. 6
Oct. 28—Merritt Wynn, Atlanta.......... Exh. 3
Oct. 28—Bob Garner, Atlanta .... Exh. 3
Oct. 29—Bob Garner, Norfolk .... Exh. 4
Oct. 31—Bob Garner, New Orleans ...... Exh. 4
Nov. 1—Bob Garner, New Orleans ...... Exh. 3
Nov. 3—Bob Garner, Nashville.......... Exh. 4
Nov. 8—Johnny Shkor, Boston .... Exh. 4
Nov. 9—Bernie Reynolds, New Haven .... Exh. 4
Nov. 17—Jimmy Bivins, Cleveland .... Exh. 6
Nov. 19—Vern Mitchell, Detroit .... Exh. 6
Nov. 23—Kid Riviera, St. Louis .... Exh. 4
Nov. 24—Ray Augustus, Oklahoma City . Exh. KO 2
Nov. 25—Curt Kennedy, Kansas City .... Exh. 4
Nov. 29—Billy Smith, Cincinnati .... Exh. 4
Dec. 10—Billy Conn, Chicago.......... Exh. 6
Dec. 14—Arturo Godoy Philadelphia .... Exh. 6
Dec. 16—Pat Comiskey, Paterson ...... Exh. 6
Dec. 20—Willie James, Lewiston .... Exh. 4

1949

Jan. 10—Sterling Ingram, Omaha .... Exh. 4
Jan. 11—Orlando Ott, Topeka .... Exh. 4
Jan. 12—Hubert Hood, Wichita.......... Exh. 4
Jan. 17—Art Swiden, Toledo .... Exh. 4

Jan. 18—Dick Hagen, Moline, Il .... Exh. 4
Jan. 19—Orlando Ott, Rochester, MN .... Exh. 4
Jan. 25—Elmer Ray, Miami .... Exh. 6
Jan. 27—George Fitch, Palm Beach....... Exh. 4
Jan. 28—Nino Valdes, Tampa .... Exh. 4
Jan. 31—Dixie Lee Oliver, Orlando .... Exh. KO 4
Feb. 1—Elmer Ray, Jacksonville .... Exh. KO 4
Feb. 3—Bill Graves, Daytona .... Exh. KO 3
Feb. 4—George Fitch, Savannah .... Exh. 4
Feb. 23—Edgar Edwards, Kingston ...... Exh. 3
      —BWI .... Exh. 3
Mar. 1—(Louis announced his retirement as un-
defeated World Heavyweight Champion)
Mar. 1—Ed Crawley, Nassau .... Exh. 4
Mar. 4—Omelio Agramonte, Havana .... Exh. 4
Mar. 5—Omelio Agramonte, Oriente, Cuba Exh. 4
Mar. 16—Elmer Ray, Houston .... Exh. KO 4
Mar. 18—Tex Brodie, Dallas............. Exh. 4
Mar. 22—Hubert Hood, St. Paul .... Exh. 6
Oct. 3—Abel Cestac, Washington DC .... Exh. 4
Oct. 10—Curtis Sheppard, Baltimore ...... Exh. 4
Oct. 24—Bill Weinberg, Providence ...... Exh. 4
Oct. 25—Joe Domonic, Hartford ...... Exh. 4
Oct. 31—Bill Gilliam, Atlantic City .... Exh. 4
Nov. 14—Johnny Shkor, Boston .... Exh.ND 10
Nov. 22—Joe Chesul, Newark .... Exh.ND 10
Nov. 28—Johnny Flynn, Kansas City ... Exh.ND 10
Dec. 7—Pat Valentino, Chicago .... Exh.KO 8
Dec. 14—Roscoe Toles, Detroit .... Exh. 5
Dec. 14—Johnny Flynn, Detroit .... Exh. 5
Dec. 19—Al Hoosman, Oakland .... Exh.KO 5
Dec. 21—Jay Lambert, Salt Lake City .. Exh. 5
Dec. 21—Rey Layne, Salt Lake City ...... Exh. 5

1950

Jan. 6—Willie Bean, Hollywood .... Exh. 6
Jan. 10—Jack Flood, Seattle .... Exh. 4
Jan. 12—Clarence Henry, Wilmington ..... Exh. 4
Jan. 13—Al Spaulding, San Diego .... Exh. 4
Jan. 20—Andy Walker, Stockton .... Exh. 4
Jan. 24—Rex Layne, Salt Lake City ...... Exh. 4
Feb. 1—Gene Jones, Miami .... Exh. 8
Feb. 7—Nino Valdes, St. Petersburgh .... Exh. 4
Feb. 8—Candy McDaniels, Orlando ...... Exh. 5
Feb. 14—Johnny Haynes, Tampa .... Exh. 4
Feb. 21—Sid Peaks, Jacksonville .... Exh. 6
Feb. 23—Dan Bolston, Macon .... Exh. 1
Feb. 23—Leo Jackson, Macon .... Exh. 3
Feb. 27—Willie Johnson, Albany, GA. .... Exh. 4
Feb. 28—Dan Bolston, Columbus, GA .... Exh. 4
Mar. 3—Leo Johnson, Waycross, GA .... Exh. 4
Mar. 18—Kid Carr, Lubbock .... Exh. 4
Mar. 20—Sterling Ingram, Odessa ...... Exh. 4
Mar. 22—Joe Santell, El Paso .... Exh. 4
Mar. 22—John McFalls, El Paso........... Exh. 4
Mar. 24—Henry Hall, Austin .... Exh. 4
Mar. 25—J. K. Homer, Austin .... Exh. 4
Apr. 22—Walter Hafer Rio de Janiero .. Exh.KO 2
Sept. 27—Ezzard Charles, New York .... L 15
(For World Heavyweight Title)
Nov. 29—Cesar Brion, Chicago .... W 10

1951

Jan. 3—Freddie Beshore, Detroit......... KO 4
Feb. 7—Omelio Agramonte, Miami .... W 10
Feb. 23—Andy Walker, San Francisco ..... KO 10

May 2—Omelio Agramonte, Detroit .... W 10
June 15—Lee Savold, New York .... KO 6
Aug. 1—Cesar Brion, San Francisco .... W 10
Aug. 15—Jimmy Bivins, Baltimore .... W 10
Oct. 26—Rocky Marciano, New York ....KO by 8
Nov. 18—U.S. Serviceman, Tokyo .... KO
Nov. 18—U.S. Serviceman, Tokyo .... KO
Nov. 18—U.S. Serviceman, Tokyo .... KO
Nov. 18—Cpt. Buford J. DeCordova, Tokyo ... Exh.
Nov.   —Cpt. Buford J. DeCordova, Tokyo ... Exh.
Nov.   —Cpt. Buford J. DeCordova, Tokyo ... Exh.
Dec.   —St. Lindy Brooks, Sendai, Japan .. Exh. 3
Dec. 14—Chang Pulu, Taipeh, Formosa Exh. KO 1
Dec. 14—Sgt. Seth E. Woodbury, Taipeh,
Formosa .... Exh. 2
Dec. 14—D.H. Camtrell (U.S. Navy) Taipeh,
Formosa .... Exh. 2
Dec. 14—Cpt. Buford J. DeCordova, Taipeh,
Formosa .... Exh. 3
Dec. 16—Cpt. Buford J. DeCordova, Taipeh,
Formosa .... Exh. 3

TB	KO	WD	WF	D	LD	LF	KO BY	ND	NC
71	54	13	1	0	1	0	2	0	0

Elected to Boxing Hall of Fame 1954.
Died April 12, 1981, Las Vegas, NV.

RON LYLE
Denver, CO. Heavyweight
Born, Feb. 11, 1942
1971

Apr. 23—A.J. Staples, Denver .... KO 2
May 22—Art Miller, Boston .... KO 5
June 22—Gary Bates, Stateline............ KO 4
July 16—Edmundo Stewart, New York ..... KO 2
July 24—Leroy Caldwell, Lake Geneva ..... W 5
Aug. 11—Frank Niglett, Las Vegas .... KO 9
Sept. 1—Eddie Land, Las Vegas .... KO 7
Oct. 10—Manuel Ramos, Denver .... W 10
Nov. 10—Joe E. Lewis, Las Vegas .... KO 3
Nov. 26—Jack O'Halloran, Denver .... KO 4
Dec. 18—Bill Drover, Denver.............. KO 2

1972

Jan. 22—Chuck Leslie, Denver .... KO 3
Mar. 25—George Johnson, Denver .... KO 3
May 10—Mel Turnbow, Las Vegas .... KO 7
May 25—Mike Boswell, Omaha .... KO 4
July 11—Vicente Rondon, Denver .... KO 2
Sept. 30—Buster Mathis, Denver .... KO 2
Oct. 29—Luis Pirez, Denver .... KO 3
Dec. 9—Larry Middleton, Denver......... KO 3

1973

Feb. 9—Jerry Quarry, New York .... L 12
Apr. 14—Bob Stallings, Missoula .... W 10
May 12—Gregorio Peralta, Denver .... W 10
June 11—Wendell Newton, Philadelphia ..... W 10
July 3—Lou Bailey, Oklahoma City .... W 10
Aug. 15—Jose Luis Garcia, Denver .... KO 8
Oct. 4—Jurgin Blin, Denver .... KO 2
Oct. 31—Larry Middleton, Baltimore........ W 10
Nov. 17—Gregorio Peralta, Frankfurt .... D 10

1974

Mar. 19—Oscar Bonavena, Denver .... W 12
May 21—Larry Middleton, Baltimore ...... W 12
July 16—Jimmy Ellis, Denver .... W 12
Sept. 17—Boone Kirkman, Seattle .... KO 8
Dec. 1—Al (Memphis) Jones, New Orleans . KO 5

1975

Feb. 11—Jimmy Young, Honolulu .... L 10
May 16—Muhammad Ali, Las Vegas ..... KO by 11
(World Heavyweight Title)
Sept. 13—Earnie Shavers, Denver.......... KO 6

1976

Jan. 24—George Foreman, Las Vegas .... KO by 4
(U.S. Heavyweight Title)
Sept. 11—Kevin Isaac, Utica .... KO 7
Nov. 6—Jimmy Young, San Francisco .... L 12

1977

Mar. 20—Joe Bugner, Las Vegas .... W 12
Sept. 14—Stan Ward, Las Vegas .... W 10

1978

June 3—Horacio Robinson, Denver .... KO 8

1979

Apr. 7—Fili Moala, San Diego .... KO 8
May 12—Scott LeDoux, Las Vegas......... W 10
Dec. 12—Lynn Ball, Phoenix .... KO by 2

ROCKY MARCIANO

(Rocco Francis Marchegiano)
(Brockton Blockbuster)

Born, September 1, 1923, Brockton, MA.
Weight, 184 pounds. Height, 5 ft. 11 in. Managed by
Gene Caggiano; later by Al Weill.

1947

Mar. 17—Lee Epperson, Holyoke .... KO 3

1948

July 12—Harry Balzerian, Providence ...... KO 1
July 19—John Edwards, Providence .... KO 1
Aug. 9—Bobby Quinn, Providence .... KO 3
Aug. 23—Eddie Ross, Providence.......... KO 1
Aug. 30—Jimmy Weeks, Providence .... KO 1
Sept. 13—Jerry Jackson, Providence........ KO 1
Sept. 20—Bill Hardeman, Providence ...... KO 1
Sept. 30—Gil Cardione, Washington, DC .... KO 1
Oct. 4—Bob Jefferson, Providence........ KO 2
Nov. 29—Patrick Connolly, Providence ..... KO 1
Dec. 4—Gilley Ferron, Philadelphia....... KO 2

1949

Mar. 21—Johnny Pretzie, Providence ...... KO 5
Mar. 28—Artie Donator, Providence........ KO 1
Apr. 11—James Walls, Providence .... KO 3
May 2—Jimmy Evans, Providence .... KO 3
May 23—Don Mogard, Providence .... W 10
July 18—Harry Haft, Providence .... KO 3
Aug. 16—Pete Louthis, New Bedford ...... KO 3
Sept. 26—Tommy DiGiorgio, Providence .... KO 4
Oct. 10—Ted Lowry, Providence .... W 10
Nov. 7—Joe Domonic, Providence .... KO 2
Dec. 2—Pat Richards, New York .... KO 2
Dec. 19—Phil Muscato, Providence .... KO 5
Dec. 30—Carmine Vingo, New York ...... KO 6

1950

Mar. 24—Roland LaStarza, New York .... W 10
June 5—Eldridge Eatman, Providence ..... KO 3
July 10—Gino Buonvino, Boston .... KO 10
Sept. 18—Johnny Shkor, Providence ...... KO 6
Nov. 13—Ted Lowry, Providence .... W 10
Dec. 18—Bill Wilson, Providence.......... KO 1

1951

Jan. 29—Keene Simmons, Providence...... KO 8
Mar. 20—Harold Mitchell, Hartford .... KO 2
Mar. 26—Art Henri, Providence .... KO 9
Apr. 30—Red Applegate, Providence .... W 10
July 12—Rex Layne New York .... KO 6
Aug. 27—Freddie Beshore, Boston .... KO 4
Oct. 26—Joe Louis, New York .... KO 8

1952

Feb. 13—Lee Savold, Philadelphia......... KO 6
Apr. 21—Gino Buonvino, Providence ...... KO 2
May 12—Bernie Reynolds, Providence ..... KO 3
July 28—Harry Matthews, New York ...... KO 2
Sept. 23—Jersey Joe Walcott, Philadelphia... KO 13
(Won World Heavyweight Title)

1953

May 15—Jersey Joe Walcott, Chicago ...... KO 1
(Title Bout)
Sept. 24—Roland LaStarza, New York ...... KO 11
(Title Bout)

1954

June 17—Ezzard Charles, New York .... W 15
(Title Bout)
Sept. 17—Ezzard Charles, New York ...... KO 8
(Title Bout)

1955

May 16—Don Cockell, San Francisco ...... KO 9
(Title Bout)
Sept. 21—Archie Moore, New York .... KO 9
(Title Bout)

1956

Announced retirement as undefeated World
Heavyweight Champion, April 27, 1956.

Elected to Boxing Hall of Fame 1959.

Killed in an airplane accident in Newton, IA,
August 31, 1969 the day before his 46th birthday.

TB	KO	WD	WF	D	LD	LF	KO BY	ND	NC
49	43	6	0	0	0	0	0	0	0

JOEY MAXIM

(Guiseppe Antonio Berardinelli)

Born, March 28, 1922, Cleveland, OH. Light-
Heavyweight. Height, 6 ft. 1 in. Managed by Jack
Kearns.

1941

Jan. 13—Bob Perry, Cleveland .... W 4
Jan. 27—Frank McBride, Chicago .... W 8
Feb. 17—Orlando Trotter, Chicago .... L 8
Apr. 29—Bob Berry, Cleveland .... W 6
July 11—Tony Paoli, Cleveland .... W 10
July 28—Johnny Trotter, Chicago .... W 8
Sept. 13—Lee Oma, Youngstown, OH .... W 8
Sept. 15—Nate Bolden, Chicago .... W 10

Oct. 6—Bill Peterson, Chicago .... W 10
Oct. 27—Oliver Shanks, Chicago .... KO 5
Dec. 1—Clarence Red Burman, Cleveland ... W 10

1942

Jan. 16—Booker Beckwith, Chicago .... L 10
Mar. 11—Herbie Katz, Cleveland .... KO 6
Mar. 23—Lou Brooks, Baltimore .... W 10
Apr. 20—Frank Green, Chicago .... KO 2
May 11—Charles Roth, Chicago ....LF 2
June 1—Charles Roth, Chicago .... KO 4
June 22—Jimmy Bivins, Cleveland ....L 10
July 10—Lou Brooks. Wilmington .... W 10
July 27—Curtis Sheppard, Pittsburgh ...... W 10
Aug. 10—Altus Allen, Chicago ....L 10
Aug. 27—Jack Marshall, Chicago .... KO 8
Sept. 22—Shelton Bell, Pittsburgh .... W 10
Oct. 5—Hubert Hood, Chicago.......... W 8
Oct. 13—Larry Lane, Akron .... W 10
Oct. 27—Ezzard Charles, Pittsburgh ......L 10
Dec. 1—Ezzard Charles, Cleveland ....L 10

1943

Jan. 18—Clarence Brown, Chicago .... W 10
Feb. 15—Clarence Brown, Chicago .... W 10
Mar. 10—Curtis Sheppard, Cleveland.....KO by 1
Mar. 31—Curtis Sheppard, Cleveland .... W 10
Apr. 26—Al Jordan, Chicago .... W 10
Aug. 9—Nate Bolden, Chicago .... W 10
Oct. 29—Buddy Scott, Chicago .... W 10
Dec. 1—Claudio Villar, Cleveland .... KO 6
In U.S. Army.
(Physical Instructor, Army Air Force)
Won 14 out of 15 service bouts.

1944

Jan. 31—Georgie Parks, Washington .... W 10
Apr. 28—John (Buddy) Walker, Detroit ..... W 10
May 29—Bob Garner, Chicago .... W 10
June 26—Frank Androff, Chicago .... W 10
July 27—Lloyd Marshall, Cleveland .... L 10
Dec. 19—Johnny Flynn, Cleveland...........L 10

1945

Feb. 2—Johnny Flanagan, Chicago .... W 8
Apr. 16—Clarence Brown, Detroit .... W 10
Nov. 26—Cleo Everett, Cleveland .... W 10

1946

Mar. 4—Howard Williams, Detroit .... W 10
Mar. 11—John Thomas, New York...........L 10
Mar. 27—Ralph De John, Buffalo.......... KO 1
Apr. 1—Buddy Walker, Baltimore .... W 10
Apr. 9—Phil Muscato, Buffalo ....L 10
May 7—Charley Eagle, Buffalo .... D 10
May 14—Phil Muscato, Buffalo .... W 12
Aug. 2—Phil Muscato, Rochester .... W 10
Aug. 14—Henry Cooper, Chicago .... W 10
Aug. 28—Jersey Joe Walcott, Camden ...... W 10
Oct. 10—Clarence Jones, Akron........... W 10
Oct. 16—Bearcat Jones, Toledo .... KO 5
Nov. 12—Jim Ritchie, St. Louis .... D 10
Dec. 3—Jimmy Webb, Houston .... KO 6
Dec. 12—Alvelez, El Paso .... W 10
Dec. 17—Jack Marshall, Houston .... W 10

1947

Jan. 6—Jersey Joe Walcott, Philadelphia.....L 10
Jan. 28—Marty Clark, Miami............. KO 7
May 12—Charlie Roth, Louisville .... KO 4

June 23—Jersey Joe Walcott, Los Angeles . . . . . L 10
Sept. 8—Clarence Jones, Wheeling,WV . . . . KO 5
Sept. 17—John Thomas, Cleveland . . . . W 10
Nov. 12—Bob Foxworth, Chicago . . . . W 10
Dec. 8—Billy Thompson, Philadelphia . . . . . . W 10

1948

Jan. 9—Olle Tandberg, New York . . . . W 10
Feb. 2—Bob Sikes, Little Rock . . . . W 10
Feb. 13—Tony Bosnich, San Francisco . . . . . . W 10
Mar. 22—Pat Valentino, San Francisco . . . . . . D 10
Apr. 27—Louis Berlier, Houston . . . . W 10
May 7—Francisco de la Cruz, El Paso . . . . . . W 10
May 27—Roy Hawkins, Tacoma . . . . W 10
June 7—Pat Valentino, San Francisco . . . . . . D 10
June 22—Joe Kahut, Portland, OR . . . . W 10
June 29—Bill Peterson, Seattle . . . . W 10
Sept. 28—Bill Peterson, Portland, OR . . . . . . W 10
Oct. 19—Joe Kahut, Portland, OR . . . . L 15
Nov. 12—Bob Satterfield, Chicago . . . . W 10
Dec. 7—Jimmy Bivins, Cleveland . . . . W 10

1949

Feb. 28—Ezzard Charles, Cincinnati . . . . L 15
May 23—Gus Lesnevich, Cincinnati . . . . W 15
(For vacant American Light-
Heavyweight Title)
Oct. 25—Joe Kahut, Cincinnati . . . . KO 5
Nov. 30—Pat McCafferty, Wichita . . . . KO 4
Dec. 9—Bill Petersen, Grand Rapids . . . . . . W 10
Dec. 9—Bill Petersen, Grand Rapids . . . . . . W 10

1950

Jan. 24—Freddie Mills, London . . . . KO 10
(Won Light-Heavyweight Title)
Apr. 19—Joe Dawson, Omaha . . . . KO 2
Apr. 27—Jack Marshall, Dallas . . . . Exh. 4
May 12—Bill Petersen, Memphis . . . . KO 6
Sept. 25—Johnny Swanson, Huntington . . . . . KO 3
Oct. 10—Bill Petersen, Salt Lake City . . . . . . W 10
Nov. 22—Big Boy Brown, Moline, IL . . . . W 10
Dec. 11—Dave Whitlock, San Francisco . . . . KO 4

1951

Jan. 27—Hubert Hood, Indianapolis . . . . . . KO 3
May 30—Ezzard Charles, Chicago . . . . L 15
(Heavyweight Title Bout)
Aug. 22—Bob Murphy, New York . . . . W 15
(Won Light-Heavyweight Title)
Dec. 12—Ezzard Charles, San Francisco . . . . . . L 12

1952

Mar. 6—Ted Lowry, St. Paul . . . . W 10
June 25—Ray Robinson, New York . . . . KO 14
(Retained Light-Heavyweight Title)
Dec. 17—Archie Moore, St. Louis . . . . L 15
(Lost Light-Heavyweight Title)

1953

Mar. 4—Danny Nardico, Miami . . . . W 10
June 24—Archie Moore, Ogden . . . . L 15
(For World Light-Heavyweight Title)

1954

Jan. 27—Archie Moore, Miami . . . . L 15
(For World Light-Heavyweight Title)
June 7—Floyd Patterson, Brooklyn, ... W 8
Nov. 24—Paul Andrews, Chicago . . . . W 10

1955

Apr. 13—Bobo Olson, San Francisco . . . . L 10
June 28—Willie Pastrano, New Orleans . . . . . . L 10

1956

Sept. 29—Edgardo Romero, Vancouver . . . . . . W 10

1957

Jan. 25—Eddie Machen, Miami Beach . . . . . . L 10
May 3—Eddie Machen, Louisville . . . . L 10
June 18—Bobo Olson, Portland, OR . . . . L 10

1958

Apr. 11—Heinz Neuhaus, Stuttgart . . . . L 10
Apr. 27—Mino Bozzano, Milan . . . . L 10
May 17—Ulli Ritter, Mannheim . . . . L 10

1959

Announced Retirement.

TB	KO	WD	WF	D	LD	LF	KO BY	ND	NC
115	21	61	0	4	27	1	1	0	0

Elected to Boxing Hall of Fame 1976 .

RICHIE MITCHELL
(Richard Harvey Mitchell)
Born, Milwaukee, WI, July 14, 1895. Height, 5
ft. 8 7/8 in. Weight, 133 lbs. Managed by Billy Mitchell.

1912

Nov. 16—Jimmy Kelly, Milwaukee . . . . KO 3

1913

Jan. 15—Kid Smith, Milwaukee . . . . KO 3
Jan. 18—Young Krause, Milwaukee . . . . W 4
Feb. 3—Young Krause, Milwaukee . . . . ND 6
Apr. 6—Gene Gannon, Milwaukee . . . . D 4
May 2—Gene Gannon, Stoughton . . . . ND 10
Sept. 30—Young Kilbane, Superior . . . . KO 1
Nov. 3—Frankie Rowan, Milwaukee . . . . . ND 6
Nov. 24—Bobby Hayes, Milwaukee . . . . . . ND 6

1914

Jan. 1—Kid Burns, Milwaukee . . . . KO 5
Jan. 12—Dick Loadman, Milwaukee . . . . . . ND 8
Feb. 2—Dick Loadman, Milwaukee . . . . . . ND 10
Feb. 23—Fred Yelle, Milwaukee . . . . ND 10
Mar. 12—Kid Mahoney, Milwaukee . . . . . . ND 10
Apr. 13—Cal Delaney, Milwaukee . . . . ND 10
Aug. 18—Benny Chavez, Denver . . . . D 20
Sept. 23—Patsy McMahon, Columbus, OH . . . ND 12
Sept. 28—Benny Chavez, Milwaukee . . . . . . KO 2
Oct. 5—Bryan Downey, Columbus . . . . . . ND 12
Nov. 23—Peanuts Schriebel, Milwaukee . . . ND 10

1915

Feb. 14—Freddie Andrews, Milwaukee . . . . . ND 10
Mar. 8—Charles Scully, Milwaukee . . . . . . ND 10
Mar. 19—Mel Coogan, Milwaukee . . . . ND 10
May 18—Ad Wolgast, Milwaukee . . . . ND 10
Aug. 30—Johnny Dundee, Milwaukee . . . . . ND 10
Sept. 21—Johnny Kilbane, Milwaukee . . . . . ND 10
Oct. 18—Joe Azevedo, Milwaukee . . . . ND 10
Dec. 21—Benny Palmer, Milwaukee . . . . . . ND 10

1916

Jan. 1—Johnny Kilbane, Cincinnati . . . . . . ND 10
Jan. 24—Joe Rivers, Cincinnati . . . . ND 10
Apr. 7—Freddie Welsh, Milwaukee . . . . . . ND 10
June 2—Charley White, Milwaukee . . . . . . ND 10
Sept. 13—Shamus O'Brien, Milwaukee . . . . . ND 10
Oct. 7—Eddie McAndrews, Philadelphia . . . ND 6
Dec. 8—Joe Rivers, Milwaukee . . . . ND 10

Dec. 18—Joe Wellings, Racine, WI . . . . ND 10

1917

Jan. 16—Freddie Welsh, Milwaukee . . . . ND 10
Apr. 19—Benny Leonard, Milwaukee . . . . KO by 7
(After serving several months as civilian boxing
instructor of 35th Infantry Division of U.S. Army,
Mitchell enlisted in U.S. Navy.)

1918

Mar. 7—Solly Burns, Rock Island . . . . ND 10
Apr. 5—Clonie Tait, Milwaukee . . . . KO 8
Apr. 17—Solly Burns, Rock Island . . . . ND 10
May 24—Joe Welling, Milwaukee . . . . ND 10
Dec. 11—J. Miller, London . . . . L 4
(Mitchell competed as member of American ser-
vice team in Inter-Allied Games.)

1919

Jan. 10—Sailor Friedman, Milwaukee . . . . . . ND 10
Feb. 14—Johnny Schauer, Milwaukee . . . . . . KO 2
Apr. 11—Mike Paulson, Superior . . . . ND 10
Apr. 18—Eddie Pinkman, Seattle . . . . NC 1
(Pinkman floored as bell ended round; both men
declared guilty of fighting after the gong.)
May 9—Johnny Dundee, Milwaukee . . . . . . ND 10
June 9—Jimmy Hanlon, Indianapolis . . . . . . ND 10
Aug. 9—Sailor Friedman, Benton Harbor . . NC 6
(Friedman was disqualified.)
Sept. 20—Harvey Thrope, Detroit . . . . ND 10
Oct. 1—Joe Welling, Cincinnati . . . . ND 10
Nov. 1—Willie Doyle, Grand Rapids . . . . . . ND 10
Nov. 19—Irish Patsy Cline, Detroit . . . . ND 10
Dec. 20—Pete Hartley, Philadelphia . . . . . . ND 6

1920

Feb. 13—Johnny Sheppard, Milwaukee . . . . . ND 10
Feb. 26—Llewelyn Edwards, Milwaukee . . . . KO 7
Mar. 29—Willie Jackson, Milwaukee . . . . . . ND 10
Apr. 7—Mel Coogan, Detroit . . . . ND 10
June 9—Lew Tendler, Milwaukee . . . . ND 10
Sept. 6—Mel Coogan, Youngstown . . . . W 12
Sept. 15—Jimmy Hanlon, Fort Worth . . . . . . W 12
Oct. 4—George Young Erne, Milwaukee . . KO 2
Oct. 11—Joe Welling, Philadelphia . . . . . . ND 8
Nov. 6—Ray Pryel, Pittsburgh . . . . ND 10
Nov. 12—Joe Benjamin, Milwaukee . . . . . . KO 9

1921

Jan. 14—Benny Leonard, New York . . . . . KO by 6
Feb. 10—Joe Tiplitz, Milwaukee . . . . ND 10
Feb. 18—Rocky Kansas, Buffalo . . . . KO by 1
Mar. 9—Rocky Kansas, Milwaukee . . . . . . ND 10
May 16—Johnny Mendelsohn, Milwaukee . . . ND 10
Sept. 23—Ernie Rice, Milwaukee . . . . KO by 4
(Mitchell broke arm.)

1922

May 12—Ever Hammer, Milwaukee . . . . ND 10
Dec. 15—Charley White, New York . . . . . KO by 10

1923

May 25—Joe Jawson, Milwaukee . . . . ND 10
June 12—Johnny Dundee, Milwaukee . . . . . . ND 10
July 9—George Russell, Philadelphia . . . . . ND 8
July 18—Charley White, New York . . . . . KO by 4
Sept. 11—Phil Salvatore, Los Angeles . . . . L 4

TB	KO	WD	WF	D	LD	LF	KO BY	ND	NC
79	10	3	0	2	2	0	6	54	2

Died, Milwaukee, June 26, 1949.

BOB MONTGOMERY
Born, February 10, 1919, Sumter, SC
Lightweight. Height, 5 ft. 8 in.

1937
Amateur fights—24—won 22, lost 2.

1938
(As professional)
10 fights—8 knockouts—2 wins.

Oct. 23—Johnny Buff, Atlantic City .... KO 2
Oct. 27—Pat Patucci, Atlantic City .... KO 2
Nov. 4—Eddie Stewart, Philadelphia ...... KO 2
Nov. 10—Joe Beltrante, Atlantic City ...... KO 3
Nov. 17—Red Rossi, Atlantic City .... KO 2
Dec. 8—Jackie Sheppard, Atlantic City..... W 8

1939
Jan. 19—Harvey Jacobs, Atlantic City ..... KO 1
Feb. 2—Charley Burns, Atlantic City ...... W 8
Feb. 23—Jay Macedon, Atlantic City ...... W 8
Mar. 9—Billy Miller, Atlantic City .... KO 2
Mar. 16—Frank Saia, Philadelphia .... KO 4
Mar. 30—Benny Berman, Atlantic City ..... W 3
Apr. 13—Young Raspi, Atlantic City ...... KO 6
Apr. 20—Eddie Guerra, Atlantic City ..... W 8
May 1—George Zengaras, Philadelphia ..... D 10
May 23—Norment Quarles, Philadelphia .... KO 4
June 15—Charley Burns, Atlantic City ..... KO 2
June 21—Tommy Rawson, Philadelphia..... KO 1
July 3—Frankie Wallace, Philadelphia ..... W 10
Aug. 14—Jimmy Murray, Philadelphia ..... KO 3
Aug. 24—Ray Ingram, Atlantic City .... W 10
Oct. 5—Charley Gilley, Philadelphia ..... KO 6
Oct. 23—Mike Evans, Philadelphia .... W 10
Nov. 10—Tommy Spiegel, Philadelphia ...... L 10
Nov. 27—Mike Evans, Philadelphia .... KO 1

1940
Jan. 29—Al Nettlow, Philadelphia .... D 10
Mar. 11—Al Nettlow, Philadelphia .... W 10
June 3—Al Nettlow, Philadelphia .... W 12
July 5—Jimmy Vaughn, Atlantic City .... KO 2
Sept. 16—Lew Jenkins,Philadelphia .... L 10
Nov. 7—Norment Quarles, Atlantic City..... D 10
Nov. 25—Sammy Angott, Philadelphia....... L 10

1941
Jan. 28—Julie Kogon, Brooklyn............ W 8
Feb. 7—Al Nettlow, New York............. W 8
Mar. 3—George Zengaras, Philadelphia .... KO 3
Apr. 28—Nick Peters, Philadelphia .... KO 3
May 16—Louie Jenkins, New York .... W 10
June 16—Manuel Villa, Baltimore .... KO 1
June 30—Wishy Jones, Washington, DC .... KO 4
July 3—Frankie Wallace, Atlantic City .... KO 3
July 14—Slugger White, Baltimore.......... W 10
Sept. 8—Mike Kaplan, Philadelphia .... W 10
Oct. 10—Davey Day, Chicago .... KO 1
Oct. 24—Julie Kogon, Chicago............ W 10
Oct. 30—Frankie Wallace,Williamsport, PA. KO 5
Dec. 8—Jimmy Garrison, Philadelphia ..... KO 4

1942
Jan. 5—Mayon Padlo, Philadelphia .... KO 8
Mar. 6—Sammy Angott, New York .... L 12
Apr. 20—Joey Peralta, Philadelphia .... W 10
May 8—Carmen Notch, Toledo .... W 10
July 7—Sammy Angott, Philadelphia....... L 12

Aug. 13—Bobby Ruffin, New York .... W 10
Oct. 6—Maxie Shapiro, Philadelphia .... L 10
Dec. 1—Maxie Shapiro, Philadelphia ...... W 10

1943
Jan. 8—Chester Rico, New York .... KO 7
Feb. 22—Lulu Costantino, Philadelphia..... W 10
Apr. 5—Roman Alvarez, Philadelphia ..... KO 4
Apr. 30—Gene Johnson, Scranton .... W 10
May 3—Henry Vasquez, Holyoke......... W 8
May 21—Beau Jack, New York .... W 15
(Won NY Commission Lightweight Title)
July 4—Al Reasoner, New Orleans .... KO 6
July 20—Frankie Wills, Washington, DC .... W 10
Aug. 23—Fritzie Zivic, Philadelphia........ W 10
Oct. 25—Pete Scalzo, Philadelphia .... KO 6
Nov. 19—Beau Jack, New York .... L 15
(Lost NY Commission Lightweight Title)

1944
Jan. 7—Joey Peralta, Detroit .... W 10
Jan. 25—Ike Williams, Philadelphia .... KO 12
Feb. 18—Al Davis, New York .... KO by 1
Mar. 3—Beau Jack, New York .... W 15
(Won World Lightweight Title recognized by NY)
Apr. 28—Joey Peralta, Chicago .... W 10
Aug. 4—Beau Jack, New York .... L 10
In U.S. Army.

1945
Feb. 13—Cecil Hudson, Los Angeles .... W 10
Mar. 20—Genaro Rojo, Los Angles .... KO 8
May 8—Nick Moran, Los Angeles .... L 10
July 9—Nick Moran, Philadelphia .... W 10

1946
Feb. 3—Bill Parsons, New Orleans .... W 10
Feb. 15—Leo Rodak, Chicago .... W 10
Mar. 8—Tony Pellone, New York .... W 10
Mar. 21—Ernie Petrone, New Haven ...... KO 4
June 28—Allie Stolz, New York .... KO 13
(Title Bout)
July 29—George LaRover, Springfield...... W 10
Aug. 19—Wesley Mouzon, Philadelphia ..KO by 2
Nov. 26—Wesley Mouzon, Philadelphia, ... KO 8
(Title Bout)

1947
Jan. 20—Eddie Giosa, Philadelphia........ KO 5
Feb. 7—Tony Pellone, Detroit ....L 10
Feb. 25—Joey Barnum, Los Angeles ...... KO 7
Mar. 31—Jesse Flores, San Francisco ...... KO 3
May 12—George LaRover, Philadelphia .... W 10
June 2—Julie Kogan, New Haven .... W 10
June 9—Frankie Cordino, Springfield ...... W 10
Aug. 4—Ike Williams, Philadelphia .....KO by 6
(Lost Lightweight Title)
Nov. 24—Livio Minelli, Philadelphia ...... L 10
Dec. 22—Joey Angelo. Boston .... L 10

1950
Feb. 3—Aldo Minelli, Washington ....L 10
Feb. 27—Johnny Greco, Montreal .... L 10
Mar. 9—Don Williams, Worcester .... L 10
Mar. 27—Eddie Giosa, Philadelphia .... L 10

TB	KO	WD	WF	D	LD	LF	KO BY	ND	NC
97	37	38	0	3	16	0	3	0	0

ARCHIE MOORE
(Archibald Lee Wright)
Born, December 13, 1913, Benoit, MS (Moore claims he was born Dec. 13, 1916 at Collinsville, IL. His mother gives the earlier date). Height, 5 ft. 11 in. Managed by Kid Bandy, George Wilsman, Cal Thompson, Felix Thurman, Jack Richardson, Jimmy Johnston, Charley Johnston and Jack Kearns.

1936
Jan. 31—Poco Kid, Hot Springs .... KO 2
Feb. 7—Dale Richards, Poplar Bluffs ..... KO 1
Feb. 18—Ray Halford, St. Louis .... KO 3
Feb. 20—Willie Harper, St. Louis .... KO 3
Feb. 21—Courtland Sheppard, St. Louis ......L 6
—Kneibert Davidson .... KO 2
—Ray Brewster .... KO 3
—Billy Simms .... KO 2
—Johnny Leggs................. KO 1
Apr. 15—Peter Urban, Cleveland, ... KO 6
Apr. 16—Frankie Nelson, Clevealnd ....L 6
May 4—Tiger Brown, St. Louis ....L 6
May 18—Thurmond Martin, St. Louis ...... W 5
—Ferman Burton .... KO 1
—Billy Simms .... KO 1
July 14—Murrray Allen, Quincy, IL .... KO 6
—Julius Kemp .... KO 3
—Four H. Posey .... KO 6
Oct. 9—Sammy Jackson,St. Louis .... W 6
—Dick Putnam .... KO 3
Dec. 8—Sammy Jackson, St. Louis........ D 5
—Sammy Christian, St. Louis..... KO 6

1937
Jan. 5—Dynamite Payne, St. Louis ...... KO 1
Jan. 18—Johnny Davis, Quincy, IL .... KO 3
Feb. 2—Joe Huff, St. Louis .... KO 2
—Murray Allen, Keokuk, IA ...... KO 2
Apr. 9—Charlie Dawson, Indianapolis .... KO 5
Apr. 23—Karl Martin, Indianapolis .... KO 1
—Frank Hatfield................ KO 1
—Al Dublinsky .... KO 1
Aug. 19—Deacon Logan, St. Louis .... KO 3
Sept. 9—Sammy Slaughter, Indianapolis .... W 10
Nov. 16—Sammy Christian, St. Louis....... W 5
—Sammy Jackson .... KO 8

1938
Jan. 7—Carl Lautenschlger, St. Louis ..... KO 2
—Frank Rowsey, San Diego........ KO 2
May 20—Jimmy Brent, San Diego .... KO 1
May 27—Ray Vargas, San Diego .... KO 3
June 24—Johnny Romero, San Diego ......L 10
July —Johnny Sikes, San Diego ...... KO 4
Aug. 5—Lorenzo Pedro, San Diego ...... W 10
Sept. —Johnny Romero, San Diego ...... KO 8
Sept. 27—Tom Henry, San Diego .... KO 4
Nov. 22—Ray Lyle, St. Louis .... KO 2
Dec. 7—Irish Bob Turner, St. Louis ...... KO 2
—Bobby Yannes .... KO 2

1939
Jan. 20—Jack Moran, St. Louis .... KO 1
Mar. 2—Domenic Ceccarelli, St. Louis ..... KO 1
Apr. 1—Marty Simmons, Minneapolis ...... W 10
Apr. 20—Teddy Yarosz, St. Louis ....L 10
July 21—Jack Coggins, San Diego .... NC 8
Sept. 22—Bobby Seaman, San Diego .... KO 7

Dec. 7—Honeyboy Jones, St. Louis .... W 10
Dec. 21—Shorty Hogue, San Diego ....L 6
1940
Mar. 30—Jack McNamee, Melbourne .... KO 4
Apr. 18—Ron Richards, Sydney .... KO 10
May 9—Atilio Sabatino, Sydney .... KO 5
May 12—Joe Delaney, Adelaide .... KO 7
June 2—Frank Lindsay, Tasmania .... KO 4
June 27—Fred Henneberry, Sydney .... KO 7
July 11—Ron Richards, Sydney .... W 12
Oct. 18—Pancho Ramierez, San Diego ..... KO 5
Dec. 5—Shorty Hogue, San Diego ....L 6
1941
Jan. 17—Clay Rowan, San Francisco ...... KO 1
Jan. 31—Shorty Hogue, San Diego ....L 10
Feb. —Clay Rowan, San Diego .... KO 1
Feb. 26—Billy Smith, Cincinnati ...... D 10
Retired because of extended illness.
1942
Jan. 28—Bobby Britt, Phoenix.......... KO 3
Feb. 27—Guero Martinez, San Diego ..... KO 2
Mar. 17—Jimmy Casino, San Francisco ..... KO 5
Oct. 30—Shorty Hogue, San Diego ...... KO 2
Nov. 6—Tabby Romero, San Diego ..... KO 2
Nov. 27—Jack Chase, San Diego .... W 10
Dec. 11—Eddie Booker, San Diego .... D 10
1943
May 8—Jack Chase, San Diego .... W 15
July 28—Eddie Cerda, San Diego .... KO 3
Aug. —Big Boy Hogue, Lane Field ..... KO 5
Aug. 2—Jack Chase, San Francisco ....L 15
Aug. 16—Aaron Wade, San Francisco ....L 10
Nov. 5—Kid Hermosillo, San Diego ..... KO 5
Nov. 26—Jack Chase, San Diego .... W 10
1944
Jan. 7—Amado Rodriquez, San Diego ..... KO 1
Jan. 21—Eddie Booker, Hollywood ......KO by 8
Mar. 24—Roman Starr, Hollywood .... KO 2
Apr. 21—Charles Burley, Hollywood ......L 10
May 19—Kenny LaSalle, San Diego ..... W 10
Sept. 1—Battling Monroe, San Diego ..... KO 6
Dec. 18—Nate Bolden, New York .... W 10
1945
Jan. 11—Joey Jones, Boston............. KO 1
Jan. 29—Bob Jacobs, New York .... KO 9
Feb. 12—Nap Mitchell, Boston.......... KO 6
Apr. 2—Nate Bolden, Baltimore .... W 10
Apr. 23—Teddy Randolph, Baltimore ...... KO 9
May 21—Lloyd Marshall, Cleveland ...... W 10
June 18—George Kochan, Baltimore ...... KO 6
May 21—Lloyd Marshall, Baltimore ...... W 10
Aug. 22—Jimmy Bivins, Cleveland ......KO by 6
Sept. 17—Cocoa Kid, Baltimore .... KO 8
Oct. 22—Holman Williams, Baltimore.......L 10
Nov. 12—Odell Riley, Detroit .... KO 6
Nov. 26—Holman Williams, Baltimore ...... KO 11
Dec. 13—Colion Chaney, St. Louis........ KO 5
1946
Jan. 28—Curtis Sheppard, Baltimore........ W 12
Feb. 5—Georgie Parks, Washington....... KO 1
May 2—Verne Escoe, Orange........... KO 7
May 20—Ezzard Charles, Pittsburgh ....L 10
Aug. 19—Buddy Walker, Baltimore .... KO 4
Sept. 9—Shamus O'Brien, Baltimore....... KO 2

Oct. 23—Billy Smith, Oakland............. D 12
Nov. 6—Jack Chase, Oakland .... D 10
1947
Mar. 18—Jack Chase, Los Angeles .... KO 9
Apr. 11—Rusty Payne, San Diego .... W 10
May 5—Ezzard Charles, Cincinnati ......L 10
May 5—Ezzard Charles, Cincinnati ....L 10
June 16—Curtis Sheppard, Washington, DC .. W 10
July 14—Bert Lytell, Baltimore .... W 10
July 30—Bobby Zander, Oakland .... W 12
Sept. 8—Jimmy Bivins, Baltimore .... KO 9
Nov. 10—George Fitch, Baltimore .... KO 6
1948
Jan. 13—Ezzard Charles, Cleveland .....KO by 8
Apr. 12—Dusty Wilkerson, Baltimore ...... KO 7
Apr. 19—Doc Williams, Newark .... KO 7
May 5—Billy Smith, Cincinnati .... W 10
June 2—Leonard Morrow, Oakland .....KO by 1
June 28—Jimmy Bivins, Baltimore .... W 10
Aug. 2—Ted Lowry, Baltimore .... W 10
Sept. 20—Billy Smith, Baltimore........... KO 4
Oct. 15—Henry Hall, New Orleans ....L 10
Nov. 1—Lloyd Gibson, Washington, DC. ....LF 4
Nov. 15—Henry Hall, Baltimore........... W 10
Dec. 6—Bob Amos, Washington, DC .... W 10
Dec. 27—Charley Williams, Baltimore ...... KO 7
1949
Jan. 10—Alabama Kid, Toledo .... KO 4
Jan. 31—Bob Satterfield, Toledo .... KO 3
Mar. 4—Alabama Kid, Columbus .... KO 3
Mar. 23—Dusty Wilkerson, Philadelphia .... KO 6
Apr. 11—Jimmy Bivins, Toledo .... KO 8
Apr. 26—Harold Johnson, Philadelphia ...... W 10
June 13—Clinton Bacon, Indianapolis ....LF 6
June 27—Bob Sikes, Indianapolis .... KO 3
July 29—Esco Greenwood, No. Adams ..... KO 2
Oct. 4—Bob Amos, Toledo............ W 10
Oct. 2—Phil Muscato, Toledo .... W 10
Dec. 6—Doc Williams, Hartford .... KO 8
Dec. 13—Leonard Morrow, Toledo........ KO 10
1950
Jan. 31—Bert Lytell, Toledo .... W 10
July 31—Vernon Williams, Chicago........ KO 2
1951
Jan. 2—Billy Smith, Portland .... KO 8
Jan. 28—John Thomas, Panama .... KO 1
Feb. 21—Jimmy Bivins, New York .... KO 9
Mar. 13—Abel Cestac, Toledo............. W 10
Apr. 26—Herman Harris, Flint .... KO 4
May 14—Art Henri, Baltimore........... KO 4
June 9—Abel Cestac, Buenos Aires ...... KO 10
June 23—Karel Sys, Buenos Aires .... D 10
July 8—Alberto Lovell, Buenos Aires ..... KO 1
July 15—Vicente Quiroz, Montevideo ..... KO 6
July 26—Victor Carabajal, Cordoba ...... KO 3
July 28—Americo Capitanelli, Tucuman .... KO 3
Aug. 5—Rafael Miranda, Argentine .... KO 4
Aug. 17—Alfredo Lagay, Bahia Blanca ..... KO 3
Sept. 5—Embrell Davison, Detroit .... KO 1
Sept. 24—Harold Johnson, Philadelphia ...... W 10
Oct. 29—Chubby Wright, St. Louis .... KO 7
Dec. 10—Harold Johnson, Milwaukee ....L 10
1952
Jan. 29—Harold Johnson, Toledo .... W 10

Feb. 27—Jimmy Slade, St. Louis .... W 10
May 19—Bob Dunlap, San Francisco....... KO 6
June 26—Clarence Henry, Baltimore .... W 10
July 25—Clint Bacon, Denver .... KO 4
Dec. 17—Joey Maxim, St. Louis .... W 15
(Won World Light-Heavyweight Title)
1953
Jan. 27—Toxie Hall, Toledo.............. KO 4
Feb. 16—Leonard Dugan, San Francisco ... KO 8
Mar. 3—Sonny Andrews, Sacramento...... KO 5
Mar. 11—Nino Valdes, St. Louis .... W 10
Mar. 17—Al Spaulding, Spokane .... KO 3
Mar. 30—Frank Buford, San Diego .... KO 9
June 24—Joey Maxim, Ogden.............. W 15
(Title Bout)
Aug. 22—Reinaldo Ansaloni, Buenos Aires .. KO 4
Sept. 12—Dogomar Martinez, Buenos Aires ... W 10
1954
Jan. 27—Joey Maxim, Miami .... W 15
(Title Bout)
Mar. 9—Bob Baker, Miami Beach .... KO 9
June 7—Bert Whitehurst, New York ...... KO 6
Aug. 11—Harold Johnson, New York ...... KO 14
(Title Bout)
1955
May 2—Nino Valdes, Las Vegas .... W 15
June 22—Bobo Olson, New York .... KO 3
(World Light-Heavyweight Title Bout)
Sept. 21—Rocky Marciano, New York ....KO by 9
(For World Heavyweight Title)
Oct. 22—Dale Hall, Philadelphia......... Exh. 4
1956
Feb. 2—Dale Hall, Fresno .... Exh. 4
Feb. 20—Howard King, San Francisco ..... W 10
Feb. 27—Bob Dunlap, San Diego .... KO 1
Mar. 17—Frankie Daniels, Hollywood ...... W 10
Mar. 27—Howard King, Sacramento .... W 10
Apr. 10—Willie Bean, Richmond .... KO 5
Apr. 16—George Parmentier, Seattle ...... KO 3
Apr. 26—Sonny Andrews, Edmonton ...... KO 4
Apr. 30—Gene Thompson, Tucson........ KO 3
June 5—Yolande Pompey, London ...... KO 10
(Light-Heavyweight Title Bout)
July 25—James J. Parker, Toronto .... KO 9
Sept. 8—Roy Shire, Ogden .... KO 3
Nov. 30—Floyd Patterson, Chicago ......KO by 5
(For Vacant World Heavyweight Title)
1957
May 1—Hans Kalbfell, Essen............. W 10
June 2—Alain Cherville, Stuttgart .... KO 6
Sept. 20—Tony Anthony, Los Angeles ...... KO 7
(World Light-Heavyweight Title)
Oct. 31—Bob Mitchell, Vancouver........ KO 5
Nov. 5—Eddie Cotton, Seattle............ W 10
Nov. 29—Roger Rischer, Portland .... KO 4
1958
Jan. 18—Luis Ignacio, Sao Paulo.......... W 10
Feb. 1—Julio Neves, Rio de Janeiro....... KO 3
Mar. 4—Bert Whitehurst, San Bernardino .. KO 10
Mar. 10—Bob Albright, Vancouver .... KO 7
May 2—Willi Besmanoff, Louisville .... W 10
May 17—Howard King, San Diego .... W 10
May 26—Charlie Norkus, San Francisco ..... W 10
June 9—Howard King, Sacramento .... W 10

Aug. 4—Howard King, Reno .... D 10
Dec. 10—Yvon Durelle, Montreal .... KO 11
(World Light-Heavyweight Title)
1959
Feb. 2—Eddie Cotton, Victoria .... Exh. 5
Mar. 9—Sterling Davis, Odessa .... KO 3
Aug. 12—Yvon Durelle, Montreal .... KO 3
(Title Bout)
1960
May 25—Willi Besmanoff, Indianapolis ..... KO 10
Sept. 13—George Abinet, Dallas .... KO 4
Oct. 29—Giulio Rinaldi, Rome ....L 10
Nov. 28—Buddy Turman, Dallas .... W 10
Oct. 25—NBA withdrew recognition from Moore.
1961
Mar. 25—Buddy Turman, Manila .... W 10
May 8—Dave Furch, Tucson .... Exh. 4
May 12—Cliff Gray, Nogales, Mex. .... KO 4
June 10—Giulio Rinaldi, New York .... W 15
(Title Bout)
Oct. 23—Pete Rademacher, Baltimore, ... KO 6
1962
Feb. 10—NY and EBU withdrew recognition from Moore.
Mar. 30—Alejandro Lavorante, Los Angeles . KO 10
May 7—Howard King, Tijuana .... KO 1
May 28—Willie Pastrano, Los Angeles ...... D 10
Nov. 15—Cassius Clay, Los Angeles ......KO by 4
1963
Mar. 15—Mike DiBiase, Phoenix .... KO 3
Retired in 1964 to enter cinema and television fields.
1965
Aug. 27—Nap Mitchell, Michigan City .. Exh KO 3

TB	KO	WD	WF	D	LD	LF	KO BY	ND	NC
229	141	53	0	8	17	2	7	0	1

MATTHEW SAAD MUHAMMAD
(AKA MATTHEW FRANKLIN)
Philadelphia, PA, Light-Heavyweight
1974
Jan. 14—Billy Early, Philadelphia .... KO 2
Feb. 25—Bele Apolosa, Paris .... W 4
Mar. 11—Roy Ingram, Philadelphia .... W 4
May 22—Joe Middleton, Philadelphia ..... KO 5
July 15—Joe Jones, Philadelphia .... KO 3
Sept. 10—Lloyd Richardson, Philadelphia ... KO 4
Oct. 22—Joe Middleton, Alexandria .... KO 2
Dec. 10—Wayne McGee, Philadelphia .... L 6
1975
Feb. 25—Vandell Woods, Philadelphia ..... KO 6
July 24—Roosevelt Brown, Philadelphia .... KO 4
Oct. 21—Wayne McGee, Philadelphia .... D 6
1976
Feb. 13—Harold Carter, Baltimore .... W 10
May 21—Mate Parlov, Milan .... W 8
July 17—Marvin Camel, Stockton .... W 10
Sept. 15—Bobby Walker, Scranton .... KO 4
Oct. 23—Marvin Camel, Missoula ....L 10
Dec. 3—Mate Parlov, Trieste .... D 10
1977
Mar. 11—Eddie Gregory, Philadelphia .... L 10
Apr. 21—Joe Maye, Wilmington .... W 10
June 23—Ed Turner, Philadelphia .... KO 6
July 26—Marvin Johnson, Philadelphia ..... KO 12
Sept. 17—Billy Douglas, Philadelphia .... KO 6
Nov. 1—Lee Royster, Philadelphia .... W 10
1978
Feb. 10—Richie Kates, Philadelphia .... KO 6

June 19—Dale Grant, Philadelphia........ KO 5
Aug. 16—Freddie Bright, Newark .... KO 8
Oct. 24—Alvaro Lopez, Philadelphia ...... KO 11
(U.S. Light-Heavyweight Title)
1979
Apr. 22—Marvin Johnson, Indianapolis ..... KO 8
(WBC Light-Heavyweight Title)
Aug. 18—John Conteh, Atlantic City .... W 15
(WBC Light-Heavyweight Title)
1980
Mar. 29—John Conteh, Atlantic City ...... KO 4
May 11—Lewis Pergaud, Halifax .... KO 5
July 13—Yaqui Lopez, Great Gorge ...... KO 14
Nov. 28—Lotte Mwale, Los Angeles ...... KO 4
1981
Feb. 28—Vonzell Johnson, Atlantic City.......KO 4
(Retained WBC Light Heavyweight Title)
Apr. 25—Murray Sutherland, Atlantic City..KO 9
(Retained WBC Light Heavyweight Title)
Sept. 26—Jerry Martin, Atlantic City.............KO 11
(Retained WBC Light Heavyweight Title)
Dec. 19—Dwight Braxton, Atlantic City..KO by 10
(Lost WBC Heavyweight Title)
1982
Apr. 17—Pete McIntyre, Atlantic City ....KO 2
Aug. 7—Dwight Braxton, Philadelphia..KO by 6
(For WBC Light Heavyweight Title)
1983
Mar. 23—Eric Winbush, Atlantic City ..... KO by 3

TB	KO	WD	WF	D	LD	LF	KO BY	ND	NC
40	24	8	0	2	3	0	3	0	0

JOSE NAPOLES
Cuban Welterweight
Born, April 13, 1940 Santiago de Cuba, Oriente
1958
Aug. 2—Julio Rojas, Havana .... KO 1
Oct. 11—Eurispides Guerra, Havana .... KO 4
Nov. 29—Felix Pomares, Havana .... KO 2
1959
Feb. 21—Armando Castillo, Havana .... W 4
May 16—Juan Bacallao, Havana .... KO 4
July 11—Cloroaldo Hernandez, Havana..... KO 3
July 25—Cristobal Gonzalez, Havana....... W 8
Aug. 22—Hilton Smith, Havana ....L 10
Oct. 3—Cristobal Gonzalez, Havana ...... W 8
1960
Jan. 2—Isaac Espinosa, Havana .... W 10
Feb. 20—Diwaldo Ventosa, Havana ....L 10
May 21—Angel Garcia, Havana .... W 10
July 2—Leslie Grant, Havana .... W 10
Oct. 15—Tony Pardon, Havana .... W 10
Nov. 26—Chico Morales, Havana .... W 10
1961
Jan. 28—Guillermo Valdez, Havana ...... W 10
Mar. 19—Chico Morales, Havana .... W 10
Mar. 29—Enrique Carabeo, Havana ...... KO 9
1962
July 21—Enrique Camarena, Mexico City ... KO 2
Aug. 25—Kid Anahuac, Mexico City ...... KO 2
Sept. 29—Bobby Cervantes, Mexico City ... KO 1
Nov. 10—Tony Perez, Los Mochis .... W 10
1963
Jan. 5—Tony Perez, Hermosillo...........L 10

Feb. 9—Jorge Gutierrez, Mexico City ..... KO 7
Mar. 30—Baby Vasquez, Mexico City .... W 10
Apr. 27—Alfredo Urbina, Mexico City.......L 10
May 27—Raul Soriano, Tijuana .... KO 4
Aug. 19—Pulga Serrano, Tijuana .... KO 10
Oct. 23—Francisco Cancio, Mexico City .... KO 1
Nov. 16—Tony Perez, Mexico City .... KO 3
Nov. 30—L.C. Morgan, Caracas .... KO 7
1964
Mar. 1—Taketeru Yoshimoto, Tokyo ...... KO 1
Apr. 25—Alfredo Urbina, Mexico City ...... KO 1
June 22—Carlos Hernandez, Caracas ...... KO 7
Aug. 15—Eduardo Moreno, Culiacan ...... KO 5
Nov. 14—Alfredo Urbina, Mexico City ..... KO 3
1965
Jan. 1—Carlos Rios, Laguna .... KO 7
Feb. 28—L.C. Morgan, Monterrey .... KO 3
Mar. 25—Giordano Campari, Caracas ...... KO 2
Aug. 1—Eddie Perkins, Juarez .... W 10
Dec. 11—Adolph Pruitt, Mexico City ...... KO 3
1966
Feb. 12—Johnny Santos, Mexico City ..... KO 3
Apr. 17—Al Grant, Reynosa .... KO 4
July 27—Humberto Trottman, Juarez ...... KO 2
Aug. 22—L.C. Morgan, Reynosa.........KO by 4
Oct. 30—Jimmy Fields, San Luis .... KO 10
Dec. 17—Eugenio Espinoza, Mexico City ... KO 6
1967
June 4—Johnny Brooks, Merida .... KO 7
July 10—L.C. Morgan, Tijuana .... KO 2
Sept. 11—Johnny DePeiza, Ciudad .... KO 10
Dec. 3—Charlie Watson, Merdia .... KO 5
1968
Feb. 18—Mike Cruz, Tampico .... KO 4
Apr. 29—Herbie Lee, Tijuana .... KO 4
June 2—Peter Cobblah, Mexico City ...... W 10
June 14—Leroy Roberts, Los Angeles ...... KO 1
July 15—Eddie Pace, Tijuana .... W 10
Nov. 5—Des Rea, Los Angeles .... KO 5
Dec. 23—Lennox Beckles, Mexico City .... KO 1
1969
Feb. 15—Fate Davis, Mexico City .... KO 7
Apr. 18—Curtis Cokes, Los Angeles ...... KO 13
(Won World Welterweight Title)
June 29—Curtis Cokes, Mexico City .... KO 10
(Retained World Welterweight Title)
Oct. 12—Emile Griffith, Los Angeles ...... W 15
(Retained World Welterweight Title)
1970
Feb. 15—Ernie Lopez, Los Angeles .... KO 15
(Retained World Welterweight Title)
Aug. 14—Fighting Mack, Los Angeles ..... KO 3
Oct. 5—Pete Toro, New York .... KO 9
Dec. 3—Billy Backus, Syracuse ....KO by 4
(Lost World Welterweight Title)
1971
Mar. 27—Manuel Gonzalez, Mexico City .... KO 6
June 4—Billy Backus, Los Angeles........ KO 4
(Regained World Welterweight Title)
July 2—David Melendez, Los Angeles .... KO 5
Aug. 23—Jean Josselin, Los Angeles ...... KO 5
Oct. 17—Esteban Osuna, Mexico City ..... W 10
Dec. 14—Hedgemon Lewis, Los Angeles ..... W 15
(Retained World Welterweight Title)
1972
Mar. 28—Ralph Charles, London .... KO 7
(Retained World Welterweight Title)
June 10—Adolph Pruitt, Monterrey .... KO 2
(Retained World Welterweight Title)

Aug. 5—Edmundo Leite, Mexico City ..... KO 2

1973

Feb. 28—Ernie Lopez, Los Angeles .... KO 7
(Retained World Welterweight Title)
June 23—Roger Menetrey, Grenoble .... W 15
(Retained World Welterweight Title)
Sept. 22—Clyde Gray, Toronto .... W 15
(Retained World Welterweight Title)

1974

Feb. 9—Carlos Monzon, Paris ...... KO by 7
(World Middleweight Title)
Aug. 3—Hedgemon Lewis, Mexico City .... KO 9
(Retained World Welterweight Title)
Dec. 14—Horacio Saldano, Mexico City ..... KO 3
(Retained World Welterweight Title)

1975

Mar. 30—Armando Muniz, Acapulco ...... T.W. 12
(Retained World Welterweight Title)
July 12—Armando Muniz, Mexico City ..... W 15
(Retained World Welterweight Title)
Dec. 6—John Stracey, Mexico City ..... KO by 6
(Lost World Welterweight Title)

TB	KO	WD	WF	D	LD	LF	KO BY	ND	NC
84	54	21	1	0	4	0	4	0	0

BATTLING NELSON
(Oscar Nielson)

Born, June 5, 1882, Cophenhagen, Denmark.
Weight, 133 lbs. Height, 5 ft. 7½ in. Managed by John
Robinson, Ted Murphy and Billy Nolan.

1896

Sept. 3—Wallace's Kid, Hammond .... KO 1

1897

June 5—Ole Oleson, Hegewisch .... W 3

1898

May 10—Freddy Green, Sioux Falls .... W 7
May 11—Soldier Williams, Sioux Falls ..... KO 3

1899

Jan. 1—Eddie Herman, Hegewich .... D 6
Apr. 6—Eddie Penny, Chicago .... KO 1
May 3—Bull Winters, Chicago .... KO 1
June 1—Unknown John Smith, Chicago .... KO 2

1900

July 4—Feathers Vernon, West Pullman ... ND 6
Aug. 30—Chas. Dougherty, Chicago .... KO 1
Sept. 14—Joe Headmark, Chicago...........L 6
Sept. 21—Harry Griffin, Chicago .... W 6
Oct. 8—Young Bay, Chicago .... W 6
Nov. 2—Clarence Class, Chicago .... D 6
Nov. 12—Jack Readle, Chicago .... Exh. 3
Nov. 12—Joe Curtin, Chicago .... Exh. 3
Nov. 15—Black Griffo, Chicago .... KO 3
Nov. 22—Ed Burley, Chicago .... KO 5
Dec. 1—Pete Boyle, Chicago...........LF 4
Dec. 1—Danny McMahon, Chicago .... D 4
Dec. 7—Joe Percente, Chicago .... WF 2
Dec. 8—Jack Martin, Chicago............. W 6

1901

Mar. 17—Black Griffo, Chicago .... KO 3

Apr. 19—Mickey Riley, Milwaukee ....L 6
May 3—Charles Berry, Milwaukee .... D 6
May 18—Harry Fails, Omro, WI .... ND 6
May 24—Harry Fails, Rhinelander .... D 10
Nov. 10—Billy Heck, West Pullman........ ND 4
Nov. 15—Joe Percente, Milwaukee...........L 6
Nov. 29—Eddie Santry, Chicago ....L 6
Dec. 2—Joe Percente, Milwaukee .... D 6
Dec. 16—Mike Walsh, Chicago .... KO 6
Dec. 17—Charles Berry, Milwaukee ....L 6

1902

Jan. 13—Frank Colifer, West Pullman ..... KO 5
Jan. 21—Charles Berry, Fond du Lac ....L 8
Mar. 13—Joe Percente, Oshkosh .... W 8
Mar. 18—Kid Ryan, Chicago .... KO 5
Mar. 21—Johnnie Thompson, Chicago .... W 6
Apr. 5—William Rossler, Harvey, IL...... KO 1
Apr. 12—Danny McMahon, West Pullman ... D 6
May 17—Pudden Burns, Hegewisch .... W 6
June 14—Billy Hurley, Hammond .... D 6
Dec. 2—Elmer Mayfield, Hot Springs ...... W 10
Dec. 26—Christy Williams, Hot Springs .... KO 17

1903

Jan. 3—Geo. Brownford, Hot Springs ..... ND 4
Jan. 6—Sammy Maxwell, Hot Springs ....KO 10
Mar. 18—Adam Ryan, Little Rock .... D 20
Apr. 5—Jack Robinson, Hot Springs ...... ND 6
Apr. 24—Johnnie Thompson, Milwaukee ... ND 6
May 22—Stocking Kelly, Milwaukee .... KO 4
June 16—Young Scotty, Fond du Lac .... W 8
June 19—Mickey Riley, Milwaukee .... D 6
June 20—Larry McDonald, Harvey, IL...... KO 4
June 27—Clarence English, Kansas City ..... D 15
July 15—Mickey Riley, Ashland .... NC 11
July 24—Mickey Riley, Hurley, WI........ D 15
Aug. 26—Eddie Sterns, Michigan City ....L 9
Oct. 16—Charles Neary, Milwaukee ....L 6
Nov. 10—George Memsic, Milwaukee .... W 6
Dec. 28—Clarence English, St. Joe, MO ..... W 15

1904

Jan. 16—Art Simms, Milwaukee .... KO 3
Feb. 5—Jack O'Neil, Milwaukee .... W 6
Apr. 6—Spider Welsh, Salt Lake City ..... KO 16
Apr. 12—Tom Markham, Eureka .... Exh. 3
May 20—Martin Canole, San Francisco ..... KO 18
July 29—Eddie Hanlon, San Francisco ..... KO 19
Sept. 5—Aurelio Herrera, Butte .... W 20
Nov. 29—Young Corbett, San Francisco .... KO 10
Dec. 20—Jimmy Britt, San Francisco ....L 20

1905

Feb. 28—Young Corbett, San Francisco .... KO 9
May 22—Abe Attell, Philadelphia .... ND 6
June 2—Kid Sullivan, Baltimore .... D 6
June 6—Jack O'Neil, Philadelphia .... ND 6
Sept. 9—Jimmy Britt, Colma, CA .... KO 18

1906

Mar. 14—Terry McGovern, Philadelphia .... ND 6
Sept. 3—Joe Gans, Goldfield, NV ....LF 42
(For Lightweight Title)

1907

July 31—Jimmy Britt, San Francisco.........L 20
Oct. 19—Tom Freebury, Red Lodge ...... Exh. 4
Oct. 23—Charlie Berry, Billings, Mont .... Exh. 4
Oct. 26—Mark Nelson, Minot, ND .... Exh. 4

1908

Jan. 13—Jack Clifford, Ogden, UT .... KO 5
Feb. 4—Ruddy Unholz, Los Angeles ...... ND 10
Mar. 3—Jimmy Britt, Los Angeles .... ND 10
Mar. 31—Abe Attell, San Francisco .... D 15
July 4—Joe Gans, San Francisco .... KO 17
(Won Lightweight Title)
Sept. 9—*Joe Gans, Colma, CA .... KO 21
*Title Bout.
(From 1896 to 1908 Nelson's ring earnings
amounted to $121,486.80.)

1909

May 29—*Dick Hyland, Colma, CA .... KO 23
June 22—*Jack Clifford, Oklahoma City .... KO 5
July 13—Ad Wolgast, Los Angeles .... ND 10
*Title Bout.

1910

Jan. 21—Eddie Lang, Memphis .... KO 8
Feb. 22—*Ad Wolgast, Pt. Richmond ....KO by 40
(Lost Lightweight Title)
*Referee Eddie Smith gave Wolgast knockout
decision over Nelson.
Oct. 10—Monte Dale, Kansas City........ KO 3
Oct. 31—Anton LaGrave, San Francisco ..... D 15
Nov. 26—Owen Moran, San Francisco ....KO by 11

1911

July 3—Ned Whitman, North Bend, WA.. Exh. 6
July 4—Percy Cove, Bellingham, WA .... Exh. 6
Aug. 4—Tommy Gaffney, Medford, OR .... KO 5
Sept. 19—Billy Nixon, Boston .... KO 10
Oct. 3—Young Saylor, Boston ....L 12
Oct. 11—Willie Beecher, New York .... ND 10
Oct. 17—Pal Moore, Boston ....L 12
Oct. 19—Geo. Alger, Augusta, ME .... ND 6
Oct. 25—Monte Dale, Manchester, NH ...... W 15
Nov. 6—Frank Loughrey, Watervliet, NY .. ND 10
Nov. 10—Tommy Moore, Buffalo .... KO 9
Nov. 25—Louis de Ponthieu, Buffalo .... ND 10
Nov. 30—Joseph Spero, Toronto, ... KO 6
Dec. 4—Andy Bezenah, Jeffersonville ..... ND 10
Dec. 15—Bobby Wilson, Utica, NY .... ND 10
Dec. 18—Willie Howard, Brooklyn .... ND 10
Dec. 22—One Round Hogan, Brooklyn ..... ND 10
Dec. 31—Jack Redmond, New Orleans ...... W 20

1912

Jan. 9—Tommy O'Rourke, Springfield, MO ND 10
Feb. 26—Young Togo, Ft. Smith, AR .... W 6
Mar. 1—Sammy Trott, Dayton, OH ...... D 15
July 1—Andy Bezenah, Winnipeg .... ND 12
July 12—Mickey McIntyre, Winnipeg ...... ND 12
Sept. 2—Steve Ketchel, St. Joseph, MO ..... D 15
Nov. 14—Art Stewart, Hammond, IN.......ND 10
Nov. 28—Leach Cross, New York .... ND 10
Dec. 13—Teddy Maloney, Philadelphia ..... ND 6
Dec. 20—Jim Bonner, Tamaqua, PA .... ND 10
Dec. 31—Yankee Schwartz, Columbus, OH .. ND 8

1913

Jan. 3—Frankie Russell, New Orleans ..... ND 10
Feb. 5—Ray Sorenson, Racine, WI .... ND 10
Feb. 11—Harry Dillon, Tamaqua, PA ...... KO 10
Feb. 17—Joe Burke, Easton, PA .... ND 10
Feb. 22—Ray Woods, New Bedford .... D 12
Mar. 5—Frank Whitney, Atlanta, GA ..... ND 10
Mar. 27—Mike Malone, Pueblo, CO .... ND 10

Apr. 19—Ray Wood, New Bedford......... D 12
Apr. 29—Gilbert Gallant, Boston...........L 12
May 3—Pat Bradley, Philadelphia........ ND 6
Oct. 13—Ad Wolgast, Milwaukee......... ND 10

1914

Aug. 19—Cliff Ford, Sault Ste. Marie....... W 6

1915

Mar. 18—Young Donnelly, Havana, Cuba ... KO 3
Mar. 24—Jimmy Freyer, Havana, Cuba..... W 25
Sept. 6—Bobby Waugh, Juarez, Mex........L 20
Nov. 5—Jimmy Regan, Kansas City........L 10

1917

Apr. 17—Freddy Welsh, St. Louis........ ND 12

1923

Jan. 23—Dick Hyland, Fresno........... Exh. 3
June 10—Phil Salvatore, Los Angeles..... Exh. 3
Nelson's largest purse fought for was with Joe Gans at Goldfield, Sept. 3, 1906, $34,000. Of this Nelson received $23,000, irrespective of decision, and Gans, $11,000. George Siler refereed. For lightweight championship.

TB	KO	WD	WF	D	LD	LF	KO BY	ND	NC
132	38	20	1	19	15	2	2	35	0

Died, February 7, 1954, Chicago, IL
Elected to Boxing Hall of Fame 1957.

KEN NORTON
San Diego, CA, Heavyweight
Born, August 9, 1945

1967

Nov. 14—Grady Brazell, San Diego........ KO 5

1968

Jan. 16—Sam Wyatt, San Diego.......... W 6
Feb. 6—Harold Dutra, Sacramento....... KO 3
Mar. 26—Jimmy Gilmore, San Diego....... KO 7
July 23—Wayne Kindred, San Diego....... KO 6
Dec. 5—Cornell Nolan, Los Angeles....... KO 6

1969

Feb. 11—Joe Hemphill, Wooded Hills...... KO 3
Feb. 20—Wayne Kindred, Los Angeles..... KO 9
Mar. 31—Pedro Sanchez, San Diego....... KO 2
May 29—Bill McMurray, Los Angeles..... KO 7
July 25—Gary Bates, San Diego.......... KO 8
Oct. 21—Julius Garcia, San Diego........ KO 3

1970

Feb. 4—Aaron Eastling, Las Vegas....... KO 2
Mar. 13—Stanford Harris, San Diego...... KO 3
Apr. 7—Bob Mashburn, Cleveland........ KO 4
May 8—Ray Ellis, San Diego........... KO 2
July 2—Jose Luis Garcia, Los Angeles...KO by 8
Aug. 29—Cookie Wallace, San Diego...... KO 4
Sept. 26—Chuck Leslie, Woodland Hills..... W 10
Oct. 16—Roby Harris, San Diego........ KO 2

1971

Apr. 24—Steve Carter, Woodland Hills..... KO 3
June 12—Vic Brown, Santa Monica....... KO 5
Aug. 10—Chuck Haynes, Santa Monica..... KO 10
Sept. 30—James J. Woody, San Diego....... W 10

1972

Feb. 17—Charlie Harris, San Diego....... KO 3
Mar. 17—Jack O'Halloran, San Diego....... W 10

June 5—Herschel Jacobs, San Diego....... W 10
June 30—James Woody, San Diego........ KO 8
Nov. 21—Henry Clark, Stateline......... KO 9
Dec. 13—Charlie Reno, San Diego......... W 10

1973

Mar. 31—Muhammad Ali, San Diego....... W 12
May 8—Mole Williams, Washington, DC... Exh. 4
Sept. 10—Muhammad Ali, Los Angeles.......L 12

1974

Mar. 26—George Foreman, Caracas......KO by 2
(World Heavyweight Title)
June 25—Boone Kirkman, Seattle......... KO 8

1975

Mar. 4—Reco Brooks, Oklahoma City..... KO 1
Mar. 24—Jerry Quarry, New York........ KO 5
Aug. 14—Jose Luis Garcia, St. Paul....... KO 5

1976

Jan. 3—Pedro Lovell, Las Vegas........ KO 5
Apr. 30—Ron Stander, Landover.......... KO 5
July 10—Larry Middleton, San Diego...... KO 10
Sept. 28—Muhammad Ali, New York.......L 15
(World Heavyweight Title)

1977

May 11—Duane Bobick, New York....... KO 1
Sept. 14—Lorenzo Zanon, Las Vegas....... KO 5
Nov. 5—Jimmy Young, Las Vegas........ W 15

1978

June 9—Larry Holmes, Las Vegas........L 15
(WBC Heavyweight Title)
Nov. 10—Randy Stephens, Las Vegas...... KO 4

1979

Mar. 23—Earnie Shavers, Las Vegas.....KO by 1
Aug. 19—Scott LeDoux, Bloomington........ D 10

1980

Nov. 7—Randall (Tex) Cobb, El Paso....... W 10

TB	KO	WD	WF	D	LD	LF	KO BY	ND	NC
48	33	8	0	1	3	0	3	0	0

FLOYD PATTERSON
Born, Jan. 4, 1935, Waco, NC. Weight, 182 lbs. Height, 6 feet. Managed by Cus D'Amato.

1951

New York Golden Gloves 160-lb. Open Champion.

Eastern Golden Gloves 160-lb. champion.
Lost Inter-City Golden Gloves 160-lb. title bout to Richard Guerrero.

1952

New York Golden Gloves 175-lb. Open Champion.

Eastern Golden Gloves 175-lb. Champion, stopping Harold Carter in one round.
Inter-City Golden Gloves 175-lb. Champion, defeating Eddie Jones.
Olympic Middleweight Champion. Defeated O. Tebbaka (France); L. Jansen (Holland); S. Sjolin (Sweden), disq., 1; Vasili Tita (Rumania), knockout, 1 (finals).
Sept. 12—Eddie Godbold, New York....... KO 2
Oct. 6—Sammy Walker, Brooklyn........ KO 2

Oct. 21—Lester Jackson, New York....... KO 3
Dec. 29—Lalu Sabotin, Brooklyn.......... KO 5

1953

Jan. 28—Chester Mieszala, Chicago....... KO 5
Apr. 3—Dick Wagner, Brooklyn........... W 8
June 1—Gordon Wallace, Brooklyn....... KO 3
Oct. 19—Wes Bascom, Brooklyn.......... W 8
Dec. 14—Dick Wagner, Brooklyn.......... KO 5

1954

Feb. 15—Yvon Durelle, Brooklyn......... W 8
Mar. 30—Sam Brown, Washington....... KO 2
Apr. 19—Alvin Williams, Brooklyn....... W 8
May 10—Jesse Turner, Brooklyn......... W 8
June 7—Joe Maxim, Brooklyn.............L 8
July 12—Jacques Royer-Crecy, New York... KO 7
Aug. 2—Tommy Harrison, Brooklyn..... KO 1
Oct. 11—Esau Ferdinand, New York....... W 8
Oct. 22—Joe Gannon, New York.......... W 8
Nov. 19—Jimmy Slade, New York........ W 8

1955

Jan. 7—Willie Troy, New York......... KO 5
Jan. 17—Don Grant, Brooklyn............ KO 5
Mar. 17—Esau Ferdinand, Oakland....... KO 10
June 23—Yvon Durelle, Newcastle....... KO 5
July 6—Archie McBride, New York....... KO 7
Sept. 8—Alvin Williams, Moncton........ KO 8
Sept. 29—Dave Whitlock, San Francisco.... KO 3
Oct. 13—Calvin Brad, Los Angeles........ KO 1
Dec. 8—Jimmy Slade, Los Angeles........ KO 7

1956

Mar. 12—Jimmy Walls, New Britain....... KO 2
Apr. 10—Alvin Williams, Kansas City..... KO 3
*June 8—Tommy Jackson, New York...... W 12
Nov. 30—Archie Moore, Chicago.......... KO 5
(Won vacant World Heavyweight Title)
*Elimination bout for heavyweight title.

1957

Apr. 13—Julio Mederos, Kansas City...... Exh. 4
Apr. 17—Julio Mederos, Minneapolis...... Exh. 4
Apr. 19—Julio Mederos, Joplin........... Exh. 4
Apr. 23—Alvin Williams, Wichita........ Exh. 4
Apr. 26—Alvin Williams, Fort Smith...... Exh. 4
July 29—Tommy Jackson, New York...... KO 10
(World Heavyweight Title)
Aug. 22—Pete Rademacher, Seattle........ KO 6
(World Heavyweight Title)

1958

Feb. 4—Dusty Rhodes, Houston......... Exh. 3
Feb. 25—Dusty Rhodes, Philadelphia..... Exh. 3
Mar. 25—Dusty Rhodes, London........ Exh. 3
Aug. 18—Roy Harris, Los Angeles........ KO 12
(World Heavyweight Title)

1959

May 1—Brian London, Indianapolis...... KO 11
(World Heavyweight Title)
June 26—Ingemar Johansson, New York...KO by 3
(Lost World Heavyweight Title)

1960

June 20—Ingemar Johansson, New York.... KO 5
(First man to regain World Heavyweight Title)
Went to Europe and engaged in exhibitions in Sweden, Germany, England and Italy.

1961

Mar. 13—Ingemar Johansson, Miami Beach.. KO 6
(World Heavyweight Title)

Dec. 4—Tom NcNeeley, Toronto .... KO 4
(World Heavyweight Title)

1962

Sept. 25—Sonny Liston, Chicago .... KO by 1
(Lost World Heavyweight Title)

1963

July 22—Sonny Liston, Las Vegas .... KO by 1
(For World Heavyweight Championship)

1964

Jan. 6—Sánte Amonti, Stockholm .... KO 8
July 5—Eddie Machen, Stockholm .... W 12
Dec. 12—Charley Powell, San Juan .... KO 6

1965

Feb. 1—George Chuvalo, NY .... W 12
May 14—Tod Herring, Stockholm .... KO 3
Nov. 22—Muhammad Ali, Las Vegas ..... KO by 12
(World Heavyweight Title)

1966

Sept. 20—Henry Cooper, London .... KO 4

1967

Feb. 13—Willie Johnson, Miami Beach ..... KO 3
Mar. 30—Bill McMurray, Pittsburgh ...... KO 1
June 9—Jerry Quarry, Los Angeles ...... D 10
Oct. 28—Jerry Quarry, Los Angeles .... L 12

1968

Sept. 14—Jimmy Ellis, Stockholm............ L 15
(WBA Heavyweight Title)

1969

Inactive

1970

Sept. 15—Charlie Green, New York .... KO 10

1971

Jan. 16—Levi Forte, Miami Beach .... KO 2
Mar. 29—Roger Russell, Philadelphia ...... KO 9
May 26—Terry Daniels, Cleveland .... W 10
July 17—Charlie Polite, Erie .... KO 6
Aug. 21—Vic Brown, Buffalo .... W 10
Nov. 23—Charlie Harris, Portland .... KO 6

1972

Feb. 11—Oscar Bonavena, New York, ... W 10
May 16—Charlie Harris, Washington, DC .. Exh. 5
July 14—Pedro Agosto, New York........ KO 6
Sept. 20—Muhammad Ali, New York ..... KO by 7

TB	KO	WD	WF	D	LD	LF	KO BY	ND	NC
64	40	15	0	1	3	0	5	0	0

Elected to Boxing Hall of Fame 1977

WILLIE PEP

(Guglielmo Papaleo)
(Will o' the Wisp)
Born, Sept. 19, 1922, Middletown, CT. Feather-
weight. Height. 5 ft. 5 ½ in. Managed by Lou Viscusi.
Started amateur in 1937.

1938

Won the Connecticut State Amateur Flyweight
Championship.

1939

Won the Connecticut State Amateur Bantamweight Championship.

1940

July 3—James McGovern, Hartford .... W 4
July 25—Joey Marcus, Hartford........... W 4
Aug. 8—Joey Wasnick, New Haven ...... KO 3
Aug. 29—Tommy Burns, Hartford .... KO 1
Sept. 5—Joey Marcus, New Britain ...... W 6
Sept. 18—Jack Moore, Hartford .... W 6
Oct. 3—Jimmy Riche, Waterbury ...... KO 3
Nov. 22—Carlo Duponde, New Britain ..... KO 6
Nov. 29—Frank Topazio, New Britain ..... KO 5
Dec. 6—Jim Mutane, New Britain ...... KO 2

1941

Jan. 28—Augie Almeda, New Haven ...... KO 6
Feb. 3—Joe Echevarria, Holyoke .... W 6
Feb. 10—Don Lyons, Holyoke .... KO 2
Feb. 17—Ruby Garcia, Holyoke .... W 6
Mar. 3—Ruby Garcia, Holyoke .... W 6
Mar. 25—Marty Shapiro, Hartford .... W 6
Mar. 31—Ruby Garcia, Holyoke .... KO 2
Apr. 14—Henry Vasquez, Holyoke ...... W 6
Apr. 22—Mexican Joey Silva, Hartford ...... W 6
May 6—Lou Puglose, Hartford .... KO 2
May 12—Johnny Cockfield, Holyoke ...... W 6
June 24—Eddie De Angelis, Hartford ...... KO 3
July 16—Jimmy Gilligan, Hartford .... W 8
Aug. 1—Harry Hitlian, Manchester .... W 6
Aug. 5—Paul Frechette, Hartford .... KO 3
Aug. 12—Eddie Flores, Thompsonville ..... KO 1
Sept. 26—Jackie Harris, New Haven....... KO 1
Oct. 10—Carlos Manzana, New Haven ...... W 8
Oct. 22—Connie Savoie, Hartford .... KO 2
Nov. 7—Billie Spencer, Los Angeles ...... W 4
Nov. 24—Dave Crawford, Holyoke .... W 8
Dec. 12—Ruby Garcia, New York .... W 4

1942

Jan. 8—Joey Rivers, Fall River .... KO 4
Jan. 16—Sammy Parrota, New York ...... W 4
Jan. 27—Abie Kaugman, Hartford.......... W 8
Feb. 10—Angelo Callura, Hartford .... W 8
Feb. 24—Willie Roach, Hartford .... W 8
Mar. 18—Johnny Compo, New Haven ...... W 8
Apr. 14—Spider Armstrong, Hartford ...... KO 4
May 4—Curley Nichols, New Haven ...... W 8
May 12—Aaron Seltzer, Hartford .... W 8
May 26—Joey Iannotti, Hartford .... W 8
June 23—Joey Archibald, Hartford........ W 10
July 21—Abe Denner, Hartford .... W 12
Aug. 1—Joey Silva, Waterbury .... KO 7
Aug. 10—Pedro Hernandez, Hartford ...... W 10
Aug. 20—Nat Litfin, West Haven .... W 10
Sept. 1—Bobby Ivy, Hartford .... KO 10
Sept. 10—Frank Franconeri, New York ..... KO 1
Sept. 22—Vince Dell'Orto, Hartford .... W 10
Oct. 16—Joey Archibald, Providence .... W 10
Oct. 5—Bobby McIntire, Holyoke .... W 10
Oct. 27—George Zengaras, Hartford .... W 10
Nov. 20—Chalky Wright, New York ...... W 15
(Won World Featherweight Championship)
Dec. 14—Joe Aponte Torres, Washington, DC KO 7
Dec. 21—Joey Silva, Jacksonville.......... KO 9

1943

Jan. 4—Vince Dell'Orto, New Orleans...... W 10
Jan. 19—Bill Speary, Hartford............. W 10
Jan. 29—Allie Stolz, New York .... W 10

Feb. 11—Davey Crawford, Boston .... W 10
Feb. 15—Bill Speary, Baltimore .... W 10
Mar. 2—Lou Transparenti, Hartford....... KO 6
Mar. 19—Sammy Angott, New York ...... L 10
Mar. 29—Bobby McIntire, Detroit .... W 10
Apr. 9—Sal Bartolo, Boston .... W 10
Apr. 19—Angel Aviles, Tampa .... W 10
Apr. 26—Jackie Wilson, Pittsburgh .... W 12
June 8—Sal Bartolo, Boston .... W 15
(Title Bout)
In U.S. Navy after having served in Army. Hon-
orably discharged—Jan., 1944

1944

Apr. 4—Leo Francis, Hartford .... W 10
Apr. 20—Harold Snooks Lacey, New Haven .. W 10
May 1—Jackie Leamus, Philadelphia....... W 10
May 19—Frankie Rubino, Chicago .... W 10
May 23—Joey Bagnato, Buffalo .... KO 2
June 6—Julie Kogon, Hartford .... W 10
July 7—Willie Joyce, Chicago .... W 10
July 17—Manuel Ortiz, Boston .... W 10
Aug. 4—Lulu Constantino, Waterbury ...... W 10
Aug. 29—Joey Peralta, Springfield .... W 10
Sept. 19—Charley Cabey Lewis, Hartford .... W 8
Sept. 29—Chalky Wright, New York .... W 15
(Title Bout)
Oct. 25—Jackie Leamus, Montreal .... W 10
Nov. 14—Charley Cabey Lewis, Hartford..... W 10
Nov. 27—Pedro Hernandez, Washington ..... W 10
Dec. 5—Chalky Wright, Cleveland .... W 10

1945

Jan. 23—Ralph Walton, Hartford .... W 10
Feb. 5—Willie Roache, New Haven ...... W 10
Feb. 19—Phil Terranova, New York .... W 15
(Title Bout)
Mar. 14—Inducted into U.S. Army.
Oct. 30—Paulie Jackson, Hartford.......... W 8
Nov. 5—Mike Martyk, Buffalo .... KO 5
Nov. 26—Eddie Giosa, Boston .... W 10
Dec. 5—Harold Gibson, Lewiston........ W 10
Dec. 13—Jimmy McAllister, Baltimore....... D 10

1946

Jan. 15—Johnny Virgo, Buffalo .... KO 2
Feb. 13—Jimmy Joyce, Buffalo .... W 10
Mar. 1—Jimmy McAllister, New York ..... KO 2
Mar. 26—Jackie Wilson, Kansas City ...... W 10
Apr. 8—Georgie Knox, Providence .... KO 3
May 6—Ernie Petrone, New Haven ...... W 10
May 13—Joey Angelo, Providence .... W 10
May 22—Aponte Torres, St. Louis .... W 10
May 27—Jimmy Joyce, Minneapolis........ W 8
June 7—Sal Bartolo, New York .... KO 12
(Title Bout)
July 10—Harold Gibson, Buffalo .... KO 7
July 25—Jackie Graves, Minneapolis ...... KO 8
Aug. 26—Doll Rafferty, Milwaukee .... KO 6
Sept. 4—Walter Kolby, Buffalo .... KO 5
Sept. 17—Lefty LaChance, Hartford .... KO 3
Nov. 1—Paulie Jackson, Minneapolis .... W 10
Nov. 15—Tomas Beato, Waterbury......... KO 2
Nov. 27—Chalky Wright, Milwaukee .... KO 3

1947

Jan. 8—Severely injured in airplane crash.
June 17—Victor Flores, Hartford .... W 10

244

July   1—Joey Fortuna, Albany .... KO   5
July   8—Leo LeBrun, Norwalk .... W   8
July   1—Jean Barriere, North Adams ..... KO   4
July   15—Paulie Jackson, New Bedford ..... W 10
July   23—Humberto Sierra, Hartford .... W 10
Aug.   22—Jock Leslie, Flint .... KO 12
                    (Title Bout)
Oct.   21—Jean Barriere, Portland, ME ..... KO   1
Oct.   27—Archie Wilmer, Phila. .... W 10
Dec.   22—Alvara Estrada, Lewiston .... W 10
Dec.   30—Lefty La Chance, Manchester ..... KO   8
                    1948
Jan.   6—Pedro Biesca, Hartford .... W 10
Jan.   12—Jimmy McAllister, St. Louis ..... W 10
Jan.   19—Joey Angelo, Boston .... W 10
Feb.   24—Humberto Sierra, Miami .... KO 10
           (Won World Featherweight Title)
May   7—Leroy Willis, Detroit .... W 10
May   19—Charley (Cabey) Lewis, Milwaukee .. W 10
June   17—Miguel Acevedo, Minneapolis ..... W 10
June   25—Luther Burgess, Flint .... W 10
July   28—Young Junior, Utica .... KO   1
Aug.   3—Ted Davis, Hartford .... W 10
Aug.   17—Ted Davis, Hartford .... W 10
Sept.   2—Johnny Dell, Waterbury .... KO   8
Sept. 10—Paddy DeMarco, New York ...... W 10
Oct.   12—Chuck Burton, Jersey City .... W   8
Oct.   19—John LaRusso, Hartford .... W 10
Oct.   29—Sandy Saddler, New York ..... KO by   4
          (Lost World Featherweight Title)
Dec.   20—Hermie Freeman, Boston .... W 10
                    1949
Jan.   17—Teddy Davis, St. Louis .... W 10
Feb.   11—Sandy Saddler, New York .... W 15
          (Regained World Featherweight Title)
Apr.   27—Elis Ask, Detroit .... Exh.   4
May   25—Mel Hammond, St. Paul .... Exh.   4
June   6—Luis Ramos, New Haven .... W 10
June   14—Al Pennino, Pittsfield .... W 10
June   20—John LaRusso, Springfield .... W 10
July   12—Jean Mougin, Syracuse .... W 10
Sept.   2—Miguel Acevedo, Chicago ...... Exh.   4
Sept. 20—Eddie Compo, Waterbury .... KO   7
                    (Title Bout)
Dec.   12—Harold Dade, St. Louis .... W 10
                    1950
Jan.   16—Charley Riley, St. Louis .... KO   5
                    (Title Bout)
Feb.   6—Roy Andrews, Boston .... W 10
Feb.   22—Jimmy Warren, Miami .... W 10
Mar.   17—Ray Famechon, New York .... W 15
                    (Title Bout)
May   15—Art Llanos, Hartford .... KO   2
June   1—Terry Young, Milwaukee .... W 10
June   26—Bobby Timpson, Hartford .... W 10
July   25—Bobby Bell, Washington .... W 10
Aug.   2—Proctor Heinold, Scranton ...... W 10
Sept.   8—Sandy Saddler, New York ..... KO by   8
              (Lost Featherweight Title)
                    1951
Jan.   30—Tommy Baker, Hartford .... KO   4
Feb.   26—Billy Hogan, Sarasota .... KO   2
Mar.   5—Carlos Chavez, New Orleans ...... W 10
Mar.   26—Pat Iacobucci, Miami .... W 10

Apr.   17—Baby Ortiz, St. Louis .... KO   5
Apr.   27—Eddie Chavez, San Francisco ...... W 10
June   4—Jesus Compos, Baltimore .... W 10
Sept.   4—Corky Gonzales, New Orleans ..... W 10
Sept. 26—Sandy Saddler, New York ..... KO by   9
          (For Featherweight Title)
                    1952
Apr.   29—Santiago Gonzales, Tampa .... W 10
May   5—Kenny Leach, Columbus, GA ..... W 10
May   10—Buddy Baggett, Aiken, SC ...... KO   5
May   21—Claude Hammond, Miami Beach ... W 10
June   30—Tommy Collins, Boston .... KO by   6
Sept.   3—Billy Lima, Pensacola .... W 10
Sept. 11—Bobby Woods, Vancouver .... W 10
Oct.   1—Armand Savoie, Chicago .... W 10
Oct.   20—Billy Lima, Jacksonville .... W 10
Nov.   5—Manny Castro, Miami Beach ..... KO   5
Nov.   19—Fabala Chavez, St. Louis .... W 10
Dec.   5—Jorge Sanchez, West Palm Beach ... W 10
                    1953
Jan.   19—Billy Lauderdale, Nassau .... W 10
Jan.   27—Davey Mitchell, Miami Beach ..... W 10
Feb.   2—Jose Alvarez, San Antonio .... W 10
Mar.   31—Joey Gambino, Tampa .... W 10
Apr.   7—Noel Paquette, Miami Beach ...... W 10
May   13—Jackie Blair, Dallas .... W 10
June   2—Pat Marcune, New York .... KO 10
Nov.   21—Sonny Luciano, Charlotte .... W 10
Dec.   4—Davey Allen, West Palm Beach .... W 10
Dec.   8—Billy Lima, Houston .... KO   2
Dec.   15—Tony Longo, Miami Beach .... W 10
                    1954
Jan.   19—David Seabrooke, Jacksonville ..... W 10
Feb.   26—Lulu Perez, New York .... KO by   2
July   24—Mike Turcotte, Mobile .... W 10
Aug.   18—Til LeBlanc, Moncton .... W 10
Nov.   1—Mario Colon, Daytona Beach ...... W 10
                    1955
Mar.   11—Myrel Olmstead, Bennington, VT ... W 10
Mar.   22—Charley Titone, Holyoke .... W 10
Mar.   30—Gil Cadilli, Parks Airforce Base, CA .. L 10
May   18—Gil Cadilli, Detroit .... W 10
June   1—Joey Cam, Boston .... KO   4
June   14—Mickey Mars, Miami Beach ...... KO   7
July   12—Hector Rodriquez, Bridgeport ..... W 10
Sept. 13—Jimmy Ithia, Hartford .... KO   6
Sept. 27—Henry (Pappy) Gault, Holyoke ..... W 10
Oct.   10—Charley Titone, Brockton .... W 10
Nov.   29—Henry (Pappy) Gault, Tampa ...... W 10
Dec.   12—Leo Carter, Houston .... KO   4
Dec.   28—Andy Arel, Miami Beach 10
                    1956
Mar.   13—Kid Campeche, Tampa .... W 10
Mar.   27—Buddy Baggett, Beaumont .... W 10
Apr.   17—Jackie Blair, Hartford .... W 10
May   22—Manuel Armenteros, San Antonio .. KO   7
June   19—Russ Tague, Miami Beach .... W 10
July   4—Hector Bacquettes, Lawton, OK ... KO   4
                    1957
Apr.   23—Cesar Morales, Ft. Lauderdale ..... W 10
May   10—Manny Castro, Florence, SC ...... W 10
July   16—Manny Castro, El Paso .... W 10
July   23—Russ Tague, Houston .... W 10
Dec.   17—Jimmy Connors, Boston .... W 10

                    1958
Jan.   14—Tommy Tibbs, Boston .... L 10
Mar.   31—Prince Johnson, Holyoke .... W 10
Apr.   8—George Stephany, Bristol .... W 10
Apr.   14—Cleo Ortiz, Providence .... W 10
Apr.   29—Jimmy Kelly, Boston .... W 10
May   20—Bobby Singleton, Boston .... W 10
June   23—Pat McCoy, New Bedford .... W 10
July   1—Bobby Soares, Athol .... W 10
July   17—Bobby Bell, Norwood .... W 10
Aug.   4—Luis Carmona, Presque Isle ...... W 10
Aug.   9—Jesse Rodrigues, Painesville ...... W 10
Aug.   26—Al Duarte, North Adams .... W 10
Sept. 20—Hogan (Kid) Bassey, Boston ....KO by   9
                    1959
Jan.   26—Sonny Leon, Caracas .... L 10
       Announced retirement, January 27, 1959.
       Decided on a comeback, January 12, 1965.
                    1965
Jan.   28—Jerry Powers, Miami .... Exh.   4
Mar.   12—Hal McKeever, Miami .... W   8
Apr.   26—Jackie Lennon, Philadelphia ...... W   6
May   21—Johnny Gilmore, Norwalk .... W   6
May   28—Irish Bob Shaugnessy .... Exh.   4
July   26—Benny Randell, Quebec .... W 10
Sept. 28—Johnny Gilmore, Philadelphia ..... W   6
Oct.   1—Willie Little, Johnston .... KO   3
Oct.   4—Tommy Haden, Providence .... KO   3
Oct.   14—Sergio Musquiz, Phoenix .... KO   5
Oct.   25—Ray Coleman, Tucson .... KO   5
                    1966
Mar.   16—Calvin Woodland, Richmond L   6

TB   KO   WD   WF   D   LD   LF   KO BY   ND   NC
241 65 164   0   1   5   0   6   0   0
       Elected to Boxing Hall of Fame 1963.

                    JOE RIVERS
                    (JOSE YBARRA)
                    Junior Lightweight
           Born, March 19, 1892, Los Angeles, CA
             Weight: 130 lbs. Height: 5 ft. 5 in.
                  Managed by Joe Levy
                   Began boxing 1908
              (Previous record unavailable)
                    1910
Mar.   20—Billy Cappalle, Los Angeles .... W 10
Apr.   14—Red Corbett, Los Angeles .... W 10
May   13—Red Corbett, San Diego .... KO 11
May   27—Martin Leahy, Los Angeles .... KO   3
Nov.   24—Frankie Sullivan, Vernon .... KO   9
                    1911
Jan.   1—Billy Cappalle, Vernon .... KO   6
Jan.   14—Danny Webster, Vernon .... KO 13
Feb.   22—Jimmy Reagan, Vernon .... KO 13
May   6—Johnny Kilbane, Vernon .... W 20
May   19—George Kirkwood, San Francisco ... D   4
June   10—Tommy Dixon, Vernon .... WF 16
July   4—Joe Coster, Vernon .... KO 13
Sept.   4—Johnny Kilbane, Vernon ....KO by 16

245

Oct. 28—George Kirkwood, Vernon .... KO 8
Nov. 18—Frankie Conley, Vernon 20
1912
Jan.   1—Frankie Conley, Vernon .... KO 11
Mar.   6—Jack White, Vernon............. KO 12
July   4—Ad Wolgast, Vernon ....KO by 13
      (World Lightweight Title)
Sept. 2—Joe Mandot, Vernon .... L 20
Nov. 28—Joe Mandot, Vernon .... W 20
1913
Jan. 14—Leach Cross, New York........ ND 10
Feb. 22—K. O. Brown, Vernon .... KO 10
Apr.   8—Leach Cross, New York........ ND 10
July   4—Willie Ritchie, San Francsco....KO by 11
      (World Lightweight Title)
Oct. 28—Frankie Russell, New Orleans .... ND 10
Nov. 27—Leach Cross, Vernon .... W 20
1914
Jan. 23—Ad Wolgast, Milwaukee .... ND 10
Mar. 17—Freddie Welsh, Vernon .... L 20
July   4—Matty McCue, Vernon .... W 20
Aug. 11—Leach Cross, Vernon .... W 20
Sept. 7—Willie Beecher, Vernon .... W 20
Oct.   4—Joe Mandot, New Orleans .... L 20
Oct. 12—Frankie Russell, Memphis........ W 8
Dec.   8—Johnny Dundee, Los Angeles .... L 20
1915
Jan. 18—Frankie Callahan, Memphis ....KO by 2
Apr.   9—Frankie Burns, Kansas City ...... ND 10
Apr. 22—Frankie Burns, Kansas City ...... W 10
May   12—Harvey Thorpe, Kansas City ...... W 10
June 15—Johnny Harvey, New York .... ND 10
July   6—Gilbert Gallant, Boston .... D 12
July 23—Johnny Dundee, Brooklyn .... ND 10
Aug. 16—Stanley Yoakum, Denver .... W 15
Nov.   8—Johnny Dundee, Milwaukee .... ND 10
1916
Jan. 24—Richie Mitchell, Cincinnati .... ND 10
Sept. 1—Johnny Griffiths, Akron .... ND 12
Oct.   9—Joe Sherman, Cincinnati .... WF 3
Nov. 20—Joe Thomas, New Orleans .... KO 3
1917
Feb. 19—Frankie Murphy, Columbus ...... KO 2
Mar. 19—Johnny O'Leary, Columbus ...... KO 11
Mar. 23—Jimmy Duffy, New York .... ND '10
Apr.   2—Johnny Harvey, New York .....KO by 7
June   7—Al Young, Ogden .... WF 5
July   4—Frankie Burns, Oakland .... W 4
Aug. 15—Willie Hoppe, Oakland .... D 4
Aug. 24—Johnny McCarthy, San Francisco ....L 4
Oct.   6—Johnny McCarthy, Reno .... D 10
Nov.   4—Bobby Waugh, Silver City........LF 13
1918
Mar. 22—Chief Abernathy, San Diego .... L 4
May   3—Tilly Kid Herman, San Francisco ....L 4
July   4—Joe Benjamin, Turlock .... D 4
July   5—Tilly Kid Herman, San Francisco ....L 4
July   9—Johnny McCarthy, San Francisco .. D 4
July 19—Johnny McCarthy, San Francisco ....L 4
Aug. 16—Willie Robinson, San Francisco .... W 4
Sept. 2—Joe Miller, San Francisco .... D 4
1920
Dec. 14—Phil Salvadore, Los Angeles .... K 4
1923
Apr.   3—Pete McCarthy, Albuquerque ..... KO 3

246

Died June 25, 1957, Inglewood, CA.

TB	KO	WD	WF	D	LD	LF	KO BY	ND	NC
67	15	13	3	8	11	1	5	11	0

RAY ROBINSON
(Walker Smith)
(Sugar Ray)

Born, May, 3, 1920, Detroit, MI. Height 5 ft. 11 in. Managed by George Gainford.

Won Golden Gloves featherweight title in 1939 and lightweight title in 1940 in New York and in inter-city competition.

Engaged in 85 amateur bouts. Had 69 KO's (40 first round). Boxed as Walker Smith.

Oct.   4—Joe Escheverria, New York ...... KO 2
Oct.   8—Silent Stefford, Savannah .... KO 2
Oct. 22—Mistos Grispos, New York ...... W 6
Nov. 11—Bobby Woods, Philadelphia ..... KO 1
Dec.   9—Norment Quarles, Philadelphia... KO 4
Dec. 12—Oliver White, New York .... KO 3
1941
Jan.   4—Henry La Barba, Brooklyn ...... KO 1
Jan. 13—Frankie Wallace, Philadelphia ... KO 1
Jan. 31—George Zengaras, New York ..... W 6
Feb.   8—Benny Cartegena, Brooklyn ..... KO 1
Feb. 21—Bobby McIntire, New York ..... W 6
Feb. 27—Gene Spencer, Detroit .... KO 5
Mar.   3—Jimmy Tygh, Philadelphia ..... KO 8
Apr. 14—Jimmy Tygh, Philadelphia ..... KO 1
Apr. 24—Charley Burns, Atlantic City ... KO 1
Apr. 30—Joe Ghnouly, Washington .... KO 3
May   10—Vic Troise, Brooklyn .... KO 1
May   19—Nick Castiglione, Philadelphia .. KO 1
June 16—Mike Evans, Philadelphia .... KO 2
July   2—Pete Lello, New York .... KO 4
July 21—Sammy Angott, Philadelphia..... W 10
Aug. 27—Carl Red Guggino, Long Island City KO 3
Aug. 29—Maurice Arnault, Atlantic Cy..... KO 1
Sept. 19—Maxie Shapiro, New York ...... KO 3
Sept. 25—Marty Servo, Philadelphia ...... W 10
Oct. 31—Fritzie Zivic, New York .... W 10
1942
Jan. 16—Fritzie Zivic, New York .... KO 10
Feb. 20—Maxie Berger, New York .... KO 2
Mar. 20—Norman Rubio, New York ...... KO 7
Apr. 17—Harvey Dubs, Detroit .... KO 6
Apr. 30—Dick Banner, Minneapolis....... KO 2
May   28—Marty Servo, New York .... W 10
July 31—Sammy Angott, New York ...... W 10
Aug. 21—Ruben Shank, New York ...... KO 2
Aug. 27—Tony Motisi, Chicago .... KO 1
Oct.   2—Jake LaMotta, New York .... W 10
Oct. 19—Izzy Jannazzo, Philadelphia .... W 10
Nov.   6—Vic Dellicurti, New York .... W 10
Dec.   1—Izzy Jannazzo, Cleveland ...... KO 8
Dec. 14—Al Nettlow, Philadelphia .... KO 3
1943
Feb.   5—Jake LaMotta, Detroit .... L 10
Feb. 19—Jackie Wilson, New York .... W 10
Feb. 26—Jake LaMotta, Detroit .... W 10
Apr. 30—Freddie Cabral, Boston .... KO 1

July   1—Ralph Zannelli, Boston .... W 10
Aug. 27—Henry Armstrong, New York ..... W 10
1944
Oct. 13—Izzy Jannazzo, Boston .... KO 2
Oct. 27—Sgt. Lou Woods, Chicago .... KO 9
Nov. 17—Vic Dellicurti, Detroit .... W 10
Dec. 12—Sheik Rangel, Philadelphia...... KO 2
Dec. 22—Georgie Martin, Boston .... KO 7
      In U.S. Army
1945
Jan. 10—Billy Furrone, Washington, DC .. KO 2
Jan. 16—Tommy Bell, Cleveland .... W 10
Feb. 14—George Costner, Chicago .... KO 1
Feb. 23—Jake LaMotta, New York....... W 10
May   14—Jose Basora, Philadelphia .... D 10
June 15—Jimmy McDaniels, New York .... KO 2
Sept. 18—Jimmy Mandell, Buffalo .... KO 5
Sept. 26—Jake LaMotta, Chicago .... W 12
Dec.   4—Vic Dellicurti, Boston .... W 10
1946
Jan. 14—Dave Clark, Pittsburgh .... KO 2
Feb.   5—Tony Riccio, Elizabeth .... KO 4
Feb. 15—O'Neill Bell, Detroit .... KO 2
Feb. 26—Cliff Beckett, St. Louis .... KO 4
Mar.   4—Sammy Angott, Pittsburgh ...... W 10
Mar. 14—Izzy Jannazzo, Baltimore ...... W 10
Mar. 31—Freddy Flores, New York ...... KO 5
June 12—Freddy Wilson, Worcester ..... KO 2
June 25—Norman Rubio, Union City ..... W 10
July 12—Joe Curcio, New York .... KO 2
Aug. 15—Vinnie Vines, Albany........... KO 6
Sept. 25—Sidney Miller, Elizabeth .... KO 3
Oct.   7—Ossie Harris, Pittsburgh .... W 10
Nov.   1—Cecil Hudson, Detroit .... KO 6
Nov. 15—Artie Levine, Cleveland .... KO 10
Dec. 20—Tommy Bell, New York .... W 15
      (Won vacant World Welterweight Championship)
1947
Mar. 27—Bernie Miller, Miami........... KO 3
Apr.   3—Fred Wilson, Akron .... KO 3
Apr.   8—Eddie Finazzo, Kansas City...... KO 4
May   16—George Abrams, New York ...... W 10
June 24—Jimmy Doyle, Cleveland .... KO 8
      (Title Bout)
      Doyle died of injuries.
Aug. 21—Sammy Secreet, Akron .... KO 1
Aug. 29—Flashy Sebastian, New York ..... KO 1
Oct. 28—Jackie Wilson, Los Angeles...... KO 1
Dec. 10—Billy Nixon, Elizabeth .... KO 6
Dec. 19—Chuck Taylor, Detroit .... KO 6
      (Title Bout)
1948
Mar.   4—Ossie Harris, Toledo .... W 10
Mar. 16—Henry Brimm, Buffalo.......... W 10
June 28—Bernard Docusen, Chicago .... W 15
      (Title Bout)
Sept. 23—Kid Gavilan, New York .... W 10
Nov. 15—Bobby Lee, Philadelphia .... W 10
1949
Feb. 10—Gene Buffalo, Wilkes-Barre .... KO 1
Feb. 15—Henry Brimm, Buffalo .... D 10
Mar. 25—Bobby Lee, Chicago .... W 10
Apr. 11—Don Lee, Omaha .... W 10
Apr. 20—Earl Turner, Oakland .... KO 8
May   16—Al Tribuani, Wilmington........Exh. 4

June	7—Freddie Flores, New Bedford	KO	3
June	20—Cecil Hudson, Providence	KO	5
July	1—Kid Gavilan, Philadelphia........	W	15

(Title Bout)

Aug.	24—Steve Belloise, New York	KO	7
Sept.	2—Al Mobley, Chicago ....Exh.		4
Sept.	9—Benny Evans, Omaha	KO	5
Sept.	12—Charley Dotson, Houston	KO	3
Nov.	9—Don Lee, Denver	W	10
Nov.	13—Vern Lester, New Orleans	KO	5
Nov.	15—Gene Burton, Shreveport ......Exh.		6
Nov.	16—Gene Burton, Dallas .... Exh.		6

1950

Jan.	30—George LaRover, New Haven	KO	4
Feb.	13—Al Mobley, Miami	KO	6
Feb.	22—Aaron Wade, Savannah	KO	3
Feb.	27—Jean Walzack, St. Louis	W	10
Mar.	22—George Costner, Philadelphia	KO	1
Apr.	21—Cliff Beckett, Columbus, OH.....	KO	3
Apr.	28—Ray Barnes, Detroit	W	10
June	5—Robert Villemain, Philadelphia....	W	15

(Won Pennsylvania Middleweight Title)

| Aug. | 9—Charley Fusari, Jersey City .... | W | 15 |

(Welterweight Title Bout)

| Aug. | 25—Jose Basora, Scranton .... | KO | 1 |

(Pennsylvania middleweight title)

Sept.	4—Billy Brown, New York	W	10
Oct.	16—Joe Rindone, Boston	KO	6
Oct.	26—Carl Olson, Philadelphia	KO	12

(Pennsylvania Middleweight Title)

Nov.	8—Bobby Dykes, Chicago	W	10
Nov.	27—Jean Stock, Paris	KO	2
Dec.	9—Luc Van Dam, Brussels	KO	4
Dec.	16—Jean Walzack, Geneva	W	10
Dec.	22—Robert Villemain, Paris........	KO	9
Dec.	25—Hans Stretz, Frankfort	KO	5

1951

| Feb. | 14—Jake LaMotta, Chicago ...... | KO | 13 |

(Won World Middleweight Title)

Apr.	5—Holly Mims, Miami	W	10
Apr.	28—Don Ellis, Oklahoma City	KO	1
May	21—Kid Marcel, Paris	KO	5
May	26—Jean Wanes, Zurich	W	10
June	10—Jan deBruin, Antwerp	KO	8
June	16—Jean Walzack, Liege	KO	6
June	24—Gerhard Hecht, Berlin..........	ND	2

(Robinson disqualified by referee for kidney punch. Commission later reversed it to a no decision bout.)

| July | 1—Cyrille Delannoit, Turin .... | KO | 3 |
| July | 10—Randy Turpin, London .... | L | 15 |

(Lost World Middleweight Title)

| Sept. | 12—Randy Turpin, New York ...... | KO | 10 |

(Regained World Middleweight Title)

1952

| Mar. | 13—Carl (Bobo) Olson, San Francsico .. | W | 15 |

(Retained Middleweight Title)

| Apr. | 16—Rocky Graziano, Chicago ...... | KO | 3 |

(Retained Middleweight Title)

| June | 25—Joey Maxim, New York ...... | KO by | 14 |

(For Light-Heavyweight Title)

Announced Retirement December 18, 1952.

1954

| Oct. | 20—Announced return to ring. | | |
| Nov. | 29—Gene Burton, Hamilton ....Exh. | | 6 |

1955

Jan.	5—Joe Rindone, Detroit	KO	6
Jan.	19—Ralph Jones, Chicago	L	10
Mar.	29—Johnny Lombardo, Cincinnati	W	10
Apr.	14—Ted Olla, Milwaukee	KO	3
May	4—Garth Panter, Detroit	W	10
July	22—Rocky Castellani, San Francisco ...	W	10
Dec.	9—Carl (Bobo) Olson, Chicago......	KO	2

(Won World Middleweight Title)

1956

| May | 18—Carl (Bobo) Olson, Los Angeles .. | KO | 4 |

(Retained Middleweight Title)

| No. | 10—Bob Provizzi, New Haven .... | W | 10 |

1957

| Jan. | 2—Gene Fullmer, New York .... | L | 15 |

(Lost World Middleweight Title)

| May | 1—Gene Fullmer, Chicago .... | KO | 5 |

(Regained World Middleweight Title)

Sept.	10—Otis Woodard, Philadelphia .....Exh.		2
Sept.	10—Lee Williams, Philadelphia......Exh.		2
Sept.	23—Carmen Basilio, New York	L	15

(Lost World Middleweight Title)

1958

| Mar. | 25—Carmen Basilio, Chicago .... | W | 15 |

(Regained World Middleweight Title)

1959

| Dec. | 14—Bob Young, Boston .... | KO | 2 |

1960

| Jan. | 22—Paul Pender, Boston .... | L | 15 |

(Lost World Middleweight Title)

| Apr. | 2—Tony Baldoni, Baltimore .... | KO | 1 |
| June | 10—Paul Pender, Boston .... | L | 15 |

(For World Middleweight Title)

| Dec. | 3—Gene Fullmer, Los Angeles ...... | D | 15 |

(For NBA Middleweight Title)

1961

| Mar. | 4—Gene Fullmer, Las Vegas ...... | L | 15 |

(For NBA Middleweight Title)

Sept.	25—Wilf Greaves, Detroit	W	10
Oct.	21—Denny Moyer, New York	W	10
Nov.	20—Al Hauser, Providence	KO	6
Dec.	8—Wilf Greaves, Pittsburgh........	KO	8

1962

Feb.	17—Denny Moyer, New York	L	10
Apr.	27—Bobby Lee, Port of Spain, Trinidad	KO	2
July	9—Phil Moyer, Los Angeles	L	10
Sept.	25—Terry Downes, London	L	10
Oct.	17—Diego Infantes, Vienna	KO	2
Nov.	10—Georges Estatoff, Lyons	KO	6

1963

Jan.	30—Ralph Dupas, Miami Beach	W	10
Feb.	25—Bernie Reynolds, Santo Domingo .	KO	4
Mar.	11—Billy Thornton, Lewiston.......	KO	3
May	5—Maurice Rolbnet, Sherbrooke	KO	3
June	24—Joey Giardello, Philadelphia	L	10
Oct.	14—Armand Vanucci, Paris	W	10
Nov.	9—Fabio Bettini, Lyon	D	10
Nov.	16—Emile Sarens, Brussels	KO	8
Nov.	29—Andre Davier, Grenoble	W	10
Dec.	9—Armand Vanucci, Paris	W	10

1964

May	19—Gaylord Barnes, Portland	W	10
July	8—Clarence Riley, Pittsfield	KO	6
July	27—Art Hernandez, Omaha	D	10
Sept.	3—Mick Leahy, Paisley	L	10

Sept.	28—Yolande Leveque, Paris	W	10
Oct.	12—Johnny Angel, London	KO	6
Oct.	24—Jackie Caillau, Nice	W	10
Nov.	7—Baptiste Rolland, Calen	W	10
Nov.	14—Jean Beltritti, Marseilles	W	10
Nov.	27—Fabio Beltini, Rome	D	10

1965

Mar.	6—Jimmy Beecham, Kingston, Jamaica	KO	2
Apr.	4—Ray Basting, Savannah	KO	1
Apr.	28—Rocky Randell, Norfolk	KO	3
May	24—Memo Ayon, Tijuana	L	10
June	1—Stan Harrington, Honolulu	L	10
June	24—Young Joe Walcott, Richmond	W	10
July	12—Fred Hernandez, Las Vegas	L	10
July	27—Young Joe Walcott, Richmond ...	W	10
Aug.	10—Stan Harrington, Honolulu	L	10
Sept.	15—Bill Henderson, Norfolk ......NC		2
Sept.	23—Young Joe Walcott, Philadelphia ..	W	10
Oct.	1—Peter Schmidt, Johnston	W	10
Oct.	5—Neil Morrison, Richmond	KO	2
Oct.	20—Rudolph Bent, Steubenville	KO	3
Nov.	10—Joey Archer, Pittsburgh	L	10

TB	KO	WD	WF	D	LD	LF	KO BY	ND	NC
201	109	65	0	6	18	0	1	1	1

Announced retirement—December 10, 1965, at farewell party.

Became an actor in Hollywood in 1968.

Elected to Boxing Hall of Fame 1967.

BARNEY ROSS

(Barnet Rosofsky)

Born, December 23, 1909, New York, NY. Weight, 145 lbs. Height, 5 ft. 7 in. Managed by Sam Pian and Art Winch.

Started as an amateur in 1926. Won Golden Gloves and Inter-City titles in 1929 and turned pro.

1929

Virgin Tobin, KO 2; Ray Lugo, W 6; Joe Borola, W 6 and 6; Joe Harth, W 5; Mickey Genaro, W 6; Al de Rose, W 6.

1930

Young Terry, KO 8; Harry Dublinsky, KO 8; Louis New, W 6; Johnny Andrews, W 4; Jiro Kumagay, W 4; Eddie Koppy, W 8; Young Terry, D 8; Harry Dublinsky, D 8; Carlos Garcia, L 6; Eddie Rojack, KO 2; Petey Mack, KO 1; Sammy Binder, KO 2; Louis Perez, KO 1.

1931

Jan.	14—Henry Faligano, Chicago..........	W	8
Feb.	20—Young Terry, Chicago	W	10
Mar.	20—Jackie Davis, Chicago	W	6
Mar.	27—Roger Bernard, Chicago	L	8
Apr.	8—Midget Mike O'Dowd, Moline	W	8
Apr.	24—Lul Abella, Chicago	KO	2
May	1—Jackie Dugan, Moline	KO	2
May	13—Billy Shaw, Chicago	W	10
July	15—Babe Ruth, Benton Harbor, MI ..	KO	4
July	30—Jimmy Alvarado, Detroit	KO	8
Oct.	2—Glen Kamp, Chicago	W	10
Nov.	4—Lou Jallos, Chicago	W	8
Nov.	13—Young Terry, Moline	W	8
Nov.	18—Jimmy Lundy, Kansas City	W	8

1932

Feb.	8—Mickey O'Neill, Milwaukee	W 6
Feb.	18—Billy Gladstone, Chicago	W 6
Mar.	2—Nick Ellenwood, Muncie	W 10
Apr.	5—Frankie Hughes, Indianpolis	W 10
May	20—Dick Sisk, Chicago	KO 6
July	28—Henry Perlick, Chicago	KO 3
Aug.	26—Ray Miller, Chicago	W 10
Sept.	15—Frankie Petrolle, Chicago	KO 2
Oct.	21—Battling Battalino, Chicago	W 10
Nov.	11—Goldie Hess, Chicago	W 10
Nov.	25—Johnny Farr, Milwaukee	W 10

1933

Jan. 20—Johnny Dato, Pittsburgh .... KO 2
Feb. 22—Tommy Grogan, Chicago .... W 10
Mar. 22—Billy Petrolle, Chicago.......... W 10
May 4—Joe Ghnouly, St. Louis .... W 10
June 23—Tony Canzoneri, Chicago........ W 10
(Won Lightweight & Jr. Welterweight Titles)
July 26—Johnny Farr, Kansas City .... KO 6
Sept. 12—Tony Canzoneri, New York .... W 15
(Retained Lightweight Title)
(Gave up Lightweight Title)
Nov. 17—Sammy Fuller, Chicago .... W 10
(Retained Jr. Welterweight Title)

1934

Jan. 24—Billy Petrolle, New York .... W 10
Feb. 7—*Pete Nebo, Kansas City .... W 12
Mar. 5—*Frankie Klick, San Francisco ..... D 10
Mar. 14—Kid Morro, Oakland .... W 10
Mar. 27—Bobby Pacho, Los Angeles .... W 10
May 28—Jimmy McLarnin, New York ..... W 15
(Won World Welterweight Title)
Sept. 17—Jimmy McLarnin, New York ...... L 15
(Lost World Welterweight Title)
Dec. 10—*Bobby Pacho, Cleveland .... W 12
*Jr. Welterweight Title Bout.

1935

Jan. 28—*Frankie Klick, Miami .... W 10
Mar. 9—*Henry Woods, Seattle .... W 12
May 28—Jimmy McLarin, New York ...... W 15
(Regained World Welterweight Championship)
(Gave up Jr. Welterweight Title)
Sept. 6—Baby Joe Gans, Portland .... KO 2
Sept. 13—Ceferino Carcia, San Francisco .... W 10
Nov. 29—Ceferino Garcia, Chicago .... W 10
*Jr. Welterweight Title Bout.

1936

Jan. 27—Lou Halper, Philadelphia .... KO 8
Mar. 11—Gordon Wallace, Vancouver ...... W 10
May 1—Chuck Woods, Louisville .... KO 5
June 10—Laddie Tonelli, Milwaukee ...... KO 5
June 22—Morrie Sherman, Omaha .... KO 2
July 22—Phil Furr, Washington .... W 10
Nov. 27—Izzy Janazzo, New York .... W 15
(Retained Welterweight Title)

1937

Jan. 29—Al Manfredo, Detroit........... W 10
June 17—Chuck Woods, Indianapolis ..... KO 4
June 27—Jackie Burke, New Orleans ...... KO 5
Aug. 19—Al Manfredo, Des Moines .... ND 10
Sept. 23—Ceferino Garcia, New York .... W 15
(Retained Welterweight Title)

1938

Apr. 4—Henry Schaft, Minneapolis ...... KO 4
Apr. 26—Bobby Venner, Des Moines...... KO 7
May 31—Henry Armstrong, Long Island City . L 15
(Lost World Welterweight Title)

1942

Joined U. S. Marines. Wounded at Guadalcanal.

TB	KO	WD	WF	D	LD	LF	KO BY	ND	NC
82	24	50	0	3	4	0	0	1	0

Entered advertising business.
Elected to Boxing Hall of Fame 1956.
Died January 17, 1967, in Chicago after a long illness. Death was caused by cancer.

SANDY SADDLER

Born, June 25, 1926, Boston, MA. Height, 5 ft. 7 ½ in. Managed by Charley Johnston.

1944

Mar. 7—Earl Roys, Hartford............. W 8
Mar. 21—Jock Leslie, Hartford .... KO by 3
Mar. 27—Al King, Holyoke .... KO 2
Apr. 17—Joe Landry, Holyoke .... KO 1
May 8—Joe Aponte Torres, Trenton ..... W 6
May 15—Joe Aponte Torres, Holyoke ..... W 6
May 23—Domingo Diaz, Jersey City ..... W 6
June 13—Joe Aponte Torres, Union City .... W 8
June 15—Lou Alter, Fort Hamilton .... L 6
June 23—Lou Alter, New York City .... D 4
July 11—Clyde English, Dexter .... W 6
July 18—Joe Saladino, Brooklyn .... KO 3
July 25—Al Pennino, Brooklyn .... W 6
Aug. 8—Georgie Knox, Brooklyn .... KO 3
Aug. 18—Clifford Smith, New York .... W 6
Nov. 11—Manuel Torres, Brooklyn .... W 6
Nov. 13—Ken Tempkins, Newark .... KO 1
Nov. 24—Manuel Torres, New York ...... KO 5
Nov. 28—Percy Lewis, Jersey City .... KO 1
Dec. 12—Young Tony, Jersey City .... KO 2
Dec. 16—Earl Mintz, Brooklyn.......... KO 2
Dec. 26—Midget Mayo, Newark .... KO 3

1945

Jan. 13—Tony Oshiro, Brooklyn .... W 6
Jan. 15—Lucky Johnson, Newark .... KO 1
Jan. 22—Joey Puig, New York .... KO 1
Jan. 26—Benny May, New Brunswick ...... W 6
Feb. 19—Joey Gatto, New York .... KO 1
Mar. 10—Harold Gibson, Brooklyn .... W 6
Mar. 19—Joe Montiero, New York .... KO 4
Mar. 22—Georgie Knox, Camden .... KO 4
Apr. 2—Jimmy Allen, Newark .... KO 1
Apr. 19—Melvin Anderson, Detroit....... KO 5
Apr. 30—Chillendrina Valencia, Detroit ... KO 9
June 18—Caswell Harris, Baltimore ...... KO 3
June 25—Bobby Washington, Allentown ... KO 2
June 29—Leo Methot, New York .... KO 1
July 23—Herbert Jones, Baltimore .... KO 3
July 24—Joe Monteiro, Brooklyn .... KO 5

July 30—Lou Rivers, New York .... KO 4
Aug. 16—Louis Langley, Brooklyn .... KO 1
Aug. 20—Bobby English, Providence ...... KO 3
Aug. 27—Earl Mintz, Providence .... KO 1
Sept. 21—Ritchie Myashiro, New York..... W 6
Dec. 3—Benny Daniels, Holyoke .... W 6
De. 14—Joe Monterio, Boston .... W 8
Dec. 21—Filbert Osario, New York ...... W 6

1946

Jan. 17—Sam Zelman, Orange.......... KO 1
Feb. 18—Bobby McQuillan, Detroit...... L 10
Apr. 8—Ralph LaSalle, New York ...... W 8
Apr. 11—Johnny Wolgast, Atlantic City.... W 8
Apr. 25—Pedro Firpo, Atlantic City........ W 8
June 13—Cedric Flournoy, Detroit .... KO 4
July 10—George Cooper, Brooklyn ...... KO 7
July 23—Phil Terranova, Detroit .... L 10
Aug. 5—Dom Amoroso, Providence ...... KO 2
Aug. 22—Pedro Firpo, Brooklyn .... W 10
Oct. 26—Jose Rodriguez, Atlantic City .... W 10
Nov. 12—Art Price, Detroit .... W 10
Dec. 9—Clyde English, Holyoke........ KO 3
Dec. 26—Lou Marquez, Jamaica......... KO 2
Dec. 30—Leonard Caesar, Newark .... KO 2

1947

Jan. 20—Dusty Brown, Holyoke .... KO 4
Jan. 27—Humberto Zavala, New York .... KO 7
Feb. 7—Larry Thomas, Asbury Park .... KO 2
Mar. 8—Leonardo Lopez, Mexico City .... KO 2
Mar. 29—Carlos Malacra, Mexico City .... W 10
Apr. 14—Charley Cabey Lewis, New York... W 10
May 2—Joe Brown, New Orleans .... KO 3
May 9—Melvin Bartholomew, New Orleans. W 10
June 3—Jimmy Carter, Washington, DC .. D 10
July 26—Oscar Calles, Caracas .... KO 5
Aug. 14—Leslie Harris, Atlantic City ..... KO 5
Aug. 29—Miguel Acevedo, New York ..... KO 8
Sept. 17—Angelo Ambrosano, Jamaica .... KO 2
Oct. 3—Humberto Sierra, Minneapolis ..... L 10
Oct. 13—Al Penninno, New York .... KO 4
Oct. 26—Lino Garcia, Caracas .... KO 5
Nov. 9—El Barquerito, Caracas .... KO 5
Dec. 5—Lino Garcia, Havana .... KO 3
Dec. 13—Orlando Zuluta, Havana .... W 10

1948

Feb. 2—Charlie Noel, Holyoke .... W 10
Feb. 9—Joey Angelo, New York .... W 10
Mar. 5—Archie Wilmer, New York .... W 8
Mar. 8—Thompson Harmon, Holyoke .... KO 8
Mar. 23—Bobby Thompson, Hartford .... W 10
Arp. 10—Luis Monagas, Caracas .... KO 3
Apr. 17—Jose Diaz, Caracas .... KO 8
Apr. 26—Young Tanner, Aruba, D.W.I. ... KO 5
May 24—Harry LaSane, Holyoke .... W 10
June 29—Chico Rosa, Honolulu .... L 10
Aug. 16—Kid Zefine, Panama .... KO 2
Aug. 23—Aguila Allen, Panama .... KO 2
Oct. 11—Willie Roache, New Haven .... KO 3
Oct. 29—Willie Pep, New York .... KO 4
(Won World Featherweight Title)
Nov. 19—Tomas Beato, Bridgeport .... KO 2
Nov. 29—Dennis Pat Brady, Boston .... W 10
Dec. 7—Eddie Giosa, Cleveland .... KO 2

Dec. 17—Terry Young, New York .... KO 10
1949
Jan. 17—Young Finnegan, Panama ...... KO 5
Feb. 11—Willie Pep, New York .... L 15
    (Lost World Featherweight Title)
Mar. 21—Felix Ramierz, Newark .... W 10
Apr. 18—Ermano Bonetti, Philadelphia .... KO 2
June 2—Jim Keery, London .... KO 4
June 23—Luis Ramos, New York .... KO 5
July 15—Gordon House, New York .... KO 5
Aug. 2—Chuck Burton, Pittsfield .... KO 5
Aug. 8—Johnny Rowe, Brooklyn .... KO 8
Aug. 24—Alfredo Escobar, Los Angeles .... KO 9
Sept. 2—Harold Dade, Chicago .... W 10
Sept. 20—Proctor Heinold, Schenectady .... KO 2
Oct. 28—Paddy DeMarco, New York..... KO 9
Nov. 7—Leroy Willis, Toledo .... W 10
Dec. 6—Orlando Zulueta, Cleveland ..... W 10
1950
Jan. 16—Paulie Jackson, Caracas .... KO 1
Jan. 22—Pedro Firpo, Caracas .... KO 1
Feb. 6—Chuck Burton, Holyoke .... KO 1
Feb. 20—Luis Ramos, Toronto .... KO 3
Apr. 10—Reuben Davis, Newark .... KO 8
Apr. 18—Lauro Salas, Cleveland .... KO 9
Apr. 29—Jesse Underwood, Waterbury ... W 10
May 25—Miguel Acevedo, Minneapolis .... KO 6
June 19—Johnny Forte, Toronto.......... KO 3
June 30—Leroy Willis, Long Beach ...... KO 2
Sept. 8—Willie Pep, New York .... KO 8
    (Regained Featherweight Title)
Oct. 12—Harry LaSane, St. Louis .... W 10
Nov. 1—Charley Riley, St. Louis .... W 10
Dec. 6—Del Flanagan, Detroit .... L 10
1951
Jan. 23—Jesse Underwood, Buffalo .... W 10
Feb. 28—Diego Sosa, Havana .... KO 2
Mar. 27—Lauro Salas, Los Angeles ...... KO 6
Apr. 3—Freddie Herman, Los Angeles ... KO 5
May 5—Harry LaSane, Hershey, PA ..... W 10
June 2—Alfredo Prada, Buenos Aires..... KO 4
June 16—Oscar Flores, Buenos Aires ..... KO 1
June 22—Mario Salinas, Santiago .... KO 5
June 30—Angel Olivieri, Buenos Aires ... KO 5
Aug. 20—Hermie Freeman, Philadelphia ... KO 5
Aug. 27—Paddy DeMarco, Milwaukee ...... L 10
Sept. 26—Willie Pep, New York .... KO 9
    (Retained World Featherweight Title)
Dec. 7—Paddy DeMarco, New York........ L 10
1952
Jan. 14—George Araujo, Boston .... L 10
Mar. 3—Armand Savoie, Montreal .... LD 4
Mar. 17—Tommy Collins, Boston .... KO 5
    In U.S. Army.
1954
Jan. 15—Bill Bossio, New York.......... KO 9
Mar. 4—Charlie Slaughter, Akron ...... KO 4
Apr. 1—Augie Salazar, Boston .... KO 7
May 17—Hoacine Khalfi, New York ...... L 10
July 5—Libby Manzo, New York .... KO 10
Aug. 30—Jackie Blair, Caracas .... KO 1
Sept. 27—Baby Ortiz, Caracas.......... KO 3
Oct. 25—Ray Famechon, Paris .... KO 6
Dec. 10—Bobby Woods, Spokane .... W 10

1955
Jan. 17—Lulu Perez, Boston .... KO 4
Feb. 25—Teddy Davis, New York .... W 15
    (Retained World Featherweight Title)
Apr. 5—Kenny Davis, Butte .... KO 5
May 24—Joe Lopes, Sacramento .... L 10
July 8—Shigeru Kaneko, Tokyo .... KO 6
July 20—Flash Elorde, Manila........... L 10
Dec. 12—Dave Gallardo, San Francisco.... KO 7
1956
Jan. 18—Flash Elorde, San Francisco ..... KO 13
    (Retained World Featherweight Title)
Feb. 13—Georgie Monroe, Providence .... KO 3
Apr. 14—Larry Boardman, Boston .... L 10
1957
    Relinquished World Featherweight Title and announced retirement from ring because of eye injury suffered in automobile crash.

TB KO WD WF D LD LF KO BY ND NC
162 103 41 0 2 14 1 1 0 0
Elected to Boxing Hall of Fame 1971

MAX SCHMELING
(Maximillian Adolph Otto
Siegried Schmeling)
(Black Uhlan)
    Born, Sept. 28, 1905, Klein Luckaw (Brandenburg) Germany. Weight 196 lbs. Height, 6 ft. 1 in. Managed by Arthur von Bulow and Joe Jacobs.
1924
Aug. 2—Czapp, Dusseldorf .... KO 6
Sept. 19—Vanderryver, Cologne .... KO 3
Sept. 20—Louis Dyisburg, Bochum .... KO 1
Oct. 4—Rocky Knight, Cologne .... W 8
Oct. 10—Max Diekmann, Berlin ....KO by 4
Oct. 31—Fred Hammer, Cologne .... KO 3
Dec. 4—Breur, Cologne .... KO 1
Dec. 17—Battling Mather, Dusseldorf ..... KO 3
Dec. 21—Hartig, Berlin .... KO 1
Dec. 26—Jimmy Lygget, Berlin .... WF 2
1925
Jan. 14—Joe Mehling, Berlin .... W 6
Jan. 18—Johnny Kloudts, Cologne ...... KO 2
Mar. 1—Randall, Cologne .... KO 3
Mar. 14—Alf Baker, Cologne .... KO 3
Apr. 3—Jimmy Lygget, Berlin .... D 8
Apr. 28—Fred Hammer, Bonn .... W 8
May 9—Jack Taylor, Cologne .... L 10
June 14—Randall, Brussels .... D 10
Aug. 28—Larry Gains, Cologne ....KO by 2
Nov. 8—Compere, Cologne .... W 8
1926
Feb. 12—Max Diekmann, Berlin .... D 8
    (For Light-Heavyweight Title of Germany)
Mar. 19—W. Louis, Cologne .... KO 1
July 13—A. Vongohr, Berlin .... KO 1
Aug. 24—Max Diekmann, Berlin .... D 8
    (German Light Heavyweight Title)
Oct. 1—Hermann van t'Hoff, Berlin ...... WF 8

1927
Jan. 23—Wilms, Brealau .... KO 8
Jan. 27—Jack Stanley, Berlin .... KO 8
Feb. 4—Mehling, Dresden .... KO 3
Mar. 12—Sebillo, Dortmund .... KO 2
Apr. 8—Francis Charles, Berlin .... KO 8
Apr. 26—Stanley Glen, Hamburg.......... KO 1
May 8—Robert Larsen, Frankfurt .... W 10
May 17—Paillaux, Hamburg .... KO 1
June 19—Fernard Delarge, Dortmund ..... KO 14
    (Won European Light-Heavyweight Title)
July 31—Jack Taylor, Hamburg............ W 10
Aug. 7—W. Westbrook, Essen .... KO 1
Sept. 3—Robert Larsen, Berlin .... KO 4
Oct. 1—L. Clement, Dortmund............ KO 6
Nov. 6—Hein Domgoerger, Leipzig .... KO 7
    (European Light-Heavyweight title)
Dec. 2—Gypsy Daniels, Frankfurt .... W 10
1928
Jan. 6—Michele Bonaglia, Berlin........ KO 1
Feb. 25—Gypsy Daniels, Frankfurt ......KO by 1
Mar. 11—Ted Moore, Dortmund .... W 10
Apr. 4—Franz Diener, Berlin .... W 15
    (German Heavyweight Title)
Nov. 23—Joe Monte, New York .... KO 5
1929
Jan. 4—Joe Sekyra, New York .... W 10
Jan. 22—Pietro Corri, Newark .... KO 1
Feb. 1—Johnny Risko, New York .... KO 9
June 27—Paolino Uzcudun, New York ...... W 15
1930
June 12—Jack Sharkey, New York........ WF 4
    (Won vacant World Heavyweight Championship.)
1931
July 3—Young Stribling, Cleveland .... KO 15
    (Retained Heavyweight Title)
1932
June 21—Jack Sharkey, Long Island ...... L 15
    (Lost Heavyweight Title)
Sept. 26—Mickey Walker, Long Island ..... KO 8
1933
June 8—Max Baer, New York..........KO by 10
1934
Feb. 13—Steve Hamas, Philadelphia ...... L 12
May 13—Paolino Uzcudun, Barcelona ...... D 12
Aug. 26—Walter Neusel, Hamburg......... KO 8
1935
Mar. 10—Steve Hamas, Hamburg .... KO 9
July 7—Paolino Uzcundun, Berlin .... W 12
1936
June 19—Joe Louis, New York .... KO 12
1937
Dec. 14—Harry Thomas, New York........ KO 8
1938
Jan. 30—Ben Foord, Hamburg .... W 12
Apr. 16—Steve Dudas, Hamburg .... KO 5
June 22—Joe Louis New York ....KO by 1
    (Lost World Heavyweight Title)
1939
July 2—Adolf Heuser, Stuttgard .... KO 1
    (Won European Heavyweight Title)
1941
    Joined German Army and was assigned to Parachute Troops. Injured in Battle of Crete.

1947
Returned to ring after absence of eight years.
Sept. 28—Werner Vollmer, Frankfurt....... KO 7
Dec. 7—Han Joachim Dreagestein, Hamburg. W 10
1948
May 23—Walter Neusel, Hamburg...........L 10
Oct. 2—Han Joachim Dreagestein, Kiel.... KO 9
Oct. 31—Richard Vogt, Berlin.............L 10

TB	KO	WD	WF	D	LD	LF	KO BY	ND	NC
70	39	14	3	4	5	0	5	0	0

Elected to Boxing Hall of Fame 1970.

JOHN L. SULLIVAN
(John Lawrence Sullivan)
(The Boston Strong Boy)
Born, October 15, 1858, Roxbury, MA. Weight, 190 lbs. Height, 5 ft. 10 in.
1878
—Cockey Woods, Boston .... KO 5
1879
—Dan Dwyer, Boston .... KO 3
—Tommy Chandler, Boston .... W 4
—Jack (Patsy) Hogan, Boston .... W 4
1880
Feb. —Mike Donovan, Boston .... ND 3
Apr. 6—Joe Goss, Boston .... W 3
June 28—George Rooke, Boston........... KO 2
Dec. —John Donaldson, Cincinnati ...... KO 4
Dec. 24—John Donaldson, Cincinnati ...... KO 10
1881
Jan. 3—Jack Stewart, Boston .... KO 2
Mar. 31—Steve Taylor, New York .... KO 2
May 16—John Flood, New York .... KO 8
July 11—Fred Crossly, Philadelphia .... KO 1
July —Dan McCarty, Philadelphia .... KO 1
Sept. 14—James Dalton, Chicago .... KO 4
Sept. 27—Jack Burns, Chicago .... KO 1
1882
Feb. 7—Paddy Ryan, Mississippi City ..... KO 9
(Won Bareknuckle World Heavyweight Title)
Mar. 27—Jack Douglas, New York .... KO 3
Apr. 20—John McDermott, Rochester ...... KO 3
July 4—Jimmy Elliott, Brooklyn .... KO 3
July 17—Joe (Tug) Wilson, New York ...... W 4
1883
May 14—Charley Mitchell, New York ...... KO 3
Aug. 6—Herbert Slade, New York .... KO 3
Oct. 17—James McCoy, McKeesport, PA ... KO 1
Nov. 3—Jim Miles, East St. Louis .... KO 1
Nov. 25—Morris Hefey, St. Paul .... KO 1
Dec. 4—Mike Sheehan, Davenport........ KO 1
1884
Jan. 14—Fred Robinson, Butte .... KO 2
Mar. 6—George Robinson, San Francisco ... W 4
Apr. 10—Al Marks, Galveston............. KO 1
Apr. 28—William Fleming, Memphis ...... KO 1
Apr. 29—Dan Henry, Hot Springs .... KO 1
May 2—Enos Phillips, Nashville .... KO 4
Nov. 10—John Laflin, New York .... KO 3
Nov. 17—Alf Greenfield, New York ...... KO 2

1885
Jan. 12—Alf Greenfield, Boston .... W 4
Jan. 19—Paddy Ryan, New York .... KO 1
June 13—Jack Burke, Chicago .... W 5
Aug. 29—Dominick McCaffrey, Cincinnati .. W 6
(Won Queensberry World Heavyweight Title)
1886
Sept. 18—Frank Herald, Alleghany, PA .... KO 1
Nov. 13—Paddy Ryan, San Francisco ..... KO 3
Dec. 28—Duncan McDonald Denver .... D 4
1887
Jan. 18—Patsy Cardiff, Minneapolis .... D 6
1888
Mar. 10—Charley Mitchell, Chantilly, France . D 39
(Retained Bareknuckle World Heavyweight Title)
1889
July 8—Jake Kilrain, Richburg, MS ..... KO 75
(Retained Bareknuckle World Heavyweight Title)
1892
Sept. 7—James J. Corbett, New Orleans . KO by 21
(Lost Queensberry World Heavyweight Title)
1896
Aug. 31—Tom Sharkey, New York........ND 3
1905
Mar. 1—Jack McCormick, Grand Rapids .. KO 2

TB	KO	WD	WF	D	LD	LF	KO BY	ND	NC
48	34	8	0	3	0	0	1	2	0

GENE TUNNEY
(James Joseph Tunney)
(Fighting Marine)
Born, May 25, 1897, New York City. Weight, 190 lbs. Height 6 ft. ½ in. Managed by Sammy Kelly, Billy Roche, Frank (Doc) Bagley and Billy Gibson.
1915
July 2—Bobby Dawson, New York ...... KO 7
Dec. 15—Young Sharkey, New York ...... KO 6
Dec. 29—Sailor Wolfe, New York .... KO 2
1916
—Billy Rowe, New York ....ND 6
—George Lahey, New York ...... ND 6
—Young Guarini, New York ...... WF 3
—George Lahey, New York ...... KO 3
1917
Feb. 9—Victor Dahl, New York ....ND 10
Oct. 2—K.O. Jaffe, New York ....ND 10
Dec. 21—Young Joe Borrell, New York .... KO 2
1918
Jan. 15—Hughey Weir, New York ...... KO 2
July 8—Young Guarini, Jersey City ...... KO 1
May 2—Enlisted in U.S. Marine Corps.
Dec. —Tommy Gavigan, Romorantin ...... D 12
Dec. —Howard Morrow, Romorantin .... KO 6
Dec. —Marchand, Paris .... KO 2
1919
Won AEF Light-Heavyweight Championship in France defeating K. O. Sullivan and Ted Jamieson in final rounds after defeating 20 opponents in elimination series, staged throughout France. Also defeated AEF Heavyweight Champion, Bob Martin, in special 4-round bout.

Nov. 14—Dan Dowd, Bayonne, NJ ....ND 8
Dec. 15—Bob Pierce, Jersey City .... KO 2
1920
Jan. 1—Whitey Allen, Jersey City .... KO 2
Jan. 10—Bud Nelson, Bayonne .... KO 1
Feb. 4—K. O. Sullivan, Newark .... KO 1
Jan. 26—Jim Monahan, Jersey City ...... KO 1
Mar. 4—Ed Kinley, Jersey City.......... KO 5
Apr. 5—Al Roberts, Newark............ KO 7
June 7—Jeff Madden, Jersey City ...... KO 2
June 28—Ole Anderson, Jersey City ...... KO 3
Oct. 7—Paul Sampson, Paterson .... ND 8
Oct. 22—Sgt. Ray Smith, Camden .... KO 2
Nov. 25—Leo Houck, Philadelphia ....ND 6
Dec. 7—Leo Houck, Jersey City .... W 10
1921
June 30—Young Ambrose, New York ...... KO 1
July 2—Soldier Jones, Jersey City ...... KO 7
Aug. 16—Martin Burke, New York .... W 10
Aug. 29—Eddie Joseph, New York .... W 12
Sept. 15—Herbert Crossley, New York ..... KO 7
Oct. 15—Jack Burke, New York .... KO 2
Nov. 22—Wolf Larsen, New York .... KO 7
Dec. 22—Eddie O'Hare, New York .... KO 6
1922
Jan. 13—Battling Levinsky, New York ..... W 12
(Won American Light-Heavyweight Title)
Feb. 11—Jack Clifford, New York .... KO 6
Feb. 14—Whitey Wenzel, Philadelphia .... KO 4
Mar. 3—Fay Keiser, Grand Rapids........ND 10
Apr. 10—Jack Burke, Pittsburgh .... KO 9
May 23—Harry Greb, New York .... L 15
(Lost American Light-Heavyweight Title)
July 7—Fay Keiser, Rockaway .... W 12
Aug. 4—Ray Thompson, Long Branch .... KO 3
Aug. 17—Charlie Weinert, Newark ....ND 12
Aug. 24—Tommy Loughran, Philadelphia .. ND 8
Oct. 25—Chuck Wiggins, Boston .... W 10
Nov. 3—Jack Hanlon, New York .... KO 1
Nov. 29—Charlie Weinert, New York ..... KO 4
1923
Jan. 29—Jack Renault, Philadelphia ....NC 4
Feb. 3—Chuck Wiggins, New York ...... W 12
Feb. 23—Harry Greb, New York .... W 15
(Regained American Light-Heavyweight Title)
May 7—Jack Clifford, Detroit........... KO 8
May 23—Jimmy Delaney, Chicago.........ND 10
July 31—Dan O'Dowd, Long Island ..... W 12
Dec. 10—Harry Greb, New York .... W 15
(American Light-Heavyweight Title)
1924
Jan. 15—Harry Foley, Grand Rapids.......ND 10
Jan. 24—Ray Thompson, Lakeworth, FL .. KO 2
Feb. 15—Martin Burke, New Orleans ..... W 15
Mar. 17—Jimmy Delaney, St. Paul ....ND 10
June 26—Erminio Spalla, New York ...... KO 7
July 24—Georges Carpentier, New York ... KO 15
Aug. 18—Joe Lohman, Columbus, OH ...... W 8
Sept. 17—Harry Greb, Cleveland ....ND 10
Oct. 27—Harry Foley, Memphis .... KO 2
Nov. 10—Buddy McHale, Memphis .... KO 2
Dec. 8—Jeff Smith, New Orleans ....ND 15
1925
Mar. 27—Harry Greb, St. Paul .... ND 10

June   5—Tommy Gibbons, New York ..... KO 12
July   3—Italian Jack Herman, Kansas City. KO 2
Sept.   25—Bartley Madden, Minneapolis .... KO 3
Nov.   18—Johnny Risko, Cleveland .... W 12
1926
Sept.   23—Jack Dempsey, Philadelphia ...... W 10
(Won World Heavyweight Title)
1927
Sept.   22—Jack Dempsey, Chicago .... W 10
(Retained World Heavyweight Title)
Referee: Dave Barry; receipts, $2,658,660; Tunney's share $990,000; Dempsey's share $447,500. Attendance: 104,943.
1928
July   26—Tom Heeney, New York .... KO 11
(Retained World Heavyweight Title)
1941
Appointed Commander U.S. Naval Aviation and Commissioned Chief Recreation Officer in U.S. Navy.

TB	KO	WD	WF	D	LD	LF	KO BY	ND	NC
76	41	14	1	1	1	0	0	17	1

Died Nov. 7, 1978, in Greenwich, CT.
Elected to Boxing Hall of Fame 1955.

RANDY TURPIN
(Randolph Adolphus Turpin)
Born, Leamington, England, June 7, 1928. Height 5 ft. 10 in. Middle- and light-heavyweight. Managed by George Middleton.
Won five British amateur titles.
1946
Sept.   17—Gordon Griffiths, London .... KO 1
Nov.   19—Des Jones, London .... W 6
Dec.   26—Bill Blything, Birmingham ...... KO 1
1947
Jan.   14—Jimmy Davis, London .... KO 4
Jan.   24—Dai James, Birmingham .... KO 3
Feb.   18—Johnny Best, London .... KO 1
Mar.   18—Bert Hyland, London .... KO 1
Apr.   1—Frank Dolan, London .... KO 2
Apr.   15—Tommy Davies, London .... KO 2
Apr.   28—Bert Saunders, Walthamstow ... W 6
May   12—Ron Cooper, Oxford .... KO 4
May   27—Jury VII, London.............. W 6
June   3—Mark Hart, London .... W 6
June   23—Leon Foquet, Coventry .... KO 1
Sept.   8—Jimmy Ingle, Coventry .... KO 3
Oct.   20—Mark Hart, London .... D 6
1948
Jan.   26—Freddie Price, Coventry .... KO 1
Feb.   17—Gerry McCready, London ...... KO 1
Mar.   16—Vince Hawkins, London .... W 8
Apr.   26—Albert Finch, London .... L 8
June   28—Alby Hollister, Birmingham ..... W 8
Sept.   21—Jean Stock, London .... KO by 5
1949
Feb.   7—Jackie Jones, Coventry .... KO 5
Feb.   21—Doug Miller, London .... W 8
Mar.   25—Mickey Laurent, Manchester ..... KO 3

May   3—Bill Poli, London .... WF 4
June   20—Cyrille Delannoit, Birmingham ... KO 8
Aug.   22—Jean Wanes, Manchester .... KO 3
Sept.   19—Roy Wouters, Coventry .... KO 5
Nov.   15—Pete Mead, London .... KO 4
1950
Jan.   31—Gilbert Stock, London .... W 8
Mar.   6—Richard Armah, London .... KO 6
Apr.   24—Gus Degouve, Nottingham ...... W 8
Sept.   5—Eli Elandon, London .... KO 2
Oct.   17—Albert Finch, London .... KO 5
(Won British Middleweight Title)
Nov.   13—Jose Alamo, Abergavenny ...... KO 2
Dec.   12—Tommy Yarosz, London .... WF 8
1951
Jan.   22—Eduardo Lopez, Birmingham .... KO 1
Feb.   27—Luc van Dam, London .... KO 1
(Won vacant European Middleweight Title)
Mar.   19—Jean Stock, Leicester .... KO 5
Apr.   16—Billy Brown, Birmingham ...... KO 2
May   7—Jan de Bruin, Coventry .... KO 6
June   5—Jackie Keough, London .... KO 7
July   10—Ray Robinson, London .... W 15
(Won World Middleweight Title)
Sept.   12—Ray Robinson, New York ..... KO by 10
(Lost World Middleweight Title)
1952
Feb.   12—Alex Buxton, London .... KO 7
Apr.   22—Jacques Hairabedian, London .... KO 3
June   10—Don Cockell, London .... KO 11
(Won British and Empire Light-Heavyweight Title)
Oct.   21—George Angelo, London .... W 15
(Won vacant British Empire Middleweight Title)
1953
Jan.   19—Victor d'Haes, Birmingham ..... KO 6
Feb.   16—Duggie Miller, Leicester .... W 10
Mar.   17—Walter Cartier, London .... W Dis. 2
June   9—Charley Humez, London .... W 15
(Retained European Middleweight Title)
Oct.   21—Bobo Olson, New York .... L 15
(For vacant World Middleweight Title)
1954
Mar.   30—Olle Bengtsson, London .... W 10
May   2—Tiberio Mitri, Rome .... KO by 1
(Lost European Middleweight Title)
1955
Feb.   15—Ray Schmidt, Birmingham ...... WF 8
Mar.   8—Jose Gonzales, London .... KO 7
Apr.   26—Alex Buxton, London .... KO 2
(British and Empire Light-Heavyweight Titles)
Sept.   19—Ed Polly Smith, Birmingham ..... W 10
Oct.   18—Gordon Wallace, London ...... KO by 4
1956
Apr.   17—Alessandro D'Ottavio, Birmingham KO 6
June   18—Jacques Bro, Birmingham .... KO 5
Sept.   21—Hans Stretz, Hamburg .... L 10
Nov.   26—Alex Buxton, Leicester .... KO 5
(Won vacant British Light-Heavyweight Title)
1957
June   11—Arthur Howard, Leicester .... W 15
(Retained British Light-Heavyweight Title)
Sept.   17—Ahmed Boulgroune, London ..... KO 9
Oct.   28—Sergio Burchi, Birmingham...... KO 2
Nov.   25—Uwe Janssen, Leicester .... KO 8

1958
Feb.   11—Wim Snoek, Birmingham .... W 10
Apr.   21—Eddie Wright, Leicester .... KO 7
July   22—Redvers Sangoe, Oswestry ...... KO 4
Sept.   9—Yolande Pompey, Birmingham . KO by 2
1963
Mar.   18—Eddie Marcano, Wisbech .... KO 6
1964
Aug.   22—Charles Seguna, Malta.......... KO 2

TB	KO	WD	WF	D	LD	LF	KO BY	ND	NC
75	45	17	4	1	3	0	5	0	0

Died May 17, 1966, in Warwickshire, England.

JERSEY JOE WALCOTT
(Arnold Raymond Cream)
Born, January 31, 1914, Merchantville, NJ. Weight, 194 lbs. Height 6 ft. Managed by Felix Bocchicchio. Previous record unavailable.
1930
Sept.   9—Cowboy Wallace, Vineland, NJ ... KO 1
1933
—Bob Norris, Camden .... KO 1
—Henry Taylor, Camden .... KO 1
1934
—Pat Roland, Camden .... KO 5
—Louis LaPage, Camden .... KO 3
—Al King, Camden.............. KO 4
1935
—Roxie Allen, Camden .... KO 7
—Al Lang, Camden .... KO 1
Sept.   —Lew Alva, Camden .... KO 3
1936
Jan.   21—Al Ettore, Camden........... KO by 8
Mar.   16—Willie Reddish, Philadelphia ... W 10
June   22—Phil Johnson, Philadelphia ..... KO 3
June   —Joe Colucci, Camden .... KO 4
July   1—Billy Ketchell, Camden .... D 10
—Young Carmen Passarella, Camden W 8
—Billy Ketchell, Camden .... W 10
Sept.   1—Billy Ketchell, Pensauken, NJ ..... L 10
1937
May   22—Tiger Jack Fox, New York .... KO by 8
Sept.   3—Joe Lipps, Atlantic City........ KO 2
Sept.   5—Elmer Ray, New York .... KO 3
Oct.   9—George Brothers, New York ..... L 8
1938
Jan.   10—Freddie Fiducia, Philadelphia ..... W 8
Mar.   28—Art Sykes, Philadelphia ...... KO 4
Apr.   12—Lorenzo Pack, Camden .... KO 4
May   10—Tiger Jack Fox, Camden ...... L 10
June   14—Roy Lazer, Fairview, NJ .... L 8
Dec.   13—Bob Tow, Camden .... W 8
1939
Aug.   14—Al Boros, Newark .... W 8
Nov.   18—Curtis Sheppard, New York ..... W 8
1940
Jan.   19—Tiger Red Lewis, Philadelphia ... KO 6
Feb.   12—Abe Simon, Newark .... KO by 6
1941
June   27—Columbus Gant, Memphis .... KO 3

1944
June 7—Felix Del Paoli, Batesville, NJ .... W 8
June 28—Ellis Singleton, Batesville, NJ .... KO 3
1945
Jan. 11—Jackie Saunders, Camden ...... KO 2
Jan. 25—Johnny Allen, Camden .... L 8
Feb. 22—Austin Johnson, Camden .... W 6
Mar. 15—Johnny Allen, Camden .... W 8
Aug. 2—Joe Baksi, Camden .... W 10
Sept. 20—Johnny Denson, Camden .... KO 2
Oct. 23—Steve Dudas, Patterson .... KO 5
Nov. 12—Lee Q. Murray, Baltimore ..... W Dis. 9
Dec. 10—Curtis Sheppard, Baltimore ...... KO 10
1946
Jan. 30—Johnny Allen, Camden .... KO 3
Feb. 25—Jimmy Bivins, Cleveland .... W 10
Mar. 20—Al Blake, Camden .... KO 4
May 24—Lee Oma, New York .... W 10
Aug. 16—Tommy Gomez, New York ...... KO 3
Aug. 28—Joey Maxim, Camden .... L 10
Nov. 15—Elmer Ray, New York .... L 10
1947
Jan. 6—Joey Maxim, Philadelphia .... W 10
Mar. 4—Elmer Ray, Miami .... W 10
June 23—Joey Maxim, Los Angeles ..... W 10
Dec. 5—Joe Louis, New York .... L 15
(For World Heavyweight Championship)
1948
Mar. 10—Austin Johnson, Chicago .... Exh. 4
June 25—Joe Louis, New York .... KO by 11
(World Heavyweight Title Bout)
Dec. 14—Earl Griffin, Camden .... Exh. 4
1949
June 22—Ezzard Charles, Chicago .... L 15
(For NBA Heavyweight Title)
Aug. 14—Olle Tandberg, Stockholm ...... KO 5
1950
Feb. 8—Harold Johnson, Philadelphia .... KO 3
Mar. 3—Omelio Agramonte, New York ... KO 7
Mar. 13—Johnny Shkor, Philadelphia ..... KO 1
May 28—Hein Ten Hoff, Mannhein .... W 10
Nov. 24—Rex Layne, New York .... L 10
1951
Mar. 7—Ezzard Charles, Detroit .... L 15
(For World Heavyweight Title)
July 18—Ezzard Charles, Pittsburgh ...... KO 7
(Won World Heavyweight Title)
1952
Jan. 10—Jackie Burke, New Bedford ...... Exh. 5
Jan. 12—Jackie Burke, Lewiston .... Exh. 5
Jan. 21—Jackie Burke, Holyoke .... Exh. 5
Jan. 23—Jackie Burke, Portland .... Exh. 4
Jan. 24—Jackie Burke, St. Johns, NB .... Exh. 5
Jan. 25—Jackie Burke, Bangor .... Exh. 5
Jan. 26—Jackie Burke, Watery, ME ...... Exh. 5
Jan. 29—Jackie Burke, Lewistown, PA .... Exh. 5
Feb. 1—Jackie Burke, Orlando .... Exh. 5
June 5—Ezzard Charles, Philadelphia ..... W 15
(Retained World Heavyweight Title)
Sept. 23—Rocky Marciano, Philadelphia . KO by 13
(Lost World Heavyweight Title)
1953
May 15—Rocky Marciano, Chicago ..... KO by 1
(For World Heavyweight Title)

Retired to become a parole officer and a referee. Elected to Boxing Hall of Fame 1969.

TB	KO	WD	WF	D	LD	LF	KO BY	ND	NC
67	30	18	1	1	11	0	6	0	0

CLEVELAND WILLIAMS
Houston, Texas, Heavyweight
Born, June 30, 1933, Griffin, GA
1951
Dec. 11—Lee Hunt, Tampa .... KO 2
1952
Feb. 4—Paul Banks, New Orleans ...... KO 1
Feb. 26—Rudolph Wood, Ft. Hesterly ..... KO 2
Feb. 29—Roosevelt Holmes, New Orleans ... W 6
Mar. 28—Ray Banks, New Orleans .... KO 1
Apr. 15—Johnny Fowler, Tampa .... KO 5
May 28—Ray Brown, Miami .... KO 3
June 10—Paul Favorite, Tampa .... KO 4
June 17—Harry Turner, Tampa .... KO 1
June 21—Eddie Joe Williams, Daytona Beach KO 1
July 8—Jimmy Felton, Miami Beach ..... KO 3
July 22—Lee Raymond, Miami Beach ..... KO 5
July 25—Sam Harold, Macon, GA .... KO 4
Aug. 12—Candy McDaniels, Miami Beach .. KO 2
Sept. 2—Baby Booze, Tampa .... KO 1
Sept. 12—Roosevelt Holmes, New Orleans .. KO 1
Sept. 16—Art Henri, Miami Beach .... KO 8
Sept. 23—Joe McFadden, Philadelphia ..... KO 6
Oct. 3—Johnny Hollins, New Orleans .... KO 1
Nov. 25—Claude Rolfe, Tampa .... KO 9
Dec. 8—Graveyard Walters, Daytona Beach KO 2
1953
Jan. 13—Abie Gibson, Tampa .... KO 1
Mar. 4—Ponce DeLeon, Miami .... W 8
Mar. 12—Terry O'Connor, Minneapolis .... KO 3
Mar. 24—Ponce DeLeon, Tampa .... KO 2
May 12—Omelio Agramonte, Tampa, ... W 10
Sept. 1—Keene Simmons, Tampa .... W 10
Sept. 24—Sonny Jones, New York .... L 4
Oct. 1—Claude Rolfe, Charlotte .... KO 3
Oct. 20—Lloyd Wills, Miami Beach .... KO 2
1954
Mar. 9—Jimmy Walls, Tampa .... KO 1
June 8—Sonny Jones, Tampa .... KO 7
June 22—Bob Satterfield, Miami Beach .. KO by 3
1955
In U.S. Army.
1956
Aug. 6—John Hollins, Austin .... KO 3
1957
June 11—Johnny Mason, Houston .... KO 1
July 15—J. D. Marshall, Tyler .... KO 2
July 23—Cliff Gray, Houston .... KO 1
Sept. 17—John Holman, Houston .... KO 7
Oct. 15—John Holman, Houston .... KO 7
Dec. 3—Frankie Daniels, Miami Beach .... W 10
1958
Feb. 4—Gene White, Houston .... KO 1
Mar. 25—Dick Richardson, London .... W. Dis. 4
June 3—Frankie Daniels, Houston .... W 10

Dec. 9—Howie Turner, Houston .... W 10
1959
Jan. 13—Ollie Wilson, Houston .... KO 3
Apr. 15—Sonny Liston, Miami Beach ... KO by 3
May 26—Ernie Cab, Houston .... KO 3
Oct. 14—Curley Lee, Houston .... KO 10
1960
Mar. 21—Sonny Liston, Houston .... KO by 2
Oct. 24—Ben Marshall, Dallas .... KO 2
Nov. 1—George Moore, Houston .... KO 4
Dec. 7—Johnny Hayden, Miami Beach ... KO 2
1961
Feb. 7—Wayne Bethea, Houston .... W 10
Mar. 16—Alex Miteff, Houston .... KO 5
Dec. 19—Jim Wiley, Houston .... KO 1
1962
Apr. 3—Ernie Terrell, Houston .... KO 7
May 15—Alonzo Johnson, Houston ...... KO 1
July 10—Eddie Machen, Houston .... D 10
Oct. 23—Dave Bailey, Houston .... KO 5
1963
Mar. 9—Billy Daniels, Miami Beach ...... W 10
Apr. 2—Young Jack Johnson, Houston ... KO 10
Apr. 13—Ernie Terrell, Philadelphia ...... L 10
Aug. 13—Kirk Barrow, Houston .... KO 3
Oct. 8—Roger Rischer, Houston .... KO 3
1964
Apr. 7—Tommy Fields, Houston .... W 10
July 21—Sonny Banks, Houston .... KO 6
Sept. 30—Billy Daniels, Houston .... W 10
1965
(Inactive)
1966
Feb. 8—Ben Black, Houston .... KO 1
Mar. 22—Mel Turnbow, Houston .... W 10
Apr. 18—Sonny Moore, Houston .... W 10
June 28—Tod Herring, Houston .... KO 3
Nov. 14—Cassius Clay, Houston .... KO by 3
(For World Heavyweight Title)
1967
(Retired)
1968
May 21—Roy Crear, Houston .... KO 1
June 11—Mike Bruce, Houston .... KO 1
June 25—Leslie Bordon, Houston .... KO 1
Aug. 6—Jean-Claude Roy, Houston ..... W 10
Oct. 7—Moses Harrell, Tampa .... KO 7
Nov. 21—Bob Cleroux, Montreal .... L 10
1969
Mar. 18—Charley Polite, Houston ...... W 10
May 20—Al Jones, Miami Beach .... KO by 8
Sept. 14—Mac Foster, Fresno .... KO by 5
Nov. 18—Mac Foster, Houston .... KO by 3
Dec. 9—Leroy Caldwell, Orlando ...... KO 10
1970
Apr. 14—Eddie Brooks, Milwaukee ...... KO 1
May 26—Roberto Davila, Milwaukee ..... W 10
Oct. 21—Al Lewis, Detroit .... KO by 4
1971
Apr. 28—Ted Gullick, Cleveland .... W 10
Sept. 22—Jack O'Halloran, Houston .... L 10
Nov. 17—George Chuvalo, Houston .... L 10
1972
May 11—Terry Daniels, Dallas .... W 12

July   11—Bob Mashburn, Denver . . . . KO 9
Oct.   29—Roberto Davila, Denver . . . . W 10

IKE WILLIAMS

Born, Aug. 2, 1923. Brunswick, GA. Light-weight. Managed by Connie McCarthy and Frankie Palermo. Height, 5 ft. 9½ in. Started in 1938 as an amateur and won several intercity titles.

1940
Mar.   15—Carmine Fatta, New Brunswick . . . . W 4
Mar.   29—Billy George, New Brunswick . . . . . W 4
Apr.   1—Patsy Gall, Hazleton, PA . . . . D 6
May   10—Billy Hildebrand, Morristown . . . . . . L 6
June   17—Billy Hildebrand, Mt. Freedom, N J.KO 6
July   19—Joe Romero, Mt. Freedom . . . . . . KO 2
Sept.   9—Pete Kelly, Trenton . . . . KO 2
Nov.   11—Tony Maglione, Trenton . . . . L 8

1941
Jan.   6—Tommy Fontana, Trenton . . . . W 8
Feb.   19—Carl Zullo, Perth Amboy . . . . KO 2
Mar.   5—Joey Zodda, Perth Amboy . . . . L 6
Mar.   19—Joe Genovese, Perth Amboy . . . . . W 5
Apr.   9—Johnny Rudolph, Perth Amboy . . . . W 6
Apr.   14—Hughie Civatte, Trenton . . . . KO 3
Oct.   1—Freddie Archer, Perth Amboy . . . . . L 6
Oct.   27—Benny Williams, Newark . . . . D 6
Nov.   3—Vince De'Lia, Newark . . . . W 6
Dec.   16—Eddie Dowl, Perth Amboy . . . . W 6

1942
Mar.   26—Pedro Firpo, Atlantic City . . . . W 8
Apr.   10—Angelo Panatellas, Atlantic City . . KO 5
Apr.   24—Willie Roache, Perth Amboy . . . . . W 8
May   7—Abie Kaufman, Atlantic City . . . . . W 8
June   29—Ivan Christie, Newark . . . . KO 5
July   29—Angelo Maglione, Trenton . . . . . . KO 3
Sept.   10—Charley Davis, Elizabeth . . . . W 8
Oct.   20—Eugene Burton, White Plains . . . . KO 4
Dec.   7—Bob Gunther, Trenton . . . . W 8
Dec.   21—Sammy Daniels, Baltimore . . . . W 6
        —Ruby Garcia, Atlantic City . . . . W 6

1943
Jan.   29—Jerry Moore, New York . . . . W 6
Feb.   22—Sammy Daniels, Philadelphia . . . . KO 2
Feb.   23—Bob McQuillan, Cleveland . . . . KO 3
Mar.   8—Bill Speary, Philadelphia . . . . KO 2
Apr.   2—Rudy Griscombe, New York . . . . . KO 3
Apr.   5—Ruby Garcia, Philadelphia . . . . W 8
Apr.   21—Joey Genovese, Cleveland . . . . KO 4
May   7—Lefty La Chance, Boston . . . . W 8
May   14—Ray Brown, Philadelphia . . . . W 10
July   19—Jimmy Hatcher, Philadelphia . . . . KO 6
Aug.   24—Tommy Jessup, Hartford . . . . KO 5
Aug.   31—Johnny Bellus, Hartford . . . . W 10
Sept.   13—Jerry Moore, West Springfield, MA W 10
Oct.   1—Lefty LaChance, Boston . . . . KO 4
Oct.   22—Sgt. Ed Perry, New Orleans . . . . . KO 2
Oct.   29—Gene Johnson, New Orleans . . . . . . W 10
Nov.   8—Johnny Hutchinson, Philadelphia . . KO 3
Dec.   13—Mayon Padio, Philadelphia . . . . . . W 10

1944
Jan.   25—Bob Montgomery, Philadelphia . KO by 12
Feb.   28—Ellis Phillips, Philadelphia . . . . . . KO 1

Mar.   13—Leo Francis, Trenton . . . . W 8
Mar.   27—Joey Peralta, Philadelphia . . . . . . KO 9
Apr.   10—Leroy Saunders, Holyoke . . . . KO 5
Apr.   18—Mike Delia, Philadelphia . . . . KO 1
May   16—Luther Slugger White, Philadelphia W 10
June   7—Sammy Angott, Philadelphia . . . . . W 10
June   23—Cleo Shans, New York . . . . KO 10
July   10—Joey Pirrone, Philadelphia . . . . . . KO 1
July   20—Julie Kogon, New York . . . . W 10
Aug.   29—Jimmy Hatcher, Washington, DC . . W 10
Sept.   6—Sammy Angott, Philadelphia . . . . . W 10
Sept.   19—Freddie Dawson, Philadelphia . . . KO 4
Oct.   18—Johnny Green, Buffalo . . . . KO 2
Nov.   2—Ruby Garcia, Baltimore . . . . KO 7
Nov.   13—Willie Joyce, Philadelphia . . . . L 10
Dec.   5—Lulu Costantino, Cleveland . . . . . . W 10
Dec.   11—Dave Castilloux, Buffalo . . . . . . KO 5

1945
Jan.   8—Willie Joyce, Philadelphia . . . . W 12
Jan.   22—Maxie Berger, Philadelphia . . . . . KO 4
Mar.   2—Willie Joyce, New York . . . . L 12
Mar.   26—Dorsey Lay, Philadelphia . . . . . . KO 3
Apr.   18—Juan Zurita, Mexico City . . . . KO 2
        (NBA Lightweight Championship)
June   8—Willie Joyce, New York . . . . L 10
Aug.   14—Charley Smith, Union City . . . . . . W 10
Aug.   28—Gene Burton, Philadelphia . . . . . . W 10
Sept.   7—Nick Moran, New York . . . . W 10
Sept.   19—Sammy Angott, Pittsburgh . . . . KO by 6
Nov.   26—Wesley Mouzon, Philadelphia . . . . . D 10

1946
Jan.   8—Charley Smith, Trenton . . . . W 10
Jan.   20—Johnny Bratton, New Orleans . . . . W 10
Jan.   28—Freddie Dawson, Philadelphia . . . . D 10
Feb.   14—Cleo Shans, Orange . . . . W 10
Feb.   22—Ace Miller, Detroit . . . . W 10
Mar.   11—Eddie Giosa, Philadelphia . . . . . KO 4
Apr.   8—Eddie Giosa, Philadelphia . . . . . . KO 1
Apr.   30—Enrique Bolanos, Los Angeles . . KO 8
June   12—Bobby Ruffin, Brooklyn . . . . KO 5
Aug.   6—Ivan Christie, Norwalk . . . . KO 2
Sept.   4—Ronnie James, Cardiff, Wales . . . KO 9
        (NBA Title Bout)

1947
Jan.   27—Gene Burton, Chicago . . . . L 10
Apr.   14—Frankie Conti, Allentown . . . . . . KO 7
Apr.   25—Willie Russell, Columbus . . . . W 10
May   9—Ralph Zanelli, Boston . . . . W 10
May   26—Juste Fontaine, Philadelphia . . . . KO 4
June   20—Tippy Larkin, New York . . . . KO 4
Aug.   4—Bob Montgomery, Philadelphia . . KO 6
        (Won World Lightweight Title)
Sept.   29—Doll Rafferty, Philadelphia . . . . . KO 4
Oct.   10—Talmadge Bussey, Detroit . . . . . . KO 9
Dec.   12—Tony Pellone, New York . . . . W 10

1948
Jan.   13—Doug Carter, Camden . . . . W 10
Jan.   26—Freddie Dawson, Philadelphia . . . . W 10
Feb.   9—Livio Minelli, Philadephia . . . . W 10
Feb.   27—Kid Gavilan, New York . . . . W 10
May   1—Rudy Cruz, Oakland . . . . W 10
May   25—Enrique Bolanos, Los Angeles . . . . W 15
        (Retained World Lightweight Title)
July   12—Beau Jack, Philadelphia . . . . KO 6

(Retained World Lightweight Title)
Sept.   23—Jesse Flores, New York . . . . KO 10
        (Retained World Lightweight Title)
Nov.   8—Buddy Garcia, Philadelphia . . . . . KO 1
Nov.   18—Billy Nixon, Philadelphia . . . . KO 4

1949
Jan.   17—Johnny Bratton, Philadelphia . . . . W 10
Jan.   28—Kid Gavilan, New York . . . . L 10
Apr.   1—Kid Gavilan, New York . . . . L 10
Apr.   22—Vince Turpin, Cleveland . . . . KO 6
June   21—Irvin Steen, Los Angeles . . . . W 10
July   21—Enrique Bolanos, Los Angeles . . . KO 4
Aug.   3—Benny Walker, Oakland . . . . W 10
Sept.   2—Arthur King, Chicago . . . . .Exh. 4
Sept.   10—Freddie Dawson, Philadelphia . . . . W 10
Oct.   24—Al Mobley, Trenton . . . . W 10
Nov.   14—Jean Walzack, Philadelphia . . . . . . W 10
Dec.   5—Freddie Dawson, Philadelphia . . . . W 15
        (Retained World Lightweight Title)
Dec.   20—Midget Taylor, Phoenixville, PA . . Exh. 6

1950
Jan.   20—Johnny Bratton, Chicago . . . . KO 8
Feb.   8—Sonny Boy West, New York . . . . . KO 8
Feb.   27—John L. Davis, Seattle . . . . W 10
June   2—Lester Felton, Detroit . . . . W 10
July   12—George Costner, Philadelphia . . . . . L 10
Aug.   7—Charley Salas, Washington, DC . . . L 10
Sept.   26—Charley Salas, Washington, DC . . . W 10
Oct.   2—Joe Miceli, Milwaukee . . . . L 10
Nov.   23—Joe Miceli, Milwaukee . . . . W 10
Dec.   12—Dave Marsh, Akron . . . . KO 9
Dec.   18—Rudy Cruz, Philadelphia . . . . W 10

1951
Jan.   5—Jose Gatica, New York . . . . KO 1
Jan.   22—Ralph Zanelli, Providence . . . . . . KO 5
Jan.   31—Vic Cardell, Detroit . . . . KO 9
Feb.   19—Joe Miceli, Philadelphia . . . . L 10
Mar.   5—Beau Jack, Providence . . . . W 10
Apr.   11—Fitzie Pruden, Chicago . . . . W 10
May   25—James Carter, New York . . . . . KO by 14
        (Lost World Lightweight Title)
Aug.   2—Don Williams, Worcester . . . . L 10
Sept.   10—Gil Turner, Philadelphia . . . . . KO by 10

1952
Mar.   17—Johnny Cunningham, Baltimore . . KO 5
Mar.   26—Chuck Davey, Chicago . . . . KO by 5
Nov.   24—Pat Manzi, Syracuse . . . . KO 7

1953
Jan.   12—Carmen Basilio, Syracuse . . . . L 10
Mar.   9—Claude Hammond, Trenton . . . . . . W 10
Mar.   28—Vic Cardell, Philadelphia . . . . W 16
Apr.   20—Billy Andy, Trenton . . . . W 10
May   18—Billy Andy, Erie, PA . . . . W 10
June   8—Georgie Johnson, Trenton . . . . . KO by 8
Sept.   17—Dom Zimbardo, Newark . . . . KO 2
Nov.   9—Jed Black, Ft. Wayne . . . . L 10

1954
July   2—Rafael Castre, Havana . . . . L 10

1955
Apr.   9—Beau Jack, Augusta . . . . D 10
Aug.   12—Beau Jack, Augusta . . . . KO 9

TB	KO	WD	WF	D	LD	LF	KO BY	ND	NC
153	60	64	0	5	18	0	6	0	0

JESS WILLARD
(Pottawatomie Giant)

Born, December 29, 1881, Pottawatomie County, KS. Weight, 250 lbs. Height, 6 ft. 6¼ in. Managed by Tom Jones.

1911
Feb.   15—Louis Fink, Sapulpa, OK . . . . LF 10
Mar.   7—Ed Burke, El Reno, OK . . . . KO 3
Mar.   28—Louis Fink, Oklahoma City . . . . . . KO 3
Apr.   14—Al Mendeno, Oklahoma City . . . . . KO 4
Apr.   29—Joe Cavanaugh, Oklahoma City . . . KO 11
June   8—Bill Shiller, Oklahoma City . . . . . . KO 4
July   4—Frank Lyons, Elk City, OK . . . . W 10
July   16—Mike Comiskey, Hammond, OK . . . W 10
Oct.·   11—Joe Cox, Springfield, MO . . . . KO by 5
(Willard claimed he was warned not to box and retired.)

1912
May   23—John Young, Fort Wayne, IN . . . . KO 6
June   29—Frank Bowers, St. Charles, IL . . . . KO 3
July   2—John Young, So. Chicago, IL . . . . KO 5
July   29—Arthur Pelkey, New York . . . . ND 10
Aug.   19—Luther McCarthy, New York . . . . . . ND 10
Dec.   2—Sailor White, Buffalo, New York . KO 1
Dec.   27—Soldier Kearns, New York . . . . . . KO 8

1913
Jan.   22—Frank Bauer, Ft. Wayne, IN . . . . . KO 5
Mar.   5—Jack Leon, Ft. Wayne, IN . . . . KO 4
May   20—Gunboat Smith, San Francisco . . . L 20
June   27—Charley Miller, San Francisco . . . . . . D 4
July   4—Al William, Reno, NV . . . . W 8
Aug.   22—Bull Young, Vernon, CA . . . . KO 11
        Died of broken neck after bout.
Nov.   17—George Rodel, Milwaukee . . . . ND 10
Nov.   24—Jack Reed, Ft. Wayne, IN . . . . . . KO 2
Dec.   3—Carl Morris, New York . . . . ND 10
Dec.   12—George Davis, Buffalo, New York . . . K 2
Dec.   29—George Rodel, New Haven . . . . . . KO 9

1914
Mar.   27—Tom MacMahon, Youngstown . . . . . . L 12
Apr.   13—Dan Daily, Buffalo . . . . KO 9
Apr   28—George Rodel, Atlanta . . . . KO 6

1915
Apr.   5—Jack Johnson, Havana . . . . KO 26
(Won World Heavyweight Championship)
Referee, Jack Welch. Scheduled for 45 rounds.

1916
Mar.   25—*Frank Moran, New York . . . . ND 10
Aug.   8—Soldier Kearns, Plattsburg . . . . . . Exh. 2
        *Title bout.
Sept.   12—Sailor Burke, Bridgeport . . . . Exh. 6

1918
July   4—Jim Golden, Ft. Riley, KS . . . . Exh. 10
July   18—Tim Logan, Chester, PA . . . . Exh. 10

1919
July   4—Jack Dempsey, Toledo . . . . KO by 3
(For heavyweight championship of the world, Willard received $100,000 Dempsey, $27,5000.)

1922
Exhibitions: Lom Kennedy, 2; Joe Bonds, 2; Scotty Messer, 2; Tom Barnson, 2; Frank Farmer, 3; Alden Schumacher, 3.

1923
May   12—Floyd Johnson, New York . . . . KO 11
July   12—Luis Firpo, Jersey City . . . . KO by 8

1926
—Jimmy O'Gatty, New York . . . . . . Exh. 3
Died in Los Angeles, December 15, 1968.

TB	KO	WD	WF	D	LD	LF	KO BY	ND	NC
35	20	3	0	1	2	1	3	5	0

AD (ADOLPH WOLGUST) WOLGAST
(Michigan Wildcat)

Born, Feb. 8, 1888, Cadillac, MI. Weight 122–126 lbs. Height, 5 ft. 4¼ in. Managed by Tom Jones.

1906
June   10—Kid Moore, Petoskey . . . . W 6
June   28—Young Nelson, Grand Rapids . . . . KO 3
July   12—Young Nelson, Grand Rapids . . . . . . L 4
Aug.   3—Young Kilrain, Grand Rapids . . . . W 4
Aug.   5—Young Detrick, Grand Rapids . . . . KO 2
Aug.   6—Kid Bond, Grand Rapids . . . . KO 4
Aug.   9—Ted Smith, Grand Rapids . . . . W 4
Sept.   3—Ed Smith, Petoskey . . . . KO 7
Sept.   15—Kid Cannon, Grand Rapids . . . . . . W 6
Sept.   29—Young Kilrain, Grand Rapids . . . . KO 5
Oct.   15—Young Mitchell, Grand Rapids . . . KO 3
Oct.   19—Young Kelly, Grand Rapids . . . . . . KO 3
Nov.   15—Johnny De Forest, Lansing . . . . . . KO 5

1907
Feb.   1—Gene McGovern, Milwaukee . . . . . . W 6
Feb.   12—Jack Nolan, Milwaukee . . . . D 6
Feb.   26—Young Kilrain, Fond du Lac . . . . KO 2
Mar.   12—Jack Nolan, Milwaukee . . . . W 6
Mar.   15—Buddy Glover, Milwaukee . . . . WF 6
Mar.   19—Buck Plotell, St. Joe, MO . . . . D 15
Mar.   29—Kid Brady, Milwaukee . . . . KO 1
Apr.   9—Jeff O'Connell, Milwaukee . . . . . . W 6
Apr.   13—Young Redmonds, Milwaukee . . . . . . D 6
Apr.   30—Tom Campbell, St. Joe, MO . . . . . . W 15
May   21—Buddy Glover, Fond du Lac . . . . KO 7
May   25—Kid Morris, Milwaukee . . . . KO 3
June   12—Percy Cove, Oshkosh . . . . D 8
June   28—Danny Goodman, Milwaukee . . . . KO 4
Aug.   23—Jeff O'Connell, Racine . . . . D 6
Sept.   10—Frank Connelly, Milwaukee . . . . . . W 8
Sept.   15—Jeff O'Connell, St. Joe, MO . . . . . . W 15
Oct.   10—Irish Landers, Waukegan . . . . . . KO 5
Oct.   15—Frank Connelly, Milwaukee . . . . . . D 6
Nov.   21—Biz Mackay, Davenport . . . . ND 6
Dec.   30—Ole Nelson, Milwaukee . . . . KO 1

1908
Jan.   1—Buck Plotell, St. Joe, MO . . . . KO 5
Jan.   17—Willie Sullivan, Milwaukee . . . . . . KO 5
Jan.   18—Jack Nolan, Milwaukee . . . . KO 1
Feb.   14—Harry Baker, Milwaukee . . . . W 10
Mar.   30—Jack Redmond, Milwaukee . . . . . . W 6
Apr.   6—Owen Moran, New York . . . . ND 6
Apr.   24—Kid Beebe, Milwaukee . . . . W 10
May   6—Frankie Neil, Milwaukee . . . . W 10
May   26—Jeff O'Connell, Fond du Lac . . . . W 8
May   29—Frank Conley, Racine . . . . D 8
July   10—Charles Greeley, Cadillac . . . . . . Exh. 6
Aug.   26—Danny Goodman, Racine . . . . D 8
Sept.   29—Danny Webster, Los Angeles . . . . KO 18

Nov.   13—Bub. Robinson, Los Angeles . . . . . ND 10
Dec.   4—Young Kid McCoy, Los Angeles . . KO 2
Dec.   11—Abe Attell, Los Angeles . . . . . . ND 10

1909
Feb.   23—Danny Webster, Los Angeles . . . . . ND 10
Feb.   26—Walter Little, Los Angeles . . . . . . KO 4
Mar.   9—Harry Baker, Los Angeles . . . . ND 10
Mar.   30—Frank Picato, Los Angeles . . . . . . ND 10
Apr.   16—George Memsic, Los Angeles . . . . ND 10
June   5—Tommy Langdon, Philadelphia . . . KO 1
June   1—Teddy Peppers, Kansas City . . . . . . KO 10
June   19—Tommy O'Toole, Philadelphia . . . . ND 6
July   13—Battling Nelson, Los Angeles . . . . . ND 10
Sept.   1—Tommy Murphy, Pittsburgh . . . . . ND 6
Sept.   7—Matty Baldwin, Boston . . . . D 12
Sept.   14—Joe Galligan, Grand Rapids . . . . . . ND 3
Sept.   15—Pete Savoy, Grand Rapids . . . . ND 3
Sept.   16—Eddie Nelson, Grand Rapids . . . . . . ND 3
Sept.   17—Jack Ashley, Grand Rapids . . . . . . ND 3
Sept.   17—Johnny Wirth, Grand Rapids . . . . . ND 3
Nov.   14—Henri Piet, New Orleans . . . . KO 2
Nov.   29—Lew Powell, San Francisco . . . . W 20
Dec.   21—Frank Picato, Los Angeles . . . . ND 10

1910
Jan.   7—Geo. Memsic, Los Angeles . . . . ND 10
Feb.   22—Battling Nelson, Pt. Richmond . . . KO 40
(Won World Lightweight Title)
(Referee Eddie Smith gave knockout decision over Nelson)
May   6—Buck Crouse, Pittsburgh . . . . ND 4
May   30—Charlie White, Cadillac . . . . Exh. 6
June   10—Jack Redmond, Milwaukee . . . . ND 10
Aug.   9—Freddie Cole, Muncie, IN . . . . ND 6
Sept.   29—Tommy McFarland, Fond du Lac . . ND 10

1911
Feb.   8—K.O. Brown, Philadelphia . . . . ND 6
Mar.   3—K.O. Brown, New York . . . . ND 10
Mar.   17—George Memsic, Los Angeles . . . . KO 9
Mar.   31—Antonio LaGrave, San Francisco . . KO 5
Apr.   26—One Round Hogan, New York . . . KO 2
May   27—Frankie Burns, San Francisco . . . . KO 16
July   4—Owen Moran, San San Francisco . KO 13

1912
May   11—Willie Ritchie, San Francisco . . . . . ND 4
May   17—Freddie Daniels, St. Joe, MO . . . . W 4
May   31—Young Jack O'Brien, Philadelphia . ND 6
July   4—Joe Rivers, Vernon CA . . . . KO 13
        (Title Bout)
Sept.   16—Kid Black, Grand Rapids . . . . Exh. 3
Sept.   16—Eddie Wosinski, Grand Rapids . . . Exh. 3
Oct.   16—Teddy Maloney, Philadelphia . . . . . ND 6
Oct.   25—Freddy Daniels, Quincy, IL . . . . ND 6
Nov.   4—Joe Mandot, New Orleans . . . . ND 10
Nov.   28—Willie Ritchie, Daly City, CA . . . . . LF 16
(Lost World Lightweight Championship)
Jim Griffin, referee.

1913
Feb.   22—"Harlem" Tommy Murphy, Daly City,
CA . . . . D 20
Apr.   19—"Harlem" Tommy Murphy, Daly City,
CA . . . . L 20
Sept.   1—Joe Azevedo, Oakland, CA . . . . L 10
Oct.   13—Battling Nelson, Milwaukee . . . . . ND 10
Dec.   19—Charlie White, Milwaukee . . . . ND 10

1914

Jan.	1—Jack Redmond, Milwaukee	W 5
Jan.	23—Joe Rivers, Milwaukee	ND 10
Jan.	29—Rudie Unholz, Fond du Lac	KO 2
Feb.	16—Tommy Gary, Cincinnati	ND 10
Feb.	23—Jack Lepper, Ionia, MI	KO 4
Mar.	12—Willie Ritchie, Milwaukee	ND 10
Sept.	18—Joe Mandot, Milwaukee	ND 10
Oct.	23—Billy Wagner, Flint, MI	ND 10
Oct.	26—Tommy Gary, Streator, IL	ND 10
Nov.	2—*Freddy Welsh, New York	KO by 8

*Wolgast broke bone in arm. Couldn't continue.

1915

Feb.	8—Cy Smith, Columbus, OH	ND 12
May	18—Ritchie Mitchell, Milwaukee	ND 10
June	2—Leach Cross, New York	ND 10
June	9—Young White, Appleton, WI	KO 7
July	23—Rocky Kansas, Buffalo	ND 10
July	31—Steve Ketchel, Forest Park, IL	D 6
Aug.	2—Dauber Jaeger, Oshkosh	KO 7
Aug.	6—Joe Welling, Duluth	ND 10
Aug.	30—Packey Hommey, New York	ND 10
Sept.	27—Bobby Waugh, Shreveport, LA	LF 6
Oct.	11—Leach Cross, Memphis	W 8
Oct.	28—Hal Stewart, Ft. Wayne, IN	ND 6
Nov.	8—Eddy McAndrews, Philadelphia	ND 6
Nov.	17—Jimmy Murphy, LaCrosse	ND 10
Dec.	14—Frank Whitney, Atlanta	L 5
Dec.	17—Leach Cross, New York	L 2

1916

Feb.	7—Frankie Burns, Kansas City	D 10
Mar.	6—Freddy Welsh, Milwaukee	ND 10
Mar.	31—Ever Hammer, Racine	ND 10
Apr.	28—Joe Flynn, Denver	W 15
May	3—Young Gradwell, Windsor, Ont.	KO 6
May	17—Young Gilbert, Salt Lake City, UT	KO 6
June	2—Frankie Murphy, Denver	W 5
June	13—Frankie Russell, St. Louis	LF 4
June	20—Stewart Donnelly, Richmond, IN	KO 3
July	4—Freddy Welsh, Denver	LF 11

(For World Lightweight Title)

Aug.	25—Frankie Callahan, Brooklyn	ND 10
Sept.	4—Lee Morrissey, Idaho Falls, ID	D 20
Sept.	29—Battling Nick, San Diego, CA	L 4

1917

	—Young Francis, Yuma, AZ	KO by 2

1920

Sept.	6—Lee Morrissey, San Bernadino, CA	D 4

Wolgast was later taken ill and had loss of memory. He was cared for by Jack Doyle of Los Angeles, CA, and sent to a sanitarium.

TB	KO	WD	WF	D	LD	LF	KO BY	ND	NC
135	38	21	1	14	6	4	2	49	0

Died April 14, 1955, Camarillo, CA
Elected to Boxing Hall of Fame 1958.

TONY ZALE
(Anthony Florian Zaleski)
(Man of Steel)

Born, May 29, 1913, Gary, IN. Middleweight. Height, 5 ft. 8 in. Managed by Sam Pian and Art Winch.

1931

Won the Golden Gloves Lightweight Championship of Indiana.

1932

Lost in finals Chicago Golden Gloves Welterweight Tournament.

Amateur record: 95 fights: Won 37, 50 KO's, lost 8.

1934 (Amateur)

	•—Melio Bettina, NYCMSG	L 3

1934

June	11—Eddie Allen, Chicago	W 4
June	15—Johnny Simpson, Chicago	W 4
June	21—Bobby Millsap, Chicago	KO 1
June	25—Johnny Liston, Chicago	KO 3
July	2—Ossie Jefferson, Chicago	KO 3
July	9—Lou Bartell, Chicago	W 4
July	16—Einar Headquist, Chicago	KO 4
July	30—Bobby Millsap, Chicago	W 4
Aug.	6—Bruce Wade, Peoria	KO 2
Aug.	13—Billy Hood, Chicago	L 6
Aug.	20—Billy Black, Chicago	L 6
Aug.	27—Wilbur Stokes, Chicago	W 8
Sept.	3—Mickey Misko, Chicago	L 8
Sept.	17—Mickey Misko, Chicago	KO 4
Oct.	8—Jack Blackburn, Chicago	W 8
Oct.	19—Jackie Schwartz, Milwaukee	KO 4
Oct.	22—Frankie Misko, Chicago	KO 6
Oct.	28—Jackie Schwartz, Milwaukee	KO 4
Nov.	5—Jack Charvez, Chicago	W 8
Nov.	26—Kid Leonard, Peoria	L 10
Dec.	17—Jack Gibbons, Chicago	L 10
Dec.	28—Joey Bazzione, Chicago	L 6

1935

Jan.	7—Max Elling, Chicago	W 8
Feb.	4—Joe Bazzione, Chicago	L 6
Feb.	11—Roughhouse Glover, Cincinnati	KO 9
Feb.	25—Jack Blackburn, Chicago	W 6
Mar.	11—Max Elling, Chicago	W 8
May	6—Johnny Phagan, Chicago	KO by 6
July	2—Dave Clark, Chicago	L 6

1936

Apr.	13—Jack Moran, Chicago	D 5

(Worked in Gary Steel Mills part of 1935 and 1936)

1937

July	26—Elby Johnson, Chicago	W 4
Sept.	17—Elby Johnson, Chicago	KO 3
Oct.	11—Billy Brown, Chicago	KO 1
Oct.	18—Bobby Gerry, Chicago	KO 2
Nov.	1—Nate Bolden, Chicago	L 5
Nov.	22—Nate Bolden, Chicago	W 6
Dec.	2—Leon Jackson, Gary	W 6

1938

Jan.	3—Nate Bolden, Chicago	W 8
Jan.	24—Henry Schaft, Chicago	W 8
Feb.	21—Jimmy Clark, Chicago	KO by 1
Mar.	28—King Wyatt, Chicago	W 8
May	16—Bobby LaMonte, Chicago	W 5
June	13—Jimmy Clark, Chicago	KO 8
July	18—Billy Celebron, Chicago	D 10
Aug.	22—Billy Celebron, Chicago	L 10
Oct.	10—Tony Cisco, Chicago	W 10
Oct.	31—Jimmy Clark, Chicago	KO 2
Nov.	18—Enzo Iannozzi, Chicago	W 6

1939

Jan.	2—Nate Bolden, Chicago	L 10
May	1—Johnny Shaw, Chicago	KO 5
May	23—Babe Orgovan, New York	W 6
Aug.	14—Milton Shivers, Chicago	KO 3
Oct.	6—Sherman Edwards, Chicago	KO 3
Nov.	3—Al Wardlow, Youngstown	KO 3
Nov.	11—Eddie Mileski, Chicago	KO 1
Dec.	12—Babe Orgovan, Chicago	KO 3

1940

Jan.	29—Al Hostak, Chicago	W 10
Feb.	29—Enzo Iannozzi, Youngstown	KO 4
Mar.	29—Ben Brown, Chicago	KO 3
June	12—Baby Kid Chocolate, Youngstown	KO 4
July	19—Al Hostak, Seattle	KO 13

(Won NBA Middleweight Championship)

Aug.	21—Billy Soose, Chicago	L 10
Nov.	19—Fred Apostoli, Seattle	W 10

1941

Jan.	1—Tony Martin, Milwaukee	KO 8
Jan.	10—Steve Mamakos, Chicago	W 10
Feb.	21—*Steve Mamakos, Chicago	KO 14
May	28—*Al Hostak, Chicago	KO 2
July	23—Ossie Harris, Chicago	KO 1
Aug.	16—Billy Pryor, Milwaukee	KO 9
Nov.	28—Georgie Abrams, New York	W 15

(Won vacant World Middleweight Title)
*NBA Title Bout.

1942

Feb.	13—Billy Conn, New York	L 12

In U.S. Navy.

1946

Jan.	7—Bobby Giles, Kansas City	KO 4
Jan.	17—Tony Gillo, Norfolk	KO 5
Feb.	7—Oscar Boyd, Des Moines	KO 3
Feb.	26—Bobby Claus, Houston	KO 4
Apr.	12—Ira Hughes, Houston	KO 2
May	2—Eddie Rossi, Memphis	KO 4
Sept.	27—Rocky Graziano, New York	KO 6

(Retained World Middleweight Title)

1947

Feb.	3—Deacon Logan, Omaha	KO 6
Feb.	12—Len Wadsworth, Wichita	KO 3
Mar.	20—Tommy Charles, Memphis	KO 4
Apr.	1—Al Timmons, Kansas City	KO 5
May	8—Cliff Beckett, Youngstown	KO 6
July	16—Rocky Graziano, Chicago	KO by 6

(Lost World Middleweight Title)

1948

Jan.	23—Al Turner, Grand Rapids	KO 5
Mar.	8—Bobby Claus, Little Rock	KO 4
Mar.	19—Lou Woods, Toledo	KO 3
June	10—Rocky Graziano, Newark	KO 3

(Regained World Middleweight Title)

Sept.	21—Marcel Cerdan, Jersey City	KO by 12

(Lost World Middleweight Title)

TB	KO	WD	WF	D	LD	LF	KO BY	ND	NC
89	46	24	0	2	13	0	4	0	0

Elected to Boxing Hall of Fame 1958.

Joe Louis

Photo Credits

The photographs and illustrations appearing
in *The Great Fights* are courtesy of the photo
library of *The Ring* magazine, with the exception
of the following by United Press International:
pages 85, 86, 88, 162, 164–65, 168, and 171.